🍁 I Was a Teenage Katima-Victim!

"A very funny and touching book about that brief moment when we are on the cusp of adulthood, sensing its possibilities more than its limitations . . . Ferguson is never maudlin, and he has the skill and good sense to allow these moments their bittersweet complexity."

—*Montreal Gazette*

"Ferguson's narrative reads like a novel of the absurd, a coming-of-age tale for both Ferguson and Canada."

—*Quill & Quire*

"An entertaining, touching account of national life in miniature . . . [Ferguson] possesses a crafty eye for detail, not to mention a highly developed, properly cranky understanding of the essential folly in what passes for everyday life."

—*Edmonton Journal*

"An affectionate look back at a glandular, liquor-hunting summer youth program most of us will recognize, if not directly then approximately."

—*Fast Forward*

"A coming of age story with a fierce and nationalistic bite . . . Ferguson's style is aberrant and sharp while the humour swings between in-your-face to wildly subtle."

—*January Magazine*

"One of the funniest slice-and-dice jobs anyone has ever done of a Canadian political institution . . . Ferguson manages to encapsulate the Katimavik experience in all its maddening, infuriating but unfailingly funny glory."

—*Sea to Sky / Voice*

Will Ferguson

Bastards & Boneheads

**Canada's Glorious Leaders
Past and Present**

Douglas & McIntyre
Vancouver/Toronto

Douglas & McIntyre Ltd.
2323 Quebec Street, Suite 201
Vancouver, British Columbia
V5T 4S7

Canadian Cataloguing in Publication Data

Ferguson, Will
    Bastards and Boneheads

    Includes bibliographical references and index.
    ISBN 1-55054-737-2

    1. Canada—History—Humor. 2. Canada—Politics and government—Humor.
I. Title.
FC25.F47 1999   971'.002'07   C99-910604-X
F1005.F47 1999

Cover design by Peter Cocking
Cover photographs by Peter Bregg/Canapress (Pierre Trudeau); Canapress (Joe Clark)
Text design by Susanna Gilbert, *Descriptions Design*
Printed and bound in Canada by Transcontinental Printing
Printed on acid-free paper ∞

Canadä

The publisher gratefully acknowledges the support of the Canada Council for the Arts and of the British Columbia Ministry of Tourism, Small Business and Culture. The publisher also acknowledges the financial support of the Government of Canada through the Book Publishing Industry Development Program.

Contents

PART III
Boneheads on Parade:
A Survey of Canadian Prime Ministers, Past and Present

"History is never neutral."
—Pierre Elliott Trudeau

An Introduction to the Bastards and Boneheads Methodology

CALL IT A BREAKTHROUGH, if you will. Call it the most important sociological discovery of the century, if you must. But the fact remains: after years of research, often late into the night, I have developed a highly sophisticated scientific procedure for evaluating leadership. I call it "Bastards and Boneheads."

Among its many uses, this system allows us to determine whether any given Canadian prime minister is incompetent and ruthless, or just incompetent. The scheme can be applied to other public figures as well, the term "leader" being defined very broadly for our purposes.

I relied on complex mathematical calculations and incomprehensible algorithmic formulas to develop this system, and my research was funded by generous government grants and many wealthy benefactors. Even then, there were many lean years before I hit upon the correct paradigm. My earlier efforts—Muttonheads and Morons, Idiots and Assholes, Imbeciles and Odious Reptilian Opportunists— while helpful, ultimately proved inadequate. Those were dark days indeed. Many a night I sank into a deep despair, unshaven and slovenly and reeking of cheap cognac (a situation that remains pretty much unchanged to this day) as I struggled against all odds to unravel this riddle, this Sphinx, this Sphinx-like riddle.

Simply put: How does one begin to classify and evaluate Canada's leaders, past and present?

The breakthrough came one gloomy winter night as I read a dusty tome by Carl Jung in the tallow yellow of flickering candlelight. Suddenly! It came to me! In a burst of exclamation marks!! If I could somehow grasp the essential Jungian archetypes of leadership, the rest of the puzzle would fall into place. After further exhaustive labour on my part, and several new, lucrative Canada Council grants, I finally narrowed the archetypes down to two elemental figures: Pierre Elliott Trudeau and John George Diefenbaker.

Trudeau and Diefenbaker represent the two fundamental personality types that have, through either intent or ineptitude, shaped this great land of ours. Pierre Trudeau was a Bastard, an archetypal, purely defined Bastard. John Diefenbaker, the jowly jawed prairie populist with more passion than brains, was a Bonehead. The ultimate Bonehead. And between those two extremes lie countless degrees of bastardability and boneheadedness.

Bastards *succeed.* They are ruthless. They are active. Their cause may be noble or it may be amoral, but the Bastard is always the active principle. Boneheads *fail,* often by stumbling over their own two feet. They are reactive. Inept. Indignant. They are usually truly amazed by their failures.

Bastards screw Canada. Boneheads just screw up. Bastards cause events to unfold by an act of focussed will; Boneheads cause events to unfold mainly by accident. Bastards ride the tiger; Boneheads end up as tiger chow.

Granted, Boneheads do have a certain Charlie Brown charm about them. It is hard to hate a Bonehead. It is equally as hard to love a Bastard. (Though a few have been charming in their very Bastardness.) Boneheads join self-help groups and pyramid schemes. Bastards sell them on the idea. Boneheads are great huggers but lousy lays; Bastards could seduce a statue.

Bastards are sharp—to a fault. Boneheads are sincere—to a fault. And yet, for all their stark differences, the two groups do share one important characteristic: Bastards and Boneheads have both had an incalculable effect on Canada. As a nation, Canadians have been tossed on the wind, shunted back and forth between the two like a rowboat in a gale. And although we are basically a Nation of Well-Intentioned Boneheads, we yearn for a Bastard Redeemer to save us. This is why Canadians generally tend to elect Bastards. (The United States, in contrast, is a Nation of Complete Bastards that tends to elect and reward Boneheads.)

It should also be noted that, in a few rare cases, an individual has managed— through a congruence of raw ambition and general mismanagement—to be both a Bastard *and* a Bonehead. Brian Mulroney was the classic example of this.

With others, the verdict differs depending on whether we are discussing their private lives or their public lives. As a prime minister, Mackenzie King was a Bastard. As a seance-going, prostitute-redeeming, mother-fixated bachelor boy, he was a Bonehead Supreme with Oak Leaf Clusters.

A career may also arc from one realm to the other. Lester Pearson was a cunning, soft-spoken Bastard prior to being elected PM, but once in office, he faltered. The result? He must be judged as either a Flawed Bastard or an Incomplete Bonehead. (Pearson was, in fact, the hardest prime minister to label. It must have taken me, oh, I don't know, *minutes* to make my decision.)

Another thing worth noting is that the terms are gender neutral. Kim Campbell was a Bonehead. Sheila Copps, should she ever attain the office of prime minister, would probably be a Bastard. The system can be scientifically applied to any major public figure, past or present. Sure, it's Procrustean, but I say, better to lop off a few feet now and then than to spend time and energy trying to find a new bed for every person who shows up. Mine is an extremely efficient system, almost simplistic in its simplicity.

It also makes a great parlour game: "Jean Chrétien, Bastard or Bonehead?"

There is, however, more to this than merely an excuse to slander our leaders. Not much more, granted, but there is a point to be made. And the point is this: *Personality matters.* We have just suffered through one of the most brutal, dehumanizing eras in human history. The twentieth century was soaked in blood, misery and ideology—but guess what? The good guys won. Rather than succumbing to collective tyranny, we have rediscovered the importance of the individual. Instead of ideology, we have ideals: human rights, autonomy, freedom. This is still a chaotic, messy world we live in, but (in the West, at least) the ideological wars are finally coming to an end, university campuses being the last desperate bastion of ideologues.

History was once depicted as the conflux of vast, impersonal forces: class struggle, race, dialectical materialism. But the tide has turned, and as we leave the Age of Ideology, the impact of personality on world events has been reaffirmed. History is where character and circumstance collide, and *Bastards and Boneheads* takes this definition as a point of departure.

History is not a dusty mausoleum, though at times it is treated as such. History is, and remains, an ongoing dialogue between the past and the present. There is nothing wrong with having strong opinions about the past, because the past is never really over. Its meaning is never settled; its morals are never cut in stone. Just as we have strong opinions about Jean Chrétien's veracity, so too we are entitled to have strong opinions about John A. Macdonald's sobriety or John Diefenbaker's sanity.

This book is essentially a survey of some pivotal moments in the evolution of Canada. At any point, the country could have veered off on another course entirely, for better or for worse. The decisions made by a handful of key people—mainly men, unfortunately—have shaped the proud beliefs and noble institutions that we make fun of today.

I write about some dark chapters in our collective history, everything from genocide to exile to holocausts, but this is a fundamentally optimistic book. The lesson we learn from Canadian history is one learned the hard way by the United States, from the Invasion of 1775 to the War of 1812, right through to the present: "Canada has always beaten the odds." Maybe that should be our national motto: *We have always beaten the odds.*

The story of Canada is, above all, a success story. It is a tale of the slow triumph of human decency, the narrowing of the gap between the Ideal and the Real. We are a nation that has, through dogged effort and a bit of luck, managed to overcome geography, intolerance, ignorance and even common sense. Ours is a story of battles lost and wars won, of heroes and saints, sinners and rogues. Of bastards and boneheads.

AN OBJECTIVE OVERVIEW OF COMPETING SYSTEMS (AND WHY MINE IS THE BEST EVER)

In formulating the Bastards and Boneheads System, I am indebted to the actors and production crew of Edmonton's Union Theatre, who introduced me to a similar evaluative exercise. Before each rehearsal, someone in the cast would call out the name of a celebrity, and the others would instantly reply with either *Dink!* or *Not a Dink!* (For example: "Sting!" Everybody: "Dink!")

However, for the record, I developed my own system independently of theirs and was informed of the Dink/Not a Dink dichotomy only during the final stages of the manuscript. Which is to say, the cast at Union Theatre is not entitled to one thin dime of revenue from this book. ("Will Ferguson?" "*Dink!*")

I should also mention two books on my shelf, both out of print and neither of which influenced my analyses. For her 1982 survey of Canadian leaders, Irma Coucill chose the title *Founders & Guardians*, and in his 1984 book of Canadian political lists, Derek Black classified past leaders as *Winners and Losers*. The Founders and Guardians classification is, of course, far too respectful and deferential for a hard-nosed social historian such as myself, and although the designation of Winners and Losers may seem at first to foreshadow my own Bastards and Boneheads breakthrough, one discovers upon perusing this work that Mr. Black was speaking literally: his book is a list of electoral victories and defeats and is not descriptive of the actual personalities involved. (When Joe Clark is described as being "a loser," for example, it is only in reference to his 1980 defeat.)

Founders, Guardians, Winners, Losers, Dinks and Not Dinks: none of these systems has the encompassing utility of Bastards and Boneheads. Nor do I wish to disparage the work of current scholars, but I should point out that in *Sex in the Snow*, pollster Michael Adams required no fewer than 12 categories when he pigeonholed Canadians according to value tribes. These tribes had names like "Autonomous Post-Materialists," "Disengaged Darwinists" and "Cosmopolitan Modernists." It made for an entertaining read, true, but Adams's system lacked the brutal simplicity of Bastards vs. Boneheads.

Mr. Adams's work was based on phone surveys and statistical cluster groups, and it featured all kinds of impressive diagrams and pie charts. Here's how *my* system works: We examine something shocking, stirring or inspirational about our past; we mull it over; we scrutinize the key players; and we pass judgement.

Bastards and Boneheads is divided into three sections. Part I, "The Paths of Glory," traces Canada's early history, from the first permanent European settlement in 1604 to the completion of the transcontinental railway in 1885. This was an era of imperialism and nation building, a time of gunpowder and cannonballs, of armed uprisings and public executions, of rail barons and sword-waving generals. The title of the section comes from a line in Thomas Gray's "Elegy Written in a Country Churchyard." It is a line that General James Wolfe reportedly recited as his army slipped silently towards Québec: "The paths of glory lead but to the grave." The only problem is, Wolfe almost certainly did *not* recite those or any other prophetic poetic sentiments while on his way to battle. Like so much in our early history, this tale has become romanticized to the point of myth.

Part II, "Gristle into Bone," covers the twentieth century, when Canada's character was being set. In this section of the book, the emphasis shifts to human rights. Examining everything from the early women's movement to Native resurgence, the internment of Japanese Canadians to the rise of Québec nationalism, we look at the Bastards and the Boneheads behind these important events. The section's title was inspired by a comment made by John A. Macdonald several years after Confederation, when he noted that the newly formed union was still gristle and needed to "harden into bone."

Part III of the book, "Boneheads on Parade," provides an overview and an evaluation of our prime ministers. Included here is the definitive, very scientific and highly objective Bastards and Boneheads Official Ranking of Canadian Prime Ministers.

The bulk of my work on *Bastards and Boneheads* was done while living in the Maritimes, and I owe a debt of gratitude to David Langley of St. Andrews, New Brunswick, who let me take over his office for the final hectic months of research. I would also like to thank the Matsumoto family of Minamata, Japan, who graciously allowed me to use their family home in Okubo while I was finishing the final draft. (I was on a "working holiday.") Writing about Canada while huddling, hermitlike, in a secluded farmhouse in southern Kyushu was an odd experience—but at the same time it gave me a certain peculiar sense of perspective. Canada never seems more surreal than when you are away from it.

Finally, I would like to thank my wealthy benefactors, whose loyal support and large donations over the years have made *Bastards and Boneheads* possible. Unfortunately, many of them are in highly sensitive government and corporate positions and thus have asked to remain anonymous.

The Paths of Glory:
Canada's Formative Years

Death and Winter:
Lessons from
St. Croix Island

IN THE SOUTHWEST corner of New Brunswick, at the mouth of the St. Croix River, lies a small resort town known as St. Andrews by-the-sea.

Historic, charming, narcoleptic: St. Andrews was first settled in 1783 by Loyalist refugees fleeing the American Revolution, and the town remains something of an open-air museum, a living diorama of early Loyalist architecture and sombre Georgian homes. The church steeples that punctuate the skyline and the venerable Algonquin Resort high on its hill add a certain haughtiness to the town, but for the most part St. Andrews is remarkably understated. A sense of faded Empire and lost grandeur permeates the very air.

St. Andrews is a town of long, languid summer evenings, of promenades and sunset strolls. It is enchanting in a hypnotic sort of way. So enchanting, in fact, that the irascible rail baron William Van Horne built a sprawling summer cottage here in the 1890s, on an island connected to the mainland only at low tide. Thanks to Van Horne, St. Andrews was soon discovered by railway promoters and was transformed into a summer playground for the Victorian leisure class. A resort town it became, and a resort town it remains.

I first arrived in St. Andrews after spending five years in the Far East. I was recently married, and my wife and I, seeking to start anew, had blithely chosen St. Andrews as our destination. It was a decision made as much by default as anything else. The town sounded pretty; there was a college; there was history. St. Andrews was beside the sea. I had never been to New Brunswick before, nor had my wife, who was born and raised in southern Japan. We were living at the time in the semi-tropics of Kyushu, amid palm trees and bamboo forests.

"What do you think New Brunswick will be like?" asked my wife.

I looked out across the lush green fronds that spilled into a warm Japanese ocean. "Oh, I imagine it will be a lot like this," I said.

I wasn't the first misinformed explorer to stumble into the Maritimes, and I doubt I will be the last.

Our journey from the Mysterious Orient required no Northwest Passage, just a mind-numbing 12-hour flight and a hearty, rough-hewn diet of airline food. We arrived, jet-lagged and dishevelled, as bedraggled and defeated as any refugee. The trip may not have been on par with what the Loyalists endured, but it came awfully close.

The town was alluring. Sleepy, summery, perfect. But St. Andrews in autumn, ablaze with red maples and golden twilights, soon gave way to St. Andrews in winter. And St. Andrews, like Canada itself, does not glory in its winter; it endures it. The place hunkers down like a garrison on a windy island. It survives.

These are the images I remember best: St. Andrews in the off-season, after the tourists have left and the summer laughter has echoed into silence. The long nights and deserted alleyways. The snow drifting across Water Street. The signs creaking in the wind.

St. Andrews is a town of secret histories and hidden graveyards, and its memory is selective. While the early ordeals of the Loyalists are proudly recalled, the fact that they brought with them hundreds of slaves is conveniently forgotten. There were shackles in the basements and a lynching in the town square. The bodies of these forgotten Blacks may very well be buried in unmarked graves somewhere near the second tee of the Algonquin Golf Course.

History was never far from the surface during our sojourn in St. Andrews. All winter long, we heard rumours of discontent: the First Nations were claiming ownership of a sacred trailer park at the scenic south end of town, a lucrative little piece of real estate. Motives were questionable on both sides, and ancestral ghosts were evoked by Loyalists and Natives alike.

But the ghosts that resonated most in St. Andrews were French, if only by their very absence . . .

I think of what the poet Miriam Waddington wrote about Canada:

We look
like a geography but
just scratch us
and we bleed
history . . .

St. Andrews by-the-sea is a dead end, both geographically and historically. It lies perched at the end of a peninsula leading nowhere. If you want to unravel the past of St. Andrews, or of Canada for that matter, you must turn your attention upriver, to a small, unremarkable island.

St. Croix Island is easy to overlook; it is little more than a wooded grove and a rise of red granite. At low tide, a swath of sand and shoal lies exposed. At high tide, the island seems to float upon the water. St. Croix Island is a mass grave, a place where men died in abject misery. It is scarcely six acres across, and all of Canada rests upon its shoulders.

The tale begins 400 years ago, when not a single European settlement existed north of Mexico. Transient fishing communities had developed in Newfoundland and along the St. Lawrence River, but no permanent communities had taken root. Both France and England claimed the northern half of North America, but neither country had made much of a go at it. For them, Canada was a puzzle to be solved, not a land to be settled.

"Canada," noted Northrop Frye, "began as an obstacle, blocking the way to the treasures of the East, to be explored only in the hope of finding a passage through it."

But that was about to change. A French nobleman by the name of Pierre Du Gua de Monts had been granted authority over a wide stretch of this uncharted land, and in 1604 he set out with two ships and an eclectic crew of Protestants, Catholics, craftsmen, artisans, labourers and Swiss mercenaries. Their mission? To settle the New World and claim it for France. De Monts left Europe in the early spring and made a perilous journey through North Atlantic storms. Both of his ships almost went down off Sable Island in a wild squall, but having made a harrowing escape, they eventually reached the coast of Nova Scotia and groped their way along the shore and into the Bay of Fundy. In late June, probing deeper, they arrived at the mouth of an unnamed river and followed it inland to where it split into the crosslike formation that would give the river its designation: Ste-Croix.

One of de Monts's men climbed the highest hill the party could find, but all that stretched before them, as far as the eye could see, was forest. This was not the passage to the Far East, but it just might make a centre of operations. The group needed to build a fortress, and under the direction of a young cartographer named Samuel de Champlain, they chose as their site a small island in the middle of the river. It would prove a fateful, and near-fatal, decision.

In light of the horrifying ordeal that awaited them, the question needs to be asked: Why here? Why, of all places, did they choose this river? This island?

There were two primary reasons: fear and a need for defence. The island was elevated, and it lay at equidistance from both shores. A cannon at either end would give the French command of the entire river. "Vessels could pass only at the mercy of our cannons," noted Champlain approvingly in his journals. The island was large enough to support a settlement, but small enough to defend in the event of an attack, and the massive Fundy tidal system exposed great shelves during its retreats, allowing the men to gather shellfish at low tide. As for the climate, the island was on roughly the same latitude as the south of France. How cold could it get?

As the explorers were about to discover, only two things are certain in Canada: death and winter. (Taxes would come later.)

The men built de Monts's dwelling first, a handsome building stocked with ornaments from France, and then a storehouse, a blacksmith shop, a kiln oven, a kitchen, a barracks for the soldiers and a dwelling for "noblemen and artisans." A town plan was laid out, gardens were planted, and a chapel was built. The settlement was an odd but appropriate mix of New World and Old. Ornate woodwork, glass windows, a stately fireplace and heraldic banners from France adorned de Monts's residence, which was built alongside rough-hewn log shacks and heavy palisade walls. Cannons were secured at either end, pointing out towards invisible enemies. These were men ready for war.

That year, the snow began to fall on October 6. By early December, ice floes had appeared in the river. In an unfortunate twist of fate, de Monts had chosen to establish his camp during one of the most severe winters in a hundred years. The snow fell, the temperature plummeted, and the ice floes began crunching together and piling up. Practically all of the island's trees were cut down to feed the colony's ravenous fireplaces, removing what little shelter there was. Often, for weeks on end, the men were cut off, trapped without fresh water, food or warmth. Their island sanctuary had become a prison.

Through it all, the men lived in constant fear of an event more imaginary than real: a Native attack. Sentry duty and their perpetual state of readiness took a heavy psychological toll. A band of Welustuk Indians had temporarily encamped at the foot of the island, probably out of concern and curiosity, but to Europeans surrounded by the unknown, their presence was terrifying. Indeed, much of the Saga of Ile Ste-Croix reads like a parable: the hubris; the initial confidence; the growing dread; the stripping of the environment; the incubus fears, the horror, the horror—as Kurtz might have put it.

The explorers were surviving on salt meat and melted snow. Their cider froze and was dispensed by the pound. Inactive for weeks on end as they huddled within cold, fetid, unkempt lodgings, the crew was ripe for disease—and it came. With a vengeance. *Mal de terre*. Scurvy.

Here, in Champlain's own words, is a description of its symptoms:

There were produced in the mouths of those who had it, great pieces of superfluous and drivelling flesh (causing extensive putrification) which got the upper hand to such an extent that scarcely anything but liquid could be taken. Their teeth became very loose, and could be pulled out with the fingers without causing them pain. The superfluous flesh was often cut out, which caused them to eject much blood through the mouth. Afterwards a violent pain seized their arms and legs, which remained swollen and very hard . . . and they could not walk on account of the contraction of the muscles so that they were almost without strength and suffered intolerable pains. They experienced pain also in the loins, stomach, and bowels.

Of the 79 men on the island, 35 died and 20 more "were on the point of death." The cause of scurvy, a simple vitamin C deficiency, was still a mystery, though the men had read Jacques Cartier's earlier account of a miraculous cure provided by the Iroquois. When asked about this miracle, the Welustuk drank their spruce brew and shrugged. They had never heard of Cartier's cure. (Had de Monts's men bartered some of their weapons for the spruce drink, more of them might well have survived the winter.)

The Indians never did attack, though they could have easily wiped out the entire colony. If anything, they were probably worried about the crazy strangers who had chosen to settle on one of the coldest, windiest islands in the region.

Meanwhile, the bodies continued to pile up.

Burials were difficult in the frozen earth, especially given the near-exhaustion of the survivors. April came—and went. No supply ships appeared, and panic spread through the camp. They couldn't face another winter of ice and deprivation. They were cut off from the outside world. Powerless.

In June, the men decided to make a run for Europe. They would try to get to Newfoundland, restock, arrange transport and then escape from the New World. In the midst of these frantic plans, supply ships from France finally arrived, and de Monts's men greeted them with cannon blasts and jubilant trumpet calls. The ship's captain had expected to find a cozy, well-run little community of French settlers; he found instead a ragged band of half-starved, dead and dying refugees.

The venture might have ended right there, in utter failure, as so many had before, but de Monts was dogged, and he decided to give it one more go. He moved his fledgling colony across the Bay of Fundy to a cove he dubbed Port-Royal, on the inner shore of what is now Nova Scotia. The men dismantled what they could of the St. Croix settlement and shipped the timber and supplies across the bay. From this beginning would eventually grow the colony of Acadia: the first successful European presence on mainland Canada.

The sign outside the St. John's City Hall says it all: *Canada Begins Right Here*. Newfoundland—iceberg-infested, Titanic-sinking, cod-eating, screech-drinking Newfoundland—is where the sun rises and the Trans-Canada begins. Mile Zero. The Rock.

St. John's is closer to London, England, than to Vancouver, both geographically and psychologically. Newfoundland, after all, was where the English first launched their empire. Although they were dazzled by the prospect of gold and a passage to the Orient, their real money came first from fish (and later, fur). In Catholic Europe, there were more than 150 fast days when the eating of meat was prohibited. Eating fish, however, was deemed acceptable, and codfish, salted or sun-dried, could be stored for months and shipped throughout the world, making the east coast waters of Canada a veritable treasure trove. It was at the height of this period that Francis Bacon declared, "The fisheries of Newfoundland are inexhaustible and are of more value to the Empire than all the silver mines of Peru."

Newfoundland was already a lively, semi-lawless frontier of Basque fishing crews and Irish shoremen when Sir Humphrey Gilbert arrived in 1583. Gilbert claimed the island as England's very first overseas colony, making Newfoundland the place "where the British Empire began." Humphrey then departed on his frigate the *Squirrel*. (*Squirrel*? With a name like that you just know the expedition is doomed.) And so it was: they ran into a squall and the *Squirrel* went down with all hands. Overheard on the sister ship were Gilbert's immortal last words, "Looks like we're in for some rain!" I'm kidding, of course. What he actually cried out was, "We are as near to Heaven by sea as by land!" Although this was quite dramatic and very stirring, no one was quite sure what he meant by it. Alas, by the time anyone could ask, he had already drowned. It was not the noblest start an empire could hope for.

Samuel de Champlain returned to St. Croix Island only once, to walk among the ruins and offer prayers for those who had died. The wheat the men had planted now grew thick and wild, and Champlain found the sight strangely uplifting. It seemed like a metaphor for—for *something*.

Champlain soon shifted his attention to the St. Lawrence River valley, where he founded a settlement in 1608 in what is now Québec City. A free-booting, lawless community of Basque traders was already established at Tadoussac, and they at first refused to accept Champlain's claim to authority. But in the end, Champlain succeeded—barely—where Cartier had failed, and thus Champlain is known as the Father of New France, not Cartier.

The English, meanwhile, had established a colony in Jamestown, Virginia. In 1613, English raiders under the command of the Virginian privateer Samuel Argall sailed north, intent on driving the Acadians from the Bay of Fundy. They landed on St. Croix Island and torched the remains of de Monts's settlement in an attempt to eradicate all evidence of French claims to the region. The English raiders even went so far as to chisel the fleurs-de-lis and the names of de Monts and his captain off a large stone. Samuel Argall left a smouldering island in his wake, and he went on to lay waste to other scattered communities, including Port-Royal. But Argall did a sloppy job, and evidence of de Monts's original settlement was not completely obliterated. In later years, the scorched relics, scattered bricks and embedded cannonballs on St. Croix would play a pivotal role in the shape that Canada would take.

When the American Revolution began, more than 150 years later, the Acadians had long since been expelled from the Fundy region. Nova Scotia (which then included New Brunswick) was staunchly British. Unlike the 13 colonies to the south, it stayed loyal during the revolution, and once the shooting stopped, map-makers needed to draw a clear line between the new republic and the remaining British colonies. The border between New England and Nova Scotia was notoriously vague; no one knew exactly where one ended and the other began. The 1783 treaty between Britain and the United States set the boundary at the St. Croix River. But which St. Croix? The Americans, naturally enough, claimed a river farther east, which would have given them a sizable chunk of the Fundy coast. It would also have forced the relocation of hundreds of Loyalist families who had just arrived in the St. Andrews area.

And so it was, to settle the border dispute and to keep St. Andrews British, that a search party was launched and St. Croix Island was "rediscovered." Maps had shifted its location several times over the years, and it wasn't until the ruins of de Monts's settlement were unearthed that the issue was finally settled. (By then, the river was known as the Scoodic and the island as Dochet's, but both have since reverted to the name St. Croix, though the island is still erroneously labelled "Dochet's" in some textbooks and encyclopaedias.)

A few forgotten cannonballs, several overgrown piles of brick and mortar, a metal spoon and a rusted spike were what decided Canada's eastern border. The international boundary was settled in 1798, after a 15-year dispute, and ever since, the St. Croix River has been the dividing line between the destinies of North America: Loyalist Canada on one side, Republican America on the other. And French ghosts in between.

But what of the Welustuk Indians who had watched as the Europeans settled on that small island? Did they have an inkling of what was to come? That St. Croix Island marked both the beginning—and, for them, the end?

The invasion of Canada began at St. Croix, for our history is the story of conquest—a conquest by stealth, deceit, momentum and armed force. Canada begins with an invasion, and St. Croix Island was the beachhead. Initially, the Natives in the region attempted to use the Europeans to their advantage, and then they tried desperately to outmanoeuvre them. They harassed, attacked, made treaties and tried their damnedest, but in the end arithmetic and influenza won, and the First Nations were overwhelmed.

St. Croix Island now stands deserted. Among the trees are the remnants of a lighthouse, a navigational beacon standing like an empty flagpole, and some scattered remnants of French occupation. The island exists like an dusty trunk in an attic, long forgotten and filled with cobwebs and old bones.

January, 1998. Almost four hundred years have passed since de Monts and Champlain struggled through that first harrowing winter on St. Croix Island. Another disaster is now brewing, but this time around it will be a very different story, and the contrast between the past and present is as stark as it is revealing.

The Ice Storm of 1998 brought central Canada to a standstill. More than 4 million people were left without heat and without power in the dead of winter. Two dozen people died of hypothermia, asphyxiation and poorly managed fires. More than a billion dollars in damage was reported.

Although remembered largely as a Montréal event, the ice storm that paralyzed central Canada lashed out at the Maritimes as well. St. Andrews was where the storm hit the sea. The freezing rains collided with north Atlantic winds, the power lines went down, transformers exploded in the night, and sunny St. Andrews was plunged into dark and cold.

My wife, born of liquid blue bays and swaying stands of bamboo, had never seen real snow before she came to Canada; now she was caught in the middle of a near-arctic apocalypse. It was death by degrees. We wrapped our newborn son in layers of blankets in a bedroom as cold as a morgue. We could see our baby's breath in the candlelight, and I thought to myself: This is the way the world ends, not with a bang but a whimper.

There was a devastating beauty to it at first. Branches like icy chandeliers, a world gilt with frozen rain. Then the trees started to fall, one by one. The sound they made was like gun shots. Like bones snapping in two.

In St. Andrews, the world simply . . . stopped.

There is something quintessentially Canadian about waiting out a storm. Survival, we are told, is what makes us who we are. But surviving an ice storm is not so much heroic as it is humbling. I had had this image of myself as a protector, provider and patriarch, but all that changed. We were powerless in every sense of the word. The spices of the Far East seemed a million miles and a lifetime away.

And then, something happened. Something heroic. The venerable Algonquin Resort, the very epitome of St. Andrews' snob appeal, threw open its doors and offered unconditional sanctuary. The hotel's generators were switched on full blast, and every room was made available—without charge. Given shelter in a luxury suite in one of Canada's finest hotels, my wife and I lounged about, feeling decadent and rich, watching the crisis unfold on television. It was a far, far cry from what de Monts and Champlain had endured. Indeed, we could almost see St. Croix Island from the top of the Algonquin's highest tower.

The next morning, we woke to the sound of army helicopters landing behind the hotel and the sight of troops arriving in convoy. The Canadian Forces were there to clear the streets of debris, to chainsaw branches away from overhead lines, to restore power—in every sense of the word. St. Andrews had been declared a disaster zone, but if it was a disaster, it was a highly *civilized* disaster. A very, very Canadian disaster.

The Ice Storm of 1998 struck at the very heart of the Canadian identity: our faith in power lines, our lack of self-reliance, our fear of the dark. The first settlers would have scoffed at us. What we had suffered through was nothing compared to the hardships that Champlain and the others faced during that first horrific winter in Canada on a small island at the edge of the world. The evolution of Canada from Ile Ste-Croix to the Algonquin Resort is the triumph of comfort over geography, of summer over winter.

Champlain, of course, was a Bastard. A pure, undiluted Bastard who comes down to us in a long line of Bastards. For the early European explorers, Canada was the promise of something *more*. A treasure to be unwrapped, a cache to be uncovered—a passage to somewhere else.

Skirting the shores of North America, the Italian mariner Verrazzano saw and mapped an entire vast Inland Sea, one that would lead, he was sure, to the spice islands of the Indies and the gold and silk of China and Japan. But Verrazzano had mapped a mirage, and the Inland Sea existed only in European minds. (It was this

❦ THE HBC: HERE BEFORE CHRIST

The St. Lawrence River was the main trade and transport artery of New France. But if you look at a map, you may notice a quicker route out of the fur-trapping interior of Canada. Instead of going down the St. Lawrence, you could follow the waterways north to Hudson Bay instead, and then take a ship up around the tip of Québec. This Hudson Bay shortcut was first proposed to the king of France by a pair of real Bastards: the voyageurs Radisson and Groseilliers. When they received only vague promises of support from France, they went over to the English, where they were met with much greater enthusiasm, and on May 2, 1670, the "Company of Adventurers" was formed, otherwise known as the Hudson's Bay Company.

First Nations historian Olive Dickason has since challenged the notion that Radisson and Groseilliers were the initiators of this (literally) watershed change in transportation routes. The honour of discovering and promoting the Hudson Bay route, argues Dickason in her seminal work, *Canada's First Nations*, belongs not to a pair of rogue French-Canadian voyageurs but to the leaders of the northern Indians, who saw the opportunity and knew how to exploit it.

Either way, the company was given dominion over all the territory that drained into Hudson Bay, a vast area dubbed Rupert's Land, which was later expanded to cover almost 3 million square miles. At its peak, notes Peter C. Newman in *Empire of the Bay*, the Hudson's Bay Company's territory covered nearly a twelfth of the world's land mass, "an area ten times that of the Holy Roman Empire," making the HBC the largest private landholder in human history.

The fate of Canada over the next 200 years was irrevocably intertwined with that of the Hudson's Bay Company, and though the vast Northwest was eventually purchased by Canada, and the Bay itself no longer deals in furs, the company still wields a lasting influence in the hinterlands. I was born and raised in the former trapping community of Fort Vermilion, Alberta, which was founded by a rival band of traders but later swallowed up by the HBC. In Fort Vermilion, the Hudson's Bay Company was second only to God. It was always said that the company's motto was, "We screwed your grandfather, we screwed your father, and we're going to screw you."

that de Monts's men were searching for when they climbed the hills near St. Croix. They were searching for Verrazzano's Inland Sea, searching, in effect, for a mirage.)

Dreams of hidden treasure take a long time to die, and for years Canada remained not a Land of Opportunity but a Land of Disappointment. When Jacques Cartier first arrived in 1534, he was seeking a passage to the Orient, but he was soon tantalized by tales of a mysterious "Kingdom of the Saguenay" farther inland, where mounds of gold and rubies lay. Mind you, the same Stadacona Indians who told Cartier about the Kingdom of Saguenay also told him—no kidding—about a tribe to the west whose people had no anuses and another tribe whose members only had one leg and hopped about all day. Displaying selective gullibility, Cartier decided there was indeed gold to be found, and the king of France agreed. He granted Cartier a commission to discover "certain isles and countries where it is said there must be great quantities of gold and other riches."

Cartier never did find the Lost Kingdom of Saguenay but instead returned to France in a ship laden with diamonds and gold ore. Alas, assayers in Europe quickly discredited his claims: the samples he brought back were only common quartz, mica and iron pyrites—fool's gold. It was a humiliating end to Cartier's grand scheme, and it added a new phrase to the French language: *Faux comme un diamant du Canada*. "As fake as a Canadian diamond."

Martin Frobisher went even farther than Cartier in chasing chimerical treasures and Asian passages. Beginning in 1576, Frobisher sailed into Meta Incognita, "the Unknown Lands," and ran smack into Baffin Island. He mined tons of rock and brought it back to Europe where, in what might well be dubbed the original Bre-X scandal, his load was declared rich in gold ore by a shady evaluator. This claim unleashed a stampede of speculators and another massive mining expedition. Frobisher went back to Baffin Island and returned with more than 1,200 tons of "the black ore." But the only gold it contained was fool's gold, and once the bubble burst, this huge shipment of ore, this huge, useless piece of Canada, ended up being dumped in the sea or used to patch stone fences in England.

Still the explorers kept coming, egged on by promises of gold, glory and God: the evangelical, the greedy and the adventurous, drawn to the New World. These early journeys into the unknown were, in their day, more mysterious and far more dangerous than a moon landing. The men aboard these ships were sailing into a black hole. Into the blank spaces on the map. It was obsessive. Unhealthy. Exhilarating.

I think of poor doomed Henry Hudson, who thought he could sail across the North Pole to China and who ended up cast adrift in the bay that now bears his name. Convinced he had finally found the fabled passage to the Orient, Hudson pushed his crew to the edge of starvation, wintering deep in James Bay in 1611. Hudson was not, alas, at the edge of the Northwest Passage but was in fact lost in the heart of a vast continent. His men mutinied and set Henry adrift in a small boat with his son and a contingent of seven loyal supporters. The ragged band of mutineers then set sail for Europe, only to be ambushed in an Inuit attack that left most of the ringleaders dead. In this defeated condition, the remnants of Henry Hudson's failed expedition finally came limping into port.

The fate of Henry Hudson remains a mystery. There is the intriguing possibility that he somehow managed to sail out of the bay and make his way across the Arctic Circle to the Norwegian island of Spitsbergen, where a grave marked "Henry Hudson" was reportedly discovered in 1823. A more plausible resting place is on Danby Island, close to where the mutiny occurred; a row of stakes was discovered on Danby in 1631. Either way, it was a sad but symbolic end for Hudson and his small band of faithful followers. They fell victim to the worst possible Canadian nightmare: they were swallowed whole by the landscape.

You had to be driven to be an explorer. You had to be vainglorious, reckless, impatient. Very few became rich, and many were lost at sea. It is this ruthless bravado, this relentless human spirit that we celebrate today: the raw, defiant energy of the individual at odds with the world around him. These men were not heroes, they were adventurers, and that is a distinction worth keeping in mind. Heroes are ideals; they represent the dominant values of the cultures that create them. Heroes personify morality. They inspire youngsters and reinforce mainstream beliefs. Adventurers, by contrast, are forces of nature unleashed. They are, almost by definition, amoral.

The settler is a hero, the explorer an adventurer. In my book *Why I Hate Canadians*, I explored this pattern through the image of the habitant and the voyageur: we may honour the habitant, we may emulate the habitant, but we envy the voyageur. Champlain, in turn, represents an important transitional figure in our history, one who moves from explorer to settler, from adventurer to hero.

The strength of the adventurer, and his greatest flaw, lies in the very restlessness that defines him: his inability, in the words of Pascal, "to sit quietly in a room." Canada was founded on just such restlessness. So, before we continue, let's raise a glass to the men who first skirted our shores, Cartier and Champlain and Hudson and all the others. They kick-started this entire strange enterprise, this concept of a New World, this country called Canada. The bastards and the boneheads, the winners and the losers, the crazy and the really crazy—we salute them, en route to our climate-controlled shopping malls in the comfort of suburbia. We salute them.

Which brings us back to a small island in the St. Croix River.

Over the years, the south side of St. Croix has been slowly eroding. The graves of the 39 French colonists buried there have long since washed away. Of the many epitaphs the island has gone by over the years, one stands out in particular: *Bone Island.*

Treasure hunters, chasing fanciful rumours of French gold and buried chests, dug up whole sections of the island. Builders on shore excavated sand by the scow-load, and survey teams cut down much of the underbrush to improve sight-lines, but the biggest culprits have been time and tide. The island is slowly crumbling away. Champlain would hardly recognize it today, so reduced is it in size and importance.

St. Croix Island now belongs to the United States. You can't get to it from Canada; it lies on the other side of the Great Divide. When the international boundary was extended down the middle of the St. Croix River, the island lay right in its path. It might have been divided in half, or at least fought over, but in the end the land was simply ceded to the United States. The Americans have since designated St. Croix Island an "international historic site," but gestures aside, it now lies, irretrievably, within American waters. If you want to see St. Croix Island from Canada today, all you can do is stand on the shore and peer across and wonder at the Europeans who huddled there that first winter.

In *Who Killed Canadian History?*, J. L. Granatstein likens a nation without a past to an amnesiac "wandering the streets," but it is worse than that. Losing touch with the past is a small form of dying. We need the past in the same way we need our memories: to help define who we are. In a very real sense, we *are* our memories. History can be both an inspiration and a weapon. You can belittle the past; you can ignore it; you can romanticize it. You can attempt to rewrite it, or you can use it to advance agendas or defend traditions. But you cannot deny its importance.

Verdict

Samuel de Champlain: **Bastard**

2 *Exile:*
The Acadian Diaspora

IT IS COMMON for Canadians to prefer geography to history. We love our mountains, we are even proud of our mountains; we are often oblivious to our ghosts. But geography and history are not as different as they appear, for ours is a landscape imbued with history, myth and memory.

Consider: In the Miramichi Bay of northern New Brunswick lies a small island that is the exact size and shape of a nearby lake. The lake is as deep as the island is high, and Micmac mythology tells of a time long past when the island was torn from the earth and then dropped into the salt-water bay. A tale of exile, a missing piece of landscape: it might well serve as a symbol of this, the Land of the Dispossessed. Acadia.

Acadia no longer exists, at least not on maps. The Acadian nation today is like a ghostly overlay, straddling the Maritime provinces and parts of Maine and Québec. It is the oldest European community in North America.

The name Acadia appears to have been derived from the classic Greek "Arcadia," used to describe an idealized, pastoral woodland, but there is also evidence that it came from a Native place name, the river Shubenacadie. Perhaps a congruence of names occurred, blending the Old World with the New. That too would be symbolic.

Acadia was established in 1605 when, after that first disastrous winter on St. Croix Island, de Monts moved his fledging colony to a protected cove where he built Port-Royal, a single, extended *habitation*—a pattern so successful it would be used again a few years later at Québec, where a second French colony was established.

The first Acadian settlers made friends with the Micmac people who fished and hunted in the area under the leadership of the irrepressible and Methuselah-like figure, the *sagamo* and shaman, Membertou. (Legend has it that Membertou was over 100 years old at the time and had been on hand to greet Jacques Cartier 80 years earlier.) With the English farther down the Atlantic coast at Jamestown, Virginia, and New France inland along the St. Lawrence, the lines were drawn. In the middle was Acadia.

Acadia's greatest misfortune was one of geography; the colony was located at a crossroads, a continental cornice, where the hopes of France bordered the Imperial designs of the English. With their key strategic lands coveted and fought over, the Acadians found themselves caught between hammer and anvil in the power politics of the New Frontier. Everyone eventually had a go at conquering, capturing or razing Acadia, even the Dutch, who are, at best, a mere footnote in North American history.

In *France in America*, historian W. J. Eccles argues that Acadia developed as a distinct society *in spite* of France's best efforts, not because of them. France was never concerned with settling the area, but only with denying it to Britain. It wasn't until the 1630s that the population of Acadia began to grow, and this development was due not so much to French support as to simple good health. In the clean environment of the New World, the Acadians enjoyed a remarkable degree of longevity, high fertility and low infant mortality. Acadia may have been a neglected colony, regarded as little more than a pawn by the competing empires of Britain and France, but this very indifference led to a sense of independence and self-reliance that would become a hallmark of Acadian culture. (Early French administrators complained bitterly that the Acadians were not deferential enough to Imperial authority and were, in fact, "semi-republican." In other words, they were developing into a colony of Bastards.)

Acadian society was surprisingly complex, with interconnected extended families and a workable system of democratically selected delegates and communal councils. The Acadians rejected the feudal seigneurial system that was in effect along the St. Lawrence. (Trying to erect a landed aristocracy of seigneurs in the backwoods of Acadia among egalitarian-minded farmers would have been as absurd as it was impractical.) This was not a land of the upwardly mobile. People might go to Québec in pursuit of fortune, fame and adventure, but no one came to Acadia to get rich.

Acadia was settled by people who were seeking to create a homeland, and they recast the very landscape. The massive Fundy tides, 15 metres high in the Minas Basin, were turned back and diverted by Acadian settlers. Using a system of dykes and sluices, they drained the headlands of the Bay of Fundy and reaped grassland harvests from the sediment-rich silt. The dyke-works and the extensive lowland farming of the Acadian settlers are unique in the history of North America.

Although Acadia would later become a tranquil and peaceable society, its early years were filled with turmoil. From 1640 to 1645, the region was rocked by a dramatic and self-destructive civil war.

The roots of the conflict lay in a series of vague royal edicts that appeared to give two rival governors—the aristocrat Charles de Menou d'Aulnay and the merchant-backed Charles de Saint-Étienne de la Tour—final authority over the same area. The real star, however, was La Tour's wife, Françoise-Marie Jacquelin, better known as Madame La Tour. (This is actually a misnomer. Jacquelin, in keeping with the custom of the times, did not take her husband's name.)

In the spring of 1645, while Charles La Tour was in Boston trying desperately to raise arms and supplies for the coming showdown, d'Aulnay led a strike force against his opponent's fort (in what is now the city of Saint John). Having moved his men and cannon into position, d'Aulnay sent a demand for immediate and unconditional surrender to La Tour's wife. But instead of raising a white flag, Jacquelin ran up a defiant red war banner. The Siege of Fort La Tour was underway.

Behind the palisade walls, Jacquelin had fewer than 45 men and only a handful of guns, while d'Aulnay's flagship *Grand Cardinal* alone had 16 cannons primed and ready. When Jacquelin refused to open the gates, D'Aulnay unleashed a deafening bombardment. Salvos of grapeshot strafed the fort, and a fiery barrage of iron missiles rained down, but Jacquelin returned fire, making each shot count and exhorting her men to stand fast. As M. A. MacDonald notes in *Fortune and La Tour*, Jacquelin "proved herself to be a brave, capable and determined warrior . . . If d'Aulnay seemed a lion about to devour his prey, [Jacquelin] defended like a lioness."

The battle raged for three days and three nights, and when d'Aulnay's men finally breached the wall and swarmed inside, they plunged headlong into a nest of swords and pikes. In fierce hand-to-hand combat—led by Madame La Tour herself—d'Aulnay was held at bay. But the situation was now hopeless, and Jacquelin negotiated a truce. With a gallant flourish, d'Aulnay gave her his word of honour that no harm would come to her or her men should they lay down their weapons.

D'Aulnay, cackling like a character in a 1930s radio serial, quickly reneged on his promise, and as soon as he was in control of Fort La Tour he ordered mass executions. Jacquelin was forced to watch, with a noose around her neck, as her men were hanged one by one. More than two dozen of La Tour's most loyal followers were systematically killed. Jacquelin herself died, heartbroken, in a cold, damp prison cell just a few weeks later.

D'Aulnay, the Conqueror of Acadia, was not able to savour his victory for long. He drowned in 1650 when a canoe he was travelling in overturned. (Legend has it he was dragged under by the weight of his armour while a Micmac servant he had recently beaten watched impassively.) Charles La Tour returned to Acadia once d'Aulnay was safely out of the picture and married the dead man's widow(!). With his new bride, he spent his remaining years rebuilding the fur-trade network along the Bay of Fundy.

The d'Aulnay/La Tour feud would prove to be a fateful and far-reaching clash of personalities. At the time the civil war began, Acadia had ranked with—or even above—Québec in importance and prestige. By the time the war ended, however, Acadia was financially, materially and spiritually exhausted. It now lay exposed and vulnerable to the growing English presence on the coast, and the centre of gravity in French North America shifted irrevocably north, to the St. Lawrence River, where a new heartland was developing.

The remnants of the original dykes can still be seen in some places, and the lush Tantramar marshlands of the upper Fundy testify to Acadian ingenuity even today.

The Acadians, unfortunately, were the right people in the right place at the wrong time. They were trying to grow a garden in the middle of a battlefield.

In the seventeenth century alone, Acadia changed hands no fewer than nine times. The flags of competing nations went up and down so often the Acadians stopped worrying about it. And so, when Britain again conquered the heartland of Acadia in 1710, the inhabitants shrugged it off. The Treaty of Utrecht ceded Acadia to Britain in 1713, but the Acadians had no way of knowing that this time the takeover would be permanent.

Shortly afterwards, France began construction of a fortress at Louisbourg, built on the windswept coast of Ile Royale (Cape Breton). It would be the largest fortress in North America, and with its completion, along with strongholds in what are now Prince Edward Island and New Brunswick, the French had all but surrounded the British-held territories of inner Acadia. Britain held the Nova Scotia peninsula and little else.

In the midst of this growing Cold War, the British offered the Acadians under their rule two options: (a) they could forfeit their property, vacate their lands and move to French-held territories, or (b) they could swear an oath of undying loyalty to the king of Britain. The Acadians, faced with two options, chose a third: a *revised* oath. They would not swear loyalty to the British king, but they would agree to stay neutral in any future conflicts.

One British governor after another demanded that the Acadians sign an oath of loyalty, and one governor after another was disappointed. It was very frustrating. These conquered people, these *peasants*, were defying standard Imperial policy, and no matter how much the Brits rattled their sabres, the damned Acadians damn well refused to sign the damned oath. Damn it all anyway. Five times the order went out, and five times it was met with a firm but cheery *non*. What should have been a mere formality became a point of honour—and survival—for the Acadians. They wanted no part of future wars, and unlike the British, they got along fine with the First Nations. Were they to shift alliances, they would risk alienating their Native neighbours—and for what? The answer was still *non*.

The best the British could get was an agreement in which the Acadian settlers acknowledged the obvious: King George was indeed their ruler. But the Acadians agreed to this point only under the following conditions: (a) that Acadian history and traditions be protected, (b) that the Catholic Church be fully respected (something not allowed in anti-Catholic Britain at that time, and (c) that the Acadians be permitted to continue their relationship with the Micmac—who were, technically, still aligned with France and still occasionally ambushed British boats and plundered their supplies. The British hated the Micmac, but they eventually relented to Acadian demands. Oh yes, and one more thing, said the Acadians: Britain must never, *ever* call upon the Acadians to actually fight for Good King George, to whom they had just paid lip-service loyalty. The agreement was, in fact, merely a pact of neutrality. A promise to do nothing.

The Acadians became known as "the neutral French," and with the exception of a small number of rebels, they stuck to the terms of their agreement. When New Englanders launched an attack against the fortress at Louisbourg, the Acadians—much to the chagrin of France—continued tilling their fields and minding their cattle without ever leading the counter-insurgency that the British feared. A few Acadians did scout the situation in Cape Breton, but they were unimpressed with the rocky, infertile soil. As well, the French commander of Louisbourg insisted that Acadians taking up residence in the area would have to swear an oath of loyalty to the king of France *and* join the French militia. Failing that, they would be declared rebels. These were harsher terms than Britain had demanded and, not surprisingly, the Acadians rejected the French orders too.

In truth, the Acadians cared little which foreign flavour-of-the-month was declaring itself sovereign over their lands—and they clearly did view France as a foreign power at this point. They were working towards the day they would become a separate state, independent of both France and Britain. In this aspiration, they were the first true Canadians.

For more than 30 years, under the benign neglect of British rule, Acadia prospered. The once illicit trade with New England became legal. Acadians developed a well-integrated, mixed economy, and they enjoyed a religious freedom allowed neither Catholics in Britain nor Protestants in France. Acadia was at peace, and all was well. Only the oath of loyalty remained a bone of contention. Indeed, the years 1713–49 are often described as the Golden Age of Acadia.

But trouble was brewing beneath the surface. In *The Acadians*, historian Naomi Griffiths writes, "[By] 1748, the Acadians considered themselves Acadian, the French considered them unreliable allies, and the English, unsatisfactory citizens." This disparity in perceptions would prove to be fatal.

In 1749, Edward Cornwallis arrived from England to become governor of Nova Scotia. He surveyed the coast of the Acadian peninsula and in a deep, natural harbour he built a capital: Halifax. Fully fortified, it was designed to be a direct challenge to Louisbourg. Thousands of settlers were brought in. *English* settlers. *German* settlers. Protestants. The struggle for Empire had entered a new stage, the Cold War had moved to endgame, and war clouds were gathering on the horizon.

Cornwallis met with Acadian delegates and repeated the demand that they take an unconditional oath of loyalty. Otherwise, he would have them deported to France. The Acadians, however, stood by their policy of neutral rights. Cornwallis, his bluff called, backed down, but the incident was a forewarning of things to come. In the face of growing hysteria, the well-presented arguments of the Acadians carried less and less weight.

In 1754, Colonel Charles Lawrence was named lieutenant-governor of "Acadia or Nova Scotia," as it was then known, and although he had only six years of life left in him, he would prove to be one of the most socially destructive men in Canadian history. Lawrence was a military man, and for him the world was divided into ally and enemy, for and against, friend and foe. He summoned a contingent of Acadian delegates and again repeated the age-old demand, but this time, when the delegates refused to sign an oath, Lawrence had them thrown in jail. Even from behind bars, the Acadian delegates continued to argue their principles, stating that they were being held illegally and that they could not commit to anything without first consulting the villagers they represented.

In the Imperial world view, a conquered people did not argue. They obeyed. Yet here were these insufferable Acadians, once again presenting well-reasoned arguments against Imperial demands. The delegates offered to turn in their firearms as a gesture of goodwill, but they remained adamant that they would not sign any oath that might one day require them to go to war. And anyway, they pointed out with devastating honesty, no oath would keep Acadians loyal if they didn't want to be. The proof of their good intentions would lie not with a piece of paper but with their past record of non-involvement. For 40 years they had remained neutral. In 40 years, they had never fought against Britain.

Lawrence was seething. When a second delegation arrived, carrying petitions demanding that the jailed delegates be released at once, he switched to Plan B. On September 5, 1755, Acadian farmers gathered at the church in Grand Pré to hear a royal proclamation. It was, in Lawrence's own words, "the final resolution." As the message was read, a shocked silence descended upon the crowd. They had just been declared *personae non gratae*, prisoners of the British Crown. Their land and livestock were to be confiscated and their villages destroyed. There was a mad clamouring of protest, but British warships had already arrived and were waiting in the harbour, and the soldiers were armed and ready. More than 2,000 Acadians were rounded up, forced into boats and taken to transport ships that lay anchored in the Minas Basin. British troops fanned out into the countryside, laying waste to everything in their path.

The Great Expulsion had begun. Under the command of Colonel Robert Monckton and his rabidly anti-Catholic troops, Acadian villages were systematically emptied and their inhabitants herded onto crowded ships at bayonet point. Crops and buildings were burned, harvests ransacked, the earth scorched. Livestock was either butchered or left to starve. Of the 7,000 or so Acadians taken prisoner and sent away in cargo ships that first year, more than 3,000 died. Smallpox, typhoid and yellow fever had all been unknown in Acadia; now they took their toll. One ship, the *Cornwallis*, left Acadia with 417 prisoners on board, but only 210 were still alive by the time the ship reached South Carolina.

Hundreds of Acadians were sent to internment camps in England, but most of them were scattered throughout the 13 colonies of America. Some were exiled as far away as the Falkland Islands. Charles Lawrence didn't want to send the Acadians to French-held territories for fear of strengthening the enemy's hand, though a direct appeal from the French king eventually managed to get some of the prisoners shipped to France. But the Acadians who arrived there found themselves strangers in a strange land. They were not citizens of France, had not been for a hundred years. Even though they were offered enviable conditions for the peasantry of the day, they yearned for the New World.

And so, incredibly, more than 1,500 Acadians left France within a few years and resettled in Louisiana, a Spanish-held francophone territory. Here they found the wilderness, the lack of aristocratic conventions, the freedom, even the swamps that they had grown used to. They began dyking and draining the Louisiana marsh-lands, but they soon learned, as they died in the heat, that the cool clean air of Acadia was far different from the fever and muggy misery of the Bayou. The Louisiana settlers were joined by other Acadians who escaped and made their way, painfully, towards what was becoming an "Acadia in exile." The settlers were called 'Cadiens and, later, simply Cajuns, and their descendants number more than a million in Louisiana today. In the fiddle tunes and accents of the Cajuns are the memory of a people lost and of an exodus unprecedented in the history of the western hemisphere.

Although strong geopolitical forces were at work, in the end the responsibility for the Expulsion lies squarely with Colonel Lawrence. He was, of course, a Bastard. And the rigidness of his personality was, more than anything else, the deciding factor. Indeed, a message had been sent from King George ordering Lawrence *not* to deport the Acadians. It arrived too late, and once Lawrence's policy seemed to be working, the British Parliament changed its mind and gave its whole-hearted approval to the operation.

The instructions that Lawrence gave Colonel Monckton and the other English officers were blunt: Consider the Acadians enemies of the state. Take them prisoner. Confiscate all cattle and crops. Force those in hiding to turn themselves in, "by burning the Villages and destroying everything that can afford them the least Shelter." And although Lawrence never *demanded* that his troops separate families, he did encourage this practice as a way of breaking Acadian solidarity. "I would have you not wait for the Wives and Children coming in," he wrote, "but Ship Off the Men without them."

"The deportation was done with astonishing speed," writes historian Christopher Moore. "In a matter of months, Acadia ceased to exist."

The entire Acadian region had been almost completely depopulated. Of the estimated 13,000 inhabitants, between 9,000 and 10,000 were forcibly removed during Charles Lawrence's reign of terror. Those who were not captured fled, or tried to. More than a thousand Acadian resisters were thrown into stone-walled prison cells. One group dug a tunnel and made a bold escape. Others headed inland, northwards into uncharted forests. Many perished in the attempt.

In 1760, after the fall of Québec, a French armada trying to break through the British blockade of the St. Lawrence came upon a ragged camp of Acadian refugees, starved to the point where they were chewing beaver skins. The French commander turned over his food supplies to the poor souls. "This little help," he wrote in his journal, "rescued them from death's door."

One group of Acadians returned rather quickly. On their outward-bound voyage, they overpowered the British crew, captured the ship, turned it around and sailed for home. When Lawrence heard of this, he sent a warship to recapture them, but the rebel Acadians eluded the British and escaped into the woods. Many Acadians joined the ongoing battle for Québec as guerrillas and privateers, and they made a name for themselves as stubborn, fierce fighters, tenacious under fire.

Several hundred Acadians sought refuge on the French-held islands of St. Pierre and Miquelon, but most left in 1793 when, ironically, the recently established government of the French Revolution demanded that the settlers take an oath of loyalty to the New Republic. Rather than submit, the people moved on. For many Acadians, the Expulsion was the beginning of more than 50 years of wandering.

At least 2,000 Acadians escaped to Prince Edward Island and Louisbourg, but when these too fell to the British, the deportations began anew. It was only with the Treaty of Paris in 1763 that the deportations finally ended, and by then, there were very few Acadians left to deport. They had been scattered like spare change, a dispersed, beaten people, living in poverty and nostalgia at points far-flung.

French-speaking historians have long since labelled Charles Lawrence "a criminal soul." He was certainly cold-hearted, and he knew a good land grab when he saw one, noting that the Acadians "possess[ed] the best and largest tracts of land in this province." As ungrateful subjects, the Acadians were, in his eyes, fair game for plunder. The Expulsion cost Britain a lot of time and money, but it also released the rich farmlands of the Annapolis Valley and the reclaimed marshlands of the Bay of Fundy for new, more "loyal" citizens.

Charles Lawrence had died in 1760. The war between France and Britain ended, and slowly, like a cresting wave, the Acadians began making their way back home, on foot and by ship, along tortuous roads and routes, like a lost tribe returning.

New England opportunists, dubbed Planters, now occupied the former lands of the Acadians, and they were followed—in the wake of the American Revolution—by United Empire Loyalists. Forced to the periphery, to hard fields and untilled lands, the Acadians adapted. Farmers became fishermen and lumberjacks. The biggest single effect of the diaspora was that the Acadian centre of gravity shifted north, into what is now New Brunswick. As historian John Reid notes in his introduction to *The Acadians of Nova Scotia*, "It is one of the ironies of Acadian history that most Acadians now live outside Nova Scotia."

Isolated economically, geographically, linguistically, the Acadians became an inward-looking, almost forlorn people. The experience of their exile and the bittersweet triumph of their return, together with their burning conviction that they had been entirely in the right, gave them a new source of identity and—ultimately—strength.

At night, it became the custom for Acadians to gather to listen to tales of the Expulsion told by older members of their community, and fiction, fact and folklore mixed freely in these oral accounts. The American poet Henry W. Longfellow heard of these tales and was especially stricken by the stories of separation, of family and lovers who spent years trying to reunite after having been scattered to the winds. From this came his epic narrative poem, *Evangeline: A Tale of Acadie*, first published in 1847. It told the story of Evangeline and Gabriel, young, would-be lovers separated at Grand Pré. Evangeline, her heart "sustained by a vision," crosses mountains, deserts, woodlands, swamps, rivers and perpetual snows, searching for her lost love and always just missing him. At one point the two pass, quite literally, like ships in the night.

Evangeline ends her days as a kindly, grey-haired nun. While attending to the dying poor in an almshouse, she comes upon Gabriel, now bent and stricken with pestilence, just as he is about to breathe his last. After they share one final kiss, Gabriel's eyes roll heavenward, and he dies "as when a lamp is blown out by a gust of wind."

Evangeline was a huge success. The Victorians romanticized the Acadians as simple rural people living life in charming poverty, cheerfully wondering where their next meal would come from—and for a while it was popular among the upper class to make the trip to Acadia to gawk at the locals. It was all very condescending.

But the tale of Evangeline also had a remarkable impact upon the Acadians themselves, giving their story form and focus. Translated into French, the poem quickly went through several printings and soon replaced the traditional storytellers as a source of historical myth. *Evangeline* told of an idyllic, almost angelic way of life gone forever. "The dominating theme of Longfellow's vision," writes Naomi Griffiths, "is that of terrestrial Paradise Lost, and one lost without proven original sin."

In the mythos *de la Nation Acadienne*, history was divided into two periods, before and after, by the razor-like trauma of the Expulsion, *le grand dérangement*, the Great Upheaval. Acadians themselves came to believe in a Golden Age, an age whose passing, like that of the fictional Evangeline, "seemed like the ceasing of exquisite music."

An Acadian sense of self crystallized, and at Memramcook in 1881 the first Acadian Conference was held. Delegates gathered to forge an identity and a destiny separate from that of the French Canadians in Québec. Instead of St. John the Baptist, the Acadians chose Stella Maris as their patron saint, and the hymn *Ave*

❦ UNITED EMPIRE LOYALISTS: THE ORIGINAL BOAT PEOPLE

The American Revolution was, above all, a civil war. It divided towns and even families between those who remained loyal to the British crown and those who supported the Republican cause. Following the Republican victory in 1783, more than 50,000 Loyalists, fleeing reprisals, escaped north into what is now Canada. They were the original boat people. So many Loyalists flooded into Nova Scotia that a new colony, New Brunswick, had to be carved out to make room for them, and throughout the Maritimes, the Loyalists moved in and took possession of what had been Acadian land. Many more settled inland, along the Great Lakes and in what is now the Eastern Townships of Québec. The town of Kingston became a Loyalist heartland.

"They sacrificed everything save honour" became their epitaph, and the tale of the Loyalists—basically a saga of defeat and exile—has been romanticized over the years as a well-mannered exodus of genteel aristocrats. In *The Diverting History of a Loyalist Town* (first published in 1932), Grace Helen Mowat describes the arrival of Loyalists in St. Andrews in the following manner:

> The ships anchored in the harbour, the small boats were lowered and the gallant gentlemen, in their powdered wigs and plumcoloured coats and three-cornered hats, helped the ladies to alight. How quaint and delightful a picture . . . It must have been fun, too. A kind of vast picnic for those courageous and resourceful people.

Fun? A vast picnic? Hardly. The Loyalists landed unprepared and ill advised, bedraggled and defeated. They were also notoriously anti-French, which contributed to a rapid increase of tensions between French and English Canada. Given their "anti-papist" distrust of Catholics, that the Loyalists would hold a grudge was understandable. After all, France, in aiding the American Revolution, had been largely responsible for the rebels' victory.

The returning exiled Acadians, the Loyalist refugees and the recently conquered *Canadiens* did not make for a very harmonious mix: three peoples united only by their separate tales of defeat. Along such fault lines was Canada built.

Maria Stella as their anthem. The Feast of the Assumption on August 15 became the Acadian national holiday, and a few years later, they even chose a flag: the tricolours of France with a single gold star in the upper left corner.

And with the 1960 election of 34-year-old Acadian Louis Robichaud, one of the youngest provincial premiers in Canadian history, the province of New Brunswick entered its own Quiet Revolution, a time of sudden, exhilarating change. Another Acadian had held the position of premier for a few years in the 1920s, but only as a replacement for the ruling party's leadership; he never won an election. Robichaud did.

By the 1960s, the Acadian presence had grown to represent a full third of New Brunswick's population, but through discrimination, passive and otherwise, Acadians had languished as a lower caste. Robichaud's Liberals set out to change all this. For the first time ever, French textbooks were allowed in provincial schools. A francophone campus, Université de Moncton, opened, and in 1969 New Brunswick became the first province in Canada to declare itself officially bilingual. Robichaud set New Brunswick on its present course, one based on equality of opportunity, social commitments and a bilingual reality. In doing so, he incurred the wrath of the mighty Irving empire, which held the entire region in economic thrall and raised fierce opposition to Robichaud's initiatives. In a Battle of the Bastards, Louis Robichaud went head-to-head with K. C. Irving Himself—and won. Or at least, drew a stalemate, which, when you're up against the Dark Side of the Force, is tantamount to victory.

The Irving-owned newspapers lashed out at Robichaud's Program of Equal Opportunity, and editorial cartoonists took to depicting the premier as a sort of second-rate Louis XIV, dressed in tattered ermine, eyes wild, sword flailing. The Tories, predictably, denounced Robichaud as "a little dictator." But even K. C. Irving, with his behind-the-scenes clout and political ties, could not topple Louis Robichaud. P'Tit Louis, as he was now known, brazenly threw down the gauntlet and challenged K. C. to come out from the shadows and face Robichaud directly in an election. He should run for public office and let the people decide. "That," said Robichaud cuttingly, "is how democracy works."

Louis Robichaud was in power from 1960 to 1970, and the changes he wrought were immense. The Robichaud Formula itself would later be used as a model for Canada's national bilingualism policies (although, ironically, it was the Tories under Robichaud's successor, Richard Hatfield, who would actually implement New Brunswick's Official Languages Act.)

Against all odds, the Acadian nation has survived. Roughly 85 per cent of all Acadians now live in New Brunswick, either along the east coast or in the northern reaches of Madawaska, where a subsection of Acadia has developed: the lumberjack culture of *les Brayons*. Smaller Acadian communities exist in Nova Scotia and P.E.I., making up roughly 5 per cent of the populations of those provinces. Acadians have recently reestablished cultural and commercial ties with the Cajuns of New Orleans, and in 1999, the World Acadian Congress met in Louisiana.

Today, New Brunswick takes justifiable pride in its lively mix of Acadian and Loyalist roots. Tensions exist, to be sure, but in a country ready to rupture over English on stop signs and French on cornflakes boxes, New Brunswick stands out as a level-headed alternative. (And let me just say, for the record, that New Brunswick is *the* most underrated province in Canada.)

The principles upon which the Acadians stood are as solid today as they ever were. Theirs is a spirit captured best in the raucous *tintamarre*, "noise-making festivals," when horn blowing, bell ringing and outrageous costumes celebrate this simple fact: we are still here, and we are still very much alive. Acadia, with its own distinctive cuisine and dialect, is currently undergoing a renaissance, through theatre, music, visual art, folk crafts and literature. When Québec separatists such as author Yves Beauchemin dismiss the Acadians and other francophones living outside of Québec as "still-warm corpses," they reveal only their own profound ignorance.

Acadia *is* Canada, in a very real sense, for it has projected itself outwards onto the nation: in 1982, New Brunswick's Official Languages Act was incorporated into Canada's Charter of Rights and Freedoms. New Brunswick remains the only province in Canada that is officially bilingual and the only one whose language laws are cited specifically in our constitution. The 1982 charter, with its guarantee of freedom of speech, ideas and religion, is, in effect, an *oath*—an oath not to King or Crown but to an ideal, to a set of principles. It enshrines loyalty not to raw power but to human dignity, equality and unity.

Québec may set the national agenda, and Québec may hold the balance of political power, but the future of Canada lies elsewhere, with a people and a province who have learned to rise above animosity and unite opposing loyalties—becoming stronger in the process. The lesson of Acadia is one all Canadians could benefit from.

If we are good, if we are very, very good, we may one day become Acadians.

Verdict

Charles Lawrence, who thought he could force a community to disappear: **Bastard**

Louis Robichaud, who proved his community was still alive: **Even Bigger Bastard**

Conquest:
The Plains of Abraham

JE ME SOUVIENS. I remember . . .

This sad, stubborn motto is pressed into every licence plate, and every heart, of every Québécois. It is displayed on government banners, emblazoned on coats of arms, spelled out in flower beds and printed on bumper stickers. It can even be found on the flag of the queen's own representative in Québec. *Je me souviens.*

That Québec is a land steeped in its past is evident in this motto, both elegy and rallying cry, at once defiant and defeated. The prevailing attitude was expressed by historian Abbé Groulx as "*Notre maître, le passé.*" "Our master, the past." While the rest of the nation seems to exist in a thin veneer of the present, Québec tosses and turns with the insomnia of history. Memories of past wrongs haunt Québec, and Québec, in turn, haunts Canada.

Je me souviens was suggested as a provincial motto by architect Eugène Taché, who had the words inscribed beneath the coat of arms on Québec's National Assembly building in 1883. The words were meant to evoke French language and customs, the glories of the *ancien régime*. Today, the motto has an angry undertone, a kind of "Remember the Alamo" appeal, but the three-line poem from which it is derived is ambiguous: "*Je me souviens / Que né sous le lys / Je crois sous la rose.*" "I remember that, while under the fleur-de-lis [of France], I grow under the rose [of England]." The reference is to the Conquest of 1760.

In Québec, the significance of the conquest, *la conquête*, has changed significantly over the years. The Catholic clergy once saw it as a blessing in disguise, an event that saved guileless habitants from the evils of the atheistic French Revolution. In the 1960s, the conquest was politicized, becoming the symbol of past wrongs and Anglo oppression. Today, it is seen as either a tragedy to be lamented or a challenge to be met, but however one chooses to interpret it, it *was* conquest. "And conquest," writes historian Susan Mann Trofimenkoff, "is like rape."

In theory, Confederation erased the conquest. Confederation, after all, was a voluntary union. Myths to the contrary, a majority of Québec representatives supported it. The leader of the Parti Bleu, George-Étienne Cartier, was one of Confederation's key architects. No shots were fired. No one was conquered. In theory, after 1867, Canada ceased to be a land divided into two groups: the Conquered and the Conquerors. In theory, after 1867, we became something more. Sadly, this idea has never quite taken hold.

Christian Dufour, in *Le Défi Québécois* (translated as *A Canadian Challenge*), writes:

> People are often very surprised that Quebeckers say they are still affected by an event that took place over two hundred years ago, while other peoples have already overcome more recent, more devastating defeats. They forget the fundamental difference between defeat and conquest. A conquest is a permanent defeat, an institutionalized defeat.

In her book *Double Vision*, Lyse Champagne describes the conquest as the "Big Bang" of Canadian history, "hurling fragments of the past into the orbit of the future, and forever altering the chronicling of that past."

And so, although politically, socially and economically the key moment in Canadian history is Confederation, emotionally and psychologically the pivotal point remains the fall of New France in 1760. The Battle of the Plains of Abraham, on which the conflict turned, has never really ended. We are fighting it still.

In 1756, with the Expulsion of the Acadians fully underway, Great Britain officially declared war on France and her allies. It was, in the words of Winston Churchill, "the first world war in history," a war that would pit the two great Imperial powers of the day against each other in a struggle for supremacy.

The Seven Years War actually raged for *nine* years in North America (1754–63). In the war's early stages, the quick-running guerrilla tactics of the *Canadiens* and their Native allies proved remarkably efficient. The British redcoats, with their stiff formations and scarlet jackets, made easy targets for snipers hiding behind the cover of forest. Noting that the redcoats loaded and reloaded their weapons to the beat of a drum and on command, the *Canadiens* and the Natives quickly learned to shoot the drummers and officers first. The British forces would fall into confused disarray, and the slaughter would begin. The French army proved just as effective— in the beginning. They won battle after battle, often while greatly outnumbered. But of course the only battle that really counts is the *last* battle, and the British had a habit of winning that one.

William Pitt, Britain's new prime minister, was growing violently impatient. Pitt was an intense, at times insane, man; he was also obsessed with taking New France. As the self-styled "saviour of the British Empire," he was filled with a resolve that contrasted sharply with that of the financially strapped courts of France. For Pitt, the primary theatre of war was not Europe but North America. And thus, while France sent just 7,000 regulars to reinforce its American colonies, Britain sent 23,000.

In 1759, Pitt assembled a huge armada, almost a quarter of Britain's navy, including a strike force of 9,000 men. His goal? To blockade the St. Lawrence and capture the city of Québec, "the capital of Canada." As the British armada sailed into the mouth of the river, its ships stretched in line for 50 miles, and the habitants on shore watched nervously as they passed. Leading this massive military expedition was a thin, erratic, anaemic young man named James Wolfe. Wolfe had made a name for himself at the Battle of Louisbourg the year before, when his reckless heroics had helped win a victory for the British. He was only 32 years old. The strike force against Québec was his first independent command. It would also be his last.

New France at the time was grossly mismanaged. Corruption was rife throughout the Imperial world, but here it became something of an art form. The colony's economic manager, the intendant François Bigot, had been embezzling funds and cheating the French Crown to an unheard-of extent. Historians have shown two tendencies in their portrayal of Bigot: he is presented as either a grotesque, corrupt man whose excesses hastened the fall of the French colonies or as a miracle worker who kept New France supplied even as he lined his pockets, only to be turned into a scapegoat after the fact. Both interpretations are probably valid. Bigot *was* grotesque. He *did* keep New France supplied. He *did* steal a fortune. And he *was* made into a scapegoat. (Mind you, that doesn't mean we have to *like* the corpulent little toad.)

The governor of New France, Pierre de Rigaud, Marquis de Vaudreuil, has also been dealt with harshly by British and English-Canadian historians. True, the Marquis de Vaudreuil was not exactly a tactical genius, but neither was he the meddlesome, petty man historians often depict. What the marquis lacked in ability, he made up for in enthusiasm. Vaudreuil was the first native-born *Canadien* to govern New France, and it is important to keep that fact in mind. He was not defending a colony; he was defending his homeland. Vaudreuil put great faith in *les Canadiens* and their wilderness style of warfare, and he commanded both the trust and the respect of France's Native allies. Above all, Vaudreuil longed to take the battle to the

English, to roll them back and burn their forts. A resolute optimist, he was, at 60, at the height of a long career.

Vaudreuil stood in stark contrast to the man sent by the king of France to direct the war effort. Louis-Joseph, Marquis de Montcalm, a short, portly aristocrat, was in many ways "the reluctant general." Montcalm had given up before Wolfe ever arrived. Although an experienced soldier—a wounded war hero, no less—Montcalm was doomfully pessimistic over the fate of New France. He soon wearied of the constant bickering with Vaudreuil and asked to be recalled. Instead, he was promoted and given final authority. On all matters military, Vaudreuil, the governor of New France, was now under *his* authority. It was the worst possible arrangement. The two men openly despised one another and worked at cross-purposes. The pessimist vs. the optimist. The French general vs. the *Canadien* governor. Standard European battle formations vs. the guerrilla warfare techniques of *la petite guerre*. It was this wasteful personality clash, this destructive feud, that as much as anything else cost France its colonies in North America.

By the time Wolfe's strike force arrived in mid-June 1759, Montcalm had already drawn up tentative "Articles of Capitulation." Months before, he had confided in a letter that unless peace came soon, the colony was lost: "I can see nothing that can save it."

Vaudreuil, on the other hand, was far too confident. As the British armada arrived, he assured Montcalm that no vessel could possibly traverse the narrows of Québec once he had removed the navigational markers. But the British sent out a young navigator by the name of James Cook (who would go on to become one of the greatest explorers in naval history), and Cook sounded the channel with ease. The river was no more dangerous than the Thames, one of the captains remarked, and the armada sailed on through and anchored off Ile d'Orléans. Vaudreuil was astonished. Montcalm was dismayed.

Wolfe too was in for a surprise. Relying on out-of-date information apparently given to him by escaped prisoner Robert Stobo (whose life deserves a chapter, if not a book, all its own), Wolfe had expected to make short work of Québec. He would land on the tidal flats to the east and capture the city from the rear and the flank. What he came up against instead was a hastily erected, but fatally effective, earthwork fortification, as well as rows of half-sunken ships used as water-level cannon platforms.

The man who had overseen the construction of these defences was none other than François-Gaston, Chevalier de Lévis, arguably the most capable soldier on the field. Had Lévis been in command instead of Montcalm or Vaudreuil, Québec would almost certainly *not* have fallen—at least not that year. Unfortunately, Lévis was sent back to Montréal to ready defences against another English strike force on its way under General Jeffery Amherst.

Amherst, the methodical commander-in-chief of the British forces in North America, was slowly making his way up Lake Champlain, capturing French forts systematically, ineluctably, as he went. At the same time, a *third* strike force was approaching from the west, along Lake Ontario. The noose was tightening.

Wolfe, however, had run into a wall. Almost literally. The cliffs of Québec, the "Gibraltar of North America," were the most formidable natural defences in the New World, and the Upper Town was perched atop Cap-Diamant like a taunt. Wolfe set up an artillery camp on the south shore of the St. Lawrence with his cannons pointed straight at the city. Panic spread, but Vaudreuil was sure the English cannons would never be able to reach the opposite shore. On July 12, the first cannonball was fired at Québec City. As it splashed harmlessly into the St. Lawrence, the *Canadiens* cheered. Then a second shot was fired. It flew right over the Lower Town and crashed into the Upper. English cannons had the range after all.

In the military conventions of the day, firing on civilian targets, or even pointing artillery in their general direction, was frowned upon. War was a purely military engagement, with set pieces and unified formations. Indeed, crowds of spectators would often gather to watch well-publicized battles. But with young General Wolfe came the notion that when countries are at war, everyone is a potential target.

Wolfe was relentless. A rain of iron fell, and the city burned. In one night alone, a conflagration destroyed over 150 houses. Day and night the cannons pounded, but Wolfe was just warming up. He sent his wild, buckskin-clan American Rangers—whom he had earlier dismissed as "the dirtiest, most contemptible cowardly dogs" and the "worst soldiers in the universe"—to scour the countryside. The Rangers, like the *Canadiens* and the Indians of *la petite guerre*, were men of stealth and sudden attack. And like the *Canadiens* and the Indians, they took scalps.

Wolfe ordered the Rangers to "burn and lay waste the country," and thus every town, house, barn and garden for an 80-kilometre stretch along the densely populated south shore was torched. Livestock was slaughtered, and hundreds of settlers were rounded up and taken prisoner. Only the churches were spared, and even then only if the habitants of the local community had not resisted. It was during this campaign of terror that the now-familiar phrase "*les maudits Anglais*" first came into common usage.

All along the river and into the distance, smoke curled up like cries of anguish. The destruction continued throughout the summer. More than 1,400 farmhouses, many of them magnificent stone buildings, were systematically destroyed. At the village of St-Joachim, the Rangers lined up 30 habitant resisters, including the parish priest, and shot them all, then burned the village to the ground. This was spite, not strategy. As Bigot himself succinctly put it: "*M. Wolfe est cruel.*"

General Wolfe's war crimes, often presented in history books as the result of intense frustration, were actually coldly premeditated. On the voyage over, long before the fighting had begun, Wolfe had written to General Amherst:

> If by accident in the River, or by the Enemy's resistance, by sickness, or by slaughter in the Army, or, from any other cause, we find that Quebec is not likely to fall into our hands . . . I propose to set the Town on fire with Shells, to destroy the Harvest, Houses, & cattle, both above & below, to send off as many Canadians as possible to Europe, & to leave famine and desolation behind me.

Yet even as Wolfe attempted to hammer the French into surrender, or at least submission, Montcalm refused to come out from behind his walled city. When Wolfe feinted, Montcalm would counterstrike. When Wolfe moved, Montcalm would move. If Wolfe's tactics were those of attrition, Montcalm's were those of delay. Winter was approaching, and if the French could just hold out long enough, they might buy themselves another year.

As summer slowly bled away, Wolfe became violent and moody. He was now clashing openly with his officers. He was impatient, indecisive; he contradicted his own orders, and eventually he worried himself sick. One of his brigadiers, George Townshend, took to drawing merciless caricatures of the general. (Townshend also began compiling evidence for the court martial that he felt would inevitably follow Wolfe's failed expedition.) Soldiers had been sniped at, shot, flogged, sent into crossfires; and now they were deserting. The only thing that could save Wolfe's career was total victory. Either that, or a suitably romantic death. James Wolfe was about to earn both.

Autumn came. The air chilled. Soon the St. Lawrence would freeze over and become impassable, but Wolfe decided to make one last attempt before leaving. He turned his attention upriver: If he could somehow get his ships past the French sentries undetected, he might be able to land, scale the cliffs and line his men up on the field *behind* Québec City. And then maybe—just maybe—he would be able to draw Montcalm out from behind the walls and into a set, European-style conflict. The plan was foolhardy to the point of recklessness, and yet, incredibly, Wolfe managed to achieve every one of his objectives.

The site Wolfe chose for the landing of his troops was unlikely: the steep embarkment at Anse-au-Foulon, where a break in the rocks might possibly allow an army to climb the 53-metre cliffs. A small contingent of French troops at the top could have wiped out an advancing army with ease, so the landing would have to be done silently, and at night. Perhaps Wolfe had a death wish after all.

Fortunately for the British, the plan *was* crazy. So crazy that no one took it seriously. When a junior French officer mentioned Anse-au-Foulon as a possible landing site, Montcalm dismissed the idea with a snort. Just hours before Wolfe's landing, Montcalm had written, "We need not imagine that the enemy has wings, so that in one night they can cross the river, disembark, climb the obstructed cliffs, and scale the walls."

But as Montcalm was about to discover, the English didn't need to have wings. All they needed was a bit of luck, and they got it. Under cover of darkness, a flotilla of flat-bottomed boats drifted downstream on the tide. The British troops managed to slip past French sentries and land unopposed in the darkness. As they made the arduous climb up Anse-au-Foulon, often pulling themselves along by weeds and roots, a small French battery spotted them and began firing, but by then it was too late. The battery was quickly overpowered, and the rest of the British soldiers reached the heights unopposed. They were now across from the very walls of the city itself. The surprise was complete.

The Plains of Abraham have a suitably biblical name, one evoking sacrifice and divine judgement, but these fields were named not for the patriarch of the Old Testament but for a settler who once owned land in the area. Montcalm was having his morning tea on September 13, 1759, when he was greeted with the news that the British were on the plains. His chest tightened. The moment had arrived.

Or had it? Let's consider what Wolfe had really achieved. He had put himself and about 4,400 of his men at the edge of a cliff. They were far from their supplies, with only a couple of cannons that they had managed to drag up and an entire forest filled with Indian snipers on their flank. The British had, in fact, marched into a potential mass grave. As historian W. J. Eccles notes, "Few generals have burned their bridges more successfully than did Wolfe." Retreat was impossible; the British could only hope that Montcalm would make a serious miscalculation—which he obligingly did.

Wolfe's plan succeeded not because it was a good one, but because, on that misty morning in 1759, Montcalm was just a little bit more incompetent than the English general. Perhaps Montcalm felt insulted. Perhaps he was enraged. Perhaps he simply panicked, but he quickly scrambled together the troops he had on hand and decided to attack. All summer long, he had refused to engage the enemy. Now, when caution was called for, he decided to leave the walls and face Wolfe in the one type of battle that Wolfe would certainly win: a standard European arrangement. The decision Montcalm made that morning—to hurry out from behind the walls and engage Wolfe on the Plains of Abraham—changed the course of Canadian history forever.

The French advance was more of a ragged charge. Although Montcalm had mixed *Canadiens* in with his French regulars, he hadn't properly trained them, and it was all the *Canadiens* could do to keep formation. The French and the *Canadiens* had clearly never attacked together, either, even under simulated conditions. When the *Canadiens* flung themselves to the ground after firing and rolled to one side to reload (as was their custom), the French troops stumbled all over them. "In the fall of Québec," notes Desmond Morton in *A Short History of Canada*, "the French and the *Canadiens* discovered how little they had in common."

Here then is how the battle unfolds. The French and the *Canadiens* rush forward. The British troops wait, a thin red line two men deep. They are kneeling. Bagpipes are playing. Bullets whiz by. Men are hit. Soldiers begin to fall, but the line holds. Wolfe's fanatical, Prussian-like discipline is about to pay off. When the French and the *Canadiens* are just 30 paces away, the British stand and the command is given. The redcoats fire by volley, first one platoon, then the next. The smoke from their muskets takes seven minutes to clear. They reload, prime their guns and advance 10 paces, emerging from the smoke like ghosts. They raise their muskets and fire as one, a single thunderclap that echoes across the field . . .

This time, as the smoke cleared, bodies were lying scattered before the British troops, and French forces were falling back in disarray. The withdrawal became a retreat, and the retreat became a desperate flight. Montcalm, astride his magnificent black horse, was hit twice. He reeled in his saddle but refused to fall. Regaining his balance, he straightened himself and rode, slowly, back through the gates. The next morning the Marquis de Montcalm was dead.

James Wolfe died on the battlefield. A *Canadien* sharpshooter had fired from the forest and split open the English general's chest. As Wolfe lay dying, with only a few officers on hand, a cry went up: "They run!" Wolfe looked up anxiously. "Who runs?" "The enemy, sir. They give way everywhere."

It had been a massive, headlong clash of 9,000 men, the two sides equal in number, and the number of casualties had also been roughly the same, around 650 dead on each side. The battle itself had taken less than half an hour.

Nothing had yet been had settled, however. The British had won a field, that was all. Lévis might still arrive from Montréal and save the day. Rearguard troops might yet counterattack. Lock the gates! Send out the Indians! Bring up the reinforcements!

But Vaudreuil took none of these actions. Instead, he fled the city gates with the French army, taking a side road in an inglorious retreat. The French had abandoned the city, just as France would abandon its colonies at the end of the war. It is a historical fact worth repeating: the *Canadiens* were not so much conquered as abandoned.

The flight of the French army was demoralizing and disgraceful. When Lévis heard of it, he immediately marched his men to Québec, to crush the British once and for all, but by then the city had surrendered, and the Union Flag had replaced the fleur-de-lis. The redcoats were now in control.

The British had captured Québec City, but the war was far from over. Lévis returned the following spring, looking for a rematch, and he got it. Inside the city walls, the British had spent a hellish winter. They had come to the New World expecting a summer battle: they had only one uniform each, and the Highlanders were dressed in kilts, no less. The harsh winter punished the conquerors. Sentries froze to death. Men died of scurvy. James Murray, the tough little Scot who was now in charge, found himself in a city made largely uninhabitable by Wolfe's vindictive bombardment. Only a single building remained intact in the whole of Lower Town.

Lévis arrived with a small band of men. Incredibly, James Murray made the same mistake as Montcalm: he left the city walls and attacked. Lévis fell back, and Murray followed. Only too late did the Scot realize it was a trap. Suddenly he came face to face with the full might of Lévis's forces. Murray held his ground at first, but the tide of battle soon turned. A full retreat sounded, and the British got back inside the city barely in time, abandoning valuable artillery on the field and slamming the gates shut in the very faces of Lévis's men.

Lévis knew that the walls of Québec could be breached, but his siege needed stronger cannons and full reinforcements. Murray needed food and ammunition. Both sides were hurting, and both now turned their gaze down the St. Lawrence. It all came down to this: the arrival of supplies from Europe. The final battle would be a race across the Atlantic; whichever side's supply ships arrived first would be the victor. The men watched, and they waited.

Almost two weeks passed before a mast appeared in the distance and a ship slipped into sight. Lévis and his men cheered. But then the flag caught the wind and unfurled. It was British. Two days later, more ships arrived, and not a single one was French. A combination of French defeats in other lands, the British blockade and royal indifference had brought an end to Lévis's counteroffensive. Bitter and disheartened, he marched his army back to Montréal, where more than 17,000 British troops were about to converge from all sides.

Montréal, barely able to muster a force of 2,000 men, and with only wooden palisades to protect it, was indefensible. For Jeffery Amherst, the careful general, the time had arrived. He sent a message to Governor Vaudreuil, who was now behind the walls of Montréal. "I have come to take Canada," said Amherst. "And I will take nothing less."

It was September 8, 1760. New France had fallen. Lévis and his men burned their battle flags so that no English soldier might claim them as a prize, then marched out from the city and sailed for France. Lévis was eventually made marshal, the highest rank possible, and he died a much-loved and respected figure. During the French Revolution, however, mobs of liberators executed his widow and daughters on the guillotine and dug up his grave and scattered his bones.

Wolfe had better luck; his body was embalmed and sent home, and a romantic cult of sorts grew to envelop his name. British historians fawned over him for centuries, but common sense eventually prevailed, and Wolfe has now been critically reevaluated. Vaudreuil, meanwhile, lived to the ripe old age of 80 and died in the south of France, far from his homeland. He too had abandoned Canada.

When news of the conquest first reached the French court, the philosopher Voltaire reportedly made his celebrated quip, "Canada is a few acres of snow and not worth a soldier's bones." That stinging insult, "*quelques arpents de neige,*" has stayed with Canadians ever since, but the French court was much more astute than it appeared. In fact, it proved remarkably prescient. The French first minister predicted that, without the threat of France to unite them, the English-speaking colonies would soon start fighting amongst themselves. And that is exactly what happened.

The American colonies boiled over in revolution, and France, smiling all the while, threw its support behind George Washington's rebel army. The French assistance was crucial, and in the end the American colonies managed to defeat the might of the British Empire and establish a new republic.

For one brief, shining moment, Great Britain had held all of North America. Now it had lost its most valuable colonies. All Britain was left with was an eclectic mix of French-speaking *Canadiens,* Loyalist refugees, some fishing coves in Newfoundland, and the one Atlantic seaboard colony that had stayed loyal: Nova Scotia (formerly known as Acadia). It was from this patchwork of leftovers and tattered remains that Canada was born, an odd alliance of *Canadien* and Canadian. France's sweetest revenge and the greatest practical joke ever played on the British Empire: Canada.

The Conquest of 1760 is the Great Lament of French-Canadian history. It has traumatized and enraged and impeded the Québécois for more than 200 years. Or has it? Author Gilles Lalande calls the constant preoccupation of Québec's intellectuals with the conquest a "perpetual alibi."

What is less often acknowledged is that the conquest cuts both ways. English Canadians have never quite gotten over it either. If French Canadians lament it, English Canadians have gloried in it—have, indeed, wallowed in it. For centuries, English Canadians have insisted on claiming the rights of the conqueror and have acted like the offspring of victors: "Didn't we beat them on the Plains of Abraham?" But the only Canadians present on the Plains of Abraham spoke French. There were no English Canadians, because English Canada didn't exist. It hadn't been invented yet. *We* didn't "beat them on the Plains of Abraham," because *we* didn't exist.

Today, English Canada wants to kiss and make up, but in Québec memories die hard, and the Plains of Abraham burn with a singular intensity. The standoff has gone beyond history; it is saga, a masochistic myth, a mantra. An alibi. It can also be very tiring. As Lyse Champagne comments, "I don't know if history repeats itself, but the history of a conquered people repeats itself *ad nauseam*."

Henri Bourassa, Québec's greatest nationalist, was adamant. He did not want French Canadians to make any excuses for themselves. "It is foolish to waste our time in expressing fruitless regrets and unattainable desires," he said in a 1902 public address. And, he asked pointedly,

If the Treaty of Paris had saved us for France, what would have become of us? Assuming we would have escaped the bloody Reign of Terror [of the French Revolution], it is more than probable that Napoleon would have sold us to the Americans without even consulting us, as he did with Louisiana.

And so it goes. Two and a half centuries have passed, and the battle has still not ended. We have not even reached a consensus on whether it was a tragedy, a farce or a simple twist of fate. Ironically, the plains themselves no longer exist. Earthwork landscaping has transformed the original farm fields into rolling parkland with a brilliant blue view of the St. Lawrence.

I remember. I remember. And yet, collectively, we seem to forget all that has happened since then. Canada has become a nation of a new ideal: multicultural, bilingual, self-defining. Instead of fixating on past humiliations, shouldn't we see the *full* sweep of history, in its entirety, placed in a larger context? Unfortunately, it is that very context that seems to be lost on the Québécois, a people who can't forget and won't forgive.

Je me souviens.

Verdict

In the Battle of the Boneheads, Britain just barely came out on top. Wolfe won not because he was a Bastard but because Montcalm was just a slightly bigger Bonehead.

Louis-Joseph, Marquis de Montcalm: **Bonehead**

General James Wolfe: **Bonehead**

François-Gaston, Chevalier de Lévis: **Bastard**

General Jeffery Amherst: **Bastard**

Pierre de Rigaud, Marquis de Vaudreuil: **Bonehead**

JOHN GRAVES SIMCOE:
THE "HYPERACTIVE" FATHER OF ENGLISH CANADA

After the conquest of New France, Upper Canada became the first true inland colony in North America. Previous colonies had clung to the coasts or the seaways, but Upper Canada changed everything. Created in the wake of the American Revolution, and sheltered from further republican ideas by the vast expanse of the Great Lakes, Upper Canada flourished under the driving energy and optimism of its first governor, John Graves Simcoe, a man described by historians as "hyperactive."

If Champlain was the Father of New France, Simcoe was the Father of Upper Canada, which would one day be the heartland of Ontario. Simcoe laid out surveys with unbridled gusto; he plotted grandiose schemes and mapped wild fantasies of a great northern colony. Often his fancy ran away with him, true. But Simcoe was the first leader who could imagine a great inland colony where now there was only wilderness.

In his enthusiasm and his endless nation building, Simcoe is matched only by John A. Macdonald. So what if most of Simcoe's wilder schemes remained only that? John Graves Simcoe was a visionary. It was he who put an end to slavery in Upper Canada in 1793, making Upper Canada the first territory in North America—and indeed the first British colony in the world—to abolish the slave trade, long before the American Emancipation Proclamation of 1863. (Simcoe's declaration did not free existing slaves, but it did outlaw any future slavery as well as making it easier for current slaves to win their freedom.) Simcoe's strong anti-slavery sentiments were perhaps his greatest legacy. He was, in a way, Canada's own "Great Emancipator," our answer to Abraham Lincoln.

Simcoe is also credited with choosing a boggy, mosquito-ridden river delta on Lake Ontario as the unlikely capital of Upper Canada. The settlement, christened "York," would later be renamed Toronto. John Graves Simcoe: the Founding Father of the biggest, richest, least-loved and most-resented city in Canada!

Invasion:
The War of 1812

HUMORIST ERIC NICOL once noted that "very little is known about the War of 1812 because the Americans lost it." But surely the converse is equally true: the only reason Canadians remember that war is because we won. Kind of. In fact, nobody won. Or rather, nobody (that is, the Americans) will admit that they lost. And, as we shall see, there is some truth to their denial. If they didn't quite win, they didn't really lose, either.

The United States has long coveted Canada with a desire that borders on the lascivious. One of the first acts of George Washington's Revolutionary Army was the 1775 invasion of Canada. The Americans were hurled back in a blizzard at the very gates of Québec City, and from that moment onwards, Canadians learned to sleep with one eye open. The invasion of 1775, however, was merely a dress rehearsal. In 1812, the United States of America launched its most sustained, relentless attempt to conquer Canada.

When the United States declared war against Britain on June 18 of that year, the causes seemed clear enough: "Free Trade and Sailors' Rights!" At the time, Britain was waging a desperate war against Napoleon and, in an effort to block the French emperor's supply line, had placed Europe under a trade embargo. The British hounded American vessels that were trading with France, and they boarded ships to look for British deserters, often within view of the American coast. The Americans seethed, and when they saw their opportunity, they took it.

With Britain bogged down in Europe, the defences of its North American colonies were sparse. Canada lay open like a languid embrace. The time was ripe, and although the Americans liked to think of their offensive as "the Second War of Independence," it was really little more than a land grab.

Nor was it a struggle between equals. Seven and a half million Americans were at war with Britain's northern colonies, which, between them, had a population of scarcely half a million. In 1812, the disparity between Canada and the U.S. was even more lopsided than it is today. How could Canada possibly win?

Thomas Jefferson boasted that the conquest would be a "mere matter of marching." The speaker of the U.S. House of Representatives declared that the Kentucky militia alone was enough to deliver Canada, and the American secretary of war, brimming with bravado, predicted that the U.S. could "take Canada without soldiers. We have only to send officers, and the people will rally round our standard." The Americans were confident that the Canadians, in particular the French Canadians, would *welcome* an American invasion. After all, the dream and destiny of all Canadians was to one day become American, wasn't it?

Facing the impending American invasion were a few thousand British regulars, some hastily organized troops of French- and English-Canadian volunteers, and the affectionately overrated local militia. Also pitted against the Americans, and allied with the British for tactical, not loyalist, reasons, were the Indians.

It should be stated unequivocally: without its Native allies, Canada would have been lost. In view of this fact, it might be said that the opening battle of the War of 1812 actually occurred in 1811, when the American cavalry clashed headlong with the Shawnee Nation at Tippecanoe, south of Lake Michigan. The Battle of Tippecanoe demonstrated both the ruthlessness and the determination of the Americans. It also drove the Shawnee war chief Tecumseh into the British camp, a development that would prove to be crucial.

As we will see, Tecumseh was one of the great Bastards of Canadian history. He was also a remarkable diplomat and a gifted orator. Under his leadership, and through the divine inspiration of his shamanistic brother "the Prophet," was forged a Native alliance dedicated both to turning back white encroachment and to securing a sovereign Native state west of the Ohio River, one that would stretch from the Great Lakes to Florida.

A dozen different nations joined the Great Alliance. The Shawnee, the Ottawa, the Delaware, the Miami, the Wyandot, the Chippewa, the Fox, the Potawatomi, the Dakota, the Kickapoo, the Sauk, the Winnebago: all sent warriors in support of Tecumseh. Some, like the Chippewa and the Fox, had long been traditional enemies, but they put their tribal animosities behind them. Tecumseh was now at the head of a multinational strike force.

Tecumseh's alliance was supported by the British, who wanted to check American expansion, and by Canadians, who wanted to maintain the trade relationships of the fur trade. The borders of the Native territory were to be drawn permanently and in accordance with international standards, making the territory a third force in North America. Of the shattered aspirations and aching "might have beens" strewn along

In history, interpretation is everything. The raw facts don't change, but the way we look at them certainly does. If there is any doubt that the Americans see things differently from the way we do, consider the following, taken from two textbooks published at around the same time. The first is from an American text, the second from a Canadian. Both attempt to answer the same question: Why did the War of 1812 begin?

A:
The captains of the English warships kept stopping our merchant vessels and taking sailors off them. In this way the King of England had managed to get several thousand Americans and he made them help him fight his battles against the French. At last we could bear this no longer. We told the king that unless he stopped taking our sailors we would fight. He refused to stop and in the summer of 1812 Congress declared war.
—*An Elementary American History* by David H. Montgomery. Boston: 1904.

B:
When British vessels entered the United States ports it was very common for their sailors, induced by better pay, to desert. By pretending to be citizens of the United States they defeated legal action taken to compel them to return to their ships. Great Britain then took matters into her own hands, and authorized warships to search United States vessels on the high seas for these deserters and to take them by force. Such a course in the present day would be regarded as very offensive and a good cause for resentment, but at that time it was not contrary to international law.
—*A History of the Dominion of Canada* by John B. Calkin. Halifax: 1898.

As historian Robert Daniels notes in *Studying History*, the two textbooks seem "hardly to be talking about the same war."

history's path, none perhaps is quite as enticing or as sad as that of Tecumseh's lost dream: a modern Federation of First Nations, independent and autonomous within North America. It was because of that goal that the First Nations agreed to help the Canadians and the British win the war, but in the end, all they came away with was a handful of smoke and a trunk filled with hollow promises.

The Americans were bursting with enthusiasm. They had the gumption, the motivation and the initiative. What they didn't have was a coherent plan. (It's a bad sign when the cornerstone of your strategy is that the enemy secretly loves you and wants to join your cause.) The United States didn't even have a standing army, and the various state militia that formed their invasion force acted as semi-autonomous entities. According to the conditions of their constitution, militia were required to fight only in "defence" of their homeland, and in every major battle whole regiments simply refused to cross the border. This problem plagued the American commanders and delighted the British, who often fought the Americans on one side of the Niagara River while whole battalions of American soldiers watched, like spectators, from the far shore.

Even worse, the Americans hadn't counted on General Isaac Brock, the British commander in charge of Upper Canada's defence. While the reigning governor fretted and worried, and roving bands of traitors roamed the countryside, looting homes and demoralizing settlers, the citizens of Upper Canada seemed resigned to losing. They braced for impending annexation to the United States. But not Isaac Brock. In a message to Governor George Prevost, Brock noted, "Most of the people have lost all confidence. I however speak loud and look big." Desmond Morton, in *A Military History of Canada*, comments: "While some historians denounce the theory that 'great men' make much difference to history, it is hard to see how Upper Canada would have resisted invasion without Isaac Brock."

Brock knew that mere defence was not enough. Instead of cowering behind the waterways of the Great Lakes, he proposed taking the battle to the Americans. The word went out to Brock's commanders in the field: seize the initiative. Strike first, and strike hard. Britain would not be able to send any significant amounts of supplies or reinforcements for at least a year. Everything would depend on the opening engagements, and Canada's fate hung in the balance.

On July 12, 1812, the American general William Hull led a force of 2,500 men out of the fortified village of Detroit and crossed into Upper Canadian territory, where he issued a public proclamation, which ran in part:

Inhabitants of Canada!
   The army under my command has invaded your country, and the standard of the United States now waves over the territory of Canada. To the peaceable,

unoffending inhabitants, it brings neither danger nor difficulty . . . I come to protect, not to injure you . . . The United States offers you Peace, Liberty, and Security. Your choice lies between these and War, Slavery, and Destruction. Choose then, but choose wisely.

Far to the north, another invasion was underway. But this one went in the *other* direction. A small force of British regulars, backed up by a flotilla of French-Canadian voyageurs and an armada of Indian war canoes carrying over 300 warriors from a dozen different nations, landed under cover of darkness and surrounded the American post at Michilimackinac. "Mackinaw," as it was commonly known, was on an island at the strategic crossroads of three Great Lakes: Huron, Superior and Michigan. The American officer in charge of Mackinaw was terrified of the Indians and, fearing a massacre, surrendered without firing a shot.

The Americans' deep fear of Indians played an important role in several battles and gave the First Nations alliance a definite psychological advantage. Indian war cries alone were often enough to drive the Americans into flight. Some even leaped off cliffs to their death rather than face the "forest warriors." Tecumseh forbade the massacre and torture of prisoners, as well as the taking of scalps, but his control was limited to the men in his immediate field of influence. At the Battle of Frenchtown, the Indians would exact a terrible revenge for Tippecanoe, with the wholesale slaughter of hundreds of American prisoners. When word reached General Hull of the fall of Mackinaw he was distraught, for he now expected a force of Indian warriors to descend upon him at any moment. As General Brock and his Native allies advanced towards him, Hull retreated across the river and into the wooden palisades of Detroit.

For the first time, Brock and Tecumseh met face to face. Legend has it that Tecumseh turned to his men after meeting Brock and said, "This is a *man*!" Brock held an equally high opinion of Tecumseh. In his journals, Brock wrote, "A more sagacious or a more gallant warrior does not I believe exist."

The Shawnee chief argued for a quick assault on Detroit while the Americans were still unsettled and wavering, and Brock agreed. One of his officers, however, protested vehemently. Not only were the Americans well entrenched and well stocked with weapons, they outnumbered Brock's combined force of regulars, militia and Indian allies by more than 900 men. Brock brushed these objections aside. "We are committed to a war," said Brock, "in which the enemy will *always* be our superior in numbers and ammunition."

Earlier, Tecumseh had captured letters and communiqués from General Hull, and as Brock read through these confidential papers, it became clear just how terrified Hull was of an Indian massacre. Taking advantage of this, Brock devised a brilliant bit of psychological warfare. He sent a fictional communiqué along lines patrolled by American scouts. In the papers, which were duly captured and handed over to Hull, a cheerfully confident British commander advises his superiors that he has more than enough men to take Detroit and, really, they need send only, say, 5,000 more Indian reinforcements. That should do it. Thanks.

Hull was choked with fear. *Only* 5,000! That was more than his entire garrison!

Brock dressed hundreds of his volunteers in secondhand red jackets to fool the Americans into thinking that he had a large force of trained regulars. He then marched his men at double the normal spacing, thus "stretching" his columns and making his force appear larger still. It worked. The Americans thought they were facing an army of disciplined British regulars.

Tecumseh marched his own multination force of warriors along the shore across from Detroit in full view of the already shaken Americans. The line of Indians filed past and into the woods . . . They then hurried back to the end of the line and marched past again. And again. It was a splendid bit of deceit. The Americans peered across at this display of strength, and their estimates ranged from 2,000 to 3,000 warriors. In fact, Tecumseh had fewer than 600 men at his disposal.

General Hull, terrified beyond belief, suffered a complete mental breakdown. He huddled in his tent, compulsively chewing gobs of tobacco and rocking back and forth. A British delegation arrived with a message from General Brock demanding that the Americans surrender "to the force under my command," and a few cannonballs to back up Brock's request were all it took: Hull, once a hero in the War of Independence, was now completely cowed. He surrendered Detroit without a fight, and as the stars and stripes were lowered, Isaac Brock and Tecumseh rode in, side by side. The score now stood Bastards 2, Boneheads 0.

With the fall of Detroit, and the concurrent massacre at Fort Dearborn (Chicago), the U.S. suffered the single greatest loss of territory in its history. The entire western half of the continent was now controlled by the British. Not only had Brock and Tecumseh outbluffed an army and captured the key to the continental interior, but within Fort Detroit itself they found an impressive cache of weapons and supplies: more than 2,000 muskets, 500 rifles, 35 cannons, several bags of money, lots of ammunition, more than 100 pack horses and 300 head of cattle. It was a godsend for the materially strapped British forces.

Spirits soared in Upper Canada. The victory helped convince the remaining Six Nations of the Iroquois to abandon their previously neutral position and join the fight against the Americans. Everything had changed. Brock and Tecumseh were hailed as heroes, the "Saviours of Upper Canada."

They would never meet again.

Brock hurried back to the Niagara peninsula, where he was killed leading a foolhardy charge up the Queenston Heights. Perhaps Brock believed he led a charmed life. Perhaps he felt invincible; we'll never know. His death rocked Upper Canada. Others picked up the standard, others finished the fight, and Queenston Heights was eventually retaken, but it is Brock we remember best. Brock, the active principle. The man in the scarlet jacket, running, sword drawn, voice ringing out, front and centre ahead of his men—into gunshot and glory.

Brock's jacket, with that single fatal bullet hole in the chest, has been preserved to this day, and his towering monument near Niagara is the closest thing to a national shrine we have in Canada. The irony is sweet. Brock, after all, was a British general serving in the far-flung colonies, and he couldn't wait to get back to Europe, where the real action was. He was a *British* hero, but he died in Canada's defence and as such is claimed by Canadians as one of their own.

So too is Tecumseh. Almost a year to the day after Brock's fateful charge up Queenston Heights, Tecumseh died in a bitterly fought battle at Moraviantown, near present-day Chatham. The Americans had chased a ragged force of British soldiers and Indian warriors deep into Upper Canada. At Moraviantown, the allies reeled to face their pursuers. As the American cavalry fell upon them in waves, the redcoats broke and ran, but not Tecumseh, and not his men. They stayed and fought, hand to hand, until their leader fell.

The Americans burned the Indian village at Moraviantown to the ground, and Kentucky militiamen went among the bodies, taking scalps and mutilating corpses. When they reached the body of an Indian they mistook for Tecumseh, they skinned it, cutting souvenir strips of flesh to be used for razor straps back in Kentucky. Tecumseh's body, however, had been spirited away by his men, and his remains now lie somewhere near Thamesville, Ontario, in an unmarked grave. With his death, the resolve of the Native alliance faltered, and it never fully recovered.

The War of 1812 lasted two and a half years. It was a war of sudden bloody skirmishes, of retreats and advances, of confused armies clashing at night. It was fought mainly along the Niagara River, often within sight and sound of the falls themselves, and the Niagara frontier became the central vortex of the war, a no man's land of marauding armies and midnight ambushes. The war also threatened Lower Canada, and along the Great Lakes waterways it became a major naval engagement.

The American general Dearborn—a Bastard if ever there was one—used naval power to capture the capital of York (later renamed Toronto) *twice*, and his troops burned the Parliament Buildings, destroyed public property, robbed stores and looted homes. Later, the Americans successfully wrested control of lakes Ontario and Erie from the British, but they were never able to fully capitalize on their advantage, and the war on the Great Lakes was largely one of feint.

Both sides got caught up in an almost comical shipbuilding contest, in which they built bigger and bigger vessels, some reaching ridiculous proportions. At one point, the British built a monster ship, 20 storeys tall with 112 guns and room for a crew of 1,000 men. It was the nineteenth-century equivalent of Darth Vader's *Death Star*, and the Americans responded in turn with a 120-gun leviathan of their own. Many of these massive vessels never saw action, and their memory has faded into the footnotes of history. Like most arms races, this one had little, if any, effect on the eventual outcome of the war.

On the Atlantic coast, however, Britain had the upper hand. Even with Napoleon to consider and an entire ocean to patrol, the British navy could cast a wide net, and their blockade of the American coast was an important factor in the balance of power.

The most dramatic encounter of the entire war occurred just outside of Boston harbour, when, in a titanic Clash of Bastards, the British frigate *Shannon*, under Captain Philip Broke, met the newly refitted American warship *Chesapeake*, under Captain James Lawrence. In a gesture full of wartime swagger, the British captain Broke issued a formal challenge:

As the *Chesapeake* appears now ready for sea, I request you will do me the favour to meet the *Shannon* with her and try the fortune of our respective flags. Choose your terms but let us meet.

Lawrence's sense of honour would not allow Broke's invitation to go unanswered. On June 1, 1813, the Americans sailed out to meet the *Shannon*. And so began one of the greatest single-ship battles in maritime history.

The *Shannon* crashed in alongside the *Chesapeake*, and Broke's men swarmed over the sides and onto the American deck. In just 15 minutes of sabre sparks and musket fire, more than 220 men were either killed or wounded. Lawrence died in battle, and Broke was seriously wounded. But under the dauntless Nova Scotian seaman William Wallis, the *Shannon's* men captured the *Chesapeake* and towed it back to Halifax, where crowds lined the shore to cheer their triumphant return.

From the battle of the *Shannon* and the *Chesapeake* came Lawrence's famous last words. As he lay dying, he cried out, "Tell the men to fire faster and not to give up the ship; fight her till she sinks." And from this came the motto of the U.S. navy: "Don't give up the ship!" (The obvious irony that Lawrence's men most certainly *did* give up the ship, and in a most humiliating fashion, has never seemed to bother the Americans.)

Not all the heroes of the War of 1812 were men. Laura Secord, a 37-year-old mother of five, was one woman who played a decisive role. Secord's husband,

James, had been shot during the Battle of Queenston Heights, and he would have died if not for Laura, who sought him out on the battlefield and brought him home. The Secord house had been ransacked by Americans during her absence, and not long afterwards a force of American officers arrived and took up residence as Secord nursed her husband back to health.

One night, Secord overheard an American colonel discussing his plans to attack the British forces under Lieutenant James FitzGibbon. She decided to act. The following morning, under cover of dark, she set off on foot for FitzGibbon's headquarters, more than 30 kilometres away. Laura Secord trudged through brush and along pioneer trails, threading her way through the forests and swamplands of what was, in effect, a battle zone. By the time she climbed the steep Niagara Escarpment, night had fallen. Tired and sunburned, her feet bleeding and her dress in tatters, she arrived at FitzGibbon's camp. After an unnerving confrontation with a group of Mohawk warriors, she was finally taken to see the lieutenant. "The Americans are coming," said Laura.

FitzGibbon quickly organized an ambush, sending out a small force of Mohawks who took up position in a wooded, boggy area dammed by beavers (nationalist imagery in the making here). With the Natives at the forefront, FitzGibbon waited for the Americans to walk into the trap. His men stood ready to lead the main assault once the initial ambush had been launched. But it never came to that. The battle ended almost as soon as it began. Mohawk war cries sent abject panic through the American troops, and once the Americans lost their nerve, it was all over. Nearly 500 soldiers, including their commander, surrendered en masse to FitzGibbon and his few dozen men. "Not a shot fired on our side but by the Indians," noted FitzGibbon approvingly in his account of the battle. "They beat the American detachment into a state of terror."

The Battle of Beaver Dams, an important Native victory, would also prove to be a turning point in the war, one that stemmed the American advance and ultimately may have saved Canada.

Laura Secord's contribution was hushed up at first. The war still raged; her husband and children were behind enemy lines and faced possible reprisals. Unfortunately, the imposed silence was so effective that she remained largely uncredited even after the war ended. FitzGibbon wrote several testimonials on her behalf—she had risked her life, after all—but recognition was a long time coming. It was not until 1860, almost 50 years after her trek, that Laura Secord, then in her eighties, finally had her bravery acknowledged with a personal award from the Prince of Wales. Since then, she has become one of Canada's best-known heroines—though how much of that is due to her epic trek and how much to the chocolate fudge clusters that Canadians like to scarf down is uncertain.

(It's interesting to note that the chocolate company, which has no actual connection with the Secord family, originally used a tough old pioneer woman as their trademark. In the 1950s, however, Laura was transformed into a delicate Southern belle, and the cameo portrait of this sweet young girl has become confused in the public mind with the real Laura Secord. Author Ken Lefolii, in *The Canadian Look*, argues that the entire history of Canada's self-image is encapsulated in those two portraits, like "Before" and "After" pictures illustrating a nation that has slowly abandoned its own distinct identity in favour of a blander, more homogenized one: "a look without a country." Lefolii may be right, but then again it is axiomatic that pretty girls sell more chocolates than tough old dames.)

Canada gained another enduring Moment Heroic during the War of 1812 at the Battle of Châteauguay. Châteauguay is remembered as a purely Canadian victory, with the British playing no part in it. In Châteauguay we also have the faint stirrings of a modern nation: French Canadians and English Canadians fighting side by side in the autumn forests against an invading army of Americans. It doesn't get more symbolic than that. (Nationalist mythology even has it that the Canadians used branches of red maple leaves as camouflage, but this appears to be a legend rendered after the fact.)

The main victors at the Battle of Châteauguay were French-Canadian fencibles under the inspired leadership of Charles de Salaberry, together with a small band of Anglos and several hundred Mohawk warriors. Salaberry's small force of 500 turned back an American invasion, 4,000 strong, that was headed straight for Montréal. The victory was no fluke on Salaberry's part. Throughout the war, his volunteers played an important role, and a few weeks later, they helped the British score another decisive victory at the Battle of Crysler's Farm.

By now the tide had turned. Napoleon had abdicated, and Britain was able to focus its attention more fully on its overseas colonies. In August 1814, in a stunning counterattack, the British captured Washington, D.C. It wasn't much of a battle. The American president, his cabinet and most of the defending army fled so fast the battle became known sardonically as "a race." The British then spent a leisurely two days burning public buildings (in direct retaliation for what the Americans had done to York). Among the structures they put to the torch was the president's personal residence. The upper walls still stood, however, and whitewash was hurriedly applied to cover the black scorch marks. From this paint job came the new nickname for the building: the White House.

The myth-making doesn't stop there. Having sacked Washington, the British then made their way north to Baltimore, which they bombarded with rockets and bombs. A young lawyer watching the spectacle wrote the words to a song he called

"The Defence of Fort McHenry." It later became the American national anthem, renamed "The Star-Spangled Banner."

In between the taking of Washington and the assault on Baltimore, the British suffered a humiliating setback on Lake Champlain. George Prevost, the always cautious governor-in-chief of Canada, led a massive British expedition against Plattsburgh. What should have been a decisive victory was lost when the American navy blocked the British advance and Prevost beat a hasty and unseemly retreat. Plattsburgh was a fiasco, and Prevost's boneheaded blunder only helped strengthen the American position at the negotiation table. Had Prevost used his superior strength and fire-power competently, much of what is now upper New York State would belong to Canada. As it was, following the debacle at Plattsburgh, the British withdrew any claims to American territory.

The last battle Britain and America fought actually took place *after* the war was over. The Treaty of Ghent was signed on Christmas Eve, 1814, but in those pre-fax days, word did not get to the men in the field fast enough to prevent a major British assault on New Orleans. This battle, won in a convincing style by the Americans under Andrew Jackson, is immortalized by American patriots more than any other in song and in folklore. Its outcome also bolsters their odd claim that they did in fact win the War of 1812.

Britain had demonstrated that, even with one hand tied behind its back, it could still win a war. French Canadians had rejected American offers to "liberate" them, and English Canadians had stood firm in their resolve not to become American. Negotiations, however, were something else again. Instead of holding onto the land it had won, Britain agreed to return everything to the status quo of 1811. The Americans then gleefully extended their boundaries westward, deep into Indian territory. Britain had betrayed its First Nations allies utterly and shamelessly. Gone was the provision for a sovereign Native state. The Indians were not even allowed a place at the negotiation table. (The Americans had refused to consider such a possibility.) Canadians were also denied a spot, and thus the deal was hammered out privately between Britain and the United States.

In the strict military sense, the Americans clearly lost the war. They did not even come close to gaining their objective: the conquest of Canada. But war is a political tool, and what counts are end results, not heroics. In this sense, the Americans came out far ahead. In *The Struggle for the Border*, historian Bruce Hutchison writes, "The United States had lost a war and won a conference." Although the Americans were clearly beaten on the battlefield, the final score stands like this: the Americans ultimately won, the Canadians broke even, and the Indians lost.

The War of 1812 marked the beginning of the end for the First Nations. The possibility of full-scale Native political autonomy was lost, and British policy shifted dramatically. No longer needed as military allies, the Indians were now to be "civilized": settled, assimilated, turned into farmers. (The cost of this "civilization," incidentally, was to be covered by the sale of Native lands.)

When it came to dealing with the First Nations, the Americans were relentless and ruthless. They fought fire with fire and left the continent scattered with corpses. The British (and later Canadian) approach was more slippery, but the endgame was just the same: the Indians had the earth pulled out from under them.

And what of the Canadians? The Americans got a free rein in the West, a snappy new anthem, a navy motto and the White House nickname out of the deal. What did we get for our efforts? Well, for one thing, we gained a wellspring of nascent nationalism. The "militia myth" held sway for generations, telling Canadians that it was their own civilian boys who had won the day. This wasn't true, of course. British leadership, Native tactics and American incompetence—personified, in turn, by Brock, Tecumseh and Hull—were the deciding factors. Still, the Canadians, French and English alike, could take certain pride in the role they played in hurling back the American wolf. The number of men the United States had recruited during the War of 1812 was greater than the entire population of Canada—and they still couldn't take us.

Some historians have said that, in 1812, Canada won the right to remain British, but our victory was more subtle than that. We won the right to *not* be American. In that sense, then, the War of 1812 was our "war of independence"—independence from America. For more than 200 years the United States has remained baffled by our insistence that we don't want to be American. For more than 200 years the Americans (and more than a few hand-wringing Canadian nationalists) have been predicting our imminent annexation and absorption into the United States. And for more than 200 years their predictions have been unfulfilled.

The proximity of the United States of America is one of the great inescapable facts of being Canadian. The suffocating, exhilarating, exasperating presence of America has shaped us, defined us, defied us, helped us and hampered us immeasurably.

The forty-ninth parallel today is the longest undefended border in the world, and the two nations have long since made peace with their separate destinies. The Americans, it has been said, are our best friends—whether we like it or not. But it is also worth remembering that, French and English, we had to fight to be Canadian. We had to fight to be allowed the privilege of *not* being American.

The War of 1812 is not over yet. In 1999, all 175 Laura Secord stores, along with the Laura Secord brand name, were sold to a Chicago-based company. What the Americans failed to get through armed invasion, they are now winning through economic conquest. Poor Laura must be spinning in her grave.

Verdict

General Isaac Brock: **Bastard**

Chief Tecumseh: **Bastard**

General William Hull: **Bonehead**

Laura Secord: **Bastard**

5

Rebel Hordes:
The Armed Uprisings of 1837

THE REVOLUTION, LIKE most items of fashion, came late to Canada. The Americans had long since given Britain the boot and the French had long since stormed the Bastille by the time the Canadian version of *liberté, égalité, fraternité* rolled around in the fall of 1837.

The 1830s saw failed attempts at social revolutions in a number of European nations. Canada, appropriately enough, had two: one in English and another in French. Although not directly connected, they shared the same source of discontent: a colonial system that was outdated and out of touch.

The problem was not democracy, but partial democracy. The British colonies did have elected Assemblies, true, but these bodies were largely toothless. Governors and their self-selected Councils ran roughshod over the affairs of the colonies, and the elected assemblymen could do little more than block government bills and complain. Therein lay the central flaw of the system: it was representative government by half-measures. There was just enough to create expectations, but not enough to satisfy them.

Governors came and went but the Councils remained, and soon a closed-circle, interconnected oligarchy formed. In English Upper Canada this was called the Family Compact, a network of 1812 heroes and old Loyalist families based in the Anglican Church. In the French colony of Lower Canada, it was the Château Clique who wielded the power. (They were so named in reference to the inordinate amount of time that members spent at Château St-Louis, the governor's residence.) Although Lower Canada was a French-speaking territory, the Château Clique was almost entirely English, made up mostly of wealthy Montréal merchants. The elected Assembly, however, was predominantly French Canadian. Thus, in Lower Canada, the division of power was also drawn along cultural and linguistic lines.

A young, professional, French-Canadian elite—the yuppies of their day—came to dominate the Assembly under the reform-minded Parti Canadien. Their reforms went nowhere, however, and their resentment at being excluded from any real source of power grew. The situation was a recipe for confrontation.

By 1826, the Parti Canadien had grown increasingly radical and had changed its name to the Parti Patriote, a significant, symbolic move. In 1834, disgruntled members of the Patriotes drew up a list of every wrong ever suffered and every injustice ever endured, and they sent it to off to London, the final court of appeal. The Ninety-Two Resolutions, as the petition was known, was largely the work of one man: Louis-Joseph Papineau, leader of the Parti Patriote and Speaker of the Assembly.

Charismatic, enigmatic, handsome, forceful, eloquent, confused, cowardly: an aristocrat and a reformer, a wealthy landowner who admired the writings of Thomas Jefferson, Papineau was a self-sustained contradiction. He was, in the words of historian Fernand Ouellet, "a divided soul." In *The Dream of Nation*, Susan Mann Trofimenkoff comments: "[Papineau] waxed nostalgic about life on the land, pocketed his seigneurial dues, picked up profits from the timber trade on the Ottawa, lived in the grand manner in Montréal, and complained of poverty."

Historian George Woodcock finally gave up wrestling with the character of this monumental man. As he writes in *100 Great Canadians*,

> Louis-Joseph Papineau is one of the most puzzling men in Canadian history. No label fits him completely; there is always some contradiction that prevents exact definition. In theory he was a conservative; in practice he was a revolutionary. He believed in a republic, but he wanted it to be ruled by country gentlemen like himself.

As a growing economic depression drove habitants in Lower Canada to the brink of despair, cholera epidemics ravaged the congested cities, and with them, paranoid fears of a clandestine policy of genocide. The cholera, it was whispered, was unleashed by *les Anglais* to decimate the ranks of the French Canadians, who would then be overwhelmed by the influx of new immigrants.

All of these elements created an underrepresented, put-upon, embittered, alienated population. And the people's fears were not completely unfounded. Assimilation—though certainly not genocide—had long been the pet project of successive governors. Cruel men like James Craig had, in the past, made a name for themselves by harassing and imprisoning suspected French-Canadian nationalists. During his reign of terror, Governor Craig censored French-language newspapers, bullied the Assembly, and ordered mass arrests of reform-minded leaders. Indeed, antagonizing the locals seems to have been something of a hobby for many of the early governors.

Like today's separatists, Papineau was quick to tap into, and manipulate, these fears and feelings of rage. As his Parti Patriote grew bolder and more extremist, overt racial appeals emerged, dividing neighbours and even households. A militant youth wing, *Fils de la Liberté* (Sons of Liberty), began drilling for combat, and the equally militant English-speaking Doric Club matched them blow for blow—literally.

Lower Canada was a tinderbox, and the final spark came when, after a ponderous three-year delay, the official reply to Papineau's Ninety-Two Resolutions arrived from London. The response to French-Canadian grievances was dubbed "the Ten Resolutions," but the answer could just as easily have been summed up in one syllable: *No*. No to responsible government, no to a stronger Assembly, no to expanded powers for francophones, no to a distinct society. No, no, no. English inflexibility had come up square against French-Canadian political will. As might be expected, the results were disastrous.

At loud, wild-eyed public rallies, Papineau declared the situation of Lower Canada to be like that of the American colonies just before the revolution, and the implications hung in the air like a thunderclap. The Patriotes took the outlying counties and declared themselves part of a New Nation. Street brawls and angry speeches, a call to arms, and the promise of independence: it was the winter of our discontent, December 1837, and the conquest was about to be undone.

British militia were called in from Upper Canada and the Maritime colonies. Patriote leaders were rounded up and held without bail, but many escaped, melting into the rural domain of the habitant. The movement now had its own momentum. Surprisingly, several important English Canadians threw their support behind the Patriotes, and some even became leaders. Dr. Wolfred Nelson of St-Denis, a veteran war doctor of 1812, cried out that the time had come "to melt our spoons into bullets." What had begun as armed resistance was now open insurrection.

At St-Denis, the Patriotes, led by Nelson and badly outnumbered, fought a seven-hour, pitched battle against two British detachments—and won. The British army was forced to fall back to Montréal in disgrace, leaving six dead men and their cannon behind. The insurgents cheered, and Nelson plotted his next move.

And Papineau, grand Papineau, man of words and lofty gestures? What had become of Papineau? Not much. He had slipped away before the first shots were fired and even now was beating a hasty and ignoble retreat to the United States, abandoning the movement he had helped create and shouting all the while that he had never meant it to come to this.

The Battle of St-Denis was the Patriotes' first victory. It would also be their last.

The revolution had come too soon; the rebels were poorly organized and ill-trained, and the authorities counterpunched relentlessly.

Just two days after that first battle, British troops marched on Patriote positions at St-Charles and overwhelmed the rebels in a short, one-sided engagement. Sixty dead Patriotes were strewn across the field. On December 14, more than 1,400 British regulars and English-Canadian volunteers, armed with a dozen cannons, descended on the small town of St-Eustache. They fought the Patriotes back into a church and then set the building on fire. As the men inside rushed out to escape the flames, they were shot down one by one. Some stayed inside and were burned alive; some leaped to their death. Their leader, a young doctor by the name of Jean-Olivier Chénier, refused to surrender and went down fighting, and even today in Québec someone who is fearless against great odds is said to be "brave like Chénier." Almost 100 Patriotes died at St-Eustache.

At nearby St-Benoît, the habitants surrendered their arms and ammunition without resistance. The British army then marched out, leaving the town in the hands of English-Canadian volunteers. The volunteers ransacked the homes of habitants, looting and vandalizing property, before torching the entire town. They then moved into the surrounding area. For 15 miles in every direction, not a single building escaped destruction.

The Patriote Rebellion had been all heart and no brains, and it never stood a chance. Historian Donald Creighton described it in *The Story of Canada* as "little more than a series of armed riots, unplanned, purposeless, hopeless."

The rebellion flared up again in 1838, when Dr. Robert Nelson (Wolfred's brother) declared himself president of the Provisional Republic of Lower Canada, but this second uprising was quickly crushed as well. As Desmond Morton writes in *A Military History of Canada*, "Watchers from Montréal could see pillars of smoke behind the advancing columns of British, volunteers, and Indians. Cartloads of miserable, mud-spattered prisoners rumbled into Montréal. Passersby jeered and spat their contempt." In half a dozen battles over two years, almost 300 Patriotes and 27 soldiers had been killed.

Then came the reprisals. British regulars, English-Canadian volunteers and Iroquois warriors angry at Patriote raids on their land ravaged the Richelieu Valley in a scorched-earth policy that the French Canadians would never forget. Sir John Colborne was in charge of the campaign, and he is still known in Québec as *le vieux brûlot* ("the old firebrand"). Colborne arrested thousands of men, sending a dozen to the gallows and 58 more to the distant penal colonies of Australia. Later, to the stunned rage of French Canadians, Colborne was rewarded for his efforts by being made a British peer: he became Lord Seaton, or, as he was more popularly referred to by the habitants, "Lord Satan."

Back in the English-speaking colony of Upper Canada, a similar drama was unfolding. (It should be noted that the terms "upper" and "lower" did not, as is sometimes believed, denote the comparative status of the French-speaking and English-speaking colonies. The terms refer simply to the upper and lower reaches of the St. Lawrence River.)

If the Rebellions of Upper and Lower Canada were tragicomedies, Lower Canada provided the tragedy—and Upper Canada? Well, Upper Canada provided the comedy. Papineau's counterpart was William Lyon Mackenzie, a man of great rhetoric and rage, a crusading newspaper editor who wore a flaming red wig and had a temper to match. These two men—Papineau and Mackenzie—could not have been more unalike. Mackenzie had arrived from Scotland the penniless son of a widow. He was republican and democratic to a degree that surpassed even the democratic principles of the United States. He opposed slavery, for example, and mocked Americans for denying women the vote. Mackenzie was especially outspoken in condemning the Clergy Reserves, some three million acres of real estate scattered in large sections throughout the townships of Upper Canada, awarded free to the Anglican Church and usually left undeveloped. These reserves blocked the expansion of successful farmers and the growth of town centres; even worse, they smacked of privilege and imported notions of British hierarchy.

Although Papineau and Mackenzie had little in common, they did correspond, and Mackenzie was certainly encouraged by the initial rebellions in Lower Canada. If the two men shared anything, it was their complex, contradictory natures. Of Mackenzie, his biographer William Kilbourn writes, "He was the most unselfish of idealists; he was also a born muckraker and scandal-monger."

As in Lower Canada, the central problem in Upper Canada was a lack of responsible government. The Family Compact, together with the system of appointed ministers, had left the elected Assembly with very little authority. The government was in danger of becoming, in the words of historian Colin Read, "little more than a debating society."

In 1828, Mackenzie was elected to the Assembly as a member for York (Toronto), and he caused such a ruckus that he was promptly expelled. His supporters just as promptly reelected him, even awarded him a large gold medal. Mackenzie was again ejected from the Assembly, and again just as quickly reelected. The third time around the Assembly expelled him—literally—by the scruff of his neck. In total, he was reelected and expelled *five* times.

In 1834, Little Mac, as he was known, was elected the first mayor of the newly incorporated city of Toronto. His Worship Mayor Mackenzie, administrator of Upper Canada's capital: the Family Compact and their Tory supporters were livid. They simply could not shake this tenacious little bulldog. Several years earlier, the sons of

Much is made of the fact that slavery never really took root in Canada and that emancipation occurred here long before it did in the southern States—and without a civil war, either. The truth is, slavery had existed in Canada since the early days. The coastal Indians routinely exchanged and killed slaves during potlatch ceremonies, and when the European settlers arrived, they brought slaves with them as well. The slave trade in Canada lasted for more than 200 years. In New France, *Canadiens* preferred to capture and enslave Natives, but Blacks were also imported as early on as 1608. Here is a passage from the *Code Noire*, drawn up by French Canadians to outline the proper treatment of Black slaves:

> If a Black tries to escape, we cut off his ears and we brand a fleur-de-lis on his shoulder with a hot iron; if he tries to escape a second time, we cut the hamstrings on the back of his legs. If he is so bold as to try again, it's death.

With the conquest of New France by Britain in 1760, the slave trade actually *grew*. Article 47 of the Capitulation, when Montréal was surrendered to British forces, guaranteed slaveholders their "property." (There were more than 3,600 Black and Native slaves in New France at the time of the conquest.) Britain's talents as a slaver far surpassed those of France. Indeed, it might well be argued that slavery was one of the great "pillars of the British Empire."

In Upper Canada and in the Maritimes, shiploads of African slaves were bought and sold at auctions, and another great influx of slaves accompanied the United Empire Loyalists. Canada did ban slavery sooner than the United States did, but it is also true that the economic bases of the fur trade and fisheries relied far less on raw human power than did the labour-intensive plantations of the Deep South. We were nicer because we could afford to be. And even at that, when Governor Simcoe abolished the importing of slaves in 1793, he faced strong opposition from many colonists.

Between 1840 and 1860, the Underground Railroad, as the secret route via safe houses was called, helped funnel more than 30,000 escaped slaves north into Canada. Among them was Josiah Henson, the man who was the role model for Uncle Tom in Harriet Beecher Stowe's abolitionist novel. Henson's cabin can still be seen today outside of Dresden, Ontario.

In describing Canada's place in the mythology of the Underground Railroad, Martin Luther King, in a 1967 radio broadcast, said, "Deep in our history of struggle for freedom Canada was the North Star. The Negro slave, denied education, dehumanized, imprisoned on cruel plantations, knew that far to the north a land existed where a fugitive slave if he survived the horrors of the journey could find freedom."

It should be remembered, however, that the Underground Railroad was run largely by Americans, in particular the Quakers, who risked everything to help fugitive slaves escape. Once the former slaves reached Canada, their journey was more or less complete. But even then, Blacks often faced overt hostility from white Canadians. Canada had segregated schools, restaurants and cinemas right up until the 1960s. Race riots in Halifax erupted as recently as 1991, when a Black man was refused service at a tavern, and tensions continue to flare up in Nova Scotia schools, even today.

The North Star was always more legendary than real.

the elite had ransacked Mackenzie's office and thrown his printing press into Lake Ontario, but this crime only made him more of a hero among the people. Later, a respectable member of the Family Compact even tried to have Mackenzie assassinated, but still Little Mac kept coming: self-righteous, populist and very, very loud.

When cholera hit Toronto and no one could be found who was willing to drive the "cholera carts," Mackenzie did it himself, personally taking the sick to hospitals and even collecting corpses. For his efforts, Mackenzie contracted the disease and was a long time recovering.

He then set to work compiling his own "Report on Grievances," a staggering 500-page litany of complaints, criticisms and injustices containing every slight, real or imagined, big or small, that the citizens of Upper Canada had received at the hands of their government. The list covered everything from the crusade for responsible government to bad roads and the price of stamps. As always, Mackenzie was unable to distinguish between the important and the trivial. He never did learn to concentrate on one issue at a time, but instead he flung his invective about him in all directions.

Into this brewing storm of trouble, the British Colonial Office sent the wrong man at the wrong time: an adventurer–turned–travel writer, the flamboyant Sir Francis Bond Head. Even his name was slightly ridiculous. Bond Head knew absolutely nothing about the colonies and was naturally surprised when he was appointed lieutenant governor of Upper Canada in 1835. There is, in fact, a strong possibility that he was appointed by mistake. Someone proposed sending "young Head" over to Canada to calm things down, by which they may have meant *Edmund* Head, the brilliant Oxford don. Or maybe *George* Head, Francis's older brother, a military officer with extensive experience in North America. But not *Francis*, surely they didn't mean Francis, the one who liked to play at being an Argentinean gaucho, the one they called "Galloping Head," the one whose biggest claims to fame were the cheap adventure novels he wrote and his skills with a lasso, which he once demonstrated for the king. (The king had been so impressed he granted Francis a knighthood.) Surely they didn't mean *that* Head.

Appointing Bond Head was like turning a kangaroo loose in a minefield. Instead of appeasing the Reformers, Bond Head went on the offensive. He dissolved the Assembly, called an election and actively campaigned for the Tories. Bond Head was a handsome charmer and a born campaigner, and he used every trick in the book: promises of patronage, bribery, scare tactics, appeals to patriotism, and even "quick enfranchisement" (that is, suddenly granting land, and thus a vote, to a known supporter). It worked brilliantly. Sir Francis Bond Head swept the Reformers from the Assembly.

This was partisan politics at its worst, and it was just what Mackenzie had been warning about: irresponsible government. What Canada needed was a disinterested governor and an Executive Council chosen from *among* the elected members of the Assembly. They had neither.

Following the great election defeat of 1836, an enraged Mackenzie started up a new newspaper. His old paper had been called *The Colonial Advocate*; his new one was dubbed *The Constitution.* The shift in names was significant, as was the date he chose for the launch: the Fourth of July. Mackenzie even issued a "Toronto Declaration" that was copied almost directly from the American Declaration of Independence. The economic depression that hit Upper Canada in 1837 only added to the urgency of Mackenzie's message. He began riding through the countryside urging rebellion, and around him a small band of followers formed.

On a miserable day in early December 1837, a motley crew of would-be liberators gathered at Montgomery's Tavern on Yonge Street north of Toronto, near what is now the Eglinton subway station. "Up then, brave Canadians! Get ready your rifles, and make short work of it!" Mackenzie had cried, and, incredibly, some 600 men took him up on it. Mackenzie had expected 3,000 supporters; Sir Francis had declared that it would be impossible to scrape together even 50 people willing to take up arms against the government. Both men had deluded themselves.

Right up to the night that Mackenzie marched his ragtag army down Yonge Street, Bond Head refused to take the reports of insurrection seriously. Waving aside warnings, he sent his entire army up to Montréal to help put down the Patriote rebellion then underway, leaving Toronto practically defenceless. Only a handful of poorly organized militiamen and a few dedicated old officers remained. Among them was General FitzGibbon, the hero of 1812, the man Laura Secord trekked through the woods to warn. Several times on the night of the rebellion, General FitzGibbon had burst in on the sleeping governor with alarming reports, only to be dismissed. It was not until there had been skirmishes and gunfire, and men had been shot, that Bond Head realized he had an armed uprising on his hands.

Mackenzie, unlike Papineau, led his army personally. Unfortunately, his most able commander had been killed earlier that evening by a scouting Loyalist, the portly alderman John Powell. It was Powell who had finally convinced Bond Head to get out of bed, and it was Powell who, as he galloped past a rebel roadblock, had pointed his gun right at Mackenzie's face—only to have his pistol misfire.

Mackenzie had put on several heavy overcoats, to keep out the bullets, it was said, and mounted a white pony ("like a sort of deranged Yankee Doodle," is how William Kilbourn puts it in *The Firebrand*), before leading his band of rebels down Yonge Street. Riflemen were at the front, and behind them came an unlikely assortment of men armed with pitchforks, rifles, clubs and pikes. They were marching as to war, with the vague vision of freedom going on before. Or at least that was how Mackenzie saw it. The rebels would overthrow the colonial government of Upper Canada. They would defeat the Brits. They would establish a second republic on the continent. They would be a bastion of freedom and liberty unto the world! But first they had to get past Sheriff Jarvis's small band of volunteers waiting in the bushes near what is now the site of Maple Leaf Gardens.

Jarvis's musketeers fired only one volley and then fled in all directions, even as Jarvis ordered them, in vain, to stay and fight. Fortunately for Jarvis, the rebels too had panicked and run away, and the good sheriff was left holding an empty field. It was not a high-water mark in Canadian nationalism. It was, as poet Dennis Lee described it, "the first spontaneous mutual retreat in the history of warfare."

The authorities struck back two days later. An army of militiamen and volunteers marched out of Toronto, past cheering crowds, with banners high and drums beating. FitzGibbon, in his swan-song campaign as a hero, was in command, and Bond Head was there too. (No word if he had his lasso with him.) Three columns converged on Montgomery's Tavern, and in half an hour the battle was over. The rebels were scattered, and Bond Head had Montgomery's burned to the ground. A separate uprising at Brantford was quickly put down, and the rebellion was over.

Mackenzie was no Papineau. At Montgomery's Tavern, he kept fighting until the advancing army was within metres of his position. Only then did he flee, narrowly escaping capture. With a $5,000 reward on his head and his rebellion in ruins, he headed south, towards the American border. He forded icy streams as high as his chest, he hid in haystacks as the army searched through barns, and at one point, he was caught between two posses—one in front of him and one behind—and escaped only by slipping into the woods. Helped by sympathetic farmers along the way, Mackenzie finally made it to the Niagara River, which he crossed by boat even as a patrol along the shore was looking for him. It was said that some of the soldiers spotted Mackenzie but reported nothing.

William Kilbourn writes, "There is about Mackenzie the shadowy suggestion of an Upper Canadian Robin Hood, fighting the battles of the poor . . . But he is chiefly remembered in the manner of Bonnie Prince Charlie: always away or in hiding, the incarnation of impossible loyalties, the secret hope hidden at the heart's core."

It is a fitting comparison. Mackenzie was a proud Scot, and he often drew inspiration from the fact that both of his grandfathers had fought alongside Prince Charlie in the sad and final defeat of the clans at the Battle of Culloden. And, much like Prince Charlie, Mackenzie seems to have visited just about every cave and cottage for miles around. (As Kilbourn notes, "Few owners of a really old log barn or cabin within twenty miles of [the] escape route to the American border will not tell a stranger the story of how William Lyon Mackenzie slept there.")

Having escaped to the United States, Mackenzie found many supporters and volunteers who formed themselves into Hunters' Lodges. They now called themselves "Patriots," and the movement was clearly in American hands. The Patriots launched a series of bloody but ineffectual border raids, aimed presumably at annoying Canada into submission. The strategy didn't work.

Mackenzie himself led a force of several hundred Patriots onto Canadian soil, landing at Navy Island in the middle of the Niagara River, where he declared himself President of the Canadian Republic. A band of Canadian volunteers later snuck over to the American side and set the Patriot's supply ship, the *Caroline*, on fire, then cut her loose. The ship broke up and went over Niagara Falls as burning wreckage. In the scuffle, an American had been killed, and U.S.-Canadian relations were once again on the brink of all-out war. "Remember the *Caroline*!" became a rebel rallying cry, and Mackenzie sputtered and spewed.

Calmer heads soon prevailed, however, and the American government distanced itself from the Patriot movement. The dream of a new republic died on Navy

Island. Indeed, more men were killed, captured or executed in the Patriot border raids than in the initial rebellion. All told, more than 1,000 rebels and patriots were captured. Twenty were hanged. More than 800 were imprisoned. The rest were either banished or sent to the penal colonies of Australia.

One of the worst incidents occurred near the town of Prescott, Ontario, where more than 200 Patriots—led by the mad Finnish exile Nils von Schoultz—landed and barricaded themselves in several stone buildings. A force of nearly 800 militiamen and marines arrived and retook the town, but they couldn't dislodge the Patriots who had taken refuge in a towering stone windmill. During a two-day siege, the Canadians pounded the American position with heavy artillery, and in the end 80 Americans and 16 Canadians were killed in what would be known as the Battle of the Windmill. (The windmill, later converted into a lighthouse, still stands today.) Shoultz was captured and condemned to die. His lawyer? An idealistic young Kingston barrister by the name of John A. Macdonald.

What, you may ask, ultimately happened to Papineau and Mackenzie? Were they:

(a) arrested?
(b) imprisoned?
(c) executed?
(d) reelected?

Well, if you know anything about Canada, you probably chose (d). And you chose correctly. Both Papineau and Mackenzie were eventually granted amnesty, and both returned to Canada. In 1847, Papineau was once again elected to the Assembly, and he was soon back in the thick of things, advocating annexation to United States and helping to launch, along with English-Canadian reformers, what would one day become the Liberal Party of Canada.

Mackenzie returned in 1849, the last rebel to be granted clemency, and, like Papineau, he too was reelected. His grandson, none other than William Lyon Mackenzie King, went on to become Canada's most successful and longest-serving prime minister. And so it goes.

But what was accomplished during those bitter and strange rebellions? Did any good come of them?

Well, if nothing else, the Patriotes and the rebels of 1837 certainly managed to get the attention of their colonial masters in Great Britain. Civil rights were suspended, the Assemblies were dissolved, and a troubleshooter named Lord Durham was dispatched to the colonies to assess and report.

The Rebellions of 1837 were not, as some would have it, pure and noble struggles for democracy, but neither were they unnecessary side-shows of history that came and went like sudden neurotic outbursts. No. They were catalysts, and that is why we remember them. The Rebellions of 1837 *inadvertently* set in motion a chain of events that would alter the destiny of British North America and would ultimately call forth a new nation into existence.

Verdict

Very few of the players of 1837 rate well. The era was, in fact, a veritable Hive of Boneheads.

Louis-Joseph Papineau: **Bonehead**

William Lyon Mackenzie: **Bonehead**

Sir Francis Bond Head: "**Bone Head**"

The Ghost of Radical Jack: Responsible Government (and Other Oxymorons)

A WORD OF WARNING: If you are expecting a tale of vengeful spirits and haunted mansions in this chapter, you're in for a bit of a letdown. It isn't that kind of ghost story. The ghost of *this* tale haunts not a house, nor a home, but a nation.

I chose the above title with great care. If I had called the chapter "The Socio-Political Effects of the Durham Report of 1839," you probably would have skipped right over it, as you are no doubt now considering doing—but wait! This ghost is a real phantasm, a poltergeist who has played his tricks on Canada for long enough, and the time has come to kill him off once and for all. So stick around, it's a hell of a story . . .

Who was Jack? He was none other than John George Lambton, the first Earl of Durham, a snobbish, quick-tempered, brilliant young member of the British House of Commons. Like Louis-Joseph Papineau, Durham was an aristocratic reformer. He had been instrumental in introducing Britain's 1832 Reform Bill, and he had earned a name and a reputation as an outspoken liberal. They called him "Radical Jack."

Durham was the designated troubleshooter sent to Canada after the turmoils of 1837. The British government gave him sweeping powers, making him governor general of all of British North America, including Newfoundland, with a mandate to investigate and prescribe that was as wide as it was vague. Never before or since has any one individual wielded such authority in North America.

Fittingly, Lord Durham arrived in Canada in a grandiose manner, with a retinue of servants and assistants, and in his finest uniform, he rode a magnificent white horse through the streets of Montréal. One of his first acts was to pardon a score of political prisoners and to banish their leaders, not to the penal colonies of Australia but to sunny Bermuda. French-Canadian newspapers heralded his arrival.

Durham was not a healthy man—he was ill for much of his time in Canada—but he was a man of extravagant hospitality, and he hosted countless banquets and lavish feasts. In Lower Canada, he met mainly with English merchants; his contact with French leaders was fleeting. His time in Upper Canada was even briefer. He spent only 10 days in the area and only 24 hours in Toronto, the major site of the rebellion. The rest of his time was spent seeing the sights at Niagara Falls, where he astonished everyone by crossing over into the United States and charming the Americans with his flattery and republican sentiments.

Durham also met with the moderate reformers of Upper Canada just long enough for Dr. William Baldwin and his son Robert to present him with a novel concept: "responsible government."

Lord Durham's reign as governor was remarkably short. When the British House of Commons disallowed his Bermuda ordinance (on the not unreasonable grounds that his authority did not extend to Bermuda), Durham quit and went home to defend himself. He had only been in Canada for five months.

We might never have heard from him again had it not been for his *Report on the Affairs of British North America*, which he submitted in February 1839. In it, Durham more than lived up to his nickname. He recommended a complete overhaul of the colonial administration and a dismantling of the oligarchy in Upper Canada. And those recommendations were just the start. He also wanted Britain to grant greater powers to the colonies' elected Assemblies by requiring the governor to choose his Council from within their ranks.

At the time, governors of the colonies still had enormous powers. Today, our governors general and lieutenant governors are mere figureheads, vestigial remnants of British rule. Back then, however, governors were a force to be reckoned with. Making them choose their Councils from among popularly elected members would—in effect—have defanged them and shifted power to the colonists. Or at least, to the colonists' elected representatives.

Although Durham didn't use the term himself, what he was recommending was responsible government. The term Durham preferred was *responsive* government. The government, argued Radical Jack, had to be controlled by and responsive to the people. (A rose by any other name . . .) According to Durham's recommendations, the governor would be required to follow the dictates of the Assembly on all matters of internal importance. Only on Imperial matters could he override their authority. Like most revolutionary ideas, it was really quite simple.

Durham's report has been hailed with hyperbole as the Magna Carta of the colonies. True, it did set in motion what historian Chester New calls "the Canadian revolution—a revolution thoroughly British in character, since it worked itself out in a legal and constitutional manner—which won democracy for Canada and laid the foundations of self-government in the British Empire."

So far, so good. Lord Durham wanted better representation and greater constraints on corrupt power monopolies. But there is a darker side to his report. Consider this: In Britain today Lord Durham is still considered a minor hero. In English Canada he *used* to be a hero. And in French Canada he has long been cast as a villain. Radical Jack has had quite a posthumous career. His famous last words may have been, "Canada will one day do justice to my memory," but it is *our* memory that has changed—radically. I have three books on my shelf that illustrate this point:

- John Henderson's 1928 volume, *Great Men of Canada*
- George Woodcock's 1980 book, *100 Great Canadians*
- John Robert Colombo's 1986 reference, *1001 Questions about Canada*

An interesting and revealing shift has occurred over time. In Henderson's 1928 book, an entire chapter is dedicated to Lord Durham as "a great man of Canada." But by 1980, he has vanished from the radar screen; Durham does not make Woodcock's list of 100 Great Canadians (although other British-born figures, such as General Isaac Brock, do). In 1986, he is back with a vengeance. In *1001 Questions about Canada*, we find him listed not as one of "the greats" but rather—are you ready for this?—as one of the Top Ten Most Despised Men in Canadian History. He appears at number three, right behind Charles Lawrence, the man who deported the Acadians. From "great man of Canada" to "most despised"—what happened?

In Canada, it is not Lord Durham's political reforms we remember. Here, Durham's fame, or rather infamy, rests almost solely on his proposed solution to the unrest in Lower Canada. And his solution was simple. Painfully simple. Assimilation.

In his report, Lord Durham sought to correct what he took to be the central mistake of British policy in North America: "The vain endeavour to preserve a French-Canadian nationality in the midst of Anglo-American colonies and states." In English-speaking Upper Canada, Durham blamed an outdated oligarchy and the unresponsive system of government, but in Lower Canada, he saw something entirely different: "I expected to find a contest between a government and a people: I found two nations warring in the bosom of a single state: I found a struggle, not of principles, but of races."

The answer, then, was to anglicize the French. At first, Durham had urged a union of all of British North America (that is, confederation), but the Maritimes balked at the idea, and so instead he chose a dual union. To end what he called Canada's "national feud," Durham recommended uniting Lower Canada with Upper Canada and thus making the French, with the stroke of a pen, a minority.

Well, not quite. Even in a united colony, the French population would still outnumber the English by 30,000. But Durham was confident that the appeal of responsive government would draw English-speaking immigrants in by the score, thus accelerating the inevitable assimilation of francophones. A previous governor, the nasty and vindictive James Craig, had suggested the same thing—a larger union to swamp the French population and force them to assimilate—but Craig hadn't had the ear of the British government. Durham did.

Indeed, the British government went even further and suggested a short cut. Instead of simply combining the Assemblies of Upper and Lower Canada, they decided to make each of the former colonies a region under one administration with—and here's the catch—equal representation *regardless* of population. This change was, of course, unfair. It would underrepresent French Canadians and drown them politically. But then, that was the whole idea.

Whatever form the union might take, Durham was confident of one thing: once the French colony was submerged into the larger entity, its population would see the light of reason and start speaking English. To Durham, the French Canadians were "cheerful, honest, polite." And doomed.

As an enlightened liberal, Lord Durham could hardly recommend armed oppression; instead, he favoured a policy he called "benign neglect." In short, the French of Canada, by the stalwart example of British superiority, would, on seeing the error of their ways, assimilate because they wanted to. Not a strong thesis, but give Durham his due: at least he was up front about his plans. To Durham, the French were the flotsam of an empire that had failed, "an old and stationary society" that would have to make way for the "new and progressive world" of the English. "The superior political and practical intelligence of the English," wrote Durham, "cannot be, for a moment, disputed."

French Canadians, for all their cheerful honesty, were still, in the words of the enlightened Lord Durham, an ignorant, uneducated and superstitious people, "a people with no history and no literature." Theirs was a destiny of unskilled labour in the employ of English capitalists. The French language was to be proscribed in the Assembly, schools would reinforce only British ideals, and the cultural guarantees won after the conquest would now be curtailed.

Durham's report outraged French Canadians. It also outraged British parliamentarians, though for different reasons. "Responsive government!" sputtered the lords of Westminster. "A heretical suggestion!" But as far as assimilation was concerned, jolly good idea. Carry on. Unite the Canadas, pip pip and all that.

In February 1841, the Act of Union was proclaimed. The colonies of Upper and Lower Canada were welded together, and the capital was moved, briefly, to Kingston. (It later bounced from Toronto to Québec City to Montréal before Ottawa was finally selected.) With the Act of Union, a new Dark Age loomed, and it followed hard on the defeat of the Patriotes like insult added to injury. French Canadians would never forget Lord Durham's offhand dismissal of a people who had been living along the St. Lawrence for more than 200 years before his arrival.

Ah, but history is a lady with a wicked sense of humour, and, irony of ironies, not only did Durham's report fail to spell the end of the French in Canada, it actually worked in their favour. It was both an affront and a challenge, like a glove slapped across the face in invitation to a duel. Nothing unites people more than a shared outrage. In his book *French Canadians*, author Michel Gratton notes, "French Canadians owe Lord Durham a big one. His call for assimilation . . . became the rallying cry for those community leaders who might otherwise have given up on the nation. Durham said we were dead, or at least dying. Proving him wrong became the driving force of a nation."

The days that followed saw a renaissance of French-Canadian culture, a bursting forth of energy, ideas and art that would remain unparalleled until the Quiet Revolution of the 1960s. The first to pick up the glove and answer Lord Durham's challenge was François-Xavier Garneau, who set out to write a history of Canada in direct response to an English-speaking clerk who, echoing Durham, had scoffed at French Canadians as a people without a history. "I shall write the history," replied Garneau, "which you do not even know exists. You will see that our ancestors yielded only when out-numbered. There are defeats which are as glorious as victories."

Here then is the deep melancholy that lies just below the hedonistic veneer of French-Canadian culture. The Acadian exile, the Plains of Abraham, the noble failure of Papineau: these have bred a peculiar cult of defeat. If English Canada defines itself by what it is not—*not* American, *not* aggressive, *not* exciting—French Canada defines itself by what it has lost. In these tendencies, the two solitudes share a certain sadness: the centrality of absence, a country and a people defined by what is missing, by what has passed. *Defeats as glorious as victories.*

Garneau's *Histoire du Canada* appeared between 1845 and 1848, and it took three volumes to tell. Not only were *les Canadiens* a people with a past, they were a people of the past, a people born of struggle and shaped, as pine trees are, by harsh, hard winds. Theirs was an Age Heroic, an epic tale. They were a people under siege; that was their one inescapable reality. It was also their strength. Garneau defined the pillars of the nation: French law, the French language and the Catholic Church. On these, their future was staked.

Garneau was one of a legion of newly awakened French-Canadian nationalists who dominated that era. Under the intelligentsia of the newly formed Institute Canadien, Québec's feudalistic seigneurial system was finally laid to rest in 1854. A radical core of young idealists formed around old Papineau, who had returned from the wilderness and was as inspirational and quixotic as ever.

But Papineau had become a marginal figure, and centre stage now belonged to those who would change the system from within. The man with the vision was Louis-Hippolyte LaFontaine, a former Patriote and a veteran of the Battle of St-Denis. LaFontaine, Napoleonesque in both his features and his determination, was adept at turning adversity to his advantage. He saw the United Parliament of Canada, dark though its intent had been, as a key to French survival. It would provide a parliamentary bastion, and LaFontaine would become its master. A realist and a proud *Canadien*, LaFontaine transformed himself from armed rebel to moderate reformer, and in doing so, he became one of the most capable politicians Canada has ever produced.

The uniting of the two Canadas had an unforeseen effect: it brought English and French reformers together, and rather than blending the two cultures into one homogenous, Anglo-Saxon whole, it actually strengthened the dualism of the burgeoning nation. An alliance between English and French reformers soon developed, and from this connection a friendship grew between two remarkable men: Louis LaFontaine and Robert Baldwin. If LaFontaine was Napoleon, then Baldwin was a Heathcliff of the moors, a moody, morose individual, introspective and given to bouts of depression. Baldwin was also a man ahead of his time, an English-speaking Canadian who realized that the state would have to respect and make room for both French and English if it wished to survive.

The LaFontaine-Baldwin pact was as well coordinated and successful as the Papineau-Mackenzie duo was *un*coordinated and *un*successful. In public forum and raucous debate, LaFontaine and Baldwin won the very thing that armed rebellion had failed to secure: the end of the Family Compact and the Château Clique, and the creation of responsible government. On March 10, 1848, Louis LaFontaine, with the support of Robert Baldwin, formed the first responsible government in Canada. This date has been heralded as "the birth of democracy in Canada," but the real test was about to come. Would the elected government wield real authority? Or would it be responsible in name only?

At this crucial point in history another key personality enters the picture: Governor General James Elgin, a steadfast, fluently bilingual, Oxford-trained man. When the Assembly introduced the Rebellion Losses Bill, which awarded damages to the many habitants whose homes and belongings had been destroyed by Sir John Colborne's forces, the English-speaking residents of Montréal went on a rampage. They considered the bill a reward to traitors and demanded that Lord Elgin veto it. But Elgin refused: it was an internal matter and he would not interfere. The issue was for the elected members to decide. Enraged at Elgin's neutrality, an angry mob attacked the governor, pelting him with stones and bricks, invading his home and burning the Montréal Parliament to the ground. But Elgin did not flinch. Responsible government had, in name and in fact, arrived.

In no other British colony outside of the United States was the transition marked by such violence. The last time this level of protest had happened, Britain had lost its American colonies. In Upper and Lower Canada, the constant turmoil from the late 1820s through the rebellions of 1837 to the burning of the Parliament Buildings in 1849 was unparalleled anywhere else in the Empire. The colony of Nova Scotia, for example, had achieved responsible government a few weeks earlier than Canada, and without any of the bloodshed. But Canada had been the catalyst. Without the chain reaction set off by the rebellions and the report that followed, Nova Scotia (or Australia, for that matter) would never have been able to make the change as smoothly as it did.

Louis LaFontaine, as the elected leader of the 1848 Assembly, was in effect Canada's first true prime minister. Unfortunately, LaFontaine, like his friend and colleague Robert Baldwin, has been greatly undervalued over the years. A statue on Parliament Hill commemorates the two men, but I would bet that not one in 10,000 remembers their names. It is men like Mackenzie and Papineau whom we prefer to rally around.

If LaFontaine fails to excite the passions of the Québécois in the way that Papineau does, I suspect it is because LaFontaine was a winner, and French Canadians, God bless them, love a loser: Montcalm, Chénier, Papineau all failed nobly. But fail they did. LaFontaine believed in Canada. He believed in a bilingual, bicultural nation. Papineau, in contrast, was a man of puffed-up slogans and large, empty, dangerous gestures: the Lucien Bouchard of his day.

LaFontaine was a better man than Papineau. In Louis LaFontaine, we find the first stirrings of pan-Canadian federalism, one based on the enduring truth that it is better to work together than apart, better to be united than divided. Like most revolutionary ideas, it is really quite simple.

The drama merchants and the rebels, the Patriotes and the snake charmers: these certainly make better tragic heroes, but in the end it is the people who work persistently and in good faith who make the real advances. In Canada, radical solutions burn like phosphorus—bright, hot and short—and the lasting triumphs are carved out by stronger, calmer people. The LaFontaines, not the Papineaus. The Baldwins, not the Mackenzies.

When Louis LaFontaine first rose in the United Assembly back in 1842, he began his address in French. An Anglo backbencher yelled out, "Speak English!", to which LaFontaine replied:

> Even if I were as familiar with the English as with the French language, I should nonetheless make my first speech in the language of my French-Canadian compatriots, were it only to enter my solemn protest against the cruel injustice of that part of the Act of Union which seeks to proscribe the mother tongue of half the population of Canada.

There you have it: one of the most important turning points in Canadian history. From that moment on, the French language would not—could not—ever be fully outlawed. (Although attempts to do so were certainly made.) LaFontaine had rejected the ban on his language, and seven years later, when Lord Elgin delivered his first throne speech, he did so in English and then, with a slight smile, again in French. As historian Laurier LaPierre noted in *Canada, My Canada*, "United Canada had become bilingual. Elgin undid Durham."

And thus, within eight years of its proclamation, the Act of Union as a tool of assimilation was dead. So too, at age 48, was John Durham. Radical Jack never lived to see the act become law, and he never lived to see the triumphs of LaFontaine and Baldwin. He died in the summer of 1840, just 18 months after submitting his report—killed, some said, by the rigours of his Canadian assignment.

Like Jack, the Durham Report is dead. But not forgotten. The ghost lingers on like a house guest who just won't leave, a shape-changer that haunts us still. Both sides have helped keep the ghost alive, from the English-Canadian Orangemen of yesteryear to the Reform Party and the Bloc Québécois of today. French-Canadian nationalists still roll out dusty ol' Jack Durham whenever discussions turn to past wrongs and perceived injustices, and I don't think there is a separatist alive who does not still revel in and relish the insults heaped on French Canadians by a foppish British official some 160 years ago. Make no mistake: Québec's intellectual nationalists are as enamoured with Durham as they are with Papineau. *Je me souviens* and all that.

The only thing the Québécois love more than a French-Canadian loser is an English villain, and between Papineau and Lord Durham you have the puppet-play simplicity of the separatist appeal. All facts to the contrary, Papineau is still referred to as the "prophet of Québec independence." During the October Crisis of 1970, FLQ terrorists issued handbills bearing the picture of an 1837 Patriote, and one of the splinter groups was called "the Chénier cell." *Defeats as glorious as victories.*

It has been said that Canada is a land of survivors, and this is truer for no one than the Québécois, a people who have lived under siege for so long they do not realize the battle is long over and the victory won. Maybe, after 160 years, a revised constitution and a multicultural, redefined—*self*-defined—Canada, it is time to shelve the Durham Report once and for all, and move on to other things. But in this, the Land of the Long Grudges, that hardly seems possible.

Verdict

John George Lambton, Lord Durham: **A Handsome, Charming, Gregarious, Passionate Bonehead**

Louis-Hippolyte LaFontaine and Robert Baldwin: **Understated, Determined Bastards**

Governor James Elgin: **An Admirable Bastard**

. . . and in the game of life, Bastard always beats Bonehead.

Spiked Drinks:
John A. Macdonald and
the Invention of Canada

CANADA, LIKE MANY a child, was conceived under the influence of alcohol.

The idea of combining the remaining British colonies in North America into some sort of union had been around for years, but it would take a historic coalition, more than a few cases of champagne, a couple of turns on the dance floor and the threat of armed invasion before this vast enterprise of ours was called into being. More importantly, it would take four Bastards and one Bonehead to launch Confederation.

By the 1860s, the united colony of central Canada had become unworkable. Durham's Final Solution had backfired magnificently. Instead of undermining French Canadians and speeding up their assimilation, the Act of Union had inadvertently given them an almost unassailable power base. In a united legislature, any party that wished to hold office had to have the support of French Canadians. It was a matter of simple arithmetic. Personalities clashed, alliances shifted, coalitions came and went, but through it all French Canadians held the balance of power.

Thanks to a huge influx of immigrants, the English population of Canada had now surpassed that of the French, but English Canadians were trapped in an Assembly that gave an automatic 50/50 split to the two regions. The West (meaning Ontario) felt alienated and underrepresented, and George Brown of the Reform Party was the prophet of discontent. The demand for representation by population—"rep by pop!"—grew stronger and more strident. As Christopher Moore puts it in *1867: How the Fathers Made a Deal*, "In the 1860s, western alienation began at Yonge Street, and George Brown was the Preston Manning of the day."

Not everyone in English Canada found the situation intolerable. Amid the incessant wheeling and dealing, a Kingston lawyer by the name of John A. Macdonald had managed to manoeuvre himself into a position of power. Although he never won a solid majority from his fellow Anglos, Macdonald succeeded by relying on the support of French Canadians. More specifically, on his alliance with George-Étienne Cartier, leader of the conservative Bleu party. Together, Macdonald and Cartier dominated Canadian politics in an era of shifting loyalties.

George Brown despised the glad-handing Macdonald with a passion, and the feeling was mutual. Where Brown was unwavering, Macdonald was pliant to the point of elasticity. Although nominally a Tory, Macdonald had patched together a coalition from all directions on the political map, and when he was first elected prime minister it was under the banner of the "Liberal-Conservatives," a wonderfully oxymoronical name (and one that would be surpassed in that respect only many years later by the Progressive Conservatives).

But it was George Brown, the man labelled a bigot in Québec, who would revive the dream, long discussed but rarely pursued, of a single confederation of British North America, united against growing American encroachments and decreasing British support. By 1864, the workings of the Province of Canada's legislature had ground to a halt. In that year alone, four separate, mayfly governments had come and gone, and affairs of state were stalled. The government was once again on the verge of collapse, and no one knew how to break the log-jam. It is at this crux of events that the personal decision of one man changed everything.

On June 17, 1864, something remarkable happened. George Brown, Macdonald's implacable foe, rose in the House and announced that he was willing to cross the floor. He would join the Macdonald-Cartier government on the condition that it agreed to pursue a larger federation, one that would include the rest of British North America. (Such a federation, by making Canada East and Canada West separate entities again, would give English Canada greater autonomy. It would also create a much-needed strong central government. And thus, George Brown managed to be both a federalist *and* a regionalist.) The Great Coalition of 1864 was born.

Mind you, someone needed to convince the other colonies that the proposed union was worth pursuing. The Maritimes, prosperous and internationally minded, had much less to gain from such a federation. True, the Glory Argument, as it was called, did have a certain appeal: the chance to become part of something vaster, greater, grander. But more pressing, and far more persuasive, was the turmoil taking place south of the border. Indeed, one could argue that it was the American Civil War that created Canada.

The Civil War, raging since 1861, was now coming to a close. It would be the bloodiest and most costly conflict in U.S. history, and Britain had unwisely shown sympathy, even lent tacit support, to the slave-owning rebel armies of the South.

The North was now clearly winning, and it had not forgotten Britain's betrayal. "Wait till we're done with the rebs," came the angry cry. "Canada will be next!" It was 1775 and 1812 all over again. With a battle-hardened, belligerent, expansionist U.S. breathing down their necks, the British colonies were understandably concerned, and confederation became even more pressing. After all, there was strength in union.

As chance would have it, the three Maritime colonies were planning a conference to discuss a possible union of their own, and the Canadians decided to crash the party. The date and place were hurriedly set: Charlottetown, P.E.I., in the first week of September 1864.

The Canadian delegation, led by the Great Coalition of Brown, Cartier and Macdonald, sailed triumphantly into Charlottetown harbour to be met by—no one. The circus was in town, you see, and everyone was off to have a look at the elephants. In the excitement, the arrival of the Canadians had been largely forgotten. An embarrassed P.E.I. provincial secretary arranged for an oyster man to row him out to the Canadian ship, now anchored in the bay, where he apologized profusely and welcomed them to the island. It was not an auspicious start to Confederation, but the Canadians were unperturbed, for they had brought with them two secret weapons: the gift of the gab and a large supply of champagne.

What followed, in among the long speeches and exhortations to glory, was an almost endless procession of parties and soirées. One grows exhausted just reading about it: the banquets and dinners and dances; that relentless, almost aggressive hospitality for which Maritimers are known. In the words of historian Donald Swainson, "Confederation was floated through on champagne."

Canada: a nation partied into existence. Makes you proud to be a Canuck.

Heady on bubbly and new-found friendship, the delegates decided to—well, to keep on drinking. And dancing. And talking. Although the delegates did agree upon the broad principles involved, the specific terms of Confederation were not, as is sometimes believed, decided at Charlottetown. Or even discussed, really. The Charlottetown Conference was mainly a sales pitch by the Canadians, and the only concrete thing to come out of it was a commitment to have more meetings. It was, in its way, the most significant bureaucratic junket in Canadian history. Or, to put it even less reverentially, the Charlottetown Conference was one big schmooze-fest, the flirtatious courting of the Maritimers by a bunch of smooth-talking Canadians.

Soon after Charlottetown, the Confederation caravan travelled to Québec City, the capital of Canada at the time, where the usual round of champagne, soirées and piano tunes began anew. And through a haze of alcohol, banquets and late-night bull sessions, cajoled by John A.'s banter and easy wit, seduced by good food and good wine, a new nation began to take shape.

Québec City was where the work began in earnest. As Christopher Moore writes:

> [T]he conference at Québec in October 1864 was a remarkable event, the longest, largest, most inclusive, most productive, and most successful constitutional conference in the long history of Canadian constitutional palaver . . . In sixteen working days, the thirty-three delegates of more than a dozen political factions from six provinces negotiated, drafted, debated, and passed seventy-two resolutions that set out the essentials of the constitution that has governed Canada ever since.

Those Seventy-Two Resolutions would form the backbone of Confederation, which was in turn hammered out at a final conference in London, England. The agreement was called the British North America Act. Canada's Constitution. The Game Plan for Running a Nation.

Make no mistake: amid the social whirl and frothy galas, the idea of Confederation was hotly debated. Incredible as it may seem today, right from the start members of the Opposition were invited to take an active role, making for some very lively, but remarkably broad-based, discussions. (The glaring exception was the radical Rouge party, which was not invited to join the delegation from Québec.)

The key question in the 1860s was what shape the new state would take. Would it be a unitary model like France and Britain, with a single legislature, or an American model, with two levels of government, state and national? In the end the delegates chose a bit of both, a hybrid of the British and the American approaches. It would be a parliamentary system, in which the party with the most seats gets to field the prime minister (as opposed to the U.S. system, where the electorate votes directly for a president). But it would also have a clear federal structure; that is, a division of powers between the provinces and the federal government. If this all sounds very familiar, that's because the formula worked out in the 1860s is essentially what we have today. (Even Pierre Trudeau's Constitution Act of 1982 has been described by parliamentarian Eugene Forsey as little more than "the BNA Act with bells and whistles.")

Over the years, Confederation has been revised, repatriated and pronounced dead more times than you can imagine, but like John A. himself, it has shown a certain punch-drunk tenacity. What the Fathers of Confederation created has withstood the test of time remarkably well.

So who were they, these vaguely anonymous Fathers? Few are remembered today, and most Canadians, if pressed, could name only one or two—if any.

When British Columbia joined Confederation, Canada became a country "sea to sea." And the character of British Columbia was shaped by one man more than any other: James Douglas. If Champlain was the Father of New France, and Simcoe the Father of Upper Canada, then James Douglas was undoubtedly "the Father of British Columbia." (With women excluded from power, the early colonies were, unfortunately, the offspring of single parents.)

As chief factor of the Hudson's Bay Company's Pacific coast operations, James Douglas built Fort Victoria at the bottom of Vancouver Island in 1843. And it was Douglas, as governor of the colony of British Columbia, who later oversaw B.C.'s chaotic boom years during two successive gold strikes: first along the Fraser River and then in the Cariboo region.

Helping Douglas keep a steady, law-enforcing hand was Matthew Baillie Begbie, the "Hangin' Judge," a man who sounds more like a character from Dickens than a real person. Described by one miner as "the biggest man, smartest man, best-looking man and damnedest man that ever came down the Cariboo Road," Begbie continued the unfortunate Canadian tradition of giving authority and security preference over individual rights.

When one American outlaw, convicted of murder, yelled out that he would appeal the decision, Judge Begbie nodded thoughtfully and said, "Well, it will take six months or more for the colonial secretary to deal with the matter and months more before we learn of his decision. But you will not be interested in what he decides, for you are to be hanged Monday morning."

One of the strangest conflicts that occurred under Governor Douglas's tenure was the Pig War of 1859. It began on San Juan Island, south of Victoria, when a pig belonging to the Hudson's Bay Company got loose and began rummaging around in a garden belonging to an American settler. The American settler, being an American, carefully assessed his options: (a) chase the pig away, (b) complain to the owner, or (c) attempt to capture the pig. He then, of course, chose option (d)—shoot the pig. When the HBC demanded compensation, the American—being an American—refused. Unfortunately, San Juan Island lay in disputed territory, and the incident soon spun out of control as the U.S. sent in troops to "secure the island for American interests." James Douglas, never one to back down from a fight, responded in kind.

The armed standoff on San Juan Island wasn't resolved until 1872, when (here's a surprise) Britain ceded sole ownership to the U.S. as part of an arbitration agreement, proving once again that living next door to the United States is like getting nibbled to death by mice: a piece here, a piece there—it all adds up. (They should have sent in Judge Begbie to hang that damn pig-shootin', sabre-rattlin' Yankee troublemaker.)

Traditionally, there were 36 Fathers of Confederation, delegates who took part in one or more of the three conferences: Charlottetown, Québec and London. Of these 36 Fathers, nine went on to become provincial premiers, 12 became federal cabinet ministers, 10 became lieutenant governors, 12 were appointed to the Senate, 13 were awarded knighthoods, two were murdered, and two became prime minister.

And yet, for all their collective achievements and notoriety, most of the Fathers of Confederation *are* vaguely anonymous. And so they should be. There is no reason to know who these middle-aged men were, no need to memorize long lists of their names. As with any committee or conference, a few key players swayed the rest.

Here, then, is the short list, the Top Five Fathers of Confederation, given in order of importance:

1. Number One with a Bullet: George Brown

Without George Brown's momentous decision to put partisan politics aside and work towards a greater union, Confederation might never have taken place. Sadly, Brown never held such power again. Outplayed at every turn by his old nemesis, John A. Macdonald, Brown eventually quit politics entirely and devoted himself to his angry, reform-minded newspaper, the *Globe*. Although he was politically a failure, his ideas lived on. The new dominion was indeed based on the principles of "rep by pop," and Brown himself laid the groundwork for the division of powers between the federal and provincial governments. And thus, although he soon became disillusioned with the Great Coalition, he remains one of the primary architects of Confederation and its main catalyst.

Brown's life, however, ended ignobly. After he fired one of his employees for drunkenness, the man returned full of fury and, in the scuffle that ensued, George Brown was shot. He received a flesh wound that was not in itself life-threatening, but then gangrene set in and the poison spread. The man who had done so much for Canada took six weeks to die.

2. The Number-Two Man: George-Étienne Cartier

Without Cartier, French Canada might never have become part of the larger union. The inseparable Macdonald and Cartier were dubbed "the Siamese Twins," and indeed Macdonald referred to Cartier as "my second self." A lively, gregarious man with a sentimental streak and a flair for playing the piano, Cartier was immensely popular and persuasive, and he was in fact one of the few Fathers of Confederation capable of out-partying Macdonald.

Cartier's life cut a remarkable arc: from armed rebel in the extremist Fils de la Liberté to born-again bourgeois, from railway promoter to Father of Confederation, and, finally, to knighthood. In Canada's first federal parliament, George-Étienne Cartier, the former Patriote of 1837, was made Minister of Militia and Defence.

An ardent defender of French-Canadian interests, he claimed to be a direct descendant of the great explorer Jacques Cartier. He was also hopelessly infatuated with British traditions. (He named one of his daughters after the queen and dreamed of becoming a peer in the House of Lords.) In short, he was a man as mixed up as the country he helped bring about. Although he was routinely condemned as a traitor by Québec nationalists, the record shows quite clearly that Cartier—for all his British affectations—had a deep love of his *Canadien* roots. He was an unabashed romantic, and a songwriter to boot. When, as a young man, Cartier had composed and published the patriotic anthem "O Canada! Mon pays! Mes amours!" ("Oh, Canada! My country, my loves!"), it wasn't English Canada he had in mind.

If Macdonald's importance has sometimes been exaggerated over the years, Cartier's contribution has been vastly underplayed. He was, effectively, co–prime minister with Macdonald during the crucial first years of Confederation. Whenever Macdonald was ill, drunk or on an extended pub crawl (he was notorious for disappearing at important moments and then showing up later, dishevelled and morose), Cartier often acted as de facto leader. It was Cartier who negotiated the purchase of Rupert's Land from the Hudson's Bay Company, which gave Canada the entire Northwest, and it was Cartier who negotiated B.C.'s entry into Confederation—with the rash promise of a transcontinental railway, no less.

Accusations that Cartier "sold out" Québec are as groundless as they are revisionist. The cold hard truth is this: Confederation gave Québec control over its civil laws, its natural resources, and its social, linguistic, religious and cultural institutions, while at the same time giving it the benefits of belonging to a larger union. Separatist mythology to the contrary, it wasn't a bad deal then, and it isn't today. As Sheila McLeod Arnopoulos and Dominique Clift point out in *The English Fact in Québec*, "As a political compromise, Confederation turned out to be very astute and durable." To say the least.

3. The Teetotalling Tactician: Leonard Tilley

Leonard Tilley was the Liberal premier of New Brunswick, and if he seems out of place in this pantheon of Important People, it is only because he was such a pious man. He didn't quite fit in. He was an avowed teetotaller; the champagne never went to Tilley's head, if only because he never drank any. Make no mistake, however: Leonard Tilley was a master tactician. One look at a map shows how critical New Brunswick was to Confederation. Without the land link, the union would have been less a nation and more a scattering of trading partners. New Brunswick was the linchpin.

Tilley faced an angry legislature on his return from Québec City, and the hostility quickly reached a fever pitch. Rather than face defeat in the legislature, which would have ended New Brunswick's move towards Confederation, Tilley decided to call a snap election. He lost (of course). But just as he had predicted, the new government, made up of Royalists and Reformers alike, soon fell to squabbling amongst themselves. They foundered in office, and suddenly Tilley was perceived as the moderate voice of reason. A second election, in 1866, swept him back into power, and he brought New Brunswick into Confederation with strong public support. Macdonald himself couldn't have done a better job of finessing the electorate and outplaying his opponents.

Tilley is also remembered as the man who gave Canada both its official name and its motto. Reading his Bible one night (while the other delegates were out revelling in debauchery, no doubt), Tilley came across a passage in Psalms 72: "He shall have dominion also from sea to sea." From this line came our national title, the Dominion of Canada, and later, our motto: *A mari usque ad mare*, "from sea to sea." (The motto itself was not formally adopted until 1921.)

Leonard Tilley went on to bigger and better things. He joined Macdonald's cabinet as Finance Minister and he was instrumental in drafting the National Policy, a system of protective tariffs that managed to combine ruthless pragmatism with nationalist sentiments. In this, too, Leonard Tilley had an incalculable effect on the development of Canada.

4. From Bastard to Bonehead: The Life and Times of Charles Tupper

Charles Tupper was a man of "bluff and bully." As the premier of Nova Scotia, he too faced angry opposition to the proposed union. Like Tilley, Tupper had a ruling majority in his provincial parliament, but in the freewheeling days of the 1860s, party members were much less constrained in how they voted. Backbenchers wielded real power, and Tupper faced a revolt from both the Opposition and members of his own party. But if anyone was up to the battle, it was Charles Tupper.

Tupper was a braggart and a loud-talking, browbeating tyrant. He could also be incredibly charming and very cunning. Rather than face an electorate over the issue, he chose instead a strategy of delay and deceit, in which he began relentlessly wooing the opposition. It was a "rough wooing," to be sure, but it worked, and he eventually won over enough members to pass a bill supporting Confederation without ever having to take the issue to the voters. Legally, Tupper did nothing wrong. After all, members of the legislature were under no obligation to run to the people for approval on every bill they passed. That was the intent of representative democracy: your members spoke for you. Ethically, however, Tupper was on thin ice. To this day, Nova Scotians feel that they were railroaded into Confederation—and there is some truth to this claim. (The first separatist movement in Canada began not in Québec but in Nova Scotia.)

On the morning of July 1, 1867, the newspapers in Halifax announced, "Died! Last night at twelve o'clock, the free and enlightened Province of Nova Scotia." And when Tupper finally did call an election, two months *after* Confederation had already passed, the result was a massacre. Of the 19 members Nova Scotia sent to the first session in Ottawa, 18 were anti-Confederates. Among those members who had supported Confederation, only Tupper himself survived. But by then it was too late. Nova Scotians had been caught in a lobster trap. There was no escape, and they have been stuck with us ever since.

Tupper, one of the biggest Bastards of Confederation, went on to become Canada's shortest-reigning prime minister, leading John A.'s party to a massive defeat at the hands of an upstart named Wilfrid Laurier. As PM, he was the Joe Clark of his day. He started his career as a Bastard, he ended it as a Bonehead. Sad, really.

5. The Grand Champion of Confederation: John A. Macdonald

It may surprise you to find John A. ranked fifth in importance. Most people would assume he'd be the number-one man, but John A. was a late convert to Confederation. In fact, he originally stood opposed to George Brown's initiative, and it was only after Cartier announced his support that Macdonald quickly changed sides. Macdonald may have been a reluctant federalist, but once convinced he threw his energy into the project. He was the central player at Québec City, the key architect of Confederation and its most ardent supporter. Macdonald was a man of many flaws who nonetheless rose to the challenge of his times. Rarely have events and personality come crashing together with such an impact. John A. would prove himself to be the greatest nation builder in Canadian history, and a Bastard through and through.

Two Honourable Mentions

Although the five men listed above were the key movers of Confederation, two more Fathers deserve special mention: Alexander Tilloch Galt, the stalwart money man from Sherbrooke, and Thomas D'Arcy McGee, the silver-tongued poet and chief propagandist of the new union.

Galt, a successful businessman and an expert in investment banking, was the only person at the conferences with a solid background in economics. He tweaked the numbers, even fudged a few, and managed to make Confederation look more viable than it really was. He was, in a way, the Paul Martin of his day. He was also one of the first converts to the cause, a champion of Confederation long before it became fashionable. Indeed, he is sometimes referred as "the *true* Father." Historian P. B. Waite calls Galt "the financial genius of Confederation."

If Galt represented the head, McGee was the heart. And between the Economist and the Poet you have the full sweep of Confederation's appeal. McGee was Irish, which is to say charming, eloquent and more than a tad touched with blarney. A master orator, he had a rare passion for the idea of a new Canadian nationality, one that would encompass French *and* English, Irish *and* Scots, Catholic *and* Protestant. These high ideals would be the death of him. Literally.

Although he began as a Reformer, McGee eventually fell in with Macdonald, and the two men became drinking buddies. McGee's binges were legendary, and one story, possibly apocryphal, has John A. taking McGee aside one day and saying sternly, "Look here, McGee, this government can't afford two drunkards. So you'll have to stop."

In many ways, D'Arcy McGee was ahead of his time. He was already looking towards a true national identity, one with its own literature, its own sense of destiny. He was also one of only two Canadians ever assassinated for political reasons. (The other was Québec Labour Minister Pierre Laporte in 1970.)

One Dishonourable Mention

Although none of its members were technically delegates to the Confederation conferences, the Fenian Brotherhood played an important role in the creation of Canada. The Fenians were a band of Irish nationalists who had decided to free Ireland from British rule—by invading Canada. (This is the type of brilliant scheme for which the Irish are known.) Beginning in 1866, and led by an Irish-American mystic who had visions of dead Celtic kings showing them the way, the Fenians launched a series of quixotic and occasionally bloody raids into Canadian territory from the United States. Although never a real threat, they were perceived as such, and the panic they spread among the Canadian population helped strengthen support for a northern union. As Desmond Morton notes in *A Military History of Canada*, "Historically, the Fenians were probably a blessing to Canada. They united the country as nothing else could." They were, however, not the fun-loving buffoons they might have seemed. On April 7, 1868, less than a year after the triumph of Confederation, a suspected Fenian sympathizer, angry at D'Arcy McGee's British ties and anti-Fenian stance, followed McGee home one night and shot him dead. McGee was just 42 years old.

Finally, Two Conspicuous by Their Absence

Two very important people did *not* attend the Confederation debates, one by design and the other by accident. Antoine-Aimé Dorion, leader of the liberal, anti-clerical Rouges was shut out entirely. Dorion had once, briefly, held power under a coalition with Brown's Reformers, but the alliance soon fell apart. George-Étienne Cartier, unlike his compatriots, felt no need to include members of *his* opposition in the Confederation conferences. The Rouges in turn were not impressed with Cartier's deal, and they suggested their own symbol for Confederation: the rainbow, "an image without substance." Still, in spite of Dorion's opposition, Confederation passed with a majority of support among French-Canadian members. Unlike Nova Scotians, the people of Québec joined the union without widespread outrage or protest, and the claim that Québec too was railroaded into Confederation is both spurious and insidious, designed solely to bolster modern-day separatist rhetoric. (Dorion, it should be noted, later went to Ottawa anyway, as a minister under Alexander Mackenzie's Liberals.)

Joseph Howe, in Nova Scotia, was Charles Tupper's greatest foe. As a young man, Tupper had gone head-to-head against the formidable Howe in an electoral riding—and had won. No small feat when one considers Howe's stature as an opponent. Joseph Howe was a former premier himself, and he was indeed "the Father of Responsible Government" in Nova Scotia. Unlike Dorion, Howe had been invited to the conferences, but he could not attend due to prior commitments. Had he been involved, Howe might well have come up with a formula that suited him, but as it was, he spearheaded opposition to Confederation. His anti-union coalition won a major victory in 1867, but by then it was too late. Nova Scotia was already committed, and there was little that Howe could do to stop it, though he did manage to negotiate better terms. John A. Macdonald, always a man with an eye for talent, eventually won Howe over to the federalist cause, and within a year of Confederation, Joseph Howe had joined Macdonald's cabinet.

So there you have it, the dominant personalities behind Confederation.

Were these men heroes? Well, their achievement was certainly heroic, and their personalities were forceful, their eccentricities compelling. And yes, they did embody the spirit and ideals of their age. But were they, you know, *heroes*?

To the average American, the Declaration of Independence is a sacred document. "Words worth dying for," as they say. In Canada, we are a little less patriotic. The U.S. Constitution was baptized in blood, not floated in on champagne, and Canadians have often expressed a certain peculiar regret about this. We actually envy the Americans their bloodshed and gore. It's ghoulish, really, this notion that Canadians haven't been violent enough to inspire greatness. Ghoulish, and more than a bit neurotic.

Remember, by the 1860s the greatest battles had already been waged. The conquest of New France. The defeat of the Loyalists. The War of 1812. The Rebellions of 1837. But even more importantly, responsible government, the very cornerstone of modern democracy, had been won. Confederation was simply responsible government *in action*. It was never meant to be a revolutionary or seditious act.

Now, I suppose it would have been more entertaining had the Fathers duked it out in Charlottetown instead of drinking bubbly and trying to seduce each other's wives. And it certainly would have been more cinematic had John A. reached the top by climbing over the bloody bodies of his fellow delegates. But to claim Confederation is uninspiring simply because it came about so smoothly is odd logic indeed.

The American Declaration of Independence enshrined as its central ideals "life, liberty, and the pursuit of happiness." During the French Revolution, the trio of catchwords was "liberty, equality and fraternity." In Canada, however, Confederation enshrined as its three central goals "peace, order, and good government."

Peace. Order. Good government. Not words to die for, certainly, but maybe— just maybe—words worth living for.

On Monday, July 1, 1867, the British North America Act took effect, and Confederation became a reality. Most of Canada awoke to sunny skies and the sound of church bells ringing out. There were picnics and parades, fireworks and 101-gun salutes, but in spite of all the gushy editorials and the self-congratulations, this day did not mark the end of a journey. It was just the beginning.

Canada consisted of three and a half million people and four provinces: Ontario and Québec (both much smaller than their present size), New Brunswick and Nova Scotia. That was it. Canada was indeed a nation partied into existence, and like many a decision made under such conditions, this one had been reconsidered in the harsh cold light of dawn. Hangovers tend to sour one's mood, and Prince Edward Island ultimately rejected Confederation. Newfoundland declined the invitation to dance as well. No matter. The process had begun, and eventually the other pieces would fall into place. Canada was formed in stages.

The government of John A. Macdonald purchased the vast Northwest from the Hudson's Bay Company in 1869, making the new dominion, just two years after its creation, the second largest nation on earth. This development triggered an armed rebellion on the prairies and led to the creation of a new province: Manitoba. Carved out of the Northwest in 1870, Manitoba had, by far, the most dramatic birth of any Canadian province.

British Columbia was next. Resisting overtures of annexation to the United States, a delegation from B.C. travelled to Ottawa in 1871. Among their requests was that a wagon trail be built to the rest of Canada. To their amazement, they were offered a railway instead.

Even P.E.I. changed its mind, begrudgingly, and came on board in 1873, after new incentives were offered. (It helped that the Islanders had driven themselves to the brink of bankruptcy with their own provincial railway, which was as crooked in design as it was in intent.) The Newfoundlanders held out the longest; they didn't join Canada until 1949.

But the most important addition was British Columbia, if only because that province made the grandiose claim of *a mari usque ad mare* a reality. Even more significant was the railway B.C. was promised. The Canadian Pacific Railway would span the continent, from the St. Lawrence River to the West Coast, and the building of it would prove to be our formative epic. The Opposition called it "an act of insane recklessness." And they were right. It was the triumph of big dreams over small, of faith over common sense: a nation forged not in the fires of war but by a landscape traversed. In Canada, our single greatest victory would be not over armed enemies, but over sheer geography.

Until the railway was completed, John A. Macdonald warned, Canada would

He called himself the "General Boss of Everybody and Everything." William Cornelius Van Horne was the greatest gift the Americans ever gave us, a blustering, larger-than-life railway baron and the driving force behind the success of the CPR. He was a true renaissance man, a poker-playing, art-collecting, hard-driving capitalist aristocrat with a talent for oil painting and interests as wide-ranging as palaeontology and Japanese porcelain. John A. Macdonald may have had the vision, and John A. Macdonald may have had the dream, but it was Van Horne who made the railway run. Never has a single personality imposed itself with such force upon a landscape.

By the time the CPR was completed, Van Horne had renounced his American citizenship and become a Canadian. When asked about his decision, he said simply, "Building that railroad would have made a Canadian out of the German Emperor."

When the last spike was driven home, Van Horne was on hand. A ceremonial silver spike had been prepared for the ceremony, but it was a regular iron spike that joined Canada together on November 7, 1885. The regular workers were shooed away, and financier Donald Smith was invited to step in and finish the job. Smith bent the first spike, but he hammered the second one in without mishap. There was a deep, almost unnatural silence—followed by a loud, echoing cheer. Van Horne was urged forward with cries of "Speech! Speech!" but when the cheering stopped, he delivered no lengthy oration. "All I can say," he rasped, "is that the work has been done well in every way."

The locomotive from the east rumbled to life, and the whistle blew a single plaintive note that hung in the air. The conductor cried out, "All aboard for the Pacific!" And the train rolled west, in the words of Pierre Berton, "off to the blue Pacific and into history."

remain merely "a geographical expression." The railway would *invent* Canada as much as it would define it; of this Sir John A. was convinced.

In most frontier countries, settlers opened up the land and were then followed in by law, order and the railway. In Canada, these steps were neatly reversed. It was an odd, unnatural progression. The railway came first, crossing a land mass the size of Western Europe without a paying population to support it. Arriving just ahead of the railway was another archetypal Canadian invention: the North West Mounted Police (forerunners of the RCMP). Next came the Native treaties, and then—finally—the first great waves of settlers. All told, the CPR helped foster more than 800 different towns and cities. If the covered wagon is the symbol of the American West, then the twin tracks of steel, stretching to the horizon, are the symbol of ours. There were no wagon trains in Canadian history. We took the train out.

Indeed, the CPR made Canada possible; it made the landscape penetrable. A single, relentless spear of steel cut across the rock and bog of the Canadian Shield, over the grasslands and the prairies, and on to the Rocky and Coastal Mountains. More than 1,600 kilometres in length, it was an engineering marvel, the longest railway in human history.

Tunnels were blasted through rock, and tracks snaked through treacherous mountain gorges. Chinese workers were given the perilous job of placing nitroglycerine and dynamite. The contractor in charge of pushing the CPR through the mountains of the interior was the strong-willed, obsessive Andrew Onderdonk. To bypass the notorious Hell's Gate Rapids, Onderdonk ordered the blasting of two dozen tunnels, many of them through pure granite. His plan succeeded, against all odds, but at a great human cost. Onderdonk claimed that three Chinese workers died for every kilometre of track laid.

It took scandals and money and a thousand lives to build. It ruined men and it made men. Confederation set the stage, but it was the CPR that made the new union a reality. The railway bound this country together; it opened up the interior, and it preempted American expansion into the Northwest. (The Americans had already outflanked Canada on the Pacific Coast when they purchased Alaska from Russia.)

When was Canada born? The common answer is July 1, 1867, but I would argue that the real birthdate, the moment when the pieces fell irretrievably into place, came 18 years later: on November 7, 1885, in the interior of British Columbia, when the last spike of the CPR was driven home at Craigellachie. With that single spike, the nation *a mari usque ad mare*, from sea to sea, became a reality.

It seems so long ago.

Canada's Age of Steel has passed. John A. lies a'mouldering in his grave, and the train doesn't stop at Craigellachie any more. In 1990, Brian Mulroney performed, if not an act of murder, then one of euthanasia. The National Dream died in its sleep. The passenger line that had once bound Canada together was scrapped without ceremony and without public debate. The southern CPR route now carries only freight, not passengers.

It was a purely economic decision, and on paper it probably made perfect sense. Canadians, after all, had long since given up on the railway, and Canadians must shoulder most of the blame. (It is a pernicious myth that railways are not cost-efficient in a country as large and diverse as Canada. Quite the contrary. Far from being out of date, once the tracks are laid, trains are the most energy-efficient form of mass transit available.)

The death of the CPR was *not* inevitable. It was a matter of national and political will—or the lack thereof. In his elegiac book *Last Train to Toronto*, American author Terry Pindell, reflecting on the end of the dream, notes, "The more one reads of John A. Macdonald, the more one wonders, where have such leaders gone?"

Where indeed. If John A. was our great nation builder, Brian Mulroney was our great dismantler. Which is appropriate, because John A. was our first Conservative prime minister, and Brian Mulroney, undoubtedly, will be our last.

It took scandals and money and a thousand lives to build.

Verdict

Canada is a country created largely by Bastards. Four of the Top Five Fathers were Bastards. (Tupper faltered only later, after attaining the prime ministership.) George Brown, alas, comes down to us as a Bonehead. He was a better man than most of his opponents, but he was outplayed at every step and was swept from office in the very first post-Confederation election of 1867. (And as for Smilin' Brian? Well, let's just say he weren't no John A. Macdonald.)

John A. Macdonald: **Bastard**

George Brown: **Bonehead**

George-Étienne Cartier: **Bastard**

Leonard Tilley: **Bastard**

Charles Tupper: **Bastard**

❦ THE MOUNTIES:
CANADIAN ARCHETYPES, SPIFFY JACKETS

They were stalwart men in scarlet jackets. Created by an act of Parliament in 1873, the North West Mounted Police were sent out to assert Canadian ownership over the vast, newly acquired territory of the Northwest. The villains of the piece (as always) were Americans: the desperadoes, wolf hunters and smugglers who crossed the border with impunity. Whisky peddlers, selling rotgut to the Indians, opened illegal forts on Canadian soil with names like Whoop-up and Robber's Roost.

The North West Mounted Police were a disciplined, paramilitary police force, and their blazing red tunics had been chosen with great care: the colour was meant to differentiate them from the U.S. Cavalry, which had been waging a brutal war against the Plains Indians south of the border. The NWMP proved to be very efficient indeed. By the time the first great wave of settlers arrived, law and order had already been established. There would be no lawless Wild West in Canada.

The saga of the NWMP began with the near-disaster of the Great March West, a harrowing journey in the days before rail. When the Mounties finally did reach the infamous Fort Whoop-up, the American outlaws who ran it had already fled south, crossing the border into Montana.

Leading the Mounties on the last leg of their journey was the laconic Métis scout Jerry Potts, a man with an uncanny sense of direction. As they crossed the endless rolling grasslands, an exasperated officer finally asked Potts what he expected to find on the other side of the hill they were climbing. Potts replied, "Another hill."

The Blackfoot chief Crowfoot tested the intentions of the newly arrived Mounties by informing Commissioner James Macleod where a certain group of American outlaws was holed up. When the Mounties immediately tracked down and arrested the men, the sincerity of the red-coated officers was established. Although the NWMP's official motto was *Maintiens le droit* (translated as "Uphold the right"), the Americans quickly added a new one: "They always get their man."

For all the heroics of individual officers, the Mounties remained chiefly a tool of imperialism and settlement. If there was any doubt about their mission, poems like "Riders of the Plains" made it amply clear:

Our mission is to raise the Flag
Of Britain's Empire here,
Restrain the lawless savage,
And protect the pioneer . . .

Either way, they had really spiffy jackets.

"The ceasing of exquisite music." Longfellow's Evangeline

"A criminal soul." Governor Charles Lawrence

"Lioness of Acadia." The defiant Madame La Tour

"The reluctant general." Marquis de Montcalm

"To burn and lay waste the country." General James Wolfe

"A most sagacious and gallant warrior." Tecumseh, hero of 1812

"Sabre sparks and musket fire." Captain Philip Broke

"One of the most puzzling men in Canadian history." Patriote Louis-Joseph Papineau

"A born muckraker and scandalmonger." Rebel leader William Lyon Mackenzie

"From great man to most despised."
Lord Durham,
colonial troubleshooter

"The birth of Canadian democracy." Reformers
Louis LaFontaine and
Robert Baldwin

"The damnedest man that ever came down the Cariboo Road."
Judge Matthew Begbie

"Number one with a bullet."
Editor George Brown

"Canada! Mon pays! Mes amours!"
George-Étienne
Cartier

"Conspicuous by his absence."
Nova Scotian
Joseph Howe

"Messiah of the Grasslands."
Métis leader Louis Riel

"Behind a wall of fire."
The brilliant tactician
Gabriel Dumont

"Lover of the universe."
Bill Smith, a.k.a.
Amor de Cosmos

Heroes and Madmen:
The Many Rebellions of Louis Riel

SO WHO WAS HE? *What* was he? Was he a rebel, a reformer, a martyr? A madman? Was he all of the above, or none of the above, this strange character Louis Riel?

It would seem, like the overlapping circles in a Venn diagram, that Louis Riel contained all of these personas—and more. Condemned and hanged as a traitor, resurrected as a hero, Louis Riel managed to unite a people and divide a nation. He was both a Marat of the Grasslands and the self-proclaimed Prophet of the New World, and it is very difficult at times to separate the mythic from the historic.

The story begins in the Red River Valley, in what is now the area around Winnipeg. The valley was on the edge of a great frontier, and a lively, sprawling community had evolved: fur trappers, traders, Hudson's Bay men, Scottish settlers, Catholic missionaries, Ontario expansionists and American annexationists. But the heart of the community was the Métis Nation, the descendants of white settlers and Native brides. Of the approximately 12,000 people in Red River, more than half were French-speaking mixed-blood Catholics: the Métis.

Métis traditions centred on the buffalo hunt, organized every year with military precision; their hunting parties were comparable to a light cavalry. It was said that the Métis were French-Canadian at home and Indian on the hunt, but the buffalo were fewer and fewer every year, and the question was, could their semi-nomadic way of life survive?

In 1869, the Hudson's Bay Company agreed to sell Rupert's Land, the entire, vast northwest region, to the burgeoning Dominion of Canada. It was the largest single real estate deal in human history, and at a mere $1.5 million, the bargain of a lifetime. "We have," observed John A. Macdonald, "quietly and almost without observation annexed all the territory between here and the Rocky Mountains."

There was only one snag. No one had bothered to consult—*or even formally notify*—the people who happened to be living in the Northwest; they were to be included in the deal like a herd of cattle. Far from being a minor fringe group, the Red River Valley's population was greater than that of British Columbia. As historian W. L. Morton points out, "Red River was not a frontier, but an island of civilization in the wilderness." But where British Columbia was offered full provincial membership, financial concessions and even a railway, no such offer was made to the citizens of Red River. The Northwest would become an area without responsible government. A territory. A colony of Canada.

When news of this land grab reached Red River, opposition soon formed among the Métis, and a leader quickly emerged: a young man, just 25 years old, by the name of Louis Riel. Riel had studied theology and law in Montréal, and he was among the first to realize that Canada had no legal authority over Red River. The Northwest was to be transferred from the Hudson's Bay Company first to Britain and then to Canada, and this arrangement created a window of opportunity.

The government of Canada blithely sent in an army of surveyors and even a governor, all ahead of the land transfer. But Riel and the Métis stopped the surveyors by putting their feet down (literally) on a survey chain. "You shall go no farther," said Louis Riel.

After turning back the hapless, would-be Canadian governor, Riel seized Upper Fort Garry, the main Hudson's Bay Company post, where he set up an elected provisional government with French, English and Métis representatives. He and the other delegates drew up a list of conditions to be met before they would agree to join the new Dominion of Canada. In this sense, their actions constituted not a "Red River Rebellion" but a *Resistance*, as it is more accurately known.

The Hudson's Bay Company eagerly disentangled itself from the entire mess. Britain did not have legal ownership of the land, nor did Canada, and in this power vacuum, only the provisional government of Louis Riel had any real claim to legitimacy. (Though the legitimacy of Riel's actions is a hotly contested point to this day.) The Union Flag was lowered at Fort Garry, and in its place was raised a golden fleur-de-lis and a green Irish shamrock. A new nation had been proclaimed, and Canada now had no choice but to negotiate. John A. Macdonald sent out a delegation under a Hudson's Bay man, Donald Smith.

Within the Red River community, however, a small, vocal group of anti-Métis Ontario men, dubbed "Canada Firsters," were stirring up resistance *to* the resistance. A band of Canada Firsters attempted to lead a counter-rebellion, but they were quickly captured and taken prisoner. A Métis jury sentenced one prisoner to death, but in a show of good faith, Riel overturned the verdict and granted a pardon.

So far, everything had gone almost flawlessly. Riel was now in a position to lead his new province, to be named "Manitoba," proudly into Confederation. He would almost certainly be its first premier, and a long and illustrious career in politics seemed to beckon.

But personality has a way of imposing itself upon history at the most inopportune moments. And so it was that a belligerent labourer named Thomas Scott, by the very force of his belligerence, was able to undermine and unravel the best-laid plans of Louis Riel. Scott, a recent emigré from Northern Ireland and a fervent anti-Catholic Orangeman, was among the men arrested for plotting to overthrow Riel. Throughout his imprisonment and subsequent trial, Scott hurled insults and racial slurs at his Métis captors, hollering that they were cowards and half-breeds and dogs, and vowing that as soon as he was released he would personally kill Riel. The trial was little more than a farce. It was conducted in French, a language Scott didn't understand, and the charges against him were never clearly stated. (That he was an asshole is surely no justification for having him executed. If being an asshole were a crime, a lot of us would be in trouble.)

Riel did not personally pass the death sentence on Thomas Scott, but neither did he intervene, and on March 4, 1870, the prisoner was dragged out, screaming and kicking, to face a firing squad. Donald Smith frantically pleaded with Riel to reconsider, but Riel was adamant: "We must make Canada respect us!" Allowing Thomas Scott to be executed would prove to be the biggest single mistake Louis Riel ever made.

"This is horrible!" screamed Scott. "This is cold-blooded murder!"

Five rifles were raised. They fired as one, and Scott fell, writhing, to the ground. One of Riel's lieutenants walked over and fired a final bullet into the back of Thomas Scott's head. It would go down in history as "the shot that set the West ablaze."

The execution of Thomas Scott—a Canadian citizen and a British subject—enraged English Canada, especially Orange strongholds in Ontario, and Scott was elevated to the role of Anglo-Protestant Hero. Riel, in turn, was vilified as a dark man with savage blood in his veins. "The blood of the Martyred Scott must not cry in vain for vengeance," proclaimed rallying posters. "Let Canada speak out now and let the assassin Riel feel that a Canadian must be like an ancient Roman, free from injury wherever he goes."

All the while, the Americans were watching events unfold with a certain interest and a half-smile. If the Canadians couldn't control a small band of half-breeds, then perhaps the U.S. should step in and restore peace, no? Macdonald could see his dream of a nation stretching from sea to sea slipping away. He quickly approved almost all of Riel's demands: a new province would be created, a small territory around the Red River; its citizens would be granted responsible government;

French and English would be recognized as official languages; the rights of Catholics would be guaranteed; and limited land ownership was confirmed, with roughly 1.5 million acres reserved for the Métis.

The guarantees of Catholic schools explicitly laid out in the Manitoba Act of 1870 would be reneged on 20 years later, and French would be abolished as an official language in Manitoba in one of the greatest betrayals in Canadian history, but at the time, no one could have foreseen these events. The Métis took the government at its word and celebrated their successful entry into Canada. Québec was overjoyed at receiving a compatriot in the new province of Manitoba. Perhaps a bilingual, bicultural nation was possible after all.

There would, however, be no amnesty. Mackenzie and Papineau (and even Macdonald's faithful lieutenant George-Étienne Cartier, who had also taken up arms against the government as a Patriote) had all been involved in revolts much bloodier than Riel's and had instigated crimes far worse, but they were not "half-breeds" and they had been granted full pardons. Riel would receive no such treatment. The best he got was a verbal agreement from Cartier that no harm would come to him. Unfortunately, no one seemed to make that promise clear to the military expedition under Colonel Garnet Wolseley that was on its way to Red River to assert Canadian authority. Wolseley and his men were out for blood.

After a brutal three-month trek across the frozen muskeg and bedrock of the Canadian Shield (there was, pointedly, no transcontinental railway at that time), Wolseley's exhausted 2,000-man force finally reached Red River, only to find that Riel had slipped away hours before. It was just as well. "Had we caught him," said Wolseley, "he would have had no mercy." Instead, Wolseley's Ontario militiamen took their anger out on the other Métis; they beat one young man almost to death, chased another into the river where he drowned, and generally acted like the conquering army they took themselves for.

Riel was now the wild card in the Confederation deck. The Ontario Liberal government put a $5,000 bounty on his head, but the frontier was wide and the border porous. In 1873, Riel audaciously decided to run for parliament in a Manitoba by-election and was promptly elected. In a general election the following year, he was again elected, even though, as a fugitive, he would never be able to take his seat in the House. Still, it was a sweet victory; the same election saw the downfall of John A. Macdonald, who was turfed out of office for secretly accepting campaign donations in return for implied CPR contracts. Encouraged, Riel made his way to Ottawa, sauntered into the House, took his vow of loyalty to Queen Victoria and signed the official members' register before anyone realized who he was. (The signature of Louis Riel can still be found in the records.) An angry House had him formally expelled, but the voters in his Manitoba riding promptly reelected him.

In 1875, the federal government finally offered Riel a complete pardon on the condition that he stay in exile for the next five years, and Riel reluctantly agreed. Who knew? After his exile, he might yet be able to enter the political fray, might yet become premier of Manitoba . . .

But then it began: the visions. Clouds of flames, like those that loomed before Moses, and the voice of God, beckoning Riel onward, onward, to fulfill his earthly mission. And here the tone of the story changes, and the spiritual anguish of the individual overshadows the social context that shaped him. Riel's world began to collapse around him. A complete nervous breakdown, a descent into darkness, and he awoke in a Montréal insane asylum under an assumed name. He remained there for three years.

During his time in the asylum, he began to refer to himself as "Louis David Riel, Prophet, Infallible Pontiff and Priest-King." He worked out the tenets of a new religion, one that would pass the spiritual centre from the Old World to the New. Using complicated biblical calculations, he set the Second Coming of Christ for the year 4209. Bishop Ignace Bourget, the ultraorthodox French-Canadian Catholic nationalist, was to be elevated to the position of New World Pope. Riel would be the prophet.

The Métis Nation, meanwhile, had suffered greatly since 1870. The Red River Resistance had proven to be a hollow victory indeed. English settlers had flooded into the area and most of the Métis had been pushed back, farther west, into what would one day be Saskatchewan. The buffalo had disappeared like mist into the morning sun, and a semi-nomadic people had become settlers. Remembering the lessons of Manitoba, the Métis now wanted full deeds to their land before any new provinces were created. They also wanted to stop the large-square surveys that were once again imposing their relentless gridwork over the land on which they lived. (The Métis lived in curved plots of land along the riverbanks. Canada, however, was settled in right angles and grids; we imposed our geometry upon the landscape and, as always, geometry won.)

It was not only the Métis who suffered. The Plains Indians—the Cree, the Dakota-Sioux, the Blackfoot—were in dire straits as well, kept on starvation rations in reserves, praying for the buffalo to return, chasing rumours, sinking into despair.

Added to the mix was a group of disgruntled white settlers suffering through a bad harvest and angry over the sudden shift of the CPR route to the south. They too felt betrayed by their distant and unresponsive government. Frontier newspapers were openly calling for rebellion, and in 1884, the settlers began organizing a united protest with their Métis neighbours. At one such meeting someone said simply, "There is only one man who can help us now: Riel."

Among the Métis delegates at the meeting was a man by the name of Gabriel

Dumont. He was already a legendary figure, reportedly the greatest hunter who had ever lived, a horseman, a sharpshooter, a man able to "call" the buffalo, a skill held in almost mystical regard. He spoke six Native languages, as well as French and a smattering of English. During the original Red River Resistance, Dumont had offered Riel a force of 500 guerrilla riders to ambush Colonel Wolseley's force. He could have easily wiped the militiamen out, he said. But Riel, wisely, had declined the offer. With the buffalo gone, Dumont now tended a small store in the Métis community of Batoche and ran a ferry service across the river. Amid the growing discontent, the settlers, both Métis and white, asked Dumont to go to the United States, find Louis Riel and bring him back.

And so, as the snows melted in the spring of 1884, Gabriel Dumont and three others rode south into Montana.

After being released from the asylum, Riel had moved to the United States and become a naturalized American citizen. He was teaching at a mission school in Montana, but when Dumont and the others arrived, he readily agreed to return to the Northwest. Although his mental illnesses and religious delusions had subsided, they were never far from the surface. Like the prophet he believed himself to be, Louis Riel had spent his time in the wilderness. Fifteen years had passed since his first great triumph. Fifteen years. And now this, the avenging angel Gabriel, calling him back.

Round Two was about to begin.

The Second Coming of Louis Riel began predictably enough and with a pervasive sense of déjà vu: Riel sent a petition to his old nemesis John A. (who had since returned to power after his own exile in the political wilderness), and the two old foes once again squared off. Riel wanted provincial status for Saskatchewan, an elected government, and control over natural resources. Ottawa stalled. Riel persisted. Ottawa hemmed and hawed and stalled some more. (Due to his tactical use of delays, Macdonald had already earned the nickname "Old Tomorrow.") Finally, on March 19, 1885, fed up and frustrated with Ottawa's apparent disregard, Louis Riel declared a provisional government at the village of Batoche.

Everything seemed to be going according to plan, but in fact Louis Riel was fighting yesterday's battles. Things had changed since 1870.

In 1870, the ownership of the Northwest had not been clearly established. Now, however, the land was firmly in Canadian hands. There was a new presence on the high plains as well: the North West Mounted Police. In 1870, it had taken three hard months for the army to reach the Northwest. Now, with Macdonald's railway pushed almost to the Rockies, it would take less than a week.

As the northwest resistance drifted towards armed rebellion, the white settlers became nervous and abandoned the cause. Chief Crowfoot managed to keep his Blackfoot Confederacy neutral, but two small bands of Cree warriors, one led by Big Bear and the other by Poundmaker, together with a few Assiniboine and Dakota-Sioux, decided to join Riel's call for an uprising. Even then, the Indians' efforts were sporadic and not coordinated with Riel's. For all their claims of representing a pan-national alliance, the Métis in effect stood alone.

Louis Riel demanded the surrender of a nearby NWMP detachment, and at Duck Lake, a band of Mounted Police, backed up by volunteers, clashed headlong with a Métis force under the leadership of Gabriel Dumont. The Northwest Rebellion had begun. Among the first to die was Dumont's beloved brother Isidore, and Dumont himself was hit by a bullet that split his scalp and left a painful, lasting wound. Louis Riel, however, was miraculously untouched, even though he spent the battle riding back and forth, completely exposed and armed only with a large wooden cross, as he urged his men onward to victory. "Fire!" he cried. "In the name of the Father! In the name of the Son! In the name of the Holy Spirit! Fire!"

When the Mounties broke and ran, leaving a dozen dead officers and volunteers behind, Dumont gave the order to pursue and exterminate them, but he was restrained by Riel. Later, Dumont reproached his leader: "If you are going to give them the advantage like that, we cannot win."

Farther west, panic spread as Big Bear and Poundmaker led uprisings of their own. At the tiny hamlet of Frog Lake, Big Bear's followers, under the warrior Wandering Spirit, massacred nine whites, including two priests—all but three of the people who lived there.

At Battleford, settlers had holed up inside the fort, leaving the town to Poundmaker, who ransacked buildings looking for food. His people, it is worth remembering, were facing starvation. Behind the stockades of Fort Battleford, settlers and police waited for help to arrive—and it wasn't long coming. In fact, it was already on its way.

Ottawa, roused from its indifference, had acted with amazing speed. The army was mobilized and moved out on the nearly completed rail lines of the CPR. Within 10 days of Duck Lake, troops were in place. Within a month, the Métis and Cree rebels faced a force of 3,000 soldiers, backed up by 2,000 Mounted Police and assorted volunteers. The CPR had more than proved its worth.

From this event, understandably perhaps, came the public perception that the railway had saved Canada. In fact, it was just the opposite: Riel had saved the railway. At the time of the Northwest Rebellion, the CPR was stalled, in debt and on the verge of being declared bankrupt. Macdonald's national dream had become a national folly—and an expensive one at that. Parliament was not going to back any more loans, and the possibility of a transcontinental railway was just about to die when word came of a Métis uprising. In an instant, the railway became vital for national security. Parliament rallied, the money came through, and even as General Frederick Middleton loaded his men on board the trains, work resumed in the Rockies.

Middleton, a methodical and classically trained British officer, arrived in the Northwest and divided his force into three columns. One column moved north against Big Bear; a second column was sent to relieve the besieged settlers at Battleford. General Middleton himself led the third: a force 800-men strong, headed straight for Batoche. Each of the three columns used the main line of the CPR as its base, a fact not lost on the public.

Louis Riel fasted and prayed, and in rambling appeals, he sought divine guidance from Jesus and the Virgin Mary. Dumont wanted to launch a preemptive ambush against Middleton, but Riel delayed and delayed until it was almost too late. Instead of dealing in strategy, Riel appointed a committee he dubbed the Exovedate (from the Latin for "from the flock") to deal with esoteric points of theology. The Exovedate discussed matters such as changing the names of the days of the week, moving the Sabbath from Sunday to Saturday, and recognizing Riel as official prophet. The priests in the area refused communion to Riel and decried his heresies. They eventually excommunicated him, but it didn't matter. According to Riel, Rome had already fallen. A New Day was dawning.

And all the while, Middleton's army was advancing.

Only at the very last moment was Dumont allowed to lead a counterattack. At a narrow valley near Fish Creek, Dumont's small force of 150 men ambushed the Canadians. Dumont led Middleton's army into a classic buffalo trap; the soldiers found themselves pinned in on three sides, silhouetted against the sky, as the Métis fired on them from lower positions in a buffalo furrow. Standard strategy would have involved taking the heights, but Dumont was fighting a guerrilla war, and his approach was most effective. Later, after the army had retreated in panic, Dumont lit a fire in the grasslands and advanced towards them from behind the flames. The effect was unnerving.

Although the Battle of Fish Creek ended in a stalemate, General Middleton now realized that he was up against a small but formidable enemy in the Métis and a remarkable tactician in Gabriel Dumont. But Middleton had more men, better arms and almost endless ammunition. He also had a secret weapon: a Gatling gun, capable of firing 400 to 500 rounds a minute. No weapon like it had ever been seen in the Canadian Northwest.

Middleton also brought in a Hudson's Bay Company steamer, the *Northcote*, which had been refurbished as a gunboat. Its mission: to outflank the Métis from the river. Or at least, that was the plan. The *Northcote* was merrily chugging down the South Saskatchewan River when Dumont and his men, hiding on the banks, pulled a ferry cable taut across the water. It caught the *Northcote*'s smokestacks and tore them off, thus ending the first (and no doubt the only) naval battle ever to be fought in Saskatchewan.

Middleton closed in nonetheless, and on May 9, 1885, the Battle of Batoche began. It raged for four days. General Middleton strafed the village with the Gatling gun and bombarded it with cannon fire. The Métis returned fire from their rifle pits as Riel walked among them, wielding the crucifix like a sword, like a shield, and beseeching the Lord for the miracle that would save them. The Métis were so short of ammunition they were forced to dig out and reuse enemy bullets stuck in the walls of buildings, and by the end they were firing small rocks, nails and hammered buttons at Middleton's men. When the army finally rushed the Métis position, Dumont held back the advance almost singlehandedly for over an hour to give the others a chance to escape. Fighting alongside Dumont was Joseph Ouellette, 93 years old. Dumont ordered him to retreat, but the old man smiled and uttered those now immortal last words, "In a minute. I want to kill another Englishman."

Twenty-one Métis died at Batoche, including old Ouellette. The rest fell back into the scrubland forests. Dumont had urged Riel to escape with him, but the two became separated, and on May 15, 1885, just a few months after the uprising began, and even as Dumont was desperately trying to find him, Louis Riel surrendered to the Canadian army. Poundmaker followed 11 days later. Big Bear held out for another month and a half, with four columns of men pursuing; he evaded them all before he too surrendered.

The Northwest Rebellion was over.

Big Bear and Poundmaker were sentenced to prison, but both were released due to failing health, and both died soon after. Eight Cree Indians, including Wandering Spirit, were eventually sentenced to death and were publicly hanged in one of the largest mass executions in Canadian history.

Gabriel Dumont outlived them all. He was never captured, never taken. He escaped to the United States, where he hurriedly made plans to rescue Riel, but Dumont was unable to reach him in time, and he lived with guilt over this for years. Dumont later joined Buffalo Bill's Wild West Show, where he was advertised as "the Hero of the Half-Breed Rebellion." As historian Stephen Franklin writes in *The Heroes*, "The great captain of the buffalo hunt, the Prince of the Plains, was reduced to galloping around the sawdust ring shooting down little coloured balls."

Riel was returned in custody to Regina to stand trial on charges of treason. His counsel, rushed in from sympathetic supporters in Québec, tried desperately to persuade Riel to plead not guilty on grounds of insanity, but Riel, aware of posterity and not wanting to be denied his martyrdom, refused.

The trial of Louis Riel began in a small courtroom in Regina on July 28, 1885. The Dominion of Canada, just 18 years old, would never be the same. In Québec, Riel had already become a hero and a political flashpoint. The Liberal leader Wilfrid Laurier, fanning nationalist sentiment to score some easy political points, declared, "If I had been on the banks of the Saskatchewan, I too would have shouldered a musket!" Honoré Mercier, leader of the Parti National, took his anger to even greater heights, declaring that, were Louis Riel to be executed, it would be "a declaration of war against Québec."

So who was Louis Riel? Who was this person who set Canada ablaze? Was he, in the words of historian G. F. G. Stanley, simply "a sad, pathetic, unstable man, who led his followers in a suicidal crusade and whose brief glory rests upon a distortion of history"? Or was he something more?

"At the official, scholarly, and popular levels," writes historian Douglas Owran, "Riel has assumed mythical stature." In *Who Killed Canadian History?*, historian J. L. Granatstein insists that Riel was simply "a crazed religious fanatic." He might be a hero to the Métis, but, according to Granatstein, Riel "has no credentials as a hero to all Canadians."

Having brought Manitoba into Canada, Riel was certainly our most intriguing Father of Confederation. But of course, it is not the skillful negotiator of 1870 that we remember, but rather the doomed leader of 1885. Canadians, we are told, do not celebrate rebellion. We do, however, glory in defeat, something Margaret Atwood recognized in *Survival* when she called Riel "the perfect all-Canadian failed hero—he's French, Indian, Catholic, revolutionary and possibly insane, and he was hanged by the Establishment."

So who is right? J. L. Granatstein or Margaret Atwood? It depends on whether you are discussing the historic Louis Riel or the mythic Louis Riel. In the 1960s, it became fashionable to present Riel as a kind of northern Che Guevera. In the October Crisis of 1970, FLQ terrorists named one of their small bands the "Louis Riel Cell." This image of Riel as a modern freedom fighter and anti-establishment hero is odd indeed, especially in light of Riel's deeply theocratic rightist views—but then, the appeal of myth often has little to do with cold hard facts.

Historian Thomas Flanagan has argued, quite convincingly, that Riel must be considered a genuine religious leader, and not simply a rebel or a madman. "The Northwest Rebellion," writes Flanagan, "was as much a religious movement as a political uprising." If Riel was mad, it was the madness of the saints and the prophets. Had he lived in ancient Israel, who knows but we might be venerating him today. Stranger things have happened.

In a recent column in the *Globe and Mail*, historians David Bercuson and

Was Louis Riel a Father of Confederation? Traditionally, only the 36 delegates who attended at least one of the Charlottetown, Québec and London conferences are recognized as true Fathers. But shouldn't Louis Riel, "the Father of Manitoba," be included on the list as well?

And what of Charles Monck, Canada's first governor general, a man who supported Confederation right from the start and was instrumental in bringing about the Great Coalition of 1864? Surely Monck qualifies as a Father too.

And what of the wild, wacky and eventually insane Amor de Cosmos, "Lover of the Universe" (a.k.a. William Smith)? It was Amor de Cosmos, the flaky newspaperman, whose enthusiasm paved the way for B.C.'s entry into Canada. (Cosmos went on to became the premier of that province, proving that, yes, B.C. has always been a breeding ground for flakes and New Age self-invented personas. From Amor de Cosmos to W.A.C. "Wacky" Bennett and Bill "Bizarro World" Vander Zalm, the province has a long, proud tradition of electing eccentrics to office.) Doesn't Amor de Cosmos also qualify as a Father of Confederation?

And what of the irascible Joey Smallwood? When Newfoundland joined Canada in 1949, it was Smallwood who spearheaded the union. Following a long, acrimonious debate, Newfoundlanders finally voted for Confederation by a slim margin: 52 per cent in favour and 48 per cent against. Smallwood liked to call himself "the only living Father of Confederation," and in his day, he was. Joey was also a character in his own right. A true Bastard and a fast-talking, autocratic socialist, Smallwood had no compunction about calling in the police to act as strikebreakers. He also instituted the forced relocation of remote outpost communities, which helped doom an entire way of life. For almost 23 years straight, Premier Joey Smallwood ruled the Rock. Historian J. L. Granatstein called him "the funniest, toughest, most persistent, and possibly smartest politician in Canadian history." His biographer, Harold Horwood, dubbed him "the most loved, feared, and hated" man in Newfoundland. Either way, Joey Smallwood was a man who inspired extremes.

But Smallwood was not the *last* Father of Confederation. There is also John Amagoalik, the Inuit "Father of Nunavut." Nunavut, a vast northern territory, came into being on April 1, 1999, and John Amagoalik must rank as a Father of Confederation as well. He spent almost 20 years negotiating the sweeping land claims settlement to the eastern half of the Arctic, an area twice the size of B.C. It was the largest and richest Aboriginal land claim in Canadian history, and probably in the world. The "Arctic John A.," as he is known, redrew the map of Canada as did his Victorian counterpart, and he too ranks as a Father.

. . . And who was the "Mother" of Confederation?

More than one historian has suggested that the unsung Mother of Confederation was George Brown's young bride, Anne Nelson. Anne was a highly educated, articulate woman, and George Brown loved her deeply. The suggestion, unproven but intriguing, is that Anne convinced George to move beyond party politics and strike a coalition deal with Cartier and Macdonald. Others have credited Anne with having "a calming presence" on her husband, which thus allowed him to forge ahead with his constitutional negotiations. This claim is pure fluff, of course. Anne Nelson Brown has been vastly overrated by politically correct panels of experts. Anne was an intelligent woman who *should* have been involved in the negotiations. But she wasn't. To claim that Anne Nelson Brown was a "nation builder" is the height of p.c. silliness.

So who was the Mother of Confederation? None other than Queen Victoria Herself. Yup, that frumpy German lady with the inbred DNA. She proclaimed Canadian Confederation and she encouraged it. The British North America Act of 1867 was a product of Victorian times, and Good Queen Butterball was, indeed, "the mother of our nation."

With only one mother and who knows how many fathers, is it any wonder we're so confused? "I know who my mom is, but I'm not so sure about my dad."

Barry Cooper compared Riel and his followers to the Branch Davidian cult in Waco, Texas (which had to be burned out of existence in 1993). "Riel," wrote Bercuson and Cooper, "was more the David Koresh of his day than a national leader."

John A. Macdonald compared Louis Riel to Mahdi, the messianic Muslim prophet who was leading an uprising against the British in the Sudan at around the same time, though perhaps a better comparison would be to that other prairie visionary, Brigham Young. Inspired by visions similar to Riel's, Young had led his band of followers westward, where they carved a state for themselves out of the wilderness: the Mormon heartland of Utah. For Riel, however, there would be no Canadian Utah. There would be no Promised Land.

And yet, in so many ways, the story of Louis Riel is biblical in nature. Exiled to the wilderness, the leader of an oppressed minority, a messiah persecuted, executed, martyred: it is the story of Christ, writ large against the Canadian prairie. Perhaps that is why the image of Louis Riel has endured; he reaches beyond national issues and into the heart of the collective unconscious.

Riel died a traitor but was reborn a hero. Only Lord Durham has had a more active posthumous career. Over the years, even Ottawa has come to embrace Louis Riel. In 1969, the federal government of Canada unveiled a statue to the rebel leader in Regina. The Canadian prime minister at the time, Pierre Trudeau, personally dedicated the monument and even supplied a moral to the story: "We must never forget that, in the long run, a democracy is judged by the way the majority treats the minority. Louis Riel's battle is not yet won."

Louis Riel has even been portrayed (by the CBC, naturally), as a proponent of official bilingual federalism, which is an awfully long way from his image as a religious fanatic of the grasslands. In Québec, ironically, Riel has become less and less relevant over time. Québec nationalists, whose world view ends at their provincial boundaries, now see Riel as a minor fringe figure, a symbol of English oppression and little else. Certainly, when the Bloc Québécois, apropos of nothing, decided to champion Louis Riel in the House of Commons during the 1996 session, their stance had little to do with Riel's struggles and everything to do with besmirching the reputation of the federal government. (The Bloc wanted Riel pardoned posthumously as a French-Canadian hero, proving that Riel's value as a political tool hasn't completely disappeared.)

Conflict is always more compelling than compromise, and Louis Riel represents a chain of conflicts, one that can be charted in opposing pairs:

French	vs.	English
Native	vs.	White
Catholic	vs.	Protestant
West	vs.	East
Minority	vs.	Majority
The Prophet	vs.	The Establishment
The Revolutionary	vs.	The Bourgeois
Frontier	vs.	City

At one time or another, Louis Riel has come to symbolize every one of the above conflicts—and more. Some of the items on the list may have little resonance today, but all are part of the Riel dichotomy. (The Catholic/Protestant split, for one, may seem hopelessly antiquated, but in its time it was perhaps the most divisive of all.)

Currently, the three most common interpretations are that the story of Louis Riel personifies: (a) the mistreatment Canada's Natives, especially the Métis, (b) the beginnings of western alienation, and (c) the historic schism between French and English Canada.

Much like the Father, the Son and the Holy Ghost, Louis Riel is somehow three things at the same time: Métis, Canadian and *Canadien*. If he seems splintered, it is only because the mirror we are using to contain him is itself badly cracked. The fact that Riel is a French hero to the French, a Native hero to the Natives and a Canadian hero to the rest says more about us as a nation than it does about Riel. For meta-historian Daniel Francis, "Riel has achieved heroic status by being completely protean. His significance changes shape depending from what angle you look at him." In *National Dreams*, Francis claims Louis Riel as a kind of ultimate Canadian hero, "a shape-shifter, someone whose story is complex enough to appeal to the kind of fragmented society Canada has become."

The underlying irony is that the very people for whom Riel fought have all but been forgotten. Pushed to the margins of society, the Métis struggle continues even now. It is a sad fact that the grievances of today's Métis, their call for self-government and the recognition of land rights, have hardly changed since the days of Louis Riel.

Their battles are, indeed, not over yet.

John A. Macdonald could have pardoned Riel. He could have set him free. Louis Riel didn't have to die. Even the jury who found the Métis leader guilty recommended mercy, and appeals for clemency poured in from France, the United States and Britain. But Macdonald refused to budge.

A common suggestion is that John A. "killed" Louis Riel just to gain a few votes in Ontario, but this suggestion is as inaccurate as it is pernicious. John A. Macdonald was caught in the middle, and he knew full well that he could not win. Remember, Macdonald built his entire career, and the country, on a successful alliance with French Canadians. The accusation that he was playing base politics with Riel's life does not hold water. If Macdonald *had* intervened to appease voters in Québec, if he *had* reversed a decision of the courts—that would have been a political game. John A. Macdonald did *not* play games with Louis Riel's life. Quite the opposite. Instead, he let the law take its course. John A. Macdonald didn't cause Louis Riel's death. Louis Riel did.

Myths and nationalist symbolism aside, we are left with the fact that Riel led an armed uprising against the government that caused more than 100 people to die, including 15 police officers, numerous Métis and Indian supporters, and nine innocent settlers, among them two unarmed priests. John A. Macdonald had pardoned Riel once already; he would not be pardoned again. In Macdonald's eyes, Riel was a traitor, and the penalty for his crimes was death.

"He shall hang," Macdonald said bitterly, "though every dog in Québec bark in his favour."

Riel himself showed very little rancour when the jury found him guilty. In fact, he felt vindicated: for Riel, the verdict was proof that he wasn't insane. Nor was he angry with Macdonald's refusal to pardon him: "Sir John Macdonald is now committing me to death for the same reason I committed Scott . . . because it is necessary for this country's good."

The final rebellion of Louis Riel ended in prison, where he recanted his heresies and was given absolution by the Catholic Church. He thought he might one day be canonized as a Catholic saint, and he even composed a prayer for future worshippers to say to him.

On the seventh day of November, 1885, Donald Smith drove home the last spike of the Canadian transcontinental railway. Nine days later, Louis Riel, Prophet of the New World, leader of the Métis Nation, climbed the steps of the gallows and descended into darkness.

Verdict

Gabriel Dumont: **Bastard**

Louis Riel, founder of Manitoba and leader of the Red River Resistance of 1870: **Bastard**

Louis Riel, Prophet of the New World and mystic leader of the Northwest Rebellion of 1885: **Bonehead**

Gristle into Bone:

Canada in the Twentieth Century

Hyenas in Petticoats:
The Fight for Women's Rights

POOR SIR RODMOND ROBLIN. Put yourself in his position: It is 1914. You are the elderly, respected premier of a prosperous province, you have been knighted for your efforts, no less, and in comes a delegation of strident women demanding—of all things!—the vote. It is an affront to your sense of propriety. You, who have been raised with traditional values and a belief in womankind's inherent "gentleness."

What do you do in a situation like this? Well, first you try to reason with them as best you can. "I don't want a hyena in petticoats talking politics to me," you explain. "I want a nice gentle creature to bring me my slippers."

When this somehow fails to sway them, you bring out the big guns: motherhood. "What in the world do women want to vote for?" you ask, somewhat huffily. "Why do women want to mix in the hurly-burly of politics? My mother was the best woman in the world, and she certainly never wanted to vote!"

Well, that should settle things. End of debate, right? Wrong. The leader of the delegation, this Holy Terror named Nellie McClung, does the unimaginable. She mocks you.

Following their confrontation with Manitoba Premier Roblin, Nellie McClung and her supporters decided to stage a satirical Women's Parliament. The topic to be debated? Whether or not men deserved the vote. The parliament opened to a packed house in a Winnipeg theatre on January 28, 1914, with McClung herself playing the part of the premier.

As the curtain rises, a lacklustre debate is being held, in the middle of which a delegation of downtrodden men appears on stage pushing a wheelbarrow filled with petitions asking that they be allowed to vote. "We have brains," they argue. "Why not let us vote?" McClung stands up, and—after congratulating the men on their "splendid appearance" and fashionable clothes—she dismisses their request in a verbose, condescending, avuncular fashion.

"Man is made for something higher and better than voting," intones McClung. "Men were made to support families. What is home without a bank account? The man who pays the grocer rules the world! Why, if men start to vote, they will vote too much. Politics unsettles men, and unsettled men mean unsettled bills, broken furniture, broken vows and divorce. It may be," she concedes, "that I am old-fashioned. I may be wrong. After all, men may be human. Perhaps the time will come when men may vote with women."

As the *Winnipeg Tribune* reported, "Almost every sentence [of McClung's speech] was interrupted by gales of laughter."

Poor Sir Rodmond. Once an outspoken member of the Opposition and himself a hellraiser in his political youth, he was now being denounced in the press as old-fashioned. The poor man, he really was lost. Nellie McClung's mock parliament played a role in his defeat at the polls not long after. A government brought down by laughter. Remarkable.

It should be noted that the suffragist movement (from suffrage, "to vote") sought the franchise not as an end in itself but as a way of promoting women's rights, Christian social programs and—above all—prohibition. (The women's movement saw alcohol as the root of most social evils.)

We have to be careful not to ascribe modern motives to the suffragists. Most of the women activists accepted the "separate spheres" argument, that is, the belief that women had a special civilizing mission in society, separate from that of men. But the suffragists knew that political and legal rights were logical steps on the way to social reforms. Without the vote, how could women introduce child labour laws? How could they introduce prohibition? Or penal reforms? Gaining the vote was a means to an end. True, some activists did see it as a matter of principle that women achieve equality, but most were looking for specific, practical reforms. As the name of the leading organization—the Women's Christian Temperance Union—suggests, the emphasis was primarily upon Christian values and the banning of alcohol. Alcohol abuse was the social plague of the late nineteenth and early twentieth centuries, and banning alcoholic beverages was a simple, symptomatic approach to dealing with underlying problems.

Nellie McClung was the undisputed star of the movement, a skilled orator, witty, compelling and ruthlessly rational. Like a judo wrestler using her opponent's weight against him, she often transformed the very image of women put forward by her adversaries into an argument *in favour* of women's rights. "Women have cleaned up things since time began," she said. "And if women ever get into politics there will be a cleaning-out of pigeon-holes and forgotten corners, on which the dust of years has fallen, and the sound of the political carpet-beater will be heard in the land."

There were, in effect, two brands of feminism: one school that pursued equal rights as a worthy goal in itself, and another that advocated an expansion of women's noble mission to act as the moral guardians of society. These two schools, Equal Rights Feminism and Maternal Feminism, worked together to gain the vote in spite of their radically different ideological underpinnings. As historian Deborah Gorham wrote in *Canadian Dimension*, "Tactically, it was wise, at least in the short run, to emphasize the woman's maternal role because this technique turned the arguments of the opposition against itself."

There was a darker side to the movement as well, and one that is less commented on: racism. Strong nativist attitudes of a superior British race were implicit in much of the rhetoric. Often, the same suffragists who wanted the vote for white Anglo-Saxon women just as vehemently wanted it denied to non-white foreign men. A strain of moral self-righteousness informed a great deal of the movement. Although politically radical, the women's suffragist movement was socially very conservative: a movement fighting to preserve a decent, Christian, British morality. They stood, in their own words, for "a White Canada."

The central Canadian establishment has always been a very socially conservative place. Consider the fact that Emily Stowe, Canada's first female medical doctor and one of the leaders of the original suffragist movement in Canada, had to go to the United States in order to study medicine. New Zealand had granted women the vote in 1893, Australia in 1902. In Canada, Sir John A. had attempted to give women the vote back in 1883—and had failed miserably.

It took a firebrand crusade by a group of petticoated hyenas to finally win women's suffrage, and the breakthrough, when it came, originated not in central Canada but in the West. The prairie provinces have always been at the forefront of social reform, and it is no coincidence that the greatest strides made by women were in Alberta, Saskatchewan and Manitoba. The pioneer way of life was a great equalizer; women worked alongside men and worked just as hard. The West was a new society, young and without the baggage of social traditions and archaic hierarchy. The West was also self-selecting: the women and men who chose to settle in the frontier were generally more adventurous and high-spirited to begin with. Western Canada was, and still is, the home of the populist firebrand, the land of the political crusade.

On January 28, 1916, the recently elected Liberal government of Manitoba granted women the right to vote in provincial elections. The opening battle had been won. Nellie McClung, however, had since moved to Alberta with her husband and children, where she started the campaign anew. A best-

World War I shattered both the illusion and the allure of "benign" imperialism and opened the door for the competing ideologies of communism and fascism. The postwar era was a time of workers' rights, radical unions and evangelical socialism.

In 1919, the longest sustained general strike in North American history occurred in Winnipeg. On May 15 of that year, the entire city simply shut down. Almost 30,000 workers walked out, and sympathy strikes soon flared up across the nation: in Calgary, Edmonton, Regina, Toronto, Brandon, Prince Albert and even as far away as Amherst, Nova Scotia. Vancouver launched a full-scale general strike of its own. More working hours were lost to labour unrest in 1919 than in any other year in the nation's history.

Historian David Bercuson traces the roots of the Winnipeg General Strike back to labour disputes in 1906, but the war and its aftermath finally pushed things to the edge. As early as 1917, there had been talk of calling a city-wide general strike over conscription, and two years later, the pot finally boiled over. Following a call to solidarity, machinists, phone operators, milkmen, firefighters, train men, factory workers, streetcar operators, postmen, shippers, craftsmen, garbage collectors, street-sweepers: all joined the strike.

In *Confrontation at Winnipeg*, Bercuson writes, "The atmosphere was almost festive, the belief in ultimate victory strong. Few among them believed they were starting on a long, hard road because, after all, how long could the employers stand up to the united power of the working class?"

Of 96 unions in Winnipeg, 94 joined the strike; the only two that didn't were the typographers and the police. The police had in fact voted overwhelmingly to join the walkout, but the Central Strike Committee had asked them to stay on the job to maintain order, so that the government would not have an excuse to send in the troops.

As it turned out, the government did not need much of an excuse. The Winnipeg General Strike was, in the hysteria of the day, seen as a Bolshevik attempt at launching a socialist revolution, and it had to be stopped. Ottawa ordered dawn raids. Union leaders were imprisoned without trial, and when workers gathered to protest, the Mounties fired into the crowd, killing one man and wounding many more. The police then waded in on horseback, swinging truncheons and cracking skulls. Mass arrests followed, as workers were beaten and trampled. By dusk, martial law had been imposed on the city. It was June 21, 1919. Bloody Saturday.

The next morning, workers began drifting back to their jobs.

selling novelist and a mother of five, McClung was a force to be reckoned with. Our Nell, to her supporters. The Holy Terror to her opponents. Her personal motto: "Never retract, never explain, never apologize—just get the job done and let them howl."

Manitoba was the first province in Canada to grant women the vote, but Saskatchewan and Alberta followed suit a few months later. The following year, British Columbia and Ontario joined their enlightened ranks, and then, over the next few years, the Maritime provinces. The tide had begun to turn. (In Québec, however, women weren't allowed to vote in provincial elections until 1940, after a long-fought campaign spearheaded by activist Thérèse Casgrain.)

On a national level, Prime Minister Robert Borden had granted limited franchise to women during World War I as part of a larger gerrymandering strategy. Borden was trying to pass a war conscription bill, and he allowed the wives and relatives of men fighting overseas to vote, reasoning—correctly—that these women would back an increased war effort to help support their loved ones. Borden won the election handily. But human rights, like toothpaste, are hard to get back in once they are out. Having granted women partial suffrage, Borden found himself on a slippery slope towards full enfranchisement. On May 24, 1918, women in Canada finally became eligible to vote in federal elections.

From the start, women voters have had an immense and often underappreciated impact on the course of Canadian society. True to the predictions of Maternal Feminism, throughout the world when women gain the vote, sweeping social changes have followed. In Canada, 1918 marks a definite shift from property rights to human rights, from the use of government as an economic tool to the idea of government as a social instrument. Whether this development has been harmful or helpful is a much-debated topic, especially among neo-conservatives, but few people today would like to live in the pre-women's rights, pre-medicare, pre–social safety net days of yore. Nostalgia for the past is always myopic.

Provincially, women were elected to the Alberta legislature within a year of enfranchisement. Nellie McClung herself won a seat in Edmonton in 1921. Her victory opened the door to other career choices for women. Such was the case with Emily Ferguson Murphy, daughter of the wealthy and respected Ferguson clan of Cookstown, Ontario. (Of which I am no relation. Alas.) Murphy's father was a supporter of Sir John A., and her four brothers went on to become doctors and lawyers. But Emily outshone them all.

Although she was married to an Anglican minister, Murphy was far from pious. "I am possessed with a pagan love of life," she declared, and she soon grew beyond the limited role of pastor's wife. After a trip to Europe in 1898, she wrote a travel narrative entitled *The Impressions of Janey Canuck Abroad.* Rather than follow the usual Victorian niceties, Murphy explored both the museums and the back alleys, both tenement slums and cathedrals. She was caustic, funny, endlessly curious and unapologetically subjective.

The nickname "Janey Canuck" came from an incident that occurred while Murphy was in Europe. A loudmouthed Englishman was going on and on and on (as Englishmen are wont to do) about how Americans and Canadians were all the same. When Murphy finally took angry exception to this, the Englishman roared, "There's a Canuck for you!" The insinuation was (correctly) that the main difference between Americans and Canadians is how upset Canadians get when you mix the two up. Rather than take the term "Canuck" as an insult, Murphy decided to adopt it as a badge of honour. "I'm glad they called me a Canuck," she later confided to her husband. "That's just what I felt like." And, she reasoned, if there was a Johnny Canuck and a Jack Canuck, there should certainly be a Jane. Her persona was born.

Murphy's first book was a modest success and helped launch her career as a freelance writer. She had settled in Toronto with her family when tragedy struck: her husband fell ill with typhoid, which she later caught, and soon after, her youngest daughter died of diphtheria. Murphy was forced to support her family through her writing, until finally—in desperation, for their health, and to escape bad memories—the Murphys moved west, eventually settling in Edmonton in 1907. Murphy went on to write three more books set in the frontier, including *Janey Canuck in the West*, which helped build her reputation and earn her a comfortable salary.

But then, at the age of 40, Emily Murphy suddenly embarked on an entirely new career and a new direction. Over the years, she had became involved with the woman's suffrage movement and especially with the battle to grant women equal property and homestead rights. Murphy took up the crusade, and that decision led her to the legislature—and beyond.

Appalled at the way women were treated in all-male courtrooms, Murphy petitioned the Alberta government to set up a separate women's court. She expected to be stonewalled, but the attorney general of the province, the forward-looking

Charles Cross, agreed wholeheartedly with Murphy's proposal. He then stunned her by asking when she would be ready to begin her duties as judge. And so, in 1916, and somewhat unexpectedly, Emily Murphy became the first female magistrate in Canada—and indeed, in the entire British Empire.

She soon learned what she was up against. It began humorously enough, with the befuddled prisoners and lawyers fumbling over what to call her. They said "Sir" and "Your Worship," and one man even stammered "Your Majesty." But then the counsel for the defence, a man named Eardly Jackson, who was at that time the most popular criminal lawyer in the city, stood and challenged Murphy's right to wield authority. His reasoning was both brilliant and insidious: the British North America Act of 1867 clearly stated that only "qualified persons" could be appointed as judges; British common law in turn held that women were not considered persons in matters of rights and privileges; ipso facto, Emily Murphy's authority was invalid. She was presiding illegally.

"You are not even a person!" shouted Jackson. That insult would echo through the halls of justice from the western frontier all the way to the Supreme Court. *You are not even a person.* It may have seemed a minor semantical matter, but it had a potentially wide-reaching impact. If women were not legally persons, and only persons were eligible to hold public office, it put the possibility of future female MLAs, MPs and judges all across the country at risk.

Judge Murphy made proper note of Jackson's objection and carried on, but the man persisted. He brought it up every day, with every case, and soon other lawyers picked up on the loophole. As more women were appointed to the bench, they faced the same barrage of complaints. If they weren't persons, how could they be qualified to sit?

In her role as magistrate, Murphy sifted through tales of hardship and misery, of incest, prostitution, poverty, sexual assault, drug addiction, vagrancy, unwed mothers and daughters cast out from their families. She fought repeatedly against the notion that mental illness was a crime, sentiments that put her at the forefront of progressive thinking. Mind you, she also argued that "insane people are not entitled to progeny," and she supported the forced sterilization of the mentally ill. "Social necessity," she stated, took precedence over "private liberty." It was a chilling statement in light of the collective extremism that was to come. After all, fascism, communism and militant religious movements also put social necessity above private liberty, and we all know how much *they* have done for social justice.

Still, Emily Murphy was, by all accounts, a respected figure, at once firm and fair. She began a crusade against the opium trade, the new scourge of society. She even accompanied a police raid on a Vancouver opium den (the Edwardian equivalent of a crack house), and she wrote a series of sensationalized exposés

On a Friday night in Calgary, in the spring of 1917, a man named John Ryan took a prostitute home, plied her with beer and had sex with her. He then paid her $10 and told her to go away. A few days later, however, Ryan noticed the symptoms of sexually transmitted disease. The prostitute had apparently given him a case of the clap, and the medicine alone cost $3.50, so Ryan tracked the woman down and demanded compensation—plus the cost of the beer. She refused to pay, and Ryan, outraged, went to the police and demanded her arrest. The police happily complied.

So begins the sad tale of Lizzie Cyr (also known as Lizzie Waters).

The crusade of the Famous Five to have women recognized as "persons" is heralded in Canadian history as a great victory for women's rights—and it was. But the actual court case that triggered the campaign is all but forgotten.

I first heard about the case of Lizzie Cyr from Kirsten Olson, executive director of the Legal Archives of Alberta, who pored over the original transcripts of the trial and uncovered some rather disturbing aspects.

Lizzie Cyr was charged not with prostitution but with vagrancy, and she was taken before Calgary Police Magistrate Alice Jamieson. The charge itself was ridiculous. Many respectable women were "without visible means of support," but *they* were not deemed vagrants. And anyway, as a prostitute, Lizzie Cyr did have a means of support: her body.

So argued her lawyer, a man by the name of McKinley Cameron. In defending Lizzie, Cameron also brought forth a familiar objection: as a woman, Magistrate Jamieson didn't have any legal authority to try the case. "Your Honour has no capacity for being appointed a police magistrate," said Cameron.

The trial ended abruptly. Jamieson ignored Cameron's objection. She found Lizzie Cyr guilty as charged and sentenced her to six months' hard labour, all without allowing Cyr's lawyer a chance to present his defence.

Cameron was aghast—both at the conviction and at Jamieson's questionable grasp of what constituted a fair trial. He launched an appeal and asked for a ruling on whether Jamieson had any legal authority to hold office. On June 14, 1917, Justice David Scott of the Supreme

Court of Alberta dismissed the appeal and stated that, legally, women could be appointed as magistrates. (Though Justice Scott himself conceded that he had serious doubts about whether any woman was really up to the task.) It was a tainted victory, to say the least. In affirming Alice Jamieson's right to hold office, the Alberta Supreme Court was also upholding Lizzie Cyr's conviction.

When the Supreme Court of Canada later overturned the Alberta ruling that women were indeed "persons," the Famous Five—spearheaded by Emily Murphy—took the issue all the way to the Privy Council in London, England. But theirs was a middle-class crusade, and lost along the way was Lizzie Cyr, who had been sentenced by a female magistrate for the crime of being "a loose, idle and disorderly *person* . . . a vagrant." [Emphasis added.]

As Kirsten Olson dryly notes, while the magistrates and matrons were doing legal battle in the upper echelons of Canada's legal system, Lizzie Cyr had already experienced equal rights under the law.

on the drug trade for *Maclean's* as well as a book, *The Black Candle*, which caused an international uproar. Crime syndicates threatened her life, but Judge Murphy pushed on.

Nonetheless, the objection that women were not persons continued to rankle. A male barrister in Calgary asked for an outside ruling on the issue, and he lost. The Supreme Court of Alberta ruled that women were indeed persons. The court decided that although the BNA Act used "persons" for the plural and "he" for the singular, the legal rights of women were in no way compromised by this semantical quirk. It was simply a habit of language.

Outside of Alberta, though, nothing had changed, and Murphy decided to push the issue to a national level. In her research, she had discovered that any five concerned citizens could request a hearing from the Supreme Court of Canada on any constitutional point. So she brought together Nellie McClung and three other leading women activists, and together they launched the now-famous Persons Case. All five women were residents of Alberta, and the Alberta government provided legal counsel in support of their claim. The government of Québec stood in opposition, and the other provinces avoided taking a stand, so on one level the case came down to Alberta vs. Québec, with Canada deciding. "Does the word persons include women?" In 1928, after a month and a half of debate, the Supreme Court of Canada announced its decision: women were *not* persons. Canada had overruled Alberta.

But the Famous Five, as they were now known, decided to push on. At the time, the final court of appeal was the Privy Council in London. The women took their case to England, and the following year they won. On October 18, 1929, the Privy Council of the United Kingdom reversed the Supreme Court of Canada decision and affirmed the earlier Alberta decision: women were indeed persons. "The exclusion of women from all public offices," declared Lord Chancellor Sankey of the council, "is a relic of days more barbarous than ours."

It had been 13 years since Judge Murphy was first challenged by a lawyer in a provincial courtroom. Now, roused from her bed in her Edmonton home at three o'clock in the morning with the news of the Privy Council's decision, Judge Emily Ferguson Murphy, in her flannelette nightgown, her face flushed with victory, began dancing wildly about. "We've won!" she cried. "We've won! We've won!"

In the words of her old friend and ally, Nellie McClung, "[Emily] loved a fight, and as far as I know, never turned her back on one." Or, as Janey Canuck once put it: "Nothing ever happens by chance. Everything is pushed from behind."

The victory of those five Alberta women is one of the great triumphs of Canadian history. And one of the reasons it is so much fun to read about the early feminist movement in Canada is because the women involved were so sardonic and funny. They are eminently quotable. Theirs was a social revolution won largely by wit.

Of course, rights only exist when we use them, and it wasn't until the first female MP was elected to Ottawa that Canada really began to change course on a national level. The honour of being first fell to a schoolteacher named Agnes Macphail.

Macphail didn't have the firebrand oratory or bombast of Nellie McClung, but in her own way, she was just as eloquent and witty. Agnes Macphail was from rural, southwestern Ontario. She was single, strong-willed, Mormon and female. And as such, she was criticized for being (a) single, (b) strong-willed, (c) Mormon, and (d) female. (In fact, her religion played very little part in her political outlook, but it was held against her nonetheless.)

In 1921, an all-male delegation chose Macphail out of a field of 11 nominees to be the official candidate for the United Farmers of Ontario (U.F.O.), and she went on to win the riding with an impressive majority. She was just 31 years old, and she was about to make history.

Her arrival in Ottawa was a grand event, one that the papers of the day covered in voyeuristic detail. Into the stodgiest male domains had come a young woman from the backwoods of Ontario. In the words of biographer Doris Pennington, Agnes Macphail "was as welcome as an unexpected guest at a dinner party."

"I was intensely unhappy," Macphail recalled in later years. "Some of the members resented my intrusion, others jeered at me, while a very few were genuinely glad to see a woman in the House."

Newspapers pored over her appearance, debating whether she was "good-looking" or simply "plain," whether she was "neatly dressed" or "dowdy." Everything from the shape of her nose, the width of her forehead and "the firmness of her chin" to "the pinkness of her cheeks" was carefully analysed.

"I was a curiosity," she said. "A freak. And you know the way the world treats freaks."

The Ottawa wives were particularly cutting, and the undisguised hostility of the female reporters took Macphail by surprise. They made merciless comments about Macphail's poorly hemmed, navy-blue serge dress and plain brown coat. She had worn that same outfit, they noted, to every election stop, 50 times at least.

At one point an earnest young reporter asked Macphail (with a straight face, apparently), "Do you think it is possible to go into political life and yet keep radiant and untarnished the inner shrine of a woman's modesty, delicacy, sensitiveness?" To which Macphail replied, somewhat wearily, "I surely do. Public life broadens, not blunts, a woman's make-up."

When asked what her intentions were in Ottawa, she said simply, "I intend to do my own thinking."

In spite of the bias she faced, Macphail was a surprisingly effective presence in the House. Leading the fight for penal reforms, she decided to view prison conditions first-hand at the Kingston Penitentiary, which caused a great hubbub of hand-wringing protests. The warden and his jail-keepers attempted to turn her away, insisting that prison "was no place for a lady."

"I'm no lady," said Macphail. "I'm an MP."

Social programs, workers' rights, better health care, improved conditions for farmers: Macphail fought long and hard for all of these issues. She was an anti-imperialist back when imperialism was still a positive word. In an age of military bravado, she was an outspoken pacifist. In an era of retributive justice, she was a staunch opponent of the death penalty. In a time of raging patriotism, she objected to military training for schoolboys. (When Parliament approved a $400,000 fund to provide young boys with army cadet training, Macphail agreed on one condition: that the amount be reduced—by $399,999.)

"Patriotism," she once said, "is not dying for one's country, it is living for one's country. And for humanity. Perhaps that is not as romantic, but it is better."

In so many ways, Agnes Macphail was far ahead of her time. She lobbied for the old-age pension, disability allowance, hospital insurance and student bursaries—benefits we now take for granted, but which, in Macphail's day, were almost heretical.

Well-informed, forceful, funny and stubborn, Agnes Macphail outperformed the other MPs and in the end became something of an Ottawa institution. Journalist Marion Fox was an early fan, calling her "brave, fearless [and] true to principle."

"What do women want?" asked Macphail. "I think women just want to be individuals, as men are individuals—no more and no less."

During a 1924 debate in the House of Commons over women's rights in matters of divorce, she faced off against a persistent male MP who declared, "There has always existed and there always will exist in women, an inborn weakness, a marked inferiority. I am not saying this with the idea of depreciating woman, because we have all had mothers . . . Woman is looked upon—and with reason—as the angel of the home, as a gentler being than men."

Macphail, barely managing to restrain her temper, rose to her feet and replied, "I do not want to be the angel of any home; I want for myself what I want for other women—absolute equality. After that is secured then men and women can take turns at being angels." It was the death knell for Maternal Feminism.

When a heckler yelled out, "Don't you wish you were a man?", Macphail replied, "Yes. Don't you?"

(This latter story may be apocryphal; I have seen the same riposte attributed to Nellie McClung. Another, less pithy version of the exchange, related by Tommy Douglas, has an MP taunting Macphail: "Doesn't the honourable member wish she were a man?" To which she replies, "No. Doesn't the honourable member wish he were?")

Newspapers, once antagonistic, soon came to appreciate—and indeed, thrive upon—Macphail's "wit, satire and good humour." The press hailed her as the best speaker in the House. She was, in her own way, a media darling. A star. Macphail anecdotes became something of a journalistic subgenre, much to the chagrin of her opponents in the House, where she was considered an annoyance at best, and a radical socialist troublemaker at worst.

In 1924, a 12-year-old girl named Maxine Lyons won an essay contest and was invited to Ottawa for the opening of Parliament as a guest of Agnes Macphail. In her diary, young Maxine described the solemn eulogy delivered by Prime Minister Meighen in memory of two MPs who had recently passed away. "I asked Miss Macphail if they would say nice things about her if she were dead, and she said, 'Yes, if I were dead.'"

The election in midst of the Great Depression of a millionaire Calgary tycoon by the name of R. B. Bennett marked the start of a long, stormy relationship between Agnes Macphail and the new prime minister. Macphail had chosen never to marry, which was considered somewhat scandalous. The newspapers often commented on this fact, even while Canada was led by two consecutive bachelors: Mackenzie King and R. B. Bennett. In fact, Bennett—Macphail's conservative arch-nemesis—appears to have courted her. The two often held hands at public events, and Bennett is said to have proposed marriage. (He once complimented her on having "nice ankles.") Now, *that* would have been a volatile union: R. B. Bennett and Agnes Macphail. In truth, Macphail found it all very amusing and enjoyed playing it up to the press.

As Margaret Stewart and Doris French point out in *Ask No Quarter*, "[Macphail] genuinely liked Bennett the man, and she genuinely loathed Bennett the Prime Minister." Once, when asked to name the 10 best-looking men in the House of Commons, Macphail graciously granted Bennett an honourable mention as "most distinguished."

The key to understanding Agnes Macphail is that she never sought special privilege. She did not believe in any form of discrimination, not even well-intentioned reverse discrimination. Today's affirmative action programs would have horrified her. "I've never asked for anything on the ground that I was a woman," said Macphail. "If I didn't deserve it on my own merit I didn't want it."

The Second World War effectively ended Macphail's career as a federal MP. Earlier, she had been a delegate to the League of Nations in Geneva, where as a member of the disarmament committee she had argued for complete demilitarization. Her arguments went unheeded. The build-up continued, and in 1939 Hitler's tanks rolled into Belgium. Macphail's pacifism was now out of step with the times, and she was thoroughly trounced in the 1940 federal election.

When asked why she had lost, she said wryly, "Well, I told them the truth. They say the truth shall set you free. It's certainly set me free." Macphail later moved to provincial politics, where she served, on and off, until 1951.

Whenever you hear people—usually woefully uninformed people—lament the fact that Canadians have no heroes, no role models, ask them: What of Nellie McClung? What of Agnes Macphail? Their original battles have long been won, but both women live on as examples of a certain raw spirit, one we would do well to emulate. As Agnes Macphail often said, "Whenever I don't know whether to fight or not—I always fight." Nellie, Emily, Agnes and all the others. They fought the good fight, and they won.

Of course they won. They had all the best lines.

Verdict

Nellie McClung: **Bastard**

Emily Murphy: **Bastard**

Agnes Macphail: **Bastard**

Rodmond P. Roblin: **Bonehead**

10

Draft Dodgers:
The Conscription Crises

FOR CANADA, THE most divisive battles of World War I and II were fought not in Europe but on the home front. And yet, although the conscription crises of those two wars linger long in the memory of the Québécois, they are almost completely forgotten in the rest of Canada. Ours is a land of dual memory, and in Canada, the past is always plural.

World War I (1914-18) was a monstrous absurdity to begin with. Imperialism taken to its logical extreme, it began with a single act of terrorism and ended with more than 14 million dead, 21 million wounded and an entire generation shattered.

On June 28, 1914, Archduke Ferdinand of the Austro-Hungarian Empire, grandson of the emperor and heir to the throne, was shot and killed by a Serbian nationalist. Austria was outraged and demanded reparations from Serbia. But Serbia was allied with Russia, and Austria was allied with Germany. So Germany declared war on Russia and then immediately invaded France. Germany did this by going through Belgium, which was, technically, a neutral country. Britain dusted off a minor agreement signed 84 years earlier guaranteeing Belgian neutrality and then declared war on Germany. The Dominion of Canada, as part of Team Britain, automatically entered the war on August 4, 1914, at the same time Britain did. And everybody forgot about Serbia. That, more or less, is how the Stupidest War in Human History began.

Oddly enough, in the beginning the war actually helped bring French and English Canadians together. A few years earlier, Ontario had introduced Regulation 17, which all but eliminated French instruction in Ontario schools, and Franco-Ontarian mothers armed with hatpins had blocked government agents from interfering with bilingual classes. Anti-Catholic Orangemen raged, and insults flew from both sides.

Some French Canadians, like newspaperman Henri Bourassa, grandson of the 1837 Patriote Papineau, still believed that a bilingual, bicultural nation was possible, but things were simply not shaping up that way. First in Manitoba and the West, and now in Ontario, the French language was being actively proscribed. The underlying belief was that Canada was destined to become an English-speaking country, in which the French language was confined, like a virus, within the boundaries of Québec—where, it was hoped, it might yet die out. The spirit of mouldy old Jack Durham was still kicking from the grave.

In the middle of these escalating French-English tensions came war. And what a glorious war it was. It helped unify the nation by casting a mist of euphoria. Wilfrid Laurier, who as prime minister had distanced Canada from Imperial policy, was now swept up in the enthusiasm. "Ready. Aye, ready!" came the cry. Even the resolute anti-imperialist Henri Bourassa initially supported the war efforts, seeing in the conflict a chance for French and English Canadians to work together for a nobler cause. Bourassa even believed (naively) that Ontario might rescind the contentious Regulation 17 as a show of good faith. No such gesture was ever made, and instead of bringing the two Canadas together, the war would in fact divide them more than at any time since the execution of Louis Riel.

Recruiting men for battle was not a problem. At least not in the beginning. When the call went out for 25,000 men, more than 33,000 showed up. The big worry was that all the fighting would be over before they got there. "Back by Christmas!" was the cheer, and Sam Hughes, Canada's crotchety, incompetent, slightly mad Minister of Militia, put together the first Canadian expeditionary force in a suitably mad, incompetent, chaotic fashion. It was more of a stampede than a mobilization. (Significantly, 60 per cent of the initial force was made up of recent British immigrants off to fight for the homeland, a point that would be well noted by Bourassa later on.)

Sam Hughes armed "his boys" with long-barrelled, Canadian-built Ross rifles. The rifles, designed for leisurely marksmanship, were dangerously unsuitable for combat. Heavy and unwieldy, they had an unfortunate tendency to overheat and jam when fired too rapidly. They also clogged when used in mud. This wouldn't have been so bad, except that the war in the trenches of Europe involved (a) firing rapidly and (b) mud. Sam Hughes, bless his leathery old hide, refused to change the rifles as a point of stubborn pride, and thousands of Canadian boys died before he was finally overruled by Cabinet. More than 340,000 infamous Ross rifles were scrapped. Hughes also equipped his troops with the equally ridiculous MacAdam shovel, invented by one of his secretaries, Ena MacAdam, in her spare time. This bulky contraption was designed to double as both a shovel and a shield. Only problem was, bullets went right through it like a hot rivet through tin, which didn't make it especially useful as a shield, and it was also too awkward for use as a shovel.

"Men," declared Hughes to the first contingent of confused, enthusiastic, ill-equipped Canadians sent overseas, "the world regards you as a marvel!" He was right, but not in the way he supposed. The marvel was how they ever managed to get to Europe at all.

Meanwhile, Canada's Conservative prime minister, Robert Borden, in a burst of patriotism, had backed the creation of a War Measures Act, which stripped Canadians of civil rights and gave the government almost unlimited powers. As well, in the spirit of democracy, Canadians of German, Austrian, Turkish and Ukrainian (that is, Slavic) background who had been naturalized within the preceding 12 years were categorized as enemy aliens and forced to carry identity cards. Not long after, 8,500 of these "enemy aliens" were rounded up and imprisoned in camps across Canada. (It should be noted that the internment of enemy nationals was common military practice at that time. Many Canadian civilians were interned in Germany during the war, including a Canadian member of Parliament.) Berlin, a German-Canadian community in southern Ontario, was pressured into changing its name to something more patriotic; the name Kitchener was chosen, to honour a British war hero. Sillier still, German language classes were cancelled across the country, and the music of Wagner, Beethoven and other such sauerkraut-eatin', baby-killin' Hun composers was banned.

It was an age of black-and-white morality. A time of marching bands, music, intolerance and confetti: those heady, happy days of war. And however much it embarrasses French Canadians to admit it now, Québec supported the war with every bit as much fervour as Ontario and the rest of Canada did. At first.

But something happened on the way to victory. The Splendid Adventure turned into Black Horror. Armies bogged down. Corpses rotted in the mud. Fewer and fewer boys came back. At Ypres, on April 22, 1915, modern warfare was born as the German army released canisters of chlorine gas. Canadians were there as the green cloud rolled across no man's land. Soldiers died, gagging, their lungs on fire, their tongues swollen, their brass buttons stained green. The French army (as the French army is wont to do) ran away, but the Canadians held their ground, urinating into handkerchiefs and then holding the cloth over their mouths and noses. Against all odds, the Canadians turned back the German advance, and when the poison clouds finally dissolved, victory was theirs. And for what? A few acres of mud that weren't worth a soldier's bones.

After Ypres, writes historian Daniel Dancocks, "There was no more bravado about an early victory over the Hun, no more fears of missing out on 'the fun.' " The war ground on. During the long, drawn-out Battle of the Somme, well over

World War I was an ugly, dirty, pointless war. Bodies lay bloated and rotting in the field, cuts festered, wounds became gangrenous, and men had their spirits shattered—absolutely shattered. But high above the muck and blood, a very different battle was unfolding. It was the crisp clean war of the air, enacted by modern jousting knights.

Canada supplied more and better pilots than any other country. Of the top 27 British aces, 10 were Canadians. Among them:

Billy Barker of Dauphin, Manitoba, arguably the most fearless pilot of the war. Once, trapped alone behind enemy air space, he singlehandedly took on an entire flying circus of 60 German planes. Although wounded and bleeding badly, Barker went on the offensive, scattering the German planes and shooting down four. He then shot his way free and made a crash landing just past British lines. The fight was the most lopsided air battle in history, and it won Barker the Victoria Cross. The Germans, it was said, saluted him from the air.

Roy Brown of Carleton Place, Ontario, is credited with shooting down Germany's greatest air ace, Manfred von Richthofen, better known as "the Red Baron." Richthofen had already destroyed 80 Allied airplanes and was gunning for number 81 over the skies of northern France when he closed in on a young, inexperienced Canadian airman by the name of Wilfred "Wop" May. May, guns jammed, fled back over Allied territory with the Red Baron in deadly pursuit. But then Roy Brown came to the rescue. Swooping down, he riddled the Baron's red Fokker with bullets, killing the Baron and saving May in the process. (Australian soldiers, firing from the ground, later claimed *their* bullets actually brought down the Baron, in what historian Donald Jones has called "the most controversial 60 seconds in the history of aerial warfare.")

Wop May, from Carberry, Manitoba, went on to become one of Canada's greatest bush pilots. (His nickname was not in reference to Italians.) In 1929, May and his partner Vic Horner—in an open-cockpit, midwinter mercy flight carrying serum through -40° C temperatures—saved my hometown, Fort Vermilion, from a deadly diphtheria epidemic. A few years later, in what would be the world's first use of an airplane in a police manhunt, Wop May helped the Mounties track down Albert Johnson, "the Mad Trapper of Rat River."

Ray Collishaw of Nanaimo, B.C., flew an all-black Sopwith tri-plane into the history books as the Royal Flying Corps' second-ranked ace, shooting down an even 60 planes. But the greatest of them all was *Billy Bishop* of Owen Sound, Ontario. Canada's top pilot and the most decorated Allied airman of the war, Bishop shot down 72 planes. In his first seven months as a combat pilot, Bishop won the Military Cross and two Distinguished Service Orders, as well as the Victoria Cross, the highest honour available. The press called him the Lone Hawk, but to the German pilots who had to face him, he was known as Hell's Handmaiden.

The Lone Hawk and the Red Baron once went head to head in what has been described as the single greatest aerial dogfight in human history. They fought to a standoff; the Baron eventually withdrew, and Bishop flew his smoking plane back to base. In the long run Bishop won, though: unlike the Red Baron, he survived the war.

half a million British and Allied soldiers were killed, a monument to the staggering incompetence of the British High Command as much as anything else. On the first day alone, 720 of the 1,000-man force of the 1st Newfoundland Regiment were killed or wounded. It was one of the highest casualty rates of any force on the British side, and that first day at the Somme, July 1, 1916, remains the darkest in Newfoundland's history.

The bodies kept falling, and the costs kept rising. The Conservatives introduced the, ahem, "temporary measure" of income tax to help cover the costs of the war, and Borden found himself haunted by an earlier promise: that Canada would supply 500,000 new soldiers—from a population of just 8 million, only 1.5 million of whom were men of military age. Somehow, Borden expected a third of these men to volunteer.

During this time, the province of Manitoba decided to abolish any and all allowances for bilingual instruction in their schools. English would henceforth be the province's sole official language. Bourassa's bicultural breakthrough had not come to pass, and he now lost what little enthusiasm he had for the war—a war most French Canadians now recognized for what it was: a senseless, stupid, European conflict. The glory of Britain and France failed to captivate French Canadians. Their loyalty to Britain was tenuous at best, and they no longer identified themselves with France. They were orphans, *les Canadiens*, and they had come of age 155 years earlier, on the high Plains of Abraham. For them, the madness in Europe was a shadow-play once removed and hardly worth dying for. The real battle was being fought closer to home, in the schools and legislatures of English Canada. The irony was not lost on people like Bourassa. At the same time that French Canadians were being exhorted to help defend liberty and French culture overseas, French language rights and French culture were under assault in Canada.

English Canadians, meanwhile, began tallying up the lists of casualties by region and discovered that Québec was starkly underrepresented. Denied access to the French language outside of Québec, denied military instruction in their native tongue and denied positions in the officer corps (for the most part, French Canadians were expected to be grunts and trench rats), Canada's francophones didn't feel any moral imperative to join up. And Sam Hughes didn't help. He was an anti-French Orangeman who only begrudgingly accepted the presence of Canada's sole French-speaking battalion, the famed Royal 22nd Regiment, better known as "the Vandoos." The Vandoos and one other company aside, Canada's armed forces were disproportionately, unapologetically *English*.

Hughes was finally fired in 1916. In the spring of the following year, Prime Minister Borden toured the trenches and hospitals of France and was badly shaken by what he saw. Canada had to find more men. While Borden was in Europe, the Canadian Corps had won its greatest victory ever, at Vimy Ridge (a battle that has since entered the national mythos as something akin to the birth of a nation). At Vimy Ridge, the Canadians gained more ground and took more prisoners than any previous British offensive had done. But victory came at a terrible cost: more than 10,000 dead and wounded. That same month, fewer than 5,000 Canadians enlisted. The raw mathematics were amply clear.

Borden returned to Canada in a grim mood. The time for volunteers had passed, and the prime minister rose in the House and announced his decision: Canada would begin drafting men into the armed forces. "The battle for Canadian liberty and autonomy," he said, "is being fought today on the plains of France and Belgium." A week later, anti-conscription riots erupted in Montréal.

The debate over conscription divided Canada's House right down the middle, with almost every English-Canadian MP voting in favour and almost every French-Canadian MP voting against. On August 29, 1917, the Military Service Act, giving the government the right to conscript Canadian citizens for military duty, became law—just in time for a federal election.

In preparation for the election, one which would be fought almost exclusively on the issue of conscription, Borden gave the vote to all men serving overseas, regardless of how long they had been Canadian citizens. Soldiers would vote simply Government or Opposition, and almost to a man, they voted for the government. Borden also gave the vote to any woman who was a wife, sister or mother of a serviceman, thus introducing women's suffrage through the side door. Borden counted on—and received—support from these women. Women, you see, weren't expected to die, face-down and bleeding, in a muddy field far from home. Many women even believed that sending more boys overseas would somehow bring their own loved ones back. War does strange things to people's minds. (Borden also promised women full franchise if elected, and he kept his word. Women in Canada were granted the right to vote in federal elections on May 24, 1918—making them arguably the only real victors of World War I.)

At the same time that women were given a limited vote, "enemy aliens," pacifists, Quakers, Mennonites and other conscientious objectors were stripped of their franchise. The brainchild behind these gerrymandering tricks was Arthur Meighen, a future prime minister. With the cards thus stacked, Borden's Union government—a coalition of Tories and pro-conscription Liberals—won the most lopsided majority yet recorded in Canadian history. But, like Vimy Ridge, it was a victory gained only at great cost.

Canada was politically and emotionally polarized. Laurier had refused to join Borden's Union coalition because he saw in conscription "the seeds of discord and disunion." And he was proven right. Never had Canada's two solitudes been more at odds. Political positions hardened into caricatures: Québec was portrayed as a black blot on the map, Borden was derided as a toadying imperialist—and still is, reflexively, by many French-Canadian historians. (In fact, Borden helped forge a newer, more independent status for Canada during and after the war, based largely on the immense sacrifice Canadians had made on the battlefield.) Anglophones compared Bourassa to the Kaiser, and Québec leaders responded in kind by referring to Anglo-Ontarians as "the Prussians next door."

The election of 1917 was the most divisive in Canadian history, and it split Canada into two linguistic/geographic blocs: Québec vs. the Rest of Canada. But the conscription crisis was more than a simple French-English conflict; it was also a rural-urban divide. English-Canadian farmers didn't want to send their sons into battle any more than did the habitants; crops needed harvesting and cattle needed tending. To appease Canada's farmers, Borden had promised to exempt their sons from the draft, and soon more and more grounds for exemption were added. When conscription finally got underway in January 1918, a solid 98 per cent of men registered in Québec sought exemptions. In patriotic Ontario, 94 per cent sought exemption. And in the Maritimes, those men who hadn't run into the woods or over the border to America also sought exemptions. It turns out very few young men wanted to die, face-down and bleeding, in a muddy field far from home.

On Easter weekend in Québec City, troops fired on an angry mob of protesters, killing four civilians. All exemptions were cancelled. Draft dodgers were hunted down. Protestors were arrested without due process and without bail. In *The Dream of Nation*, historian Susan Mann Trofimenkoff comments, "Well might some Québécois wonder just where the war was being fought."

In British Columbia, labour organizer Ginger Goodwin was deemed fit for battle even though he suffered from tuberculosis. When he refused to show up for basic training, he was classified as a draft dodger, then hunted down and shot by a police officer under very suspicious circumstances. The killing of Ginger Goodwin triggered a general strike in Vancouver, the first in B.C.'s history.

All that anger and acrimony. The slander, the riots, the ill will, the killings—for what? Less than a few acres of mud. Victory, when it came, came suddenly. At Amiens, Canadian and Australian troops, counterpunching a massive German offensive, broke through enemy lines. The U.S. had entered the war the year before, but it was the Canadians who were now the spearhead to victory. In the final three months, dubbed "Canada's 100 Days," Canadian soldiers blazed a trail, liberating dozens of French and Belgian towns as the German army fell raggedly back.

At Vimy Ridge, Canadians had earned a reputation as storm troopers, an elite force brought in to lead one assault after another, and under the leadership of Canada's greatest general, Sir Arthur Currie, the Canadian Corps again proved its worth. Currie was a master tactician, one who studied the battlefield, who believed in meticulous preparations and careful rehearsals before any assault and—most commendably—who refused to throw away soldiers' lives as though they were random mortars. (Unlike the British High Command, alas, who had employed this technique throughout the war. Theirs was an incompetence that bordered on the criminal.) The official German history of the war, *Der Weltkrieg 1914-18*, refers to the "tenacious determination of Canadian troops" and describes Arthur Currie as "the greatest general the war produced." One German officer went on record as saying that, if it hadn't been for the Canadians and the tactics of General Currie, Germany might very well have won.

German staff officers considered the Canadians "the best troops the British had." And British Prime Minister David Lloyd George noted, "Whenever the Germans found the Canadian Corps coming into the line, they prepared for the worst." Arthur Currie's methodical, incisive approach worked magnificently. Suddenly, the Germans were on the run, yielding territory at a dizzying rate. And then, just as abruptly, it was all over. Germany surrendered before the Allies could reach its borders, and on the eleventh hour of the eleventh day of the eleventh month, the War to End All Wars came to an end. November 11, 1918.

If there was any doubt about the valour of French Canadians in battle, the Royal 22nd Regiment proved otherwise. Every single officer in the Vandoos was either killed or wounded in action. Among the wounded was a young major by the name of

Georges Vanier, who would go on to become governor general of Canada. Vanier had already won a Military Cross and the Distinguished Service Medal when he was shot almost to pieces during Canada's 100 Days. His right leg had to be amputated.

By the end of the First World War, the Canadian Corps had gone from being a colonial appendage of the British army to what was, effectively, a national corps. Conscription had forced around 125,000 Canadians into service, but fewer than 25,000 of these men actually made it to France before the war ended, and it is common among some historians to portray conscription as a failure because so few of the drafted troops were ever used. Hindsight is 20-20, however, and no one could have predicted such a stunning victory at that time. Many thought the war would drag on until 1920—and beyond. Had it continued, conscription would have been vital. The draft wasn't a failure in terms of its efficiency, but in its social repercussions; the damage to English-French relations caused by the Military Service Act was almost irreparable.

"For many nationalists," writes Susan Mann Trofimenkoff, "the war years turned French Canada into Québec."

Ironically, if the First World War drove French Canada back into Québec, it also turned English Canadians into, simply, Canadians. The Glory of Imperialism died in the mud of Flanders. The Oedipal lure of a glorious, sexy Motherland was gone forever. At Borden's insistence, Canada signed the Treaty of Versailles as an independent country and was later granted its own seat at the League of Nations (precursor to today's United Nations). It was a perk paid for with the lives of more than 60,000 Canadian men and 56 Canadian women (nurses who had died on the front lines).

The years passed. Confederation weathered both the resentment of French Canadians and the onslaught of Depression, dust-storms and dismay. Scars healed, bones set—often at twisted angles, true—but set nonetheless. And then, in 1939, Hitler's panzers rolled into Poland, and World War II (1939–45), the sequel, had begun.

This time, Canada did not enter the conflict automatically, as a colonial puppet. The 1931 Statute of Westminster had given Canada official independence in foreign policy, and the Canadian government purposely waited a full week before issuing its own declaration of war on September 10, 1939.

Once again the world was at war, and once again Canada found itself facing the dilemma of conscription. But this time around, it wasn't the hard-nosed Conservatives at the helm; it was the oh-so-slippery Liberals. Prime Minister William Lyon Mackenzie King, grandson of the rebel leader of 1837, headed the country, and Canada was in safe, if squishy, hands.

Mackenzie King often consulted the spirits of the dead for advice (although King apologists insist that he never let the spirits actually affect his decisions). Among the spirits he consulted was that of his late mentor, Wilfrid Laurier, and apparently the advice Laurier gave him from beyond the grave was, "When in doubt, *equivocate*"!

Conscription was once again a hot issue. King tried to play it both ways. More so than Borden, King had a genuine distaste for forcing men into battle. He also had a legitimate objection: what Britain needed was supplies, not warm bodies. "Give us the tools and we'll finish the job!" Churchill had pleaded, and this tug-of-war between Men and Materials was at the core of the controversy. Canada needed men to harvest its fields, mine its ore, log its forests. Britain desperately needed raw materials. Where should Canada's priorities lie?

Rational arguments rarely work in wartime, and as the conflict wore on and the body count climbed, pressure grew across Canada to reinstate the draft. King, however, had been elected in Québec almost solely on his pledge *not* to introduce conscription, and so it would seem that his hands were tied. But King, the Houdini of Canadian politics, simply slapped on a coat of grease and slipped himself free.

In 1942, King announced that he would hold a national plebiscite, a referendum of sorts, not on conscription, heavens no, but rather on whether to release the government from its earlier promise of not introducing conscription. Confused? So were most Canadians—which was of course the whole idea. In Québec, Mackenzie King told voters that the plebiscite was not about conscription per se but about the *possibility* of conscription, while at the same he assured English Canadians that it most definitely *was* about conscription. King summed up his incomprehensible stance with a slogan destined to go down in the history books as one of the all-time classic examples of political misdirection: *Conscription if necessary, but not necessarily conscription.*

Genius. Pure genius. A generation earlier, Borden had attempted to obfuscate the issue of conscription with a confusing slogan of his own—"Continuous consultation leading to concerted action"—but his slogan wasn't quite convoluted or wily enough. King's most certainly was.

In *Right Honourable Men*, historian Michael Bliss defends King's formulation, insisting that "the words were precise, the policy was clear, and the approach sensible." Most people, however, find King's policy to have been ambiguous, misleading and vague. Certainly, at the time, it was interpreted in radically different ways.

Québec, as could have been expected, balked at the mere mention of the word "conscription," and in the 1942 plebiscite Québec voted *no* by 73 per cent. The rest of Canada, meanwhile, voted *yes* by 80 per cent. Once again, Québec was at odds with the sentiments of the nation, and once again Québec was shouted down.

King, having won the referendum, was now free to introduce conscription. If necessary. But not necessarily. For two more years he managed to sidestep and stall.

It should be noted that registration and limited conscription *for home defence* had been underway since 1940. Thousands of men had been called up under the National Resources Mobilization Act (NRMA), and tens of thousands more volunteered. The NRMA gave the impression that the government was Doing Something, while at the same time avoiding full overseas conscription. With Canada under no real threat of invasion, save rumours of Japanese plans for the Pacific Coast, the NRMA didn't have a lot to do, and they were quickly dubbed "Zombies" by their critics. Many of the NRMA would later take defiant pride in their nickname.

King dumped his Minister of Defence, the pro-conscription Colonel J. L. Ralston, in a singularly shabby manner and brought in General Andrew McNaughton to replace him. McNaughton thought he could convince 16,000 or so Zombies to volunteer for overseas duties, but he failed miserably. King, now facing a mass resignation by his ministers, finally relented, and conscription began in late November 1944. By then, British, American and Canadian forces had already landed on the beaches of Normandy. It was a hard-won beachhead, and the liberation of Europe was proving to be a long, bloody slog. Men wounded two or three times were being patched up and sent back in. Canada was the only nation involved that didn't have the draft—even Australia had resorted to conscription. Fresh troops were needed now, in the final push, more than ever.

French-Canadian nationalists tried to rally opposition to the government's conscription bill and a few perfunctory riots broke out in Montréal, but with the waters thoroughly muddied and the issues carefully sugar-coated (that's right, Mackenzie King could sugar-coat mud), most French Canadians merely grumbled and accepted it.

Under King's directives, roughly 13,000 men were sent abroad, but they were taken from the Zombies of the NRMA Home Defence, so it didn't really *feel* like conscription. Fewer than 2,500 actually reached the battlefield, and only 69 died in action. That number compares starkly with the total number of Canadians who died in World War II: more than 42,000.

As it had during the First World War, conscription proved more destructive to Canadian unity than effective against the Germans. Mackenzie King survived the crisis and was later reelected with full support in Québec, where he was perceived as a man who had resisted conscription as long as possible, giving in only when all other options had been denied.

And so passed the storm.

The economy boomed. The boys came home. And from the detritus of an empire, Canada emerged as a nation. After World War I, Canada was no longer a colony but still not quite a country. The Statute of Westminster made us an autonomous nation; the Second World War allowed us to prove we were. As the poet F. R. Scott noted, "Canada won its independence mostly by fighting against Germans."

From 1945 on, we were on our own. We were stuck with one another, for better or for worse, in sickness and in health. Until death do we part.

Verdict

Robert Borden: **Bastard**

Mackenzie King: **Bastard**

General Arthur Currie: **Bastard**

Sam Hughes: **Blustering, Blundering Bonehead**

11

Apartheid:
The Politics of Treaty-Making

WHEN I WAS a college student, back in those swingin' Palaeolithic days we now call "the eighties," I remember dozens of mass rallies against South Africa's system of racial apartheid. I never saw a single comparable outpouring over Canada's system of exclusion.

History is always an act of selective memory, of deciding what is worth remembering and what is not, and as historian Daniel Francis points out in *National Dreams*, memory always implies its opposite: forgetting. What we choose to forget is just as revealing as what we choose to remember.

We live in a country that was captured as much by stealth as by anything else. Over the years Europeans and their Canadian descendants unleashed a multipronged assault of settlers, disease, Mounted Police, missionaries and armies of well-intentioned social workers on Canada's First Nations. But the most effective tool employed by far was one of legal double-feint, that proud tradition of bureaucratic magic we call Treaty Rights.

Treaty-making in Canada between 1763 and 1923 formed a patchwork of territorial agreements that cover much (but not all) of our nation. British Columbia, for example, was settled by whites with virtually no treaties and no pretext of legitimacy. They just moved in and set up camp.

Treaty-making is predicated on the notion of two or more autonomous groups negotiating mutually acceptable terms. One side may be better armed or more proficient at legalistic manoeuvring, but the agreement itself is based on the recognition of separate, sovereign entities. Nothing contained in any treaty changes this basic fact. So what happens when treaties, negotiated originally in poor faith, are subsequently dishonoured? The underlying autonomy of the signatories resurfaces, and you have a very, very messy situation.

Having founded Québec City and the St. Lawrence colony of New France, Samuel de Champlain made a grave tactical error: he joined a band of Native allies in a raid into Iroquoian territory. By thus aligning himself against the Iroquois Confederacy, Champlain unwittingly plunged New France into a protracted, ongoing war of attrition, though "feud" might be a more accurate description. The conflict was handed down from generation to generation, with the French and the Iroquois (most notably the Mohawk) waging an ongoing guerrilla war along the Canadian frontier.

The sudden attacks, gruesome tortures and symbolic cannibalism of the Iroquois both terrified and hardened the citizens of New France. One Jesuit missionary, soon to be martyred, said with something akin to awe, "They move like foxes through the forest. They strike like lions, and take flight like birds, disappearing before they have really appeared."

In 1660, a young officer by the name of Adam Dollard des Ormeaux led a force of 17 *Canadiens*, together with a contingent of Huron and Algonquian allies, on an armed raid against the Iroquois. Dollard had been planning to stage a small ambush, but he and his men ran into a full invasion force of Iroquois warriors. Much like what happened at the Alamo, Dollard's last stand at an abandoned fort at Long Sault is seen as an epic of outnumbered, gallant men. The battle turned into a siege that lasted for more than a week. Dollard and his men were eventually overrun and either killed outright or taken prisoner and tortured to death. But Dollard did succeed, in the eyes of nationalist historians anyway, in saving Montréal from a full-scale Iroquois invasion.

As the Great Martyred Hero of New France, Adam Dollard has long had mythical stature in Québec. But lately historians have critically reevaluated the legend. Some dispute the claim that Dollard prevented a full-scale assault, arguing that the Iroquois were clearly more interested in collecting war trophies than in trying to capture Montréal. It now seems unlikely that Dollard was even in charge; the expedition was probably led by a Huron warrior. And, as historian Daniel Francis says in *The Imaginary Indian*, "Far from saving New France, the Dollard incident probably served to provoke the Iroquois into redoubling their attacks the next season."

The French Canadians, meanwhile, launched a raid deep into Iroquois territory and burned a Seneca village to the ground. The Iroquois retaliated with a massive attack on the French settlement of Lachine, killing two dozen settlers and carrying off almost 60 more for ritualistic torture. Three years later, 14-year-old heroine Madeleine de Verchères defended her family farm with the battle cry: "Let us fight to the death! For our homeland and our religion! For God and King!" Or at least, that's how Madeleine told the story. It turns out that most of her claims were, how shall we say, a wee bit *exaggerated*. Over the years, the number of Iroquois she eluded somehow multiplied from a single brave to more than 45 bloodthirsty warriors.

Memories like these, whether accurate or not, don't exactly bring people together. Even today, the relationship between the Québécois and the Mohawk is not especially pleasant. Witness the 1990 armed standoff between Mohawk Warriors and the Québec authorities at Oka over a disputed holy ground that was slated to be turned into a golf course. It didn't take long for old animosities to come boiling to the surface.

The First Nations of Canada, contrary to common belief, were never conquered, never defeated militarily, never forced into unconditional surrender. They forfeited neither their autonomy nor their right to self-government. This is the cold, hard truth at the core of Canadian history, and the ramifications are staggering.

The politics of early treaty-making was an art in itself, in the same way that conjuring and sleight of hand can be considered arts. What the First Nations saw as covenants between autonomous groups—friendship pacts in which they offered access to land in exchange for payments and security—the whites took as outright bills of sale. And between those differences in perception lies the Great Abyss. Either Canada's land treaties were remarkably lopsided real estate deals in which the Natives got royally suckered (and the Natives would have to have been stupid beyond belief to have accepted the terms that the whites said they did), or these treaties were something else, something bigger. Writs of diplomacy between sovereign peoples, perhaps, and not simply land cessions.

Canada was founded not by two nations but by three: French, British and Aboriginal. (There were not two solitudes but dozens. The First Nations exhibited far more variety in language, culture and social arrangements than did the two European nations.) The governments of Britain and later Canada, having successfully pulled the land out from under the feet of Native Canadians, next sought to isolate them from white society, both socially and physically. This leads to Phase Two of our Conquest by Memo: the creation of land reserves.

In *Ghost Camps*, author Stephen Hume writes, "The stationary community of [the reserve] was invented by nineteenth century bureaucrats as an instrument of administrative control. It was, to all intents and purposes, a concentration camp for nomadic people."

Perhaps "holding pens" would be a more accurate description. Indian reserves were set up to contain Natives until they could be properly tamed and integrated into mainstream white society. This is not editorializing on my part; these were the specific goals of the Indian Act. To ensure that this assimilation took place, Phase Three of our conquest was invented: something called "enfranchisement."

First established in 1869, enfranchisement originally meant "the voluntary relinquishment" of Native identity. That is, if a Native person was good, if he was very good, if he learned English or French and agreed to give up Native customs, language and religion, he would be allowed to "graduate." That is, he would be granted the privilege of *not* being an Indian.

Now, you may notice something very odd about this clever scheme of ours. Phase Two: Reserves (that is, isolation) and Phase Three: Enfranchisement (that is, assimilation) actually work *against* one another. If the goal was assimilation and the method was isolation, then the method and the goal were working at stark cross-purposes. By confining the First Nations to scattered remnants of Crown land and cutting them off from their traditional methods of livelihood, the government did succeed in driving Native Canadians to poverty and despair. What it did not achieve was assimilation. Enfranchisement was a miserable failure.

If there was one thing our Victorian forebears agreed on, it was this: the First Nations were finished. Kaput. Doomed to extinction. Sad figures in the twilight . . . This assumption has been one of the biggest single delusions of Canadian society, stubbornly surviving to this day. Like Canada itself, the First Nations have beaten the odds—and the odds were stacked mightily against them. The First Nations have survived every government scheme ever thrown at them. They have survived 500 years of white encroachment and more than 200 years of treaties, and they are with us still, part of the social landscape, battered, bruised, but standing.

If only the Natives had read the script. They were supposed to fade poetically into the woods, lamented and forsaken, noble savages, an era passing. They were certainly *not* supposed to survive into the modern age, where they would employ the politics of land claims and turn the legislative process on its head. They were never supposed to win, you see. Indians, by definition, were meant to be the great tragic losers of Canadian history. It really was inconsiderate of them not to quietly expire and be kept safely in the past tense.

Consider the poet Duncan Campbell Scott (1862–1947), a man who wrote—well, *dreck*, really. Nonetheless, he is well represented in Canadian literary anthologies, and his poems, I have been told, are "still greatly admired." (I love that phrase. I think we should abbreviate it and apply it liberally. As in, "Pauline Johnson, poet, princess, S.G.A.") It would make Can-Lit courses easier to get through.

Duncan Campbell Scott's most S.G.A. poems are those dealing with the Indians. He wrote woeful elegies about the Noble Savage doomed to vanish into the night. Scott's Indians are murdered, mutilated, tossed over cliffs. Some freeze to death. Indeed, the Scott canon is littered with their corpses. Pound for pound, Duncan Campbell Scott had more dead Indians per page than any other poet. He seemed to experience a certain voyeuristic glee in coming up with new ways to kill them off, even as he bemoaned the plight of the "tragic savage," that "weird and waning race." It's no wonder he was concerned. Consider the following statement made by the director of Canada's Indian policy in 1931, at about the same time that Scott was writing his dead Indian poems:

> The Government will in time reach the end of its responsibility as the Indians progress into civilization and finally disappear as a separate and distinct people, not by race extinction but by gradual assimilation.

Chilling, don't you think? No wonder poets like Scott were concerned; no wonder they wrote mournful poems on the passing of the Native way of life.

There was just one problem. The government official who made those "Final Solution" statements was the same man who wrote the poems lamenting the fate of the Indian. Duncan Campbell Scott, as well as being a Famous Canadian Poet (S.G.A.), was also Canada's senior administrator of Indian policy from 1913 until his retirement in 1932. Dedicated to the complete eradication of Native culture, Scott was relentless in his censure of such things as the west-coast potlatch, which he condemned as immoral for its "wanton giving away of property," as well as the pow-wow and other celebrations, because they "slowed the process of assimilation." With Scott's approval, many Native ceremonies, initiation rituals and even certain types of housing were banned. (Communal houses were deemed "vile and immoral," which says more about the writhing ids of our forebears than it does about Native dwellings.) Scott also sought to outlaw "senseless drumming and dancing" and proposed a hefty fine for any Native wearing traditional dress outside the reserves.

The following synopses are included as a handy reference guide to Duncan Campbell Scott's top S.G.A. poems in the "dead Indian" category. Keep in mind that (a) this man is still highly regarded in the Canadian literary pantheon, and (b) he was responsible for setting Native policy in Canada for almost 20 years.

"Watkins"

A withered old Indian woman (Scott just *loved* writing about withered old Indian women) recalls with lip-smacking glee the pleasures she once took in slitting enemy throats, when "her long knife flashed" and "drank its fill" of blood.

"The Onondaga Madonna"

A woman of that "weird and waning race" suckles a "primal warrior" with gleaming eyes (that is, her baby). This short poem, long considered a classic of Canadian literature, describes the Native woman as "a tragic savage" with "pagan passions" who thrills at war and has "wildness in her veins."

"At Gull Lake"

A young Indian woman is tortured, mutilated and thrown over a riverbank "like a dead dog," after having been held down by a pack of withered old women who burned her eyes out with red-hot coals. (I consider this poem to be the ultimate Scott work, incorporating as it does pagan passions, savage rites, a young woman being killed gruesomely, and not just one but a whole gang of withered old Indian women.)

"Indian Place Names"

The Indians, those "dusky folk," have vanished. Gone forever. But they did leave a lot of nifty place names behind, so it wasn't all for naught.

"The Forsaken"

This has got to be one of the worst poems ever written, or, at the very least, the worst poem ever written by a respected literary figure. In it, an Indian woman baits a fish hook *with her own flesh* in order to feed her starving child. Years later, as a withered old woman (natch), she is abandoned in the woods by her people "without a word of farewell." Why? "Because she was old and useless." She dies. Of course.

"Powassan's Drum"

An angry, wizened Indian filled with hatred, his eyes burning though his eyelids, drags a severed head through murky water while storm clouds boil over and his war drum throbs and the wind blows and lightning flashes and hail falls and so on and so forth.

"On the Way to the Mission"

An Indian trapper is stalked and killed by evil whites intent on stealing what they think is a pack of furs but which—Holy O. Henry!—actually turns out to be the corpse of the dead Indian's wife, which he was carrying to the mission cemetery to be buried. The poem is a kind of "two dead Indians for the price of one" affair.

Honourable Mention in the Bad Poem Category: In addition to his celebrated dead Indian laments, Duncan Campbell Scott's oeuvre also contains a poem entitled "Dirge for a Violet." That's right, a dirge for a violet. It begins: "Here was a happy flower / Born in sun and shower." (P.S. The flower dies.)

Here is a statement of principle by Scott in 1914 on the issue of outstanding Native land claims:

> The Indian in himself had no title to the soil demanding recognition, nor, in his inferior position as a savage, had he any rights which could become the subject of treaty or negotiation.

This from the senior bureaucrat in the Department of Indian Affairs. It was kind of like putting a Ku Klux Klan Grand Dragon in charge of the National Association for the Advancement of Coloured People. (Although, in fairness, historians such as J. L. Granatstein have argued that Scott was in fact "more enlightened" than most, which is a scary thought indeed.)

Scott was an archetypal Canadian figure. As a bureaucrat and a poet, he built his career—both politically and artistically—on the hardships of the Indian. More than any other figure, he epitomizes Canada's approach to Native people: sentimental, self-righteous and utterly, utterly ruthless.

Assimilation was the objective. Assimilation was the reward. Assimilation was official government policy. Only problem was, assimilation didn't work. Native culture proved to be remarkably resilient. Not only did the Noble Indian refuse to vanish (poetically or otherwise), but the population actually began, slowly, to stabilize and then increase.

Rather than step back and reconsider the assumptions it was working under, the government decided instead to step up the campaign. The nation's resolve hardened. Throughout the 1920s, the Department of Indian Affairs tightened reserve regulations, apparently trying to make segregation so degrading that the Indians would one day just up and assimilate en masse. New rules came into effect, many of them from the pen of our beloved poet. Indians were barred from making legal claims against the government and were not allowed to leave reserve property without a pass. What is this if not apartheid? (Incredibly, the rule requiring Indians to get permission to leave the reserve was not rescinded until 1951.)

The crusades of the 1920s were relentless, and Scott had a few more poetic devices up his sleeve: voluntary enfranchisement was now enforced at will, and Indians living off reserve were forbidden to form support organizations. The darkest war waged, however, was not over legalities but over children.

Anglican and Catholic Church leaders at the turn of the century, dismayed by the slow "Christianization" of the Indians, pressured the federal government to set up residential schools where Indian children could be taken away and "civilized." Thus, with the full support of mainstream Canadian society, the state began kidnapping children.

The residential school system was started before Scott arrived on the scene, but he continued the policy with great enthusiasm. Children in these schools were routinely beaten for such crimes as speaking their Native language or following any of their tribal customs. Their culture was mocked, trivialized and outlawed. Residential schools traumatized three generations of Native Canadians, and this state-sponsored experiment in behaviour modification was not a product of some distant Dark Age; the last residential school shut its doors in 1969.

The damage those schools did to the social structure of Native society is beyond belief, and many of today's problems can be traced directly back to them. Substance abuse, violence and loss of self-esteem carry their own momentum from generation to generation.

The Native community had barely caught its breath when a new assault began. Again, it was directed at children, and again it involved state-sponsored kidnappings. This policy of legal child-snatching has been called the "Sixties Scoop," after the decade when it began, but in fact it lasted well into the 1980s. In *The First Canadians*, Pauline Comeau and Aldo Santin write:

> During a twenty-year period from the early 1960s to the 1980s, many Indian communities across Canada lost an entire generation of children to the custody of provincial child welfare agencies. Professional workers, claiming to be acting in the best interests of the children, simply scooped them up and took them away. Parents never saw their children again. These children grew into troubled teens and adults . . . Most of these children have turned to alcohol and drug abuse, many remain in psychiatric institutions and prisons, and many more chose suicide as their escape.

The First Nations have now withstood more than 160 years of overt "social engineering." What does that do to a society, to a culture? Phil Fontaine, the current head of the Assembly of First Nations, was sexually and physically abused as a child in a government residential school, and he has spent 40 years trying to come to terms with his mistreatment. More than 250 lawsuits are pending over the abuse suffered by Native children in government institutions. Where are the mass rallies in support of these complainants? Where are the protestors? If history is accumulated memory, what does this lack of public support say about our collective, selective amnesia?

In Canada, it is not the victims but the abusers who suffer from "repressed memory syndrome." *What we choose to forget is just as revealing as what we choose to remember.* Native Canadians live out their history every day of their lives; it is the rest of us who have conveniently forgotten the past.

Pop Quiz: When were Native Canadians given the right to vote?

(a) 1930, (b) 1940, or (c) 1950

Answer: (d) None of the above.

Native Canadians were not allowed to vote until 1960. At the provincial level, some areas had granted the vote earlier, but Alberta held out until 1965, and Québec until 1969—at about the same time French-Canadian nationalists were in a rage over being "oppressed" and had taken to calling themselves "the white niggers of America." That must have really cracked up the Natives living in Québec at the time.

When Canada celebrated its glorious centennial, and Montréal staged its glorious Expo 67, Native Canadians were still not allowed to vote in *la belle province.* This is a fact worth remembering.

In 1969, the federal government made another attempt at full-scale, forced assimilation. Acting on Prime Minister Pierre Trudeau's directives, a fresh young

Minister of Indian Affairs by the name of Jean Chrétien submitted a 13-page White Paper on Indian Policy. Chrétien had drafted this proposal after careful, in-depth discussions with exactly zero (o) Native groups.

The White Paper of 1969 was simply Scott's Final Solution given an extra little push. It proposed minimizing all previous treaties, disbanding all reserves, and ending any special recognition of Native people. Not surprisingly, the proposal caused such a storm of protest that it was withdrawn the following year. Natives approached the 1969 White Paper with hostility, not because they wished to remain pathetic wards of the state—as some neo-conservatives still insist—but because they understood full well that to protect their culture they needed a land base. (Québec is the example of this fact *par excellence.*)

Even then, the logic behind the White Paper defied both common sense and empirical evidence. The 1969 White Paper saw reserves and special status for Natives as being the *cause* of racism and social problems, not a symptom. In recent years, this type of thinking has come to be called "blaming the victim." The government argued that by stripping Natives of legal protection and moving them into city centres, it could end all of their woes in one fell swoop. And why not? After all, these were Natives in the abstract who were being discussed, people without a past. Unfortunately, as a survey of any downtown city core in Canada will reveal, there are thousands of Indians who, in spite of being "freed" of their special status and "freed" from reserves, are still marginalized, still ghettoized, still discriminated against. Blaming reserves is a red herring. Native people *by their very presence* challenge our notions of ownership. It is not the First Nations who have to change their way of thinking.

So when did the government finally admit defeat and strike assimilation as the explicit goal of the Indian Act? Was it in 1969, in the wake of the ill-advised White Paper? No. Not even close. Enfranchisement, the dream that the Indians would someday voluntarily vanish, was not removed as the stated objective of federal Native policy until 1985. That's right, *1985*—three years after we got our shiny new Trudeau-sponsored constitution, three years after the Canadian Charter of Rights and Freedoms was enacted. Only then was the spectre of assimilation finally officially removed.

In Canada today, there are roughly 1 million people of Aboriginal descent: Native, Inuit and Métis. Of these, more than 600,000 are legally recognized as status Indians, and of these more than 300,000 live on reserves. These reserves, owned by the federal government, are scattered across the country. They range in size from wide expanses of land covering thousands of acres to small plots of sod. It is from these far-flung, shattered remnants of Native territory that the First Nations are launching their counterattack.

What began as apartheid has been neatly subverted. Reserves, established as a tool of assimilation, have backfired. Instead of extinguishing "the Indian problem," they have instead given the First Nations both a focus and a power base from which to work. The irony is sweet and the justice is poetic, though I doubt that Duncan Campbell Scott would agree.

Scott, after all, was the perfect embodiment of the contradictory impulses Canadians have felt towards the First Nations down through the years: the Poetic vs. the Bureaucratic, the Romantic vs. the Legalistic. Or, in contemporary terms, New Age Spiritual Bunk vs. the Neo-Conservative Backlash. The common thread is the conviction that the Native community is doomed. On this the poets and the bureaucrats, the neo-conservatives and the romantics, implicitly agree. Neither side approaches Native culture with a vision of the future. It is not the present that they wish to capture, but the past. On both ends of the political spectrum, Natives are considered to be innocent, naive or spoiled. In other words, children. Not adults, and certainly not members of a modern culture.

In *Narrow Vision*, E. Brian Titley comments on how Duncan Campbell Scott-the-Bureaucrat "saw the Indians as primitive, childlike creatures in constant need of the paternal care of the government." At the same time, as critic John Flood points out, Scott-the-Poet depicts Natives who are "invariably caricatured as drunken, stupid, or 'pagan.' "

These two views reinforce rather than contradict each other. In his study *The Imaginary Indian*, historian Daniel Francis calls Duncan Campbell Scott "a patronizing bully," which, in its way, is an apt summation of the approach that Canada has always taken towards the First Nations.

Conservatives who only a few generations ago would have argued in favour of reserves are now dead set against them. Indeed, today's neo-conservatives consider reserves repugnant and racist, describing them as "a system of apartheid." Their proposed solution? Reserves need to be disassembled and treaties revoked in order to—you guessed it—assimilate the Native population. You have to give the neo-conservatives credit if only for their stubborn refusal to learn from history.

Native Canadians are not going to go away quietly. They are not going to vanish. They are not going to assimilate. And they are not going to give up. Far from being doomed, the First Nations are, in fact, in the middle of a cultural, artistic and political renaissance. Reserves may be the remnants of apartheid, but they are now also a crucial key to the First Nations' revival.

The reserve system itself can be transformed, opening the door for the devolution of power, for self-government and economic investment, for developing an infrastructure, for giving control over Native lands back to the Natives. The accusation that reserves represent some bizarre sort of self-inflicted apartheid on the part of the First Nations is incorrect.

In an article entitled "Native History, Native Claims, and Self-Determination," former justice Thomas Berger had this to say:

> At times it is suggested that native claims are based on the idea of apartheid. This suggestion misses the whole point of native demands. In South Africa the blacks [were] confined to "homelands," without any right to citizenship in South Africa itself and without any right to live, work, or own property . . . The native people in Canada are seeking access to the social, economic, and political institutions of the dominant society. What they are seeking is the exact opposite of apartheid. Only if we denied them that access could it be said that we are guilty of apartheid.

With the creation in 1999 of Nunavut, a self-governing Inuit majority territory in Canada's Arctic, the bar has been raised even higher. Aboriginal people are no longer fighting a rearguard action aimed at mere survival; they are now on the offensive, and their opponents (political indifference, bureaucratic red tape, latent racism) are now on the run.

A backlash, therefore, is almost inevitable. In *Our Home or Native Land?*, Melvin Smith, a hero among neo-conservatives and a bogey man to the politically correct, has hit a raw nerve with his tireless chronicling of government waste in what he calls "the Indian Industry," Canada's multimillion-dollar circus of negotiators, lawyers, spokesmen and government expense accounts.

As Smith points out, at least $40 billion has been spent over the last 20 years trying to end the inequality between Natives and whites. And to what effect? You've heard about the U.S. Pentagon and its $400 hammers and $2,000 toilet seats? Well, in Canada the equivalent was the Department of Indian Affairs and Northern Development. DIAND was the black hole of government departments, sucking in billions and billions of dollars, to little—or worse, harmful—effect. Of course, the easiest thing in the world is to spend other people's money, and DIAND pretty much had carte blanche to slather cash wherever it felt necessary. The department has been described by Smith as "the world's most expensive collective guilt trip." (DIAND has since been renamed INAC, Indian and Northern Affairs Canada, with a shift in emphasis towards establishing self-government and promoting economic development. Whether the change in acronyms will make any real difference remains to be seen.)

With Ottawa continuing to act as judge, jury and adversary—and remaining blithely immune to charges of conflict of interest—the government of Canada can effectively smother Native land claims with whipped cream and bullshit. Specific and comprehensive claims alike get bogged down in paperwork and are often tossed out on the pettiest of technicalities. The process consumes money, time and resources. And, as a 1990 Canadian Human Rights Commission report noted, it is a process "heavily weighted in favour of the government." Journalists Geoffrey York and Loreen Pindera, in *People of the Pines*, make a similar observation: "Federal officials admit that hundreds of Indian claims are morally valid, yet they are rejected for narrow technical reasons."

It is true that some Native claims have been absurd. One band made up of 850 people wanted the entire city of Vancouver, where almost 2 million people are apparently living as squatters. (According to some estimates, if all competing overlapping claims in B.C. were awarded, the total would amount to 111 per cent of the province's land area.) But fixating on these excesses is simply another case of argument by misdirection. It is always easy to target a movement's lunatic fringe, and it is never hard to find examples of waste and graft in a government department. Much more difficult to grapple with are the moral and historical claims Native Canadians make on our national conscience.

In fairness to Melvin Smith, who is all too often portrayed as some kind of villain, the arguments he makes are reasonable—*as long as they are taken out of social and historical context.* In many ways, Smith and other neo-conservatives are simply the champions of lofty Enlightenment ideals. These ideals, stark and clean and straightforward, can be very compelling. Why should we have special rights for one group of citizens? Why shouldn't Indians be treated just like everyone else? These are logical enough arguments—in the abstract. But they do not fit the murky, muddy world in which we live. Native Canadians are asking for distinct status because they are entitled to it legally and historically. Native claims and Native rights are a legal and moral issue, not a racial one. There are now more than 350 specific land claims either dragging their way slowly through the courts or "under review."

To my mind, the best analogy here is the gold held by Swiss banks after the Nazi Holocaust. (I am not comparing Canadians to Nazis, but rather to the Swiss, who profited handsomely from the hardships of others.) No moral person would dream of arguing that the gold hoarded by the Swiss, the gold that belonged to Jews who perished under the Nazi regime, should remain in Swiss possession. The ancestors of those victims are entitled to compensation; they have a legitimate and outstanding legal claim. The Jews who demand that the Swiss release these profits are not arguing that they deserve payment merely because they are Jewish, but because justice has not been served. The issues are legal and moral ones. In a similar vein, no one is saying that Natives should be awarded certain rights just because they are Indians. No. It is because legally, historically and morally, they are entitled to them.

This is why I have never been able to understand the vehement opposition of Canada's neo-conservatives to Native land claims. These claims are essentially about property rights, something very dear to the hearts of neo-conservatives. Property rights and government abuse: aren't these the issues that neo-conservatives usually rally around?

The other complaint one occasionally encounters, more of bleat really, is that the First Nations are living in the past. "They can't go back to hunting buffalo and living in teepees, you know." Well, we can't ride down Yonge Street in horse-drawn buggies, either. With the exception of a few Amish communities, we are all citizens of the modern age. Native land claims have never been about retreating to the past. They have always been about reclaiming the future.

Melvin Smith is not entirely unreasonable when it comes to Native rights. He proposes giving Native groups ownership of their reserves but balks at further outstanding claims. He also argues in favour of self-government on a municipal level. But the First Nations want more. They want Canadians to acknowledge their prior legal and moral rights, and to recognize Native self-government as a "third order," on par with the provinces. The question is no longer whether Native self-government will be granted—it will; the tide has already turned—but which model will be used. The principle has been won. Only the details need to be hammered out.

And the devil, as they say, is in the details.

In 1987, the chief of the Peguis band north of Winnipeg invited the South African ambassador to Canada to visit his reserve. This visit took place at the height of anti-apartheid protests around the world, and the gesture was meant (a) to embarrass the Canadian government (which it did), and (b) to make Canadians more aware of their own treatment of Aboriginal peoples (which it didn't). Indeed, that same year, 1987, Brian Mulroney unveiled the proposed Meech Lake Accord, aimed at giving Quebeckers "distinct society" status within the constitution. It was a stunning display of cultural myopia. Native Canadians were not included in the accord, which Mulroney and the provincial premiers presented at their triumphant news conference as "a breakthrough in the relations between Canada's *two* founding nations, French and English." [Emphasis added.]

The exclusion of the First Nations from the formula was not overlooked by Aboriginal activists. There was an immediate outcry from Native Canadians, and the government frantically tried to reassure them that Meech Lake was nothing more than a gesture towards Québec, a way of achieving national harmony and defusing separatism. But Native Canadians know first-hand, and all too well, the long-term ramifications of seemingly innocuous treaties and "accords." Their anger didn't abate. (For the record, I do not believe that *any* ethnic, racial or geographic group should be given "distinct society" status in our constitution. However, if we are going to start dishing out special rights, surely the First Nations are at the front of the line, not Québec.)

Meech Lake was just the latest in a long line of policies designed without Native consent or input, going back to 1763. But this time, things were different. Natives now had the vote, and they had learned to use legislative power to their advantage. Most importantly, a Native Canadian had been elected to a minor but critical provincial riding. And the entire Canadian political landscape was about to go topsy-turvy.

The deadline set for passing the Meech Lake Accord was June 23, 1990. There was just one small flaw in the scheme: all 10 provinces had to pass it before the deadline, or the accord would expire. Eight of the 10 provinces had ratified Meech Lake by the time Manitoba brought it forward for final debate. With a majority backing in the province's legislature, the accord would probably have passed—if it had ever been tabled. However, legislative procedure required a unanimous, perfunctory approval to bring the accord forward. This approval should have been granted simply as a matter of course, but there was one factor no one had counted on: an MLA by the name of Elijah Harper, a 41-year-old Cree from northern Manitoba. When called upon to give the unanimity necessary to begin debate, he said, simply, "No, Mr. Speaker."

And everything ground to a halt. The entire Canadian political machine came to a standstill.

Elijah Harper was asked eight more times over the next 10 days, and every time he answered, "No." "Never in Canadian history," wrote Pauline Comeau in an article in *The Canadian Forum*, "has a single word carried so much political weight."

In response to Harper's one-man blockade, Newfoundland followed suit, refusing to table the bill at all. The Meech Lake Accord died, and Québec was once again humiliated to the point of apoplexy. The separatists-in-Conservative-clothing had fled Mulroney's cabinet, Canada was again on the brink of breakup, and the prime minister's career was effectively over (though he lingered like a bad chest cold for three more years). All because of one disgruntled Indian.

Contrary to Québec's nationalist mythology, Meech Lake failed not because French-Canadian aspirations were rejected by evil Anglos, but because prior Native claims hadn't been acknowledged. Meech died because it had not included Canada's Third Solitude in its formula.

I was visiting a friend at the University of Calgary on the day that the Meech Lake Accord died. After all the noise and commotion, there came a vacuum. An odd silence settled. People looked around, dazed, as if having woken up from an especially comfortable dream. In the campus cafeteria a small hushed crowd watched the newscasts recount the story again and again, the volume so low it was almost a whisper.

Suddenly, in a loud voice, someone at the back declared, "They never should have given those damn Indians the vote!"

Startled, we turned to see who had spoken, and there, grinning back at us, was a Native student trying his damnedest not to laugh.

Verdict

Duncan Campbell Scott (the Poet): **Bonehead**

Duncan Campbell Scott (the Bureaucrat): **Bastard**

Elijah Harper (the MLA): **Bastard**

12

Holocausts:
Canada's Contribution to the Genocide

I WENT TO A "Jewish university." Which is to say, a university that made room for Jewish customs and culture. Which is to say, a university where you not only got Christmas off, but Yom Kippur as well. That was the good news. The bad news? The university in question was York.

York is an Ode to Cement, built back in those heady, carefree days of the early 1970s when concrete was king. The campus is located on the windblown tundra north of Toronto, far from civilization and transit lines. I don't blame the Jews for this. "We are a wandering people," my roommate said. "And at York you can see us wandering. Wandering to try and find something to do. Wandering to try and find a bus. Wandering."

York University, we were told, was all about choice. A progressive place where one could choose between, say, horrible tasteless cafeteria food on the one hand, and horrible tasteless *kosher* cafeteria food on the other. When I was there, it was also the most crowded campus in Canada.

What I am leading up to is simply this: there was something about York that engendered arguments, or, if no one got punched, "debates." It was either a dynamic campus or a volatile one, depending on your point of view, both a politically correct heartland *and* a bastion of Ayn Rand capitalists.

I was shoving my way through the gridlock of bodies wedged into the university's central square one day when I passed an information desk and a large banner that read "Holocaust Awareness Week." Sure enough, it was sponsored by the JSA (Jewish Students Association), the same fun-loving bunch who had given us—this is true—Death Awareness Week. Death, mind you. Is there anyone not aware of this? Were the other students cutting through the square looking up and saying, "Hey, *death*. You know, I never thought about it before."?

Death Awareness Week had sported a big banner as well, along with a motivational slogan: "To Know Death Is to Know Life." I had stopped and asked the person behind the table what this motto was supposed to mean and whether it was such a good slogan to promote, considering the high rate of suicide among Canadian university students.

"Well," she said, "to know death is to know life."

"How's that?" I wanted to know.

"Well, when you know death, you will know life."

"But what does that mean? It makes no sense whatsoever."

She made a noise, kind of halfway between a sigh and a growl, and I decided to peruse the display on my own. I soon discovered that it wasn't really about death, it was about *Jewish* death: funeral rites, rituals, prayers and so on. But I never did figure out that slogan.

So here I was, once again presented with a project by the York JSA: Holocaust Awareness Week. Remember, this was on a largely Jewish campus; you would be hard pressed to find anyone who *wasn't* aware of the Holocaust. It would be like having Crucifix Awareness Week at a convent.

There must be more to this, I decided, and I approached a young man standing behind the information table.

"Which holocaust?" I wanted to know.

"What?"

"Which holocaust?" I wasn't being coy. I was quite serious. Did they mean the Beothuk of Newfoundland, who were completely wiped off the face of the earth, or perhaps the Indians of Guatemala, who were facing a full-scale attempt at genocide *as we spoke*? Or the Turkish mass slaughter of more than a million Armenians? Or the 1.5 million people executed in Cambodia by the Khmer Rouge? The killing fields of Cambodia stopped only when the country was liberated, not by Western democracies but by the Communists of Vietnam, Cambodia's long-time enemy. The mountains of skulls in Cambodia surely count as a holocaust. And unlike the Nazi Party, the Khmer Rouge were, at that time, a very real political entity, just a whisper away from regaining power. So again, *which* holocaust?

His eyes narrowed and he said sharply, "*The* Holocaust."

"But this is York," I protested. "If you want to enlighten the students, hold a Palestinian Awareness Week. Or better yet, hold Holocaust Awareness Week in Eckville, Alberta. Anywhere but here. What is there left for us to learn?"

You see, I still lived under the impression that the Nazi death camps occurred on another continent, that Canada was uninvolved. Certainly, living on campus, I had gotten awfully tired of hearing about the Holocaust; it was always presented as though I should somehow feel guilty for what the Nazis did. But why should Canadians accept any responsibility for what happened in Germany more than 50 years ago? Didn't we help kick butt and free the Jews from the concentration camps? I mean, shouldn't Canada's Jewish population be, well, *grateful*?

It seemed to me that Jewish Canadians had a different memory of the war years than the rest of us. Once again, history seemed less crisp than I would have liked. And once again, I found I had much to learn.

Fascism in Canada predates the rise of Hitler. When Mussolini took power in Italy, he was hailed as a saviour by the Pope and was greatly admired in Canada. And when the Nazis gained control of Germany, they too were cheered by fascist groups around the world, including those of the Great White North. Hitler didn't invent anti-Semitism, he simply pandered to it. The Nazis were *elected* on a promise of state-enshrined persecution of Jews and Gypsies. (Jews and Gypsies were held in the same contempt. But, unlike the Gypsies, the Jews had the impolite habit of opening businesses and settling down.)

Canada was especially susceptible to the fascist call, and nowhere was this more true than in Québec. There, it fed on the racial ultranationalism of Abbé Groulx and other fascist sympathizers. Heralded by some as "the spiritual father of modern Québec," Groulx today causes difficulties among the French-Canadian intelligentsia who don't know whether to deify him or disown him. It should also be noted that the battle cry *"Achat chez nous!"* (similar in sentiment to the later slogan "Masters in our own home") began as an anti-Semitic slogan. Indeed, today's separatist cry, *"Québec pour le Québécois!"*, is an unsettling echo of the motto of English-Canadian fascists, "Canada for Canadians."

Jews were portrayed as demonic world destroyers, responsible for everything from high prices to the French Revolution. Across Canada, rage against this powerful Jewish conspiracy was vented on such diabolical figures as Jewish children, Jewish shopkeepers and Jewish families picnicking on public beaches. This worldwide conspiracy had to be stopped somehow, you see. First public beaches, and next thing you know, they would own the planet.

In Québec, these views were not presented from the fringes but grew directly out of church doctrine. The Catholic Church labelled Jews as Christ-killers and applauded Hitler's persecutions. In 1936, the Catholic daily newspaper *L'Action Catholique* declared that Hitler must be recognized for the "merit of snatching his country from the Communists by placing his iron fist on the elements of disorder that were, all too often, both in Germany and in Russia, the Jews."

The profound anti-Semitism of the Catholic Church is all too well documented. One could fill volumes with passages such as that above, together with similar xenophobic thoughts of nationalists like Abbé Groulx. These sentiments certainly paved the way for Adrien Arcand.

Adrien Arcand was Québec's self-proclaimed Fuhrer-in-waiting. He was a media star in his day, with his thin little moustache and beady dictator's eyes. His Nazi-style party churned out anti-Jewish hate "literature" and held mass meetings that featured Arcand screaming wildly in what he hoped was a Hitleresque fashion. Party members donned uniforms, drilled and dreamed of the day they would march on Ottawa—or even better, be elected. Their symbol: a swastika wreathed in maple leaves and topped by a beaver. Arcand soon had a growing list of disciples, most notably an impressionable young man named Ernst Zündel, who later credited Arcand with bringing "order into my confused mind." Arcand took Zündel under his wing and became his mentor; the Nazi gave rise to the neo-Nazi.

The thirties were Arcand's glory days. The *Globe and Mail* called him a "brilliant young French Canadian," *Maclean's* called him "a passionate fighter," and *Life* did a picture story on Arcand that described him as "tall [and] good-looking." All the while, Arcand railed at "the exploitation, thievery, perfidy, immorality, filth, corruption and bolshevik propaganda of the sons of Judas."

The respected newspaper *Le Devoir*, under the guidance of Georges Pelletier, became—in the words of Dr. Lita-Rose Betcherman, author of *The Swastika and the Maple Leaf*—"intensely anti-Semitic." It began publishing inflammatory editorials that suggested, among other things, that Jews in Canada be deported because they were a race "that refused to be assimilated." This from a French-Canadian nationalist, mind you.

In 1939, long after Hitler's pogroms of terror were underway, and long after Kristallnacht, the night when the windows of Jewish houses and stores were shattered, synagogues gutted, and Jews publicly assaulted and killed on the streets of Germany, and long after hundreds of Jewish families had already been sent to concentration camps—after all of this, the St. Jean Baptiste Society, that proud defender of French-Canadian rights, could take no more. They presented the Canadian government with a petition signed by 127,364 people to "protest vigorously against"—*what?* Nazi atrocities? Government inaction? No. "To protest vigorously against immigration of any kind whatever and especially against Jewish immigration."

Apparently, the St. Jean Baptiste boys had forgotten that John the Baptist, their patriarch, was Jewish. Should ol' St. John have shown up at Canada's gates, the St. Jean Baptiste Society would have hustled him right back to the Nazis.

English-Canadian nativist attitudes (*nativism* being an especially nasty mix of nationalism and racial ideology) were equally entrenched. Although they lacked the aura of respectability that the Catholic Church bestowed on French-Canadian fascists, the English, by virtue of their majority and access to policy, were far more effective. Canada was still a British country, Canadians were British citizens, and the government was determined to keep it that way.

Notorious "desirability lists" were in effect from the 1920s right through to 1948. The most desirable immigrants were, of course, British. If we couldn't fill our quota with them, our preferences, in descending order, were for Germans, Scandinavians and the Dutch. Then the French. These were Canada's Chosen Races. (Sound familiar? Hint: Think Hitler.) After these nationalities came Eastern Europeans. Then Asians. Then Blacks.

The Jews were a problem. They were, of course, "not desirable," but the difficulty was that there were German Jews, Scandinavian Jews, Spanish Jews, Polish Jews, even—God forbid—British Jews. So an exception had to be made. Other than British-born Jews, whom Canada would grudgingly accept, Jewish refugees, regardless of nationality or language, fell into a category called "Special Permit," meaning that each application was individually examined by immigration officials before being rejected.

Historians often blame the Depression for these racial exclusions, citing "economic uncertainty," which sounds a lot better than "racist ideology." But these regulations were in fact introduced *before* the Depression, in the boom days of the 1920s, and stayed in effect throughout the war, long after the Depression had ended.

The result of these various currents in Canadian society was a closed-door policy for Jewish refugees. Just when Jews most needed sanctuary from the forces of Nazism, sanctuary was denied. And the man given responsibility for keeping them out of Canada was a bureaucratic little reptile by the name of Frederick Charles Blair.

Blair was proud of the number of Jews he turned away. He saw himself as a loyal civil servant playing by the book. He didn't trust Jews, he didn't like Jews, and he showed a singular lack of compassion in dealing with their requests for asylum. When Jewish groups in Canada pledged to pay passage for, and then financially support, any refugees brought in, Blair accused them of lying. He never bothered to put their offer to the test. When he was begged on humanitarian grounds to allow in at least the most desperate cases, he refused, saying that if he opened the door a crack, others would try to squeeze in as well. When he was asked to accept orphans, he refused on the grounds that the children were probably not really orphans and would later use their position in Canada to try to get their parents in.

Lower-income Jewish refugees were rejected ostensibly because they would be a drain (even though the Canadian Jewish Congress had vowed to fully support them), and wealthy Jewish refugees were rejected because they would be competition for Canadian businessmen. Instead, Jews were kept in Europe, where their money enriched Nazi coffers and their bones enriched the fields of Auschwitz. Canada rejected not only Jewish millionaires with money to invest and rabbis marked for certain death, it also rejected well-educated, established businessmen, academics and scientists. One Canadian immigration officer in Europe watched in helpless rage as hundreds of Jewish refugees he had cleared for entry to Canada were systematically dismissed by the "Blair Blockade." They were later rounded up by the Germans and executed.

Canada was, in effect, aiding and abetting the Holocaust.

It is important to separate *anti-fascism* from *anti-racism* in Canada. Once Hitler became our enemy, he was hated, but that hatred had nothing to do with his persecution of the Jews. Even as we were marching off to war, anti-Semitism was gaining ground in Canada. Betcherman writes, "It might have been supposed that, in the anti-Nazi temper of the times, anti-Semitism would decline. But this was not so. Far from receding, it was actually growing."

Adrien Arcand and other fascist leaders in Canada were thrown into jail, but only after we were at war. Again, as Betcherman points out, "The fascist movement in Canada was suppressed, not out of any moral repugnance, but because Germany had become the enemy." At one point early on, when the Nazis were still willing to extradite Jews, they had offered to send as many Jewish refugees as any nation was willing to accept. There were no takers, and Hitler realized then that he could act with impunity.

"Nazi Germany," said Hitler, "places greater emphasis upon race than upon citizenship." Oh, wait. I'm sorry, that should read, "*Canada* places greater emphasis upon race than upon citizenship." And it wasn't Hitler who said that, it was our old friend Frederick Blair, in a 1941 wartime statement of immigration policy.

Canada may have boldly signed the 1942 Allied Declaration condemning Nazi war crimes, but when the chance to rescue thousands of Jewish children suddenly arose by way of an offer from the puppet-regime of Vichy France, nothing was done. Although Canada had earlier taken in thousands of Protestant British children and found good homes for them, Blair would not even admit that Jewish children were in danger. Again, the Canadian Jewish Congress guaranteed to sponsor any arrivals. Again, Canada did nothing.

And again, people perished.

As late as December 1943, there was still a chance to get 6,000 children out of France before the Gestapo arrived. The U.S. offered 4,000 open visas and asked Canada to take 1,000 of them. Canada never replied. Our country could proudly say that it had saved not a single child from the gas chambers, even when the opportunity to do so was presented. When Blair retired in 1943, the Nazi death camps were working overtime. In a moving ceremony, the Canadian government presented Blair with the highest award ever bestowed on a civil servant, "for meritorious service to the country." It didn't say which country.

Was Blair a war criminal? This is a hard question to answer. On the surface, of course, he was not. He broke no laws. He was just following orders. He was merely enforcing regulations. That he did it with such enthusiasm can't be held against him. Or can it? Blair, the cold, legalistic, career bureaucrat was, in the words of Valerie Knowles, author of *Strangers at Our Gates*, "the perfect instrument of the government's anti-immigration policy."

But while it would be nice to heap the blame solely on Blair, he was neither a rogue nor an anomaly. He was faithfully carrying out the policies of Prime Minister Mackenzie King, who wanted "to keep this part of the Continent free from unrest and from too great an intermixture of foreign strains of blood."

In German territories, Jews were being sent to concentration camps and synagogues were being destroyed. Mackenzie King, marshalling all of his moral fortitude, decided that the time had come for his government to do—*nothing*. Jews would not be allowed into Canada. When pressed further, King said the issue was really a federal/provincial matter, and he would look into it. The main thing, said King, was to avoid the sort of social strife that might follow in Canada should he allow in Jewish immigrants. (This, remember, is the man that a 1997 *Maclean's* panel ranked as "our greatest prime minister ever"!)

MacKenzie King is, without a doubt, the single most overrated politician in Canadian history. We have confused longevity with greatness. He was a cunning man. He was by no means a great man. Thousands of Jews who later perished in the ovens of Europe were turned away during King's Reign of Blandness.

Even then, it must be noted that King—who had a weather vane where most people have a heart—was merely responding to the mood of the time. In the few instances where the government did allow in Jewish refugees, the Canadian public raised a huge outcry. Québec premier and fascist supporter Maurice Duplessis ranted about an international Zionist conspiracy, and the newspapers of the day denounced any move to accept Jewish refugees. King's policy of exclusion was accepted, indeed *demanded*, by the nation. As historians Irving Abella and Harold Troper write in their book *None Is Too Many*,

> The Jews of Europe were not so much trapped in a whirlwind of systematic mass murder as they were abandoned to it. The Nazis planned and executed the Holocaust, but it was made possible by an indifference to the suffering of the victims which sometimes bordered on contempt.

Canadians can't even take comfort in assurances that we weren't as bad as some countries. The opposite is true. No other Western nation barred its doors as firmly. During the 12 years that the Nazis ran rampant (1933-45), the United States allowed 200,000 Jewish refugees to enter. The United Kingdom took in 195,000, of whom

125,000 were rerouted to British-held Palestine. Argentina gave asylum to 50,000. Brazil, 27,000. And Canada, a sparsely inhabited nation in need of skilled crafts-people, investment and immigrants? Canada allowed in fewer than 5,000 refugees. Our regulations aimed at keeping Jews out were, in the words of Abella and Troper, "probably the most stringent in the world."

In 1946, just a year after the Nazis had been defeated, a Gallup Poll asked the fol-lowing question: "If Canada does allow more immigrants are there any of these na-tionalities [a list was provided] that you would like to keep out?" The results of the poll indicated that the least desirable potential immigrants were the Japanese. Fair enough; we had just finished fighting a war against Japan, and emotions were still running high. So next on the list should be the Germans, right? After all, we had been fighting the Nazis for six straight years. But no; second on the list of undesir-able groups were Jews. The government of Canada still insisted on keeping them out, and the public agreed.

Jews may have been unwelcome, but gosh, not Nazi war criminals. Canada was a haven for Nazis after the war. The 1986 Deschênes Commission on War Criminals confirmed this. Hundreds of possible war criminals living in Canada were known to Ottawa, but until the late 1990s not a single case was brought for-ward for prosecution. Estimates of the number of Nazis who entered Canada after the war range as high as 6,000—more than the total number of Jewish refugees al-lowed in during the Nazi era. Ironic, wouldn't you say?

Canada did not fight Hitler because of his racist, relentless persecution of the Jews. We fought him because we had to. Had Hitler not forced our hands, Canada and the other Western democracies would have continued hemming and hawing and writing memos until Hitler had stuffed every last Jew into an oven. We are not nearly as noble as we like to think we are. It is only in retrospect that we be-came champions of morality, a notion based on an invalid syllogism: (a) the Nazis were evil, (b) we defeated the Nazis, therefore (c) we must have been pure and righteous.

Don't misunderstand me—the thousands upon thousands of Canadians who gave their lives fighting the Axis powers were very brave, and they deserve to be ho-noured. Canadian troops fought hard and long against an empire recognized as evil. But we saw it as evil because it was aggressive, not because it was xenophobic. Let's at least be honest about our past.

Judaism contains 613 Commandments. (Christians have the *Reader's Digest* ver-sion; the Top Ten, so to speak.) A 614th Commandment was added in 1968 by the Jewish theologian Emil Fackenheim: "We must not grant posthumous victories to Hitler." I think of the systematic mass murders that decimated the population of Cambodia under the reign of Pol Pot; those deaths are another victory for

Hitler. Like the question of the tolling bell, so often quoted and so seldom understood, the question "Which holocaust?" cannot be answered. There is only one; it repeats itself in various forms. It is the holocaust of indifference, and amnesia allows its return.

I think also of another refugee crisis, in 1979, when thousands of Vietnamese citizens were fleeing their homeland. Nation after nation rejected them, and flotillas of ships, barely afloat, waited in limbo. During the height of the crisis, historians Irving Abella and Harold Troper sent the Canadian Minister of Immigration a copy of *None Is Too Many* in manuscript form. With it they included a note: "We hope Canada will not be found wanting in this refugee crisis the way it was in the last."

Pressure to accept the Vietnamese "boat people" grew and grew. The government of Canada hesitated . . . and then swung open the gates. Church groups, volunteer organizations and private citizens rushed to sponsor refugees, and the federal government matched them sponsorship for sponsorship. Over 77,000 Indochinese refugees were given asylum in Canada during the late seventies and early eighties. Canada's contribution was second to none.

But if memory is to keep us honest, then let us remember another boat full of people seeking shelter. The year was 1939. The ocean liner *St. Louis* left Hamburg just ahead of the Gestapo. On board were 930 Jewish refugees. The Nazis had taken everything the refugees had: businesses, savings, homes, even citizenship. Cuba had granted them entrance visas, however, and they managed to escape. But their ship crossed the Atlantic only to be refused entry into Havana. The Cuban government had changed its mind and now refused to honour the visas, even as the passengers threatened to commit mass suicide.

The journey of the *St. Louis* became an odyssey: Argentina, Paraguay, Panama, Uruguay. No one would grant its passengers asylum. They sailed towards the United States, but the Americans sent a Coast Guard cutter to intercept them. The gunboat shadowed the *St. Louis* all the way to Canadian waters. Canada was now their very last hope, and they sent word, begging to be allowed entry.

Jewish groups in Canada were frantic as well. They repeated their pledge to sponsor any Jewish refugees allowed in. A telegram sent to Mackenzie King pleaded with the prime minister, asking him to show "Christian charity." But King, that paragon of manly virtue, passed the decision off to Blair, and Blair refused to grant entry. The refugees were turned away, the ship returned to Germany, and the voyage ended in cattle cars and crematoriums. It was another small contribution from Canada to the Holocaust.

Frederick Blair lost no sleep over his decision. After all, he said, "The line must be drawn somewhere."

Verdict

Adrien Arcand: **Vile Little Bonehead**

Frederick Blair and Mackenzie King: **Ice-cold Bastards** and (unintentional) Nazi collaborators

13

Refugee Camps:
The Saga of the
Japanese Canadians

"Let our slogan be for British Columbia: No Japs from the Rockies to the seas!"
—Ian Mackenzie, Canada's Minister of Pensions and Health, during a 1944 speech

FOR JAPANESE CANADIANS, the Second World War began long before Pearl Harbor and ended long after Hiroshima and Nagasaki.

From their arrival in Canada in the 1870s, the Japanese faced relentless racial hostility. The B.C. Asiatic Exclusion League was formed with the explicit intent of stopping all Oriental immigration to Canada, and in 1907 the league incited race riots in Vancouver under the battle cry of "Stand for White Canada!" The newspapers in Victoria and Vancouver warned of a Yellow Menace and declared, patriotically, "this province must be a white man's country."

In Canada, the Japanese settled almost exclusively on the west coast of British Columbia. Most lived within 70 miles of Vancouver, and the Powell Street ghetto of Little Tokyo became better known as "Japtown." Although denied the right to vote, Japanese Canadians were required to pay taxes, the principle of "No taxation without representation!" being lost on Canada. The registration and fingerprinting of Japanese Canadians, it should be noted, had already begun before the onset of the Pacific war. In history, context is everything, and it is against this backdrop of long-simmering racism that the events of World War II must be placed.

On December 7, 1941, Japan launched a surprise attack against the American naval base at Pearl Harbor. Within hours, bombs were falling on Hong Kong, and after a brutal, one-sided battle, the British colony fell. Hundreds of Canadian soldiers were taken prisoner, and the Japanese war machine continued to steamroll across Southeast Asia: Thailand, the Philippines, Indonesia, Guam, Singapore. The emperor's Imperial Army was unstoppable and had soon conquered half the Pacific. Along the way, the invaders were helped by so-called fifth columns: Japanese civilians who helped sabotage enemy defences. (At Hong Kong, civilians had cut wires, disabled equipment and worked as snipers for the advancing Imperial Army. The Canadian Forces barber turned out to be a Japanese mole.) Australia now lay within striking distance. Prior to the attack on Pearl Harbor, newspapers in Japan had confidently been predicting just such a landing: "North America must be invaded!"

In Canada, 38 suspect Japanese-Canadian citizens were rounded up and detained, and more than 1,000 fishing boats were seized. Japanese nationals were required to register with the Canadian government and take an oath of loyalty. (As were Italians and Germans in Canada during this period—their treatment was similar but much less dramatic. About 660 Germans were eventually interned, along with 480 Italians.)

It was known that Japan had been placing spies and possible saboteurs in North America for more than a decade. In 1932, a Japanese intelligence officer was sent to the West Coast specifically to gather information on local defences and to recruit "fifth-column" support from members of Japanese-Canadian and Japanese-American fishing crews. That he met with little success is beside the point. Hindsight is always 20-20, and at the time of the strike on Pearl Harbor, no one knew the extent, if any, of Japan's North American base.

Japanese submarines prowled the waters off California. A U.S. tanker was shelled and sunk. The Germans had wreaked havoc on the Atlantic Coast, and the fear—very real, though ultimately unfounded—was that Japan was about to unleash the same type of terror on the Pacific. In *The Enemy That Never Was*, historian Ken Adachi writes, "There was no invasion of Canadian soil, no landings from the sea or bombings from aircraft, nor was there any evidence that Japan ever seriously considered such enterprises." Perhaps. But none of this was known at the time.

Certainly, Japan *did* launch an Alaskan invasion with the explicit aim of striking at the North American mainland. On June 3, 1942, they attacked the U.S. naval base at Dutch Harbor. The battle raged for two days; 35 people were killed and 28 wounded. A few days later, the Japanese landed on the Aleutian islands of Kiska and Attu. It was the first time since 1812 that an enemy force had taken American territory. The Japanese managed to hold the islands for more than a year before Kiska was finally retaken following an intense U.S. naval bombardment, after which the Japanese abandoned Attu as well, falling back under cover of fog. When American and Canadian forces stormed ashore at Attu, they expected to wade into a high-pitched battle. Instead, they met only silence.

Japanese attacks on Alaskan territory may now seem like minor footnotes in his-

In the wake of their massive surprise attack on Pearl Harbor on December 7, 1941, the Japanese Imperial Forces swept across Southeast Asia and were soon within striking distance of Australia. Lost along the way was the British garrison at Hong Kong.

Although Winston Churchill was on record as stating that Hong Kong was "indefensible," the British High Command had earlier decided to add reinforcements anyway, as a token show of resistance. Thus, more than 1,900 Canadian soldiers were sent into the coming maelstrom, like lambs to the slaughter. Untried in combat, the Canadians arrived in Hong Kong just three weeks before the Japanese attacked. For them, the war would be short, sudden and brutal.

In a typhoon of steel, the battle-hardened Japanese army unleashed a withering attack on Hong Kong and quickly overran the main island. The British and Canadian troops fought back with a resolve and valour that took the Japanese by surprise. It was hand-to-hand combat and house-to-house raids. With their ammunition running low, the Canadians even managed to retake one hill with a bayonet charge. Amid the chaos and confusion, Sergeant Major John Osborn of the Winnipeg Grenadiers threw himself on a live grenade to save his men. (He was awarded a posthumous Victoria Cross for his actions.) One of the most powerful and poignant scenes of the battle took place that same day, when Canadian brigadier John Lawson, his pillbox surrounded, radioed to his superior officers that he was going outside "to fight it out." With a pistol in each hand, Lawson charged, guns blazing, into glory.

On Christmas Eve, 1941, the Canadian Royal Rifles launched a determined but desperate counterattack. They were mowed down, and the following day, the British governor formally surrendered. The victorious Japanese stormed a hospital, bayonetting wounded soldiers in their beds and ignoring flags of surrender. They raped and then murdered nurses. Many of the prisoners were tied up, tortured, shot in the back and tossed from the cliffs at Repulse Bay. Others were marched into captivity, where they were starved and beaten and forced into labour camps and coal mines. The Japanese POW camps had, by far, the worst record for atrocities and crimes against humanity. For the Canadians captured at Hong Kong, the real ordeal was just beginning.

The Japanese had signed the 1929 Geneva Convention concerning the treatment of POWs but had not ratified it—and they certainly did not take it seriously. Canadian servicemen held prisoner were starved and beaten, and they died by the score. Men were forced to eat rats, garbage and maggots to survive, and they suffered inhuman physical and emotional ordeals. As quoted in Daniel G. Dancocks's oral history of Canadian POWs, *In Enemy Hands*, one prisoner, a young private named Gordon Durrant, recalled, "After you were in there for a while, you got the idea that Canada never existed. After the years went on, you thought it was a dream, Canada was just a dream. It didn't exist. It couldn't exist. Canada and your life before was just a dream."

tory, but the intent behind them was not benign. The original plan was to enlarge the Japanese empire from Fiji to Alaska, covering a 1,600-kilometre arc of islands that formed a natural invasion route to North America—on maps, anyway. (The desolate climate of Alaska soon discouraged the scheme.)

On June 20, 1942, Japanese shells fell on Canadian territory when a submarine launched an attack on a wireless station and lighthouse on Vancouver Island. The Japanese went on to shell Santa Barbara, California, and points along the Oregon coast. They later sank two ships at the entrance of Juan de Fuca Strait. Again, these incidents seem inconsequential only in retrospect. No one knew then whether they were minor raids or the foreshadowing of worse to come. The war, after all, had begun with a massive surprise attack. In 1940, the Japanese government had held an Imperial conference which they invited loyal Japanese subjects from Manchuria, Southeast Asia and North America to attend. The Japanese in Canada sent an official delegation. Is it any wonder that their loyalties would later come under question?

Unfortunately, the RCMP's counter-intelligence was as inconsistent as it was unreliable. Some internal reports did indeed describe Japanese Canadians as posing "no threat," but others stated just the opposite. Unlike in the Italian and German communities, RCMP intelligence had failed to infiltrate. The fact was, no one knew whether Japanese Canadians were a risk or not. Some military advisors of the day declared the Japanese in Canada to be loyal citizens, others urged that extreme cautionary measures be taken.

In their book *Mutual Hostages*, a team of Japanese and Canadian historians conclude, "[T]he simple truth is that espionage and sabotage were genuine possibilities."

In British Columbia, the worst possible conflux occurred: deep-rooted racism met wartime fears, and the situation quickly escalated out of control. Panic spread. The mayor of Victoria warned of an imminent Japanese invasion. Plans were quickly drafted for the possible mass evacuation of Vancouver Island. The lieutenant governor of the province was beside himself. He wrote long, frantic letters to Ottawa. The provincial police commissioner declared publicly that all Japanese—whether Canadian-born or not—were a menace and had to be removed. Newspapers reported that Japanese fishing boats off the coast of B.C. contained concealed guns, that the fishermen themselves had been charting the coast in preparation for a landing. The rumours swirled, and the hysteria grew.

Initially, Ottawa did not intend to inter or evacuate Japanese Canadians, but B.C. delegates grew more and more frantic in their assessment, and the pressure quickly mounted. "The Japs can't be trusted." "They have to be moved." "They don't assimilate." "They are a threat to national security." "Once a Jap, always a Jap." In such an atmosphere, the voice of reason is inevitably drowned out. Escott Reid, an official with External Affairs, had a clammy, almost nauseous feeling about the way events were unfolding. The B.C. delegates, noted Reid, "spoke of the Japanese Canadians in the way that the Nazis would have spoken about Jewish Germans."

The panic grew to such a fever pitch, in fact, that when it was pointed out Japanese Canadians hadn't committed a single act of sabotage and so far had ignored any temptation to aid the Japanese empire, had in fact been going about their business quietly and without dishonour, this lack of activity was cited as a reason to step up measures against them. Their very silence indicated that they were mustering their forces and lying in wait. One Liberal MP warned ominously that the reason there had been no sabotage was because "the time was not yet ripe."

In B.C., the Kiwanis Club called for the imprisonment of all Japanese Canadians, warning that they were inscrutable, treacherous and deceitful. The Kinsmen demanded a boycott of Japanese businesses. The Rotary Club joined the chorus, as did the Provincial Council of Women and the Imperial Order Daughters of the Empire. The Canadian Legion was particularly outspoken in its rabid, anti-Japanese stance. Indeed, there are very few heroes in this story. Vancouver alderman George Buscombe wanted all Japanese, whether or not they were Canadian citizens, to be "shipped back to Japan." Such proposals were part of a massive, relentless campaign, and Ottawa caved in to the pressure. Several British Columbia MPs had been waging an anti-Japanese campaign for more than 20 years; the war just gave them added ammunition. The war was, in the words of one agitator, "a heaven-sent opportunity."

To placate fears among B.C.'s representatives—and ostensibly to protect

Japanese Canadians from race riots—it was decided to evacuate all able-bodied males of Japanese descent between the ages of 18 and 45 and to find work for them inland, away from any sensitive military areas. But that was only the beginning, the thin edge of the wedge. The diaspora of the Japanese Canadians had begun, a displacement the likes of which had not been seen in Canada since the expulsion of the Acadians.

In the House of Commons, Prime Minister Mackenzie King rose up on his hind legs and, while noting that Japanese Canadians had to this point proved loyal and trustworthy, announced that they would now be forcibly evacuated nonetheless. Those who resisted would be thrown into internment centres. He invoked the austere authority of the War Measures Act, which granted the government near-dictatorial powers. It was not the first time in Canadian history that the War Measures Act had been implemented, and it would not be the last.

Something rarely commented upon is the fact that Canada relied on forced (that is, "slave") labour during World War II. Japanese Canadians who refused the often back-breaking work assigned to them had their food rations cut until they complied. Failing that, they were locked up. More than 750 Japanese and Japanese Canadians were imprisoned during the war. A few were rabid imperialists, perhaps, but the majority of the prisoners had simply asserted their human rights and refused to comply with the relocation orders. They were branded "resisters," and after the war ended a strident campaign would be launched to have them stripped of their citizenship and deported. During their time in the camps, the prisoners were forced to wear work uniforms with large, targetlike red suns painted on their backs. This visible marking was disturbingly similar to the yellow stars that Jews were forced to wear under the Nazi regime.

The mass evacuation of Japanese Canadians from the West Coast began in February 1942, and by September of that year, virtually every man, woman and child of Japanese descent had been forcibly uprooted and relocated against their will. In the end, 22,000 people would be moved; 75 per cent of them were Canadian-born citizens.

Families were often roused from their sleep in the middle of the night and given less than 24 hours' notice before being evicted. In several cases, people had just two or three hours to pack everything, close up their homes and leave. (Their belongings, they were told, would be placed under the protection of a government custodian.) They were then herded into hastily converted livestock barns at Vancouver's Hastings Park, where they awaited evacuation, and the symbolism of the cattle pens and abattoir was not lost on them.

Japanese-Canadian refugees were forced to move time and time again. There was a violent reaction against them in communities across Canada. In Kelowna,

B.C., a sign was posted on the outskirts of town: "Kelowna Welcomes You—Coast Japs: You Are Not Wanted. Get Out." When Japanese families attempted to debark in Kelowna they were run out of town by a band of vigilantes, an act applauded by the local papers. (Indeed, the entire Okanagan Valley was virulently anti-Japanese throughout the war.) The mayor of Saskatoon publicly endorsed a proposal to put Japanese Canadians "into concentration camps." Lethbridge, Alberta, issued all kinds of mean-spirited bans on Japanese workers. The mayor of Calgary called for their expulsion from the province. In southern Ontario near-riots erupted wherever the refugees attempted to settle, and in the Niagara region, crosses were burned in front of farms employing Japanese workers. The city council in Toronto passed legislation attempting to prevent Japanese Canadians from crossing its municipal boundaries. The city of Ottawa flatly refused to have evacuees admitted, and the newspapers in Montréal wanted them driven out of Canada entirely. Québec Premier Maurice Duplessis angrily vowed that he would stop all Japanese Canadians from entering his province.

Native Canadians cheered this injustice as loudly as anyone. The mass evacuation opened up the fishing industry for west-coast Natives and allowed them to reap huge wartime profits, proving once again that greed and racism are by no means a white prerogative.

Ironically, at the same time that an entire ethnic population was being dispossessed, stripped of its belongings and carted off to relocation camps—all without trial, charges or due process—Canadians were being urged to buy Victory Bonds under the slogan, "Here, in Canada, you are free!"

> Free to live and work in peace and comfort. Free to dream, free to plan your future. Free from cruel decrees. Free from confiscation, from suffering, from wanton imprisonment without cause. Yes, you are free in Canada . . . Buy Victory Bonds!

Meanwhile, the Canadian boys captured at Hong Kong were being starved and tortured to death in Japanese camps. Almost a third of Canadian prisoners died while under Japanese "care," more men than had died in the actual Battle of Hong Kong. It was an appalling record, far worse than that of the German POW camps, and it is tempting to say, "Look how horribly the Japanese treated *their* captives. Our treatment of Japanese Canadians was much more humane." But comparing Canada's actions to those of a fascist Imperial Army is disingenuous, to say the least. Canada was a democracy. We were supposed to be better than that.

Most Japanese Canadians ended up being shipped off to ghost towns in the remote interior of B.C., where row upon row of shanty shacks awaited them.

Cramped, squalid and without insulation in the dead of winter, many of these shacks had no toilets. In most of them, several families were crowded into a single dwelling. The use of the word "camps" in connection with these relocation communities raises the hackles of some historians, because—technically speaking—they were not "internment camps" but rather "interior housing centres." There was no barbed wire; there were no armed sentries. But residents could not leave. They had been sent to these places against their will and without consultation, their movements were curtailed, and they had to carry identification papers at all times. The Japanese Canadians themselves referred to these refurbished ghost towns as both concentration camps and internment camps. A better word, perhaps, would be "refugee camps."

Living conditions were primitive and unnecessarily harsh. When the International Red Cross conveyed complaints to the Canadian government, Prime Minister King simply appointed a royal commission to investigate. The commissioners made a whirlwind tour of all six camps in less than five days and announced that things were just fine. End of controversy.

Of the Japanese Canadians forced to leave the coast, more than 12,000 were shipped to refugee camps. There, the weeks turned into months, and the months turned into years. In the words of Ken Adachi, "The removal of the Japanese became an end in itself and no longer a means of achieving national security."

The worst was yet to come.

Japanese-Canadian homes, farms, shops, fishing boats, furniture and family heirlooms had been confiscated with the promise that they would be held in trust. But within a year, the federal government began auctioning off Japanese property at fire-sale rates. The auctions were a bargain hunter's dream, and the money that was raked in was used to pay for the refugee camps, once a healthy "commission" had been taken out by the government. Often, government agencies would roll the property over, selling it for profits of 200 per cent or more.

Lifetimes of effort and hard work were auctioned off. Everything was liquidated. Items deemed "valueless," such as family altars and Buddhist shrines, were either discarded or sold for pennies. (It was not uncommon for trunks filled with kimonos, handed down from generations of mothers to their daughters, to be sold for 50 cents.) Japanese Canadians lost millions upon millions of dollars in property during the war. It was nothing short of a public looting, and it was supported right down the line by our stalwart prime minister, William Lyon Mackenzie King.

In some communities, former neighbours ransacked the homes of interned Japanese Canadians. At a Buddhist cemetery, funeral ashes were dumped on the ground and the urns stolen. A typical story—presented in *The Enemy That Never Was*—is that of a Japanese-Canadian man who was ordered by the Canadian gov-

Ironically, one of the greatest heroes to emerge during the Sino-Japanese War of 1937–45 was a Canadian: Dr. Norman Bethune.

A restless, passionate man, Bethune had already served on the front lines of the Spanish Civil War when he decided to travel to China to offer medical aid to Mao's beleaguered Communist forces. Accompanying Bethune was Jean Ewen, a nurse and fellow Canadian. Ewen had spent several years in China already; she knew the culture, and she spoke Mandarin. As Bethune's interpreter and assistant, Ewen was with the doctor when he first met Mao face to face, though she was excluded from the famous painting of that event—almost literally airbrushed out of history.

In her bitingly funny and often poignant memoir, *Canadian Nurse in China*, Ewen writes of her stormy relationship with Norman Bethune, a man who treated her with undisguised contempt and condescension. Ewen and Bethune joined a supply train that took them deep into guerrilla territory, through the front lines of the Japanese invasion. They were bombed, strafed and shot at; they hid in caves and operated on patients as shells exploded around them.

Ewen never forgot the horrors of front-line surgery or the misery she had witnessed. She recalled, years later, how she had once been reduced to digging bomb fragments out of a patient's leg with her fingers and a pair of chopsticks. "The waiting rooms were crowded with wounded from the last air raid. Halls were packed with homemade stretchers; some patients died before aid could be given them. The floors were sticky with blood and emesis and excrement. Two little ones were screaming in shock beside their dead parents. Legs, hands, and fingers were amputated; shrapnel picked out of wounds; bleeding stopped. The smell of blood is not a pleasant odour."

Throughout their ordeal, Bethune treated Ewen like a servant. He bullied and patronized her and constantly criticized her lack of commitment to the Communist cause. (Ewen's father had been an old-line Communist supporter, and Bethune denounced her as a disgrace to the Ewen family name.) Jean Ewen was opposed to the Communists' grip on medical facilities, arguing vehemently against "mixing sutures with politics." But her arguments fell on deaf ears. As Ewen wrote with dry understatement, "Dr. Bethune did not appreciate an opinionated woman."

Ewen eventually had had enough and left both Bethune and the Communist camps. Crossing back over enemy lines, she made her way south to Hong Kong. It was a trek that would take months, and one so foolhardy and fraught with danger that at one point the American press reported that she had been killed en route. But Jean Ewen survived, and she made it back to Vancouver on board "the last boat out of China," exhausted and stone broke.

In the fall of 1939, amid the fire and the shellings, Norman Bethune nicked his finger during one of his exhausting, marathon rounds of surgery. Without proper antiseptic, he soon contracted blood poisoning and died. In Communist China, he was elevated to the near-divine status of Revolutionary Hero. In Canada, he is remembered differently, as a complex, contradictory man. An ardent supporter of Joseph Stalin and Mao Zedong—two of the most notorious mass murderers in human history—Norman Bethune was a Party Communist all the way, militant and unbending.

Unlike Norman Bethune, Jean Ewen was not an ideologue or a martyr to any cause. A strong, level-headed, practical-minded woman, she got out of China alive. She did not die a hero's death; she was never turned into a Communist icon. And as a result, there have been no statues erected in her honour, no bloated bio-pics made, no postage stamps bearing her image and no posters adorning college dorm walls. She has, in fact, been all but forgotten.

ernment to leave his wife and children and report for manual labour on a road gang. He refused, citing his human rights. (Forced labour of civilians was forbidden by the Geneva Convention.) The government responded by sending him to a prison camp in northern Ontario, where he spent four years behind barbed wire, without a trial. During his imprisonment, the government confiscated the man's land, his home, his business and all of his possessions, and then sold them without his consent. The cost of his upkeep, plus a healthy commission and surcharge, took what little money was left. After the war, he had nothing. "Is this democracy?" he asked.

The Japanese-Canadian refugees had committed no crimes and no acts of treason, but Prime Minister King nonetheless announced the creation of "loyalty commissions" that would ferret out disloyal or wavering members of the Japanese community. The goal of these Stalinist committees? Mass deportations after the war ended. The plan was, in effect, to strip certain Canadian citizens of their nationality and ship them off to a foreign country. At these loyalty hearings, refugees would be offered the choice of being (a) imprisoned or (b) deported *within* Canada. Those who refused to cooperate would be sent to Japan. Gallup polls demonstrated that the majority of Canadians clearly supported mass deportations, even if they had to take place in peacetime. I say it again: Canadians are not nearly as nice as we like to think we are.

The democratic government of Canada intended to deport more than 10,000 people, almost half of the Japanese population in Canada, despite passionate pleas to reconsider. Non-cooperation itself was deemed a crime. (Does that sound like a Soviet statement, or what? "Non-cooperation is, in itself, a crime.") Any adult males who had been interned for any reason whatsoever during the war, or who had missed a retroactive deadline for appealing the decision, would—along with their wives and children—be put on a boat and sent "back" to Japan. Most of them, though, were Canadian citizens who had never *been* to Japan.

The war ended in the summer of 1945. The threat of deportation, however, would not be lifted for several years. By then, 4,000 Japanese Canadians had been hounded out of the country, among them a decorated World War I veteran who had to be forcibly removed. More than half were Canadian-born. More than a third were children under the age of 16 who spoke only English and knew no other country but Canada. "What will I do if I go to Japan?" asked one deportee. "I am a Canadian. I cannot speak the language. Who would employ me? I am a Canadian and an enemy."

And who was the Minister of Justice overseeing this entire distasteful exercise? Why, none other than happy-go-lucky Louis St. Laurent, a.k.a. "Uncle Louis," future prime minister of Canada. St. Laurent and his fellow Liberals fought long and hard in favour of the deportations. Conservatives thought Liberals should be doing even more to persecute Japanese Canadians. Indeed, the only political organization to emerge from this whole debacle with its reputation intact was the prairie-based CCF (Co-operative Commonwealth Federation). The CCF denounced government plundering of Japanese-Canadian property, as well as the plans for mass deportations, which they described as "a direct negation . . . of decent, elemental, fundamental democracy."

Not only did Canada's actions contravene the newly drafted United Nations Charter of Human Rights, but deportation based on racial grounds had actually been defined by the UN as "a crime against humanity," something that never seemed to bother either Mackenzie King or Louis St. Laurent. The *Winnipeg Free Press* and the *Toronto Star* eventually picked up on this glaring criminality and began criticizing the deportations as "a Nazi-like policy." The Jewish community echoed these worries, warning that "the ghost of Hitler still walks in Canada." King, however, defended his actions by citing instead the principles of "peace, order and good government," which he felt took precedence over human rights.

Mackenzie King did not believe in upholding human rights; he believed in staying in power. The deportations were eventually cancelled not because of a sudden moral awakening on King's part, but simply for reasons of political expediency. Public opinion had turned, so King rescinded the earlier measures. It was that simple. King then implemented an immigration policy that was explicitly racist, and one that would stand until 1962. It too is part of the great "King legacy." King never offered compensation. He never made amends. He never showed any remorse or regret for the havoc he wreaked on people's lives, all in the name of political manoeuvring. Indeed, when the atomic bomb was dropped on Hiroshima, King expressed in his journals his relief that such a weapon was used "on yellow people" and not on the decent white races of Europe.

Relocation camps. Racial segregation. Confiscation. Government-sponsored lootings. Deportation orders. Loyalty hearings. Forced labour. This is Canada?

The war was over, but Japanese Canadians were still in camps, their rights and movements still constrained. In 1947, the CCF called for a repeal of these now blatantly unnecessary measures, but they were opposed by King's Liberals and resoundingly defeated. In 1948, Mackenzie King maintained sanctions against Japanese Canadians *solely so the Liberals could win a minor by-election in B.C.* When he was warned that history would judge him harshly for maintaining restrictions against innocent civilians in peacetime, King stated, bluntly, that it was more important for the government to stay in power than it was to stand up "for certain principles." (I am not editorializing here. These are King's own thoughts, clearly stated.)

When Japanese Canadians did attempt to return to their homes, they were arrested and thrown in jail. One man went back his hometown in 1948—three years after the war had ended!—and was rooted out by the police, imprisoned and sentenced to a year's hard labour. His only crime: being of Japanese descent and attempting to travel freely during peacetime.

Unlike the saga of the Acadians 200 years earlier, there would be no Great Return, no rediscovery of community, no voyage back. In the words of Ann Sunahara, author of *The Politics of Racism*, "WW II destroyed the Japanese Canadian community in B.C."

What are the lessons here, if any, to be learned? How are we to judge our past? How much allowance should we make for the context of war in which these events took place? A limited evacuation may have been warranted, but it was not the only option available, even if the Japanese-Canadian community *had* been rife with saboteurs. In fact, it would have been far cheaper and just as effective to simply step up surveillance. (The cost of evicting, relocating and interning Japanese Canadians was more than $15 million. Surveillance—even intense surveillance—would have been much less.)

In judging historical events, we must ask ourselves not what we feel today, with the advantage of hindsight, but what any decent, reasonable person could have been expected to support as these events were unfolding. With that in mind, I would argue that the initial evacuation, wasteful though it was, *can* be defended as a wartime action. No apology is needed for legitimate measures taken by a government under the duress of war. What *cannot* be defended are the wholesale confiscation of goods, the blatant profiteering by the government in selling off the evacuees' property, the threat of mass deportation that lasted years after the war had ended, and the restrictions against Japanese Canadians that remained in place until 1949. Context explains. It doesn't excuse.

The battle for redress began as early as 1948, when evacuees in Moose Jaw, Saskatchewan, led by a fiery World War I veteran named Hirokichi Isomura, staged a sit-in to protest their treatment. The message was simple and unambiguous: "We want to be compensated for our seized businesses and homes and for our five years spent in internment camps . . . The government took us out of our homes, interned us as enemy aliens, and seized our property, all without cause." For his efforts, Isomura was arrested and given a suspended sentence.

The battle for redress began anew in the mid-eighties, fuelled in part by a 1986 Price-Waterhouse report, *Economic Losses of Japanese Canadians after 1941*, which provided the first documented calculation of the economic loss suffered by the Japanese-Canadian community, an amount "not less than $443 million." Armed with this report, the National Association of Japanese Canadians (NAJC) stepped up its campaign. In 1988, they were victorious. The Redress Agreement finally hammered out awarded surviving claimants $21,000 each; the agreement also included the establishment of a community fund, a public apology and a full pardon for those wrongly convicted.

The fight had been led by an unassuming Winnipeg school principal named Art Miki. As president of the NAJC, Miki was instrumental in bringing about a resolution to 45 years of bitterness. In that sense, VC Day—Victory in Canada Day—can be dated not to 1945 but to September 22, 1988, when Prime Minister Brian Mulroney finally conceded defeat on behalf of the Canadian government.

For Art Miki, the fight for redress was always about larger principles, about human rights and human dignity. In his introduction to *Justice in Our Time*, Miki writes, "I hope that our story will remain, for future generations of Canadians, a

In 1946, in the wake of World War II and the horrors of the Holocaust, New Brunswick–born diplomat John Humphrey was appointed the United Nations' director of human rights. As such, he was the principal architect of what would become the Universal Declaration of Human Rights, adopted by the United Nations on December 10, 1948.

The declaration, sometimes described as a "Magna Carta of mankind," established human rights as the basis for international law and justice. In doing so, it provides both the legal right and the moral force behind the United Nations' authority. (It has also been suggested that Humphrey's own personality, forged through his experiences as an amputee and an orphan, was in part responsible for both the compassion and the pragmatic idealism that runs through the declaration.) Although little known inside his own country, John Humphrey has had a greater impact on modern world history than any other Canadian before or since.

prime example of one community's struggle to overcome the devastating effects of racism, and to affirm the rights of all individuals in a democracy." In 1991, Miki was awarded the Order of Canada: a recognition of loyalty. Loyalty to Canada and to the ideals upon which the country is built.

The motto of the Order of Canada? "They desire a better country."

Verdict

Ian Mackenzie, Minister of Pensions and Health, and all the other race-baiting politicians, editors and shriekers like him: **Boneheads Hysterical**

Hirokichi Isomura: **Bastard**, Part I

Art Miki: **Bastard**, Part II

Mackenzie King: **Perennial Bastard**

The Quiet Revolution: Québec Catches Up

THEY CALLED IT *la grande noirceur*, the Dark Ages. The Great Gloom. The regime of Maurice Duplessis, premier and last feudal lord of Québec.

Duplessis was a bush-league Mussolini, but without the medals. His party, the Union Nationale, ran the province from 1936 to 1939 and then again from 1944 to 1960. They called him "the Chief," and he and his boys left a lasting impression on Québec, in much the same way that childhood trauma may leave a stutter. Duplessis and his Union Nationale thugs were hardline, strikebreaking, ballot-stuffing, corruption-ridden, ultra-conservative neo-nationalists, and their second time in office they stayed in power for 16 straight years. In *Straight from the Heart*, Jean Chrétien writes, "Duplessis seemed omnipotent."

Canadians like to pretend that the American anti-Communist witchhunts of the 1940s and 1950s could never have happened here. That isn't quite true. We had our witchhunts, but unlike in the U.S., in Canada the accusations were never debated publicly. Our witchhunts were less showy and more ruthless.

Premier Duplessis passed his infamous "Padlock Law" in 1937, long before Senator McCarthy arrived on the scene south of the border. The law gave sweeping, dictatorial powers to Québec's attorney general (a post that just happened to be filled by Duplessis Himself), allowing the government, without due process, to (a) evict any person from any building, (b) confiscate and destroy any materials discovered on the property as it saw fit, and (c) padlock the doors, all on the mere *suspicion* that a building was being used by Communists. When it was pointed out that the act contained no definition of the word "communist," Duplessis replied that no definition was needed. "Communism," said Duplessis, "can be felt."

True to his word, Duplessis relied on his unerring intuition in rooting out bolshevik subversives. These included Jehovah's Witnesses, along with their families, friends and supporters; Duplessis's political opponents; his critics; and anyone else who just, well, pissed him off. This latter group included, in the memorable words of one of his cabinet ministers, "the thousands and thousands of people who are Communists without being aware of it." Thus, in a single legislative act, Maurice Duplessis managed to incorporate religious intolerance, anti-Communist hysteria and political corruption. Quite an achievement.

Hundreds of homes and offices were raided. Newspapers were shut down, printing presses confiscated, cultural centres locked up. Suspected Commies were often evicted without notice, in the middle of the night, including women, children and even—in one notorious case—a toddler. There were no trials because there were no arrests. It was Stalinism on a Canadian scale.

The Padlock Law lasted for 20 years before it was finally overturned by the Supreme Court of Canada in 1957. By then, Duplessis had managed to purge most of his political opponents. The question that still intrigues historians is this: Was Duplessis a master or a pawn? That is, did the English elite in Québec permit Duplessis to stay in power, or vice versa? Some maintain that he was merely *le roi nègre*, "the nigger king," a puppet used by the English to oppress the poor, hapless habitants—who somehow, in spite of everything, kept reelecting him. Hmmm. There is a flaw in this conspiracy theory. In a representative democracy, the proletariat have no alibi. Duplessis did not seize power, he did not storm the Winter Palace and execute the czar; he was voted in by the electorate for four straight terms. It was the francophone majority who kept him in power, not *les Anglais*.

Not that Duplessis ever fought his elections on even ground. Heavens, no. He openly manipulated voting districts to favour the rural regions where his support was strongest. He stacked the deck, he gerrymandered electoral ridings, and his tactics worked. In Québec, Duplessis stayed in power *because* he was a domineering autocrat, not in spite of it. During election campaigns he was as blunt as he was honest. There was nothing coy about his repeated promises and threats. "Do you want a new hospital? A new bridge? A new school?" he would thunder from the bully pulpit. "Then vote Union Nationale. I would hate to force gifts upon you that wouldn't be appreciated." He also liked to keep $60,000 in ready cash in a drawer in his office, because, "You never know when constituents may drop in on a weekend."

Duplessis, no matter what Québec nationalists want to believe, was not an aberration. He was, in truth, just the latest in a long tradition of authoritarian, Alpha-male, sternly paternalistic father figures who had been taken to heart by the Québécois over the years. In a closed and hierarchal society, Maurice Duplessis simply played the game better than anyone else. "The reign of Duplessis," wrote journalist Jean-Marc Léger in 1962, "marked both the zenith and the twilight of a certain kind of traditionalism." The patterns of this traditionalism evolved following the Conquest of 1760, when the Church assumed the role of both protector and patriarch of French Canada. The two became inexorably linked: French Canadians and the Catholic Church. It was a relationship born of necessity and hard times, but the rise of the Ultramontane movement soon gave it an ideological base. What fate had delivered, Ultramontanism solidified.

Ultramontanism (from "beyond the mountains," in reference to Rome and the Vatican) was a rigidly orthodox movement, one that began as a reaction against the clear atheistic undercurrents of the French Revolution. The movement, refusing to reconcile Church tenets with modern thought, came to Canada in the 1820s and took firm root. If the French Revolution had been a conflict between Liberty and Authority, the Ultramontanes came out clearly on the side of Authority. Lower Canada (that is, Québec) had rejected the French Revolution, which led to an odd situation indeed. It was the Old World of France that had embraced the new ideals of republicanism. The New World, in contrast, clung to the old ways.

With the flow of French immigrants blocked, and English speakers flooding the land, the clergy in Québec urged families to produce more babies. The birth rate accelerated at unprecedented levels and began declining only in 1960, at which point the Québec provincial government began offering sizable cash bonuses for each new baby born, effectively buying what the Church had got on credit. The torch had been passed.

The priest-historian Abbé Groulx called the Church's original baby boom "*la revanche des berceaux*," "the revenge of the cradle." Faith, family and race were the pillars of the abandoned French colony; language would not enter into the mix until much later. As recently as 1957, Québec's separatist motto was *Dieu, Famille, Patrie*, "God, Family, Homeland." French-Canadian society saw itself as a spiritual beacon in North America, anti-materialistic, conservative and religiously pure, a society morally superior to the base capitalistic community of *les Anglais*.

"It was hardly an exaggeration," writes Gérard Pelletier in *Daedalus*, "to say that, at that time, the Catholic clergy was omnipresent and omnipotent in Québec and that no political structure could govern without the support of its bishops and clergymen."

Although xenophobic and authoritarian, the Catholic Church did maintain a sense of unity and community in Québec through some difficult, wind-tossed times. But as the world changed around it, the Church found itself increasingly estranged from reality. "Nothing must change" was both the mantra and the central commandment. "Nothing must change." Like a great, tall, dead tree, the Church was magnificent, impressive, but just one storm away from the end. Looking back, Léger would write, "We were smothering in the dust of the museum; we were becoming an anachronism in North America."

Maurice Duplessis was the last great defender of this outdated, defensive nationalism. It was a nationalism built on the twin edifices of the Church and the Union Nationale, and a grand structure it was. But structures of this kind have a way of falling. When Duplessis dedicated the immodestly named Duplessis Bridge at Trois-Rivières, he announced, "This bridge is as strong as the Union Nationale!" Six months later, the bridge collapsed. Perhaps it was an omen. Still, Duplessis's party had a lot of life left in it. The Chief had once bragged (like the Sun God of France, who declared, "I am the state") that "*L'Union Nationale, c'est moi!*" It took death to remove him. Maurice Duplessis died in office in 1959, and the Union Nationale went through two other leaders in quick succession before falling to the Liberals of Jean Lesage on June 22, 1960.

Jean Lesage would remain in power only six years, but they would prove to be the wildest, most energetic and innovative six years in Québec's history. It was an exciting time, a time of sudden prosperity and promise, a time of great social unrest. Author Michel Gratton recalls it well: "The Cold War was at its most frigid, but the space race was on. Men and women looked at a moon that was no longer unreachable. The sky was, indeed, the limit." An adaptation of Abbé Groulx's maxim "Our master, the past" now seemed possible; "Our master, the future" better captured the spirit of the age.

All that potential energy, like a coiled spring. And the harder you push down on a spring . . .

The sixties exploded in Québec like nowhere else in Canada. They called it the Quiet Revolution, but it was more of a Renaissance, and it happened on all fronts: social, political, religious, artistic. Lesage announced a project a day during his first month in power, a period *Le Devoir* dubbed "thirty days that shook the province." Québec's was one of the swiftest industrial revolutions in human history. The transformation and turnabout was breathtaking. Virtually overnight, the province went from being a "priest-ridden" rural society to a youthful, urban-based, modern entity. The time of stagnation and mere survival was over, and Québec would never be the same again. Neither would Canada.

Jean Lesage was the Pandora of Canadian history, a man who pried open the magic box and then stood back, amazed and at times aghast at what he had unleashed. He was the Father of the Quiet Revolution, which is to say, the Father of Modern Québec. He overhauled the economy, modernized Québec's mediaeval labour laws, bolstered women's rights, introduced a public pension scheme and—perhaps his greatest victory—wrested control of the school system away from the Catholic Church. He was a visionary: a workaholic, an alcoholic and a man of almost palpable pride. John Diefenbaker said Lesage was the only person he knew who could strut sitting down.

And yet, although Lesage had an abrasive personality and was often openly antag-

So far in our story we have had lots of violence, but where is the sex? Well, here goes.

It isn't much of a sex scandal, but it's the only one we've got. From 1958 to 1961, Prime Minister John Diefenbaker's associate minister of defence, Pierre Sévigny, was having an affair with a prostitute named Gerda Munsinger, a recent immigrant from Germany. (You can tell it's a Canadian sex scandal because it involves a German named Gerda and not, say, a Parisian courtesan named Mimi.)

Munsinger had also, it turned out, been sleeping with Soviet agents, and the scandal blew wide open in 1966. By then, Gerda Munsinger had returned to Germany, and the Canadian government was insisting that she had disappeared or died of leukemia. But in what was to be dubbed "the scoop of the decade," a reporter with the *Toronto Star* tracked Munsinger down in Munich, where she was working as a barmaid, alive and well and more than happy to spill the beans. "I will not be quiet about it," she said huskily. "I will tell you how it was. How it really was in my fast-living restless life, where I met the men of society who wanted to have my love."

The response to the Munsinger affair? Typically Canadian. The government appointed a royal commission to look into the matter.

onistic towards Ottawa, he was never a separatist. "He was truly, profoundly, a federalist," recalled his son in a Montréal *Gazette* interview, years after his father had died. In many ways, Lesage's Quiet Revolution, brash though it was, represented "rational" nationalism, whereas today's separatism represents "emotional" nationalism.

Maurice Duplessis had supported old-style capitalism. Lesage was actively interventionist. The state was to be an agent for change, not a mere collector of taxes. Lesage was fortunate to have a like-minded prime minister in Lester Pearson, who—scrambling to keep up with the changes that were overtaking the country—was promoting something called "co-operative federalism." (This term would later be replaced with another: "profitable federalism." In Canada, when in doubt, come up with a new name for an old idea; in this case, expanding provincial powers. In the future, I recommend "interprovincial associated federalism." I'm not sure exactly what this means, but as soon as I work it out I'll let you know.)

Lesage adopted the motto *"Maîtres chez nous! C'est l'temps qu'ça change!"*

"Masters in our own house! It's time for a change!" And while the second half of the slogan was hardly original (politicians have been calling for change since forever), that first burst—*masters in our own house*—ignited the public imagination and encapsulated the pent-up frustrations of an entire people. (As noted, the slogan also had anti-Semitic roots, though certainly Lesage never intended it that way.)

Supported by an enthusiastic and talented group of advisors, Jean Lesage had uncorked a typhoon. He and his supporters knew that they were making history, and this realization gave them a confidence that bordered on bravado. "The more I see of Premier Lesage," quipped Newfoundland premier Joey Smallwood, "the more I appreciate the humility of General de Gaulle."

In some ways, Québec was simply catching up with the rest of Canada—Lesage nationalized its hydroelectric companies, something Ontario had achieved in 1905—but in many other ways it outpaced the rest of the country. The expression "Quiet Revolution" was actually coined in Toronto, by journalist Brian Upton, but like "masters in our own house," the expression quickly became a rallying cry, a self-fulfilling prophecy. *La révolution tranquille.*

The single most dramatic change was the way the Church's authority so quickly dissipated. But power, like energy, is never really destroyed, it is simply redistributed; in this case, most of it was transferred to the state. In 1960, the number of clerics in Québec was at an all-time high. The province had, by far, more priests per capita than anywhere else in the Catholic world. Ten years later, the numbers had plummeted to half the 1960 rates. Churches were empty. Masses were only sporadically attended. Québec had become a secularized state, with not a shot fired, not a heretic hanged. In France, almost 200 years earlier, blood had flowed in the streets. In Québec, people danced.

Instead of wheeling out a guillotine, Québec's leaders appointed a commission to investigate the corruption of the Duplessis regime. Among other tidbits, it was discovered that the Union Nationale had received more than $100 million in payoffs, kick-backs and bribes during its last 16 years in office, an amount roughly equivalent to a billion dollars in today's currency. Who said crime doesn't pay?

Lately, there has been a reclamation project underway to absolve Duplessis of his guilt. It is pointed out that the Chief built a lot of highways, factories and bridges during his reign. It is even argued that he was *good* for Québec in much the same way that Bigot was actually *good* for New France. Québec's nationalist thinkers have also begun rewriting history to absolve Québec of any responsibility for its stunted growth before 1960. Just as English Quebeckers are held accountable for Duplessis (the *roi nègre* theory), so too English Canada as a whole is held accountable for just about everything else. It's excellent propaganda but very poor history.

Noted historians like Fernand Ouellet refuse to have anything to do with this persecution complex. Québec transformed itself. It solved its own problems better, more quickly and with more verve than anyone could have predicted. That should be a cause for celebration, not finger-pointing.

One such example: education. When Québec entered Confederation in 1867, it was given complete and exclusive authority over its school system. The Church, through lay organizations, controlled every level of education from elementary to university. And that control showed. In Québec, prior to the Quiet Revolution, 34 per cent of university students were studying theology; 4 per cent were studying applied science. In Ontario, during the same period, the numbers were 0.6 per cent in theology and 28 per cent in applied science. In every area and by every standard, education in Québec was subpar, almost laughable in its slant and deficiencies. The Quiet Revolution changed this. English Canadians were involved neither in the problem nor in the solution.

From the whirlwind of the Quiet Revolution emerged several dominant personalities who would, effectively, set the national agenda for the next 30 years. The first was a wealthy intellectual named Pierre Trudeau, who had been an implacable foe of Duplessis throughout the 1950s. Together with Gérard Pelletier and other activists, Trudeau had helped found *Cité libre*, perhaps the most influential small magazine in Canadian history. *Cité libre* attacked the narrow ethnic nationalism of Québec separatists, as well as the corruption of Duplessis.

In 1965, labour leader Jean Marchand, along with Trudeau and Pelletier, decided to enter the federal political arena. On an invitation from Prime Minister Pearson, the trio set off to Ottawa with the avowed goal of reconciling Québec's place in Confederation. The press quickly dubbed them "the Three Wise Men."

Trudeau rose quickly, making a name for himself as Minister of Justice before replacing Lester Pearson as both Liberal leader and prime minister in 1968. Pierre Trudeau was a hard-hitting man, and he had many enemies among Québec extremists and Anglo reactionaries. Québec's Rassemblement pour l'indépendance nationale (RIN) had the year before adopted the slogan "*Cent ans d'injustice*," "100 years of injustice," to mark Canada's centennial. Trudeau prepared for a showdown, and it wasn't long in coming.

Led by the separatist firebrand Pierre Bourgault, the RIN incited a riot during Montréal's St. Jean Baptiste Day parade. It was the eve of the 1968 election, and Pierre Trudeau—denounced by the RIN as "the traitor of Québec"—was in the reviewing stand. Bourgault and his followers charged forward, hurling bricks and bottles at the officials. As the other officials ran for cover, Pierre Trudeau held his ground. His bodyguard tried to convince him to leave, but he was sent away, and Canada watched as Pierre Elliott Trudeau sat alone, smiling at the crowds even while under attack. Bottles and stones whizzed past. Trudeau never flinched. The parade continued.

The police wrestled the rioters into submission. Bourgault was hauled away, and the other delegates gradually returned to the viewing stand. The next night, Trudeau was elected with a solid mandate, Canada's first majority government in years. The history of the nation had turned on the will of a single individual.

The RIN was broken. Many of its members drifted towards the more moderate Parti Québécois, which had only recently been founded by an energetic, chain-smoking ex-journalist named René Lévesque. Lévesque had first gained recognition as an overseas correspondent, covering distant wars and explaining them to his fellow Québécois in direct, no-nonsense terms. He entered politics at the provincial level, as one of Lesage's lieutenants, but eventually grew impatient with the premier's federalist stance.

Lévesque had a feel for the people. He was their heart, and Trudeau was their head. The two men were opposites in almost every way. Pierre Trudeau, it was said, was who the Québécois would like to be; Lévesque was who they really were. Lévesque was one of them. He understood their fears, their dreams, their aspirations. It was Lévesque who had come up with the famous battle cry "*Maîtres chez nous!*" And when he had followed this slogan to its logical conclusion—sovereignty—he realized it was time to move on. Lévesque abandoned the Liberals and in 1968 founded the Parti Québécois, a party dedicated to achieving Québec's independence through nonviolent means. In November of 1976, in an election that would shake the nation, René Lévesque, avowed separatist and populist hero, was elected premier of Québec.

It had come down to this: a federalist French-Canadian prime minister in Ottawa and a separatist premier in Québec. What followed was the most crucial clash of personalities since Montcalm and Vaudreuil battled it out in New France. On one level, politics is simply personalities in action. And personalities inevitably come down to ideas—or the lack thereof. Federalist vs. separatist, head vs. heart: it was a clash that would rage across Québec and Canada, dividing families and friends, laying waste to our energy and intellectual resources, and in the end solving very little. When the dust finally settled, René Lévesque had lost, but Trudeau hadn't really won. Canada, at the very best, had broken even.

In retrospect, the clash may not have been productive, and it may not have been healthy, but by god it made for some good television. Politics were never as passionate, as powerful, as *entertaining*, before or since, and we owe it all to the basic contradictions of the Quiet Revolution, which has always meant radically different things to different people. In *The Illustrated History of Canada*, Desmond Morton writes, "What outsiders were slower to recognize was that the prime motive for reform was not modernization but Québec nationalism."

Indeed, the Quiet Revolution marked a major shift in Québec's national movement, away from a primarily defensive, traditionalist posture to one that was more aggressive, more active and resolutely unapologetic. Québec nationalism was now on the offensive. The real question was this: Was Québec attempting to take its place in Canada, or was it moving out completely? Had Québec grown up, or outgrown the nation? What began as a series of exhilarating reforms had now become a crusade. The religious fervour of Québec's past had never really been dammed but merely rerouted, and French Canadian nationalism was given a new burst of energy. Separatism became the new religion, federalists the new heretics. There were dragons to kill and a kingdom to claim.

In his lucid study *National Identity*, Professor Anthony D. Smith of the London School of Economics discusses the nationalist movements in Wales, Scotland, Catalonia and Brittany, as well as those in Eastern Europe:

> In all these cases a cultural renaissance, literary, linguistic and historical, preceded the formation of political movements demanding ethnic autonomy . . . In each case we are dealing with perceptions of neglected or suppressed identity, and in each case it is the centralized state itself that is held to blame. One has to admit that in this matter the state can do no right; benign neglect is as much cause for grievance as crass intervention.

Sound familiar? In Québec, however, the provincial government had become identified with the ethnic group in question. Thus, the new dichotomy pitted one level of the state (provincial) against another (federal). Québec cornered the market on French-Canadian identity. The French outside of Québec, the Acadians and the Brayons and the Franco-Ontarians and the pockets of French-Canadian culture in Manitoba and elsewhere, had been abandoned, just as surely as New France had been abandoned 200 years earlier.

Franco-Ontarian writer Michel Gratton remembers that time well. The new nationalism of the 1960s and 1970s "was a movement of awesome power, as sweeping as communism in its heyday, if only because it provided simple answers for all the tough questions. Outside Québec, other French Canadians watched the procession go by, knowing it was leaving them behind."

When did the Quiet Revolution end? A stunned Jean Lesage was unceremoniously dumped by the voters in 1966, but the reforms his government had initiated were carried forward by Daniel Johnson's Union Nationale, by Robert Bourassa's Liberals and by René Lévesque's Parti Québécois.

Personally, I would put both the climax and the end (and oh, how often those two points follow one another) at June 24, 1967, Canada's centennial year. The event: St. Jean Baptiste Day. The place: Montréal.

General Charles de Gaulle, president of France, appears on a balcony at the

Montréal city hall to address the crowd. His procession through the streets of Québec had, he said, reminded him of his triumphant return to Paris after its liberation from the Nazis. The implications—and the insult—were clear. And now, looking down upon his poor oppressed brethren, and egged on by chanting separatists and Gallic pride, the general calls out to them, "*Vive le Québec!*" There is a pause, a long, hold-your-breath pause, and then he says it: "*Vive le Québec libre!*" It is the slogan of the separatists, and it sets the crowd on fire. They cheer and weep and wave the fleur-de-lis.

De Gaulle then strode right back out again and called for the liberation of France's own oppressed, separatist-minded minority: the Basques. Ha ha. Just kidding. De Gaulle, that imperialist old fart, did no such thing.

Prime Minister Pearson curtly announced that de Gaulle's actions were "unacceptable," and the president's visit was cut short. "Canadians do not need to be liberated," said Pearson. "Indeed, many thousands of Canadians gave their lives in two world wars in the liberation of France and other European countries."

Still, the damage, nearly irreparable, had been done. *Vive le Québec libre!* The power of the slogan had been confirmed, legitimatized, and while the rest of Canada fumed, the separatists in Québec rejoiced. Things had heated up, and soon the pot would boil over. A small band of would-be revolutionaries in Québec had already dedicated themselves to the violent overthrow of the government. They called themselves Le Front de Libération du Québec (FLQ), and they issued a manifesto calling for an end to "Anglo-Saxon colonization."

The FLQ began planting bombs in mailboxes and federal armouries and in the English sections of Montréal. They killed the vice-president of a firearms company during a robbery, and between 1963 and 1970 they would set off more than 200 explosions. One, at the Montréal Stock Exchange, injured 27 people.

The revolution was quiet no longer . . .

Verdict

Maurice Duplessis: **Old-style Bastard**

Jean Lesage: **New-style Bastard**

General Charles de Gaulle: **Old World Bonehead**

For the verdicts on Trudeau and Lévesque, read on.

The October Crisis:
The Revolution Turns Noisy

IT WAS, IF NOT the end of the Canadian Dream, the end of the Canadian Delusion.

In 1970 that distinctive Canadian fantasy—that Canada is an island of peace and civility in an otherwise harsh world, that Canadians are nicer than most—collapsed. We can trace the cracks in the modern Canadian mosaic back even further, but the real moment of truth or dare occurred in October 1970. It was the year we grew up, the year we lost our virginity.

The October Crisis came at the end of the Quiet Revolution, in much the same way that the French Revolution's high ideals of "liberty, equality and fraternity" degenerated into guillotines and mob madness.

The FLQ, le Front de Libération du Québec, founded in 1963, was a clandestine organization long on rhetoric but short on logic. They called themselves "a vast front of love." "We do not terrorize our people," they insisted. Rather, they were simply "impatient" for liberation, and they thus were dedicated to the violent overthrow of the government and the forcible removal of Québec from Confederation.

It begins with graffiti: *FLQ!* and *Québec libre* scrawled on the walls of government buildings. It begins with graffiti and it ends in martial law, murder and mass arrests.

In April 1963, a bomb explodes on the CNR tracks just a few hours before Prime Minister Diefenbaker's train was to have passed by. That same month, six more bombs either explode or are defused in Montréal, the last of which goes off at an army recruiting centre, killing a night watchman named Wilfrid O'Neil. He was to be the first casualty of an underground civil war.

In May, 15 bombs are planted in mailboxes throughout the city. Five detonate. In October, a revolutionary newspaper, *La Cognée*, formally announces the arrival of the FLQ. In January and February of 1964, military equipment, rifles and munitions valued at more than $40,000 are stolen from armouries in Montréal. In June, over 800 sticks of dynamite are taken from construction sites, and the significance of these thefts now becomes deadly clear: someone is stockpiling an arsenal.

For the first time, the FLQ publicly acknowledges that they are behind this wave of politically motivated crimes. A revolutionary army begins drilling at St-Boniface, Québec, and arms are stolen from a port in Montréal. During a hold-up at a firearms facility, two more people are killed.

More dynamite is stolen, more hold-ups occur. Two CNR trains are derailed and a Molotov cocktail is lobbed at a third. A bomb planted in a shoe factory explodes, killing an elderly woman and injuring three others. Revolutionary ideologue Pierre Vallières and his cohort Charles Gagnon are eventually arrested in connection with the shoe-factory blast and will spend the next few years in and out of holding cells in a drawn-out legal battle. The FLQ dismisses the dead woman as "an old spinster." The police arrest several FLQ members but cannot stem the tide.

At the Dominion Textiles factory in Montréal, Jean Corbo, a 16-year-old FLQ recruit, is killed when the bomb he is carrying goes off prematurely. The FLQ both denies and accepts responsibility, and it becomes apparent that the organization has no central authority. The FLQ is made up of small cells, each operating independently. Even as the police arrest the members of one cell, other cells continue the campaign. Corbo's family is not consoled by the Marxist rhetoric of the FLQ's regrets: "Your son died in battle."

While in jail, Vallières writes *Nègres blancs d'Amérique* (*White Niggers of America*), a manifesto for Québec independence told in autobiographical form, in which Vallières immodestly compares himself to Louis Riel and Che Guevara. The book becomes an instant best-seller.

In September 1968 a new, heightened wave of bomb attacks begins. Some—such as those planted at Eaton's, a hated symbol of English business acumen—are defused. Others are not. At the Montréal Stock Exchange, a massive "super-bomb" explodes, injuring 27 people, three seriously. Not long after, another bomb goes off behind the Montréal Reform Club, injuring four, including a small child. In March 1969, the following FLQ communiqué appears:

> In a little while the English, the Federalists, the exploiters, the toadies of the occupiers, the lackeys of imperialism—all those who betray the workers and the Québec nation—will fear for their lives and they will be right. For the FLQ will kill . . .
>
> Have you ever seen a bus full of the English blow up?
> Have you ever seen an English library blow up?

Not all of the bombings in the sixties were political. Some were just, well, bizarre. On May 18, 1966, Paul Joseph Chartier, an unemployed truck driver from Alberta, carried a powerful homemade bomb into the Parliament Buildings in Ottawa. He had a speech prepared, but he never got to give it. "Mr. Speaker, Gentlemen, I might as well give you a blast to wake you up. For one whole year, I have thought of nothing but how to exterminate as many of you as possible . . . The only bills you pass are the ones that line your pockets, while the rest of the country has to eat spaghetti and meatballs." Following this speech, Chartier planned on flinging his bomb directly into the House.

He slipped into the men's room to prime the explosives. Alas, his bomb went off prematurely, blowing Chartier apart and damaging some of the plumbing, but injuring no one else. The remnants of his speech were found among the debris.

Have you ever seen a can explode on a shelf of a supermarket in the British quarter?

Have you ever seen a Protestant church burning?

Have you ever seen Westmount without telephones or electricity and with its water supply poisoned?

Have you ever seen sharp-shooters ambushed on roofs, shooting down traitors?

Be sure you soon will!!!

Another super-bomb, 141 sticks of dynamite, is discovered under the overpass of Montréal's Metropolitan Boulevard and is defused just in time. In September 1969, a bomb explodes behind the home of Montréal mayor Jean Drapeau. A few months later another one goes off at McGill, Montréal's English university.

In February 1970, Charles Gagnon and Pierre Vallières are released from prison. Both are unrepentant, and they announce that they will "start up" the FLQ again. Not long after, a plot to kidnap the Israeli consul in Montréal is uncovered. In June, another kidnapping plot is revealed, this one aimed at the United States consul. In both cases, FLQ members are arrested.

In August 1970, FLQ terrorists begin training at guerrilla camps in Jordan under the direction of Palestinian commandos. They announce a "revival" of the FLQ and the use of "selective assassinations." And on October 5, four armed men break into the Montréal home of James Cross, the British trade commissioner. Brandishing guns and yelling, "We are the FLQ!", they abduct him. The crisis is about to come to a head.

In seven years, the FLQ has caused the death of six people and has injured more than 40 others. They have planted more than 200 bombs and have carried out more than 30 armed robberies. But with the kidnapping of James Cross, everything has changed. The situation in Québec is now an international incident; if the provincial government does not act quickly, the federal government will. The terrorists holding James Cross call themselves the Libération Cell. Among their demands: $500,000 in gold bullion, the release of 23 so-called political prisoners, all of whom have been imprisoned for criminal acts and not for their political views, and safe passage to Cuba. Incredibly, many of Québec's intellectual nationalists urge the government to comply.

The ransom demands made by the FLQ include a drawing of an armed Patriote, and as the crisis heightens the mythology of the 1837 rebellions will become increasingly intertwined with that of 1970.

The government refuses to pay the money or release any prisoners, but it does allow the FLQ Manifesto to be read on national television in both English and French. The next day the document is published in newspapers across Canada. "We live in a society of terrorized slaves!" screams the manifesto. It is certainly a lively document; in it, the FLQ refers to Trudeau as "a pansy," Premier Bourassa as "a hypocrite" and the mayor of Montréal as "Drapeau the dog." Worse yet, they refer to Molson's beer as "horse piss." It ends predictably enough with a flurry of *vives*. (*Vive le Québec libre! Vive le Front de Libération du Québec! Vive la révolution québécoise!*, etc.)

Unfortunately, by granting even this small concession to the kidnappers, the government only encourages other similar actions. A second, unrelated group calling itself the Chénier Cell (after the doomed hero of 1837) acts quickly. Just two days after the October 8 broadcast of the manifesto, they abduct Québec's Minister of Labour and Immigration, Pierre Laporte.

Laporte, a former journalist and outspoken critic of Duplessis's corrupt rule, had been a key player in the reforms and social progress that occurred during the Quiet Revolution. On the day in question, he has just arrived home and is heading for the front door when he stops to toss a football with his young nephew. That interlude will cost him his life. A car pulls up; armed men pile out, grab him and whisk him away. Ironically, in the wake of Cross's kidnapping, Laporte had attempted to assuage public fears: "This is a wind of madness blowing across the province. I hope it won't last long." Now he is a victim of that same wind.

Two days later, the army moves into Ottawa, ostensibly to protect federal cabinet ministers but in reality as a show of force and a demonstration of national will. The prime minister behind this display of armed might is Pierre Elliott Trudeau, a young intellectual who has made his name as a civil libertarian. Just the year before, at the dedication of a monument to Louis Riel, Trudeau had reminded his audience, "It is all too easy, should disturbances erupt, to crush them in the name of law and order."

Now, on the steps of the House of Commons, he is confronted by reporter Tim Ralfe, who demands an explanation. The following exchange is caught on camera:

Ralfe: Sir, what is it with all these men with guns around here?

Trudeau (dryly): Haven't you noticed?

Ralfe: Yes, I noticed them, you people decided to have them.

Trudeau: What's your worry?

Ralfe: I'm worried about living in a town that's full of people with guns running around.

Trudeau: Yes, well, there are a lot of bleeding hearts around who just don't like to see people with helmets and guns. All I can say is, go on and bleed, but it's more important to keep law and order in society than to worry about weak-kneed people who don't like the looks of—

Ralfe: At any cost? At any cost? How far would you go with that? How far would you extend that?

Trudeau: Just watch me.

On October 15, a shaken and distraught premier of Québec, the newly elected Robert Bourassa, asks for the armed forces to be sent in to maintain order in Montréal. Under the Canadian Defence Act, the federal government must comply with Bourassa's request. And so, in the early dawn of October 16, 1970, the government of Canada invokes the War Measures Act, outlawing the FLQ and suspending civil liberties throughout Canada. The act gives the police and the army sweeping powers to arrest and detain citizens without trial or due process. The same act had been used to detain enemy aliens in World War I and to forcibly relocate Japanese Canadians in World War II. This, however, would be the first time in Canadian history that it has been invoked in peacetime.

Canada is under martial law. Organizations that had been legal one minute before midnight are declared illegal one minute after, creating the dangerous precedent of "retroactive crime." By noon, over a thousand police raids have been made and more than 450 people rounded up and hauled into detention centres. But, this being Canada, it is more Keystone Kops than Gestapo. Hubert Bauch, writing in the Montréal *Gazette*, said, "The list of suspects for their pre-dawn arrests following the imposition of the War Measures Act appears to have been culled from the phone directory, and in one instance the police seized a book on cubism, convinced that it was a Cuban revolutionary tract."

Later, the police even raid the home of Gérard Pelletier, Canada's Secretary of State and the very man who had signed the War Measures Act. And yet, for all these blunders, the act will prove to be a most effective weapon. It will also provoke an immediate and cruel response from the terrorists. The day after the War Measures Act is imposed, the Chénier Cell of the FLQ murders Pierre Laporte. A note directs the police to an airport in Saint-Hubert, where Laporte's body is found in the trunk of a car. He has been strangled with a religious chain that he reportedly wore for good luck.

Laporte's murder horrifies the province and the nation, and support for the draconian War Measures Act increases. On December 3, police discover the north-end hide-out where Cross is being held by the Libération Cell. The terrorists barricade themselves in a room. After heated negotiations, and in exchange for safe passage to Cuba for themselves and their families, the kidnappers eventually surrender Cross unharmed and are flown out of Canada.

On December 27, police capture Francis Simard and the Rose brothers, Jacques and Paul, at a farmhouse south of Montréal. (Bernard Lortie, a fellow member of their group, had been arrested earlier.) The Chénier Cell has been broken, and the assassins of Pierre Laporte have been found.

From the kidnapping of James Cross to the arrest of Simard and the Rose brothers, *la crise d'octobre* lasted 84 days. Laporte's killers were tried and convicted, and for the premeditated abduction and murder of a publicly elected official, the longest sentence actually served ended up being 11 years. Several members of the Libération Cell who had fled to Cuba changed their minds once they got there ("they soon tired of the workers' paradise," is how Hubert Bauch put it), and in 1979 they returned to Québec to face charges. For the kidnapping of a foreign diplomat they served less than two years.

By 1982, everyone involved in the terrorist activities of October 1970 was back on the streets again. Jacques Lanctôt, once the leader of the Libération Cell, now owns his own publishing house. His sister Louise, the only woman implicated in the crimes, owns a communications firm. Francis Simard is a scriptwriter. Jacques Rose runs a home renovation company with fellow ex-terrorist Marc Carbonneau. (That's right. Home renovations by the former FLQ. "*Boooom!*")

In 1990, 20 years after he helped murder Pierre Laporte, Paul Rose was teaching at the Université du Québec à Rimouski. "Which is to say," comments Mordecai

It is both disturbing and revealing how often the chain of events of October 1970 get turned around in the memory of Canadians. We tend to reverse cause and effect: Pierre Laporte is killed and *then* the War Measures Act is declared, as though the killing sparked the declaration of martial law. In fact, just the opposite occurred.

Destinies: Canadian History since Confederation is one of the leading history texts on the market. Along with its companion volume, *Origins*, it is a well-respected, authoritative work, and one I recommend highly. But even here we see an unconscious, unintentional shift in chronology. Consider the impression given in the following passage [emphasis added]:

> The climax of the FLQ's activities occurred in October 1970, when members of the group kidnapped James Richard Cross, a British trade representative in Montréal, and, five days later, Pierre Laporte, a Québec cabinet minister. *Laporte was subsequently found murdered.* When Bourassa hesitated and seemed to favour negotiations with the terrorists, the federal government intervened, relegating the provincial government to a secondary role. *For the first time in peacetime, the federal government invoked the War Measures Act.*

Here is another example, from a 1991 *Maclean's* article, looking back at the events of the October Crisis [emphasis added]:

> Five days [after Cross was abducted], another FLQ cell snatched burly Québec Labour Minister Pierre Laporte from a Montréal sidewalk—later murdering him. *In response*, on October 15 a grim Prime Minister Pierre Trudeau began ordering armed troops to take up defensive positions around strategic buildings in Ottawa, Montréal and Québec City.

Jean Chrétien, in his memoir *Straight from the Heart*, makes a similar shift:

> [Trudeau's] greatest test had come during the Québec crisis in

October 1970, when the terrorist FLQ kidnapped and held to ransom the British Trade Commissioner, James Cross, and the Québec Minister of Labour, Pierre Laporte, who was eventually murdered. Trudeau responded forcefully with the War Measures Act.

Chrétien goes on to make this reversal even stronger in the next two paragraphs by dealing at length *first* with the murder of Pierre Laporte and *then* with the decision to implement the War Measures Act. (One suspects that Chrétien's confusion of cause and effect is not entirely innocent.)

And yet, collectively, that is how many Canadians remember the October Crisis. Laporte's death has even been used to *justify* the invocation of the act, even though what actually happened was completely the opposite: Laporte was killed in direct response to the government's "arrogance" (in the words of the FLQ) in invoking the War Measures Act.

Richler, "he was doing penance of a sort." Another member of the Libération Cell now works with Québec social services (!), and all of them have become law-abiding citizens, reaping the benefits of the bourgeois capitalist society they once sought to blow up. None have recanted or apologized, and with varying degrees of fervour, all remain publicly unrepentant.

Several FLQ terrorists were even appointed to high-level government positions:

- Serge Demers, co-founder of the FLQ, who was convicted of armed robbery, planting bombs and stealing firearms and explosives: named chief of staff to Québec's Minister of Employment under Lucien Bouchard in 1996
- Richard Thérrien, convicted for harbouring the FLQ terrorists who kidnapped and murdered Pierre Laporte: named a Québec Court judge in 1996
- Gaëtan Desrosiers, former FLQ bomb delivery boy (he planted the bomb that exploded in La Grenade shoe factory in 1966, killing an elderly woman and injuring three others): given a $91,000-a-year contract as an associate secretary shortly after the Parti Québécois was elected in 1994. He was later named associate deputy minister for the Greater Montréal area.

In Québec, terrorists are not just forgiven, they are promoted.

James Cross, now retired in England, can neither forget his ordeal nor forgive his kidnappers. When asked during an interview, "Who won?" he answers, "I did." And then, after a long pause, he says, "Who lost? Pierre Laporte."

Civil libertarians in Canada cannot forget the October Crisis either. It was unnerving how easily the government was able to suspend basic human rights. Many people saw the War Measures Act as a unilateral imposition by Pierre Trudeau, but in fact it was requested by Bourassa and passed overwhelmingly by the elected representatives in the House of Commons: 190 to 16. Only the NDP stood opposed.

Did the government overreact? Tommy Douglas, leader of the New Democratic Party, certainly thought so. "They used a sledge-hammer to crack a peanut" was how he put it. Today, most people would agree.

But as Gérard Pelletier writes in *The October Crisis*, "Anyone can play Monday morning quarterback. What would have happened *without* the special measures, no one will ever know. In history, the past conditional tense explains nothing." Future tense is equally untenable, as the prophecies of René Lévesque have shown. "The police and the army will have to leave someday," he said at the height of the crisis, "and Trudeau's filthy tricks will not prevent all sorts of other kidnappings." Lévesque repeated this prediction often, almost hoping—it seems to me—that he would help make it self-fulfilling, almost egging on other would-be heroes. "One day, the police and the army will be gone, and Trudeau's stupidity will not have prevented more kidnappings." It sounds not so much like a warning as an exhortation.

Lévesque, of course, was wrong. As Trudeau commented in his memoirs years later, "The facts have proven otherwise." In the last four decades, through all kinds of divisive national debates, referendums, accords and separatist bluster, there has never—*never*—been a resurgence of terrorism in Québec. Proving a causal relationship between that fact and the implementation of the War Measures Act may be theoretically impossible, but it certainly seems likely that by sending in the troops at a key moment in Canadian history, Trudeau's "filthy tricks" did indeed end political violence in Québec.

Legally, the federal government was within its rights. The War Measures Act was designed to stop any insurrection "real or apprehended," and in October 1970, the threat of insurrection was very real. Minister of Regional Affairs Jean Marchand, relying on puffed-up FLQ communiqués, estimated the group's membership in the thousands and feared that they had enough dynamite to destroy the entire inner city core of Montréal. Nor was it simply the terrorists themselves who startled the government. The sympathy and tacit approval they received from leading Québécois intellectuals was truly alarming. In 1968, France had been convulsed by prolonged, bloody student clashes that were nothing short of an uprising. In the United States, the student movement was exploding as well; at Kent State, the

National Guard had fired on university students, killing four. In Canada, in 1970, Secretary of State Pelletier was sickened with the fear that a similar situation might well be unfolding here. The FLQ was not going to disappear on its own. One couldn't make the problem go away through appeasement or warm fuzzy hugs. In his autobiography *A Life on the Fringe*, respected parliamentarian Eugene Forsey writes, "In my judgement Pierre Trudeau kept Québec in Canada when no one else could have done it. In my judgement also, he saved us from Baader-Meinhof gangs and Red Brigades."

The question is not "Did the War Measures Act work?" It did. The real question is "Do the ends justify the means?" Now, in a perfect world, and in ethical abstract musings, the end *never* justifies the means. But in the messy world in which we live, things are not always that easy. "Democracy," said Trudeau in a terse public statement, "first must preserve itself. Within Canada there is ample room for opposition and dissent, but none for intimidation and terror."

Years later, Jean Marchand admitted, "We mobilized a cannon to kill a fly." Jean Chrétien, a minister under Trudeau when the October Crisis broke, resorted to metaphor as well when he tried to explain the dilemma facing the government. "It was like we had a refrigerator to move and we had a choice between using a bicycle and a tractor-trailer truck. We weren't going to get far using the bicycle and we were bound to look foolish using the tractor-trailer."

What is most unsettling is how popular the War Measures Act was at the time. The atmosphere in the country should have been grim. A democracy forced into a corner, resorting to extreme measures: it should have been a moment of sadness and deep regret, not celebration. But celebrate is exactly what most Canadians did.

In his book *But Not in Canada!*, Walter Stewart, no stranger to controversy himself, writes of how we acted when Trudeau sent in the troops:

Canadians cheered; we went berserk with delight. We lined up for the pollsters and wrote letters to our papers and clambered aboard open-line radio shows to pour out our jubilation that the government, at last, was clamping down, that our boys, our very own boys, were just as willing to hurl people of the wrong political persuasion into the coop as any Russian commissar. At York University in Toronto, students held a large, noisy demonstration *in favour of* the repression.

"Frankly," notes Stewart, "I am not much impressed by rights that work only when the sun shines."

A Gallup poll taken in December 1970 found that 87 per cent of Canadians fully supported the War Measures Act. Another cold, hard truth? Although now denounced as an example of Anglo oppression, the War Measures Act was just as pop-

Hard to believe, but Canada's national police force, the RCMP, were originally both cops *and* spies, in charge of espionage as well as enforcing the law. The same organization that was writing traffic tickets outside of Moose Jaw was also fielding secret agent super-spies. It was a bit too much to handle, and the cloak-and-dagger branch of the Mounties was separated to form the Canadian Security Intelligence Service (CSIS) in 1984.

The move to create CSIS began with revelations in the mid-1970s that the Mounties had, how shall we say, interpreted their duty "to serve and protect" in as wide a manner as possible. An inquiry revealed that the RCMP had staged more than 400 break-ins, as well as illegal wiretappings, mail openings, electronic surveillance, political interference, the theft of explosives and the use of forged documents. And, for good measure, they burned down a barn and blamed it on the separatists.

The typical response of Canadians to these allegations of wrongdoing by the RCMP? Outrage. Absolute outrage. If police officers were committing illegal acts, then the law should be changed so that those acts would no longer be illegal! Sigh.

ular at the time among French Canadians as it was among English Canadians. In fact, it remains perhaps the single most popular piece of legislation ever passed in Canadian history. When I mention this fact to my European friends, they are always amazed. An act limiting the rights of citizens being supported by these same citizens? Isn't this how fascism begins?

Well, not quite. Canada was not poised on the brink of fascism in 1970. But it is disconcerting just how quickly Canadians were willing to sell out their birthright for a stiff drink and a lullaby.

Myths often harden into accepted fact. Many Canadians, for example, take it as a given that most of the FLQ bombs were really planted by the Mounties, who also secretly wrote the manifesto. (The RCMP did burn a barn later on and delve into dirty tricks of their own, but that is a separate story.) The RCMP did not write the FLQ Manifesto. Convicted terrorist Francis Simard has always taken proud credit as one of the authors. Simard and the Rose brothers were in a car headed for Florida when they heard their words being read on the radio. They turned the car around and headed back to Montréal where they staged a kidnapping—and a killing—of their own.

Some have suggested Laporte died by accident during an escape attempt, when he got tangled in the chain of his medallion and somehow choked to death. A common household accident. Others have Laporte still alive in the trunk, but dying because the police dawdled on their way to rescue him. Another conspiracy theory—and one that is accepted by far too many people as fact—is that the entire October Crisis was actively encouraged by the federal government as a smokescreen to hide their real, dastardly purpose: to discredit and harass the sovereignty movement in Québec.

Certainly, the October Crisis did discredit the separatist movement as a whole and the Parti Québécois in particular. (Three years after the crisis, Robert Bourassa's Liberals were returned to power with the largest electoral victory in Québec history.) And true, there were cases of abuse by the local police, who used their increased power to settle old scores. But the biggest exploitation of the crisis occurred not at a national or even a provincial level, but at the municipal. Montréal mayor Jean Drapeau held an election at the height of the October Crisis while the War Measures Act was still in effect. He labelled the opposition "terrorists" and, with his main political rival locked up behind bars, played heavily on the public's fears. On October 25, 1970, Jean Drapeau took every single seat in the city with a whopping 92 per cent of the vote. The October Crisis was very good to Jean Drapeau.

The separatists were bruised but not defeated. Extremist rhetoric was toned down, violence became less acceptable, and once it had abandoned its more strident claims, the Parti Québécois was eventually elected. However, when a referendum on "sovereignty-association" was finally held in 1980, 10 years after the October Crisis, the PQ's proposition was soundly rejected. Since then, the Québec separatist movement has risen and fallen in waves.

In the wake of the October Crisis, even Vallières denounced violence as a means of promoting Québec independence, though he wavered later in life. The fact is, the FLQ terrorists were simply *péquistes* in a hurry. And the intellectual nationalists who took out full-page statements in newspapers to proclaim loudly that freedom of speech was dead in Québec or raged at length on public airwaves that they had been "reduced to silence" were caught in a contradiction that was as obvious as it was unacknowledged. They were not up against a dictatorship. They were up against a democracy. And the single greatest Achilles' heel of democracy is democracy itself. The separatists of Québec have learned to use the system from within, and at times they have almost succeeded. If the country breaks apart it probably won't be with a bomb blast, but through a gradual erosion of public will. We will be numbed to death by compromise: killed by bureaucratic process.

Or will we?

In the wake of the divisive 1995 referendum, when separatist leader Jacques Parizeau bitterly blamed the narrow defeat on a conspiracy of "money and the ethnic vote," angry graffiti began appearing on the streets of Montréal. *Anglos go home. FLQ.*

It starts with graffiti . . .

Verdict

Robert Bourassa: **Bonehead**, singular

The FLQ: **Boneheads**, collective

(Of course the FLQ were Boneheads. Everyone knows that you don't have to use force to break up this country; Canadians are more than willing to let you do it by half-measures.)

Pierre Trudeau: **Federalist Bastard**

René Lévesque: **Separatist Bonehead**

(Lévesque may have been a good man, he may have been a sincere man, but the fact remains: he was outplayed and outsmarted at every turn by Pierre Trudeau, from the 1980 referendum to the 1982 patriation of the constitution. René Lévesque was the Joe Clark of Québec nationalism.)

16

The Oka Crisis:
The Mohawk Resistance of 1990

TO HELP CELEBRATE the twentieth anniversary of the October Crisis, the government and citizens of Québec staged a revival of sorts. A kind of "come as you were" party.

Again, the conflict was in the Montréal area. Again, it involved a minority group with a long history of grievances at the hands of an unresponsive majority. Again, a militant fringe led an armed protest against the authorities. Again, the government sent in troops. And again, it was Robert "Boo Boo" Bourassa at the helm, having been reelected premier in a 1986 by-election, after a 10-year hiatus.

In comparing the two crises, the 1990 events contrast sharply with those of 1970, and the differences are as revealing as the similarities—one was an ideological campaign, the other an armed standoff over specific land claims—but above all, there is a pervading sense of irony. In 1990, it is the Québécois who are the powerful, insensitive majority. The oppressed minority are the English-speaking Mohawks living beyond the city limits of Montréal, in the small Kanesatake settlement at Oka. (The correct name for the Mohawk people is *Kanienkehaka*, "people of the flint," but the term Mohawk is now accepted and used even within the Kanienkehaka Nation.)

The roots of the 1990 crisis are older than Canada itself. In 1717, the governor of New France first granted lands to a Catholic seminary in the Oka area to be held in trust for the Mohawks. The Church, ahem, "reinterpreted" the agreement as giving them sole ownership, and over the years the missionaries began selling off Mohawk land and timber. This practice eventually led to the *first* Oka Crisis, in 1868, just a year after Confederation, when Joseph Onasakenrat, chief of the Oka Mohawks, petitioned the Church in protest:

This land was given to you in trust for the tribe to whom it belongs; and how have you betrayed this trust? By selling the timber and filling your treasury with the proceeds of stolen property. This land is ours—ours by right of possession; ours as a heritage, given us as a sacred legacy.

The following year Onasakenrat returned with an armed force of 40 Mohawk men and gave the missionaries eight days to relinquish Native lands. The missionaries called in the police, who stormed into Oka and imprisoned the protestors, including Chief Onasakenrat. *Welcome to Confederation!*

In 1936, the seminary at Oka sold off most of the remaining territory, turned a tidy profit and left. The Mohawks protested these land sales as well, launching petition after petition, but nothing was ever resolved.

Which brings us to 1990, and the Summer of Our Discontent.

Outstanding Mohawk claims have been ignored, dismissed and put on hold for more than 260 years. Through successive, relentless encroachments and legal manoeuvres, their land has been whittled down to a few scattered remnants. In the Oka region, the Mohawks now retain a mere 1 per cent of the territory that had been originally set aside for them.

Part of the land denied the Mohawks is a beautiful wooded area called the Pines. Considered sacred, this forest of white pine is one of the oldest hand-planted stands in North America, created by the ancestors of today's Mohawks. Adjacent to the Pines is a Mohawk cemetery.

The nine-hole Club de golf Oka, built in 1961, set a dangerous precedent—land claimed by the Mohawks was sold right out from under them. The Mohawks launched a legal protest, but by the time the case was heard, bulldozers were already clearing huge tracts of forest, pushing a parking lot and greens up to within tee-off distance of the cemetery. Golf balls were often found in among the headstones.

In 1989, the mayor of Oka, a breathtakingly tactless man named Jean Ouellette, decided to finish the job. He announced that the rest of the Pines would be cut down to expand Oka's exclusive, members-only golf club. Why settle for a mere nine holes, when you could have 18? The plans also called for 60 luxury condominiums to be built along a section of the Pines, but at no time did the town of Oka ever consult with or even inform the Mohawks. ("You know you can't talk to the Indians," was how Mayor Ouellette explained himself.) The town stood to make millions, and Ouellette himself was a member of the private club that stood to benefit.

As soon as the announcement was made, the Mohawks petitioned the town council to halt the proposed expansion: "It is common knowledge that these lands are part of the Mohawk territory of Kanesatake and that our title to these lands has

The Iroquois were the Romans of the New World. A political alliance of five nations—Mohawk, Oneida, Onondaga, Cayuga and Seneca (a sixth nation, the Tuscarora, was admitted in the 1720s)—the Iroquois Confederacy waged apocalyptic wars against their neighbours and imposed a *Pax Iroquois* on a vast territory stretching from the Great Lakes to the Mississippi, across the eastern flank of North America. They negotiated treaties with the Dutch, they battled the French to a standstill, and they played a critical role in the American War of Independence. Later, allied with the British, they would turn back American invaders in the War of 1812.

Today's Longhouse traditions are based on the Great Law of Peace, the 117-article Constitution of the Iroquois Confederacy, which dates back to 1570. Benjamin Franklin was greatly impressed with the Great Law, and he and the other founding fathers incorporated key elements of it into the United States' own constitution (a fact the U.S. Senate confirmed in a 1987 report).

The Iroquois Confederacy, as a union of sovereign states governed by a mutually chosen council, provides the blueprint for the federal system adopted by the United States and later Canada. However, one key element of the Iroquois constitution was *not* adopted: women's rights. Canada's Indian Act of 1876 took *away* the right to vote from Native women—a right they had held for centuries under Iroquois law.

As author Ronald Wright points out in *Home and Away*, the Iroquois Confederacy "is in fact the oldest democracy on this continent. Its political system, which includes a voice for all and a balance of power between the sexes, existed when Europe still believed in the divine right of kings."

never been ceded or extinguished." Their protest, however, was dismissed out of hand, and plans were made to cut down the Pines.

On March 10, 1990, Mohawk protestors occupied the forest, and the crisis began to unfold. The reconstruction of events that follows comes primarily from two books, Michael Baxendale and Craig MacLaine's *This Land Is Our Land* and Geoffrey York and Loreen Pindera's *People of the Pines*, as well as from newspaper and magazine reports of the time.

At first, the protests are confined to acts of civil disobedience (the Mohawks block a dirt road leading into the Pines and begin pulling up survey stakes), but as tensions grow, the protestors arm themselves with semi-automatic rifles.

Waving a court order, the mayor of Oka demands that the protestors leave the Pines immediately. They refuse, and Québec Minister for Native Affairs John Ciaccia, recognizing how volatile the situation has become, urges Mayor Ouellette to show restraint. Ciaccia pleads, "These people have seen their lands disappear without having been consulted or compensated, and that, in my opinion, is unfair and unjust, especially over a golf course." In what would prove to be a crucial clash of personalities, Ciaccia lost, Ouellette won, and Canada suffered the consequences. Instead of showing restraint, Mayor Ouellette calls in the police, the Sûreté du Québec (SQ).

The Mohawk protestors reinforce their barricade with sandbags, logs and concrete blocks, and as the situation escalates, the Mohawk men guarding the Pines ask the women to decide whether or not the weapons they have amassed should remain. According to the Constitution of the Iroquois Confederacy, the ancient law to which the warriors subscribe, women are caretakers of the land and "progenitors of the Nation." Which is to say, ultimate responsibility falls on the women, not the men. After a long discussion, the women finally give their permission, but with the warning that the men are to use their weapons only if the Mohawks are attacked. Only then.

In the early dawn of July 11, 1990, the tactical intervention squad of the SQ moves into position. They are armed with tear gas, assault rifles, bullet-proof vests, concussion grenades and gas masks. In the clearing, behind the barricades, the Mohawk protestors are in the middle of morning prayers, burning tobacco and sweetgrass. A Sûreté officer takes up a bullhorn and barks out a command: "We want to speak to your leader!"

There are no leaders. Mohawk decisions are made by consensus and along traditional matrilineal lines. And thus, the SQ tactical squad—expecting a war chief of some sort—finds itself confronted by a dozen unarmed Mohawk women who walk out from behind the barricades. The police raise their guns and level them at the women. The officer repeats his demand. "We want to speak to your leader!"

"There is no leader," one of the woman shouts back. "You're looking at the leaders. Everyone's the leader. The people are the leaders."

The women finally send a Faithkeeper and a spokeswoman from the Turtle Clan to speak to the armed SQ officers. "You can't attack," the Faithkeeper tells the officer. "The Pines are sacred. It's like a church. And besides, there are women and children here."

Above them, the chop and whir of an SQ helicopter echoes through the Pines as the strike force moves into position. The Sûreté brings in attack dogs. A force of 100 men falls in, and a bulldozer moves up. Just before 9:00 a.m. the assault begins. As the women link arms and stand in front of the barriers, the SQ fires canisters of tear gas and concussion grenades into the crowd. One canister hits a woman in the leg, several more explode, and the women and children are sent running in panic. The SQ moves in.

And then, from the trees, a war cry goes up.

The Mohawk men are in position, hiding in the forest, and the SQ are in their sights. As one warrior later recalls, they could have killed a dozen officers if they had wanted to. The Sûreté lobs in more grenades, more tear gas, even as the Mohawk war cries echo through the Pines. Here then, reenacted, are the battles of New France, between traditional enemies. Here too is a classic conflict between two different styles of warfare: guerrilla ambush vs. formal tactics.

The SQ assault team advances behind a cloud of tear gas as a front-end loader is brought in. Then suddenly, from the forest, comes a volley of gunfire, the Mohawk and the SQ firing as one. The shots come in a continuous roar, like a cresting wave. It lasts less than 30 seconds, but that's all it takes. The battle is over. The police break rank and run—run like the wind, abandoning six vehicles and their pride to the Mohawks.

In the wake of the assault and the deafening fusillade it unleashed, a strange silence descends. The Mohawk men—eyes stinging from the tear gas, coughing, crouching in position—brace themselves for a second assault. Through the smoke, they hear a bulldozer rumbling towards them, siren wailing, but when it breaks into view, a Mohawk warrior is at the wheel, and a cheer goes up. The bulldozer siren becomes a victory cry, and in the aftermath of the battle an embarrassing array of police weapons, ammunition and communications equipment is gathered up. Using the SQ's own bulldozer, the Mohawks pile the police vehicles on top of each other, forming a new, improved and far more formidable barrier. On a cement blockade, in large letters, the Mohawk protestors write a message: "They came, they saw, they ran away."

In the brief gun battle, Corporal Marcel Lemay, a member of the tactical intervention squad, has been shot. The bullet hit between the sections of his protective vest, and he is rushed from the battlefield in an ambulance, only to die a short while later. Lemay was the father of a two-year-old girl, and his young wife is pregnant with their second child. What began as a standoff over a golf course has now become a war.

A few days later, after the funeral of Corporal Lemay, both the SQ and the Mohawks lower their flags to half-mast. The Mohawk protestors send their condolences and sorrows, but they refuse to accept the blame. It was the mayor of Oka, they point out, who ordered a full-scale armed assault on an area that contained women and children.

The SQ raid was both ill advised and poorly executed, but that no longer matters. With the death of Corporal Lemay, everything has changed. The Shoot-Out at the Oka Corral has sent shock waves across Canada and grabbed headlines around the world. Things like this aren't suppose to happen in Canada, the Peaceable Kingdom. Canada, the Land of the Very Nice People.

Meanwhile, south of Montréal, in a direct response to the attack at Oka, Mohawk protestors from the nearby Kahnawake Reserve seize the Mercier Bridge and blockade all roads leading through their territory. Traffic backs up for miles, and Mohawk steelworkers—who know how a bridge goes up and how to take one down—inform the government that if the Sûreté leads another assault at Oka, they will blow up the Mercier Bridge. The threat works. A second assault is quickly cancelled, and the attention now shifts from the golf course at Oka to the road blockades at Kahnawake. There are in fact two parallel crises, one over the disputed Pines and a second, more effective, sympathy blockade at the Mercier Bridge.

Back at Oka, Mohawk reinforcements are arriving from other reserves in Canada and the United States, most notably from the "Wild West" reserve at Akwesasne, which straddles the U.S.-Canada border near Cornwall, Ontario. Crossing an international boundary as it does, Akwesasne has become a centre for smuggling and illicit gambling. A civil war among Mohawk factions had earlier resulted in running gun battles and two deaths. (The dispute at Oka and the Mercier Bridge had nothing to do with the situation at Akwesasne, but it is surprising how many people still confuse the two and assume that Oka was a civil war of some kind, when in fact it was exactly what it appeared to be: an armed protest against a golf course expansion onto disputed land.)

When the Mohawks at Oka send out a plea for support from the other nations of the Iroquois Confederacy, the Warriors Society at Akwesasne responds in full force, but so do the other First Nations. Protest marches, hunger strikes and blockades on train tracks and highways are launched across Canada. The Assembly of First Nations issues a request to Indian bands across the country, asking them to provide financial aid. Elijah Harper, the MLA who had singlehandedly blocked the Meech Lake Accord just a few weeks prior, arrives to offer his support as well. Natives from Yukon, B.C., Saskatchewan, Ontario, New York, Wisconsin and Nova Scotia pour in, offering food, supplies, reinforcements, weapons. It is one of the most united displays of Native solidarity in recent history.

The Mohawk community itself, however, was deeply divided. On the one hand were the traditionalists under the matrilineal Longhouse Society, divided among Clan Mothers and the men's Warrior Society (more accurately called "carriers of peace"). On the advice of the Longhouse women, these traditionalists were in charge of defending the land against outside attack.

The Longhouse traditions, the Clan Mothers, the Warriors and the Faithkeepers stand in stark opposition to the government-approved Mohawk band councils. Unlike the members of the Longhouse, the band councils, dependent on federal largesse, accept the terms of the Indian Act. (Band councils actually have less autonomy and less authority than the average town council.) Although the officially sanctioned band council system was imposed upon the Iroquois, often with brute force and in armed clashes, the government of Canada now denies the legitimacy of the Longhouse traditions. The members of the Longhouse, in turn, boycott all band council elections and have in fact denounced the council as "puppets" of the federal government.

At the height of the Oka Crisis, Ottawa tried to put a particular spin on the situation by describing the original Mohawk protests as having been "hijacked" by "criminal elements." Following the disastrous SQ attack, Mohawk resistance certainly did harden, and did indeed become more militant and extreme, but the barricades—especially in those first crucial months—were strongly supported by all members of the Mohawk community, including members of the Kahnawake band council. (Which does seem to counter the claim that the councils are merely puppets.)

As the standoffs at Oka and the Mercier Bridge continued, world opinion quickly lost all sympathy for Québécois nationalism. Québec was now perceived as the bully and not the victim. When the Sûreté du Québec cut off food and medical supplies to the Mohawk protestors in an attempt to starve them out, Québec's own Ligues des Droits et Libertés condemned the SQ's actions. A convoy of Red Cross vehicles negotiated with the SQ for safe passage to bring supplies to the 150 or so protestors behind the barricades, but at one point the SQ refused to let the Red Cross through and delayed delivery of food and medicine by 24 hours, in violation of every known international human rights convention.

The confrontation at the Pines was reminiscent of trench warfare, with the two sides facing off across a no man's land. The Mohawks laid down their conditions: they wanted title to the Pines, a police withdrawal and a 48-hour amnesty after the barricades came down. They also wanted all legal disputes arising from the armed confrontation referred to the World Court in the Hague, something the federal government refused to consider. (To have agreed to the intervention of the World Court would have been tacit recognition of Mohawk sovereignty, something Ottawa could not allow.)

It is a myth, and a nasty one at that, that the Mohawk demands concerned legalized gambling or contraband cigarettes. The fact is, the demands made by the

Mohawks concerned land ownership, police reprisals and international observers. They were never about bingo or smuggling. Indeed, the only group who made money from the Oka Crisis was the town council of Oka—and they made millions.

The federal government, trying to buy its way out of the problem without having to deal directly with the underlying issues, agreed to spend a whopping $5.3 million for the section of the Pines that had been slated for the golf course expansion, thus preventing further development. Mayor Ouellette eventually agreed and, feeling generous, also threw in the Mohawk cemetery and the ancestral bones contained therein, which he sold to the federal government for $1. The Mohawks were insulted and enraged, as well they might be. Even then, the real issue of land title had not been addressed; ownership of the Pines had merely changed hands, from one level of government to another.

At the Mercier Bridge and the other Kahnawake barricades, things had quickly turned ugly. The citizens of the bedroom community of Châteauguay were now forced to take a long detour to get into Montréal, and for this inconvenience they wanted blood. (You don't mess around with a commuter's route.) Mobs gathered at the barricades, screaming for vengeance, and when a Mohawk woman was spotted shopping in a Châteauguay grocery store, a group attacked her, hurling stones and racial insults as they chased her back to the reserve.

Contrary to popular misconception, these ugly scenes at the bridge were not the result of long-simmering, pent-up frustrations. The mobs formed almost instantly. Within a day or two, crude caricatures of Indians were being strung up in effigy and set on fire. The tribal cry of *"Québec pour les Québécois"* rang out proudly and loudly. On July 13, when an ambulance tried to get through to take an injured Mohawk child to a hospital, the Québécois mob swarmed in, rocking the vehicle and attempting to flip it over. This event occurred just two days after the barricades went up. The Mohawk protest had quickly been transformed into a race war.

As reported in *People of the Pines*, the Châteauguay member of Parliament helped fan the flames, as did the francophone chapter of the KKK and the virulently anti-Indian radio host Gilles Proulx, who repeatedly reminded his angry listeners that the Mohawks "couldn't even speak French." (The Châteauguay MP had once recommended rounding up all the Indians in Québec and shipping them off to Labrador "if they want their own country so much.") Effigies of Indians in war paint and feathers continued to be strung up, and the Mohawks replied by burning the fleur-de-lis flag.

Geoffrey York and Loreen Pindera, whose book remains the definitive work on the Oka Crisis, write, "What the Mohawks saw on the faces of those who chanted beneath the burning effigies was pure racial hatred. The mobs helped to unify the Kahnawake Mohawks and solidify their support for the warriors at the barricades."

As the Mohawks soon discovered, the blockade cut both ways. The Kahnawake Reserve was now sealed off. The people there had put themselves under voluntary siege. Vans filled with Québécois vigilantes cruised the back roads "lookin' for Indians" and making sure no one managed to escape. Food shortages were real, and crowds of enraged Québécois repeatedly blocked efforts to get supplies through, while the Sûreté stood by and did very little. In fact, on several occasions SQ officers seemed to encourage the mobs. That is, until the mob turned on the SQ as well, lobbing Molotov cocktails and broken bottles at the police. The crowds even managed to set one officer on fire and put 10 RCMP constables in the hospital. (The RCMP had been called in when the SQ lost control.)

Finally, in an unnerving echo of 1970 events, Premier Robert Bourassa phoned the prime minister of Canada and asked him to send in the troops. The War Measures Act had been rescinded two years earlier, so Bourassa was not allowed to declare martial law. Instead, he invoked the National Defence Act and demanded that Prime Minister Mulroney comply. Mulroney was reluctant to send in the army because, in the words of a senior government official, Mulroney didn't want to go down in history as "the butcher of Oka." But Bourassa insisted, and the prime minister eventually relented.

In mid-August, a delegation from the International Federation of Human Rights arrived to investigate allegations of abuse. When they attempted to enter Kahnawake, the Québécois mobs refused to let them through, and the delegates had to be airlifted in to avoid being attacked by baseball-bat-wielding gangs. The protests had indeed been usurped by "criminal elements." But it was on the Québécois side of the barriers that this occurred.

Later, a member of the Human Rights Federation, a judge from Norway, described the events that were unfolding as "degrading . . . The only persons who have treated me in a civilized way in this matter here in Canada are the Mohawks. The army and police do nothing."

On August 23, the Châteauguay mobs prevented a Mohawk woman from getting to a maternity ward, and she was forced to have her baby at home, behind the barricades. During delivery she began haemorrhaging, and an ambulance was rushed in. However, rock-throwing yahoos surrounded the vehicle and tried to stop it from leaving, even pulling open the door to terrorize the bleeding mother and her newborn baby. *Québec pour les Québécois!* The mob almost cost the woman her life; had they managed to delay the ambulance much longer, she would most likely have died.

By this point, the armed forces had already moved in. Helicopters circled overhead, and Leopard tanks were loaded onto trucks. At Oka, the Sûreté had peered at the Mohawk positions from across a 1.5-kilometre no man's land, but the army boldly moved their perimeter right up to within five metres of the barricades. Tensions climbed, and no evening news broadcast was complete without the spectacle of a battle-fatigued warrior standing nose-to-nose, eyeball-to-eyeball and manhood-to-manhood with a Canadian soldier. It was all very theatrical. And desperate.

On August 28, in the face of an impending attack by the army, the Mohawks at Kahnawake decided to evacuate 200 women, children and elderly. The convoy of vehicles was stopped and searched by the police when it tried to drive past the barriers. The women inside were attempting to flee the escalating violence, but the police held them for more than two hours while an ominous crowd of Québécois grew. The vehicles were then forced to crawl past a gauntlet of bricks, rocks and bottles. A huge chunk of cement went through a car window, shattering it, and a 76-year-old man inside was hit in the chest and badly cut. More windows were shattered. Cars were pummelled. Racist taunts went up. The police made no real attempt to restrain the crowds, and among the eventual casualties was a 71-year-old Mohawk man, a veteran of World War II, who died a few days later from heart failure, his death attributed to the strain of the mob attack.

The following morning, August 29, a small group of unarmed Mohawk warriors stepped out from behind the barricades at the Mercier Bridge. One of them laid a peace pipe on the ground. An army officer went over to meet them; the men talked, shook hands, and the Kahnawake siege was over. It would take more than a week for the army and the Mohawks, working together, to dismantle the various barricades, but by September 6 the Mercier Bridge was reopened to commuter traffic.

The Mohawks across the river at Oka felt betrayed. With the Mercier Bridge now open, they had lost their only effective bargaining chip—and it showed. Once the traffic was moving smoothly again, the Québec government rejected all new Mohawk overtures.

The media, encouraged by the army and the SQ, had greatly exaggerated the Mohawks' arsenal, often to ridiculous proportions. At the peak of the crisis, newspapers circulated rumours that the Mohawks had upwards of 6,000 guns. In fact, the Native protestors had fewer than 600 rifles, the vast majority of which were legally purchased in Canada and duly registered with the Sûreté du Québec. Nor did the Mohawks have rocket launchers or anti-tank missiles or huge caches of firepower or a secret air force of Cessna planes. These too are myths. The Mohawk arsenal paled in comparison to that of the army and the police.

At Oka, the situation was getting more and more strained. The nose-to-nose confrontations, staged for news cameras and photographers, were now hurting Mohawk credibility. A few of the more extreme, showboating warriors had become media sluts, strutting and posing and feeding their egos.

During the siege, houses near the war zone, abandoned by nervous homeowners, were vandalized by a small band of warriors acting on their own. Lootings and break-ins increased as the summer wore on, and when two of the Mohawk men responsible were reprimanded by their own people, they physically attacked their accusers. One of their victims had to flee across the barricade lines, seeking refuge with the army—who promptly arrested him.

With the breakdown of order inside the Mohawk camp and the growing threat of mass violence, the army decided to act. On September 1, they rolled a convoy of trucks right up and through the barriers. The warriors had vowed not to fire first, and they kept their word. The army, by maintaining its poise in the face of taunts and death threats, slowly pushed the Mohawk warriors back. "I was waiting for that first shot," recalled one warrior later. "That's all it would have taken."

Ironically, the Mohawk system of group consensus and decentralized authority ultimately worked against them. As the army moved in from all sides, there was no central, coordinated response from the Mohawks. "Give me permission to shoot! Someone give me permission to shoot," one warrior screamed.

In stark contrast to the cowboy tactics of the SQ, the Canadian Forces moved forward in a methodical, relentless advance. The soldiers showed remarkable discipline, and in the end their self-control paid off. The Mohawk line of defence was breached, the barricades came down, and about 30 warriors, together with women and children, fell back to a treatment centre at the edge of an escarpment. The army ringed the area around the centre with razor wire, trapping the remaining Mohawks inside. The standoff had now turned into a siege.

The army commander phoned in and demanded an unconditional surrender. The warriors refused, and tensions grew. During the night, Canadian soldiers crept across and beat a sleeping warrior senseless. He was forced to leave the centre to seek outside medical treatment—and was promptly arrested.

The army then cut all phone lines, save their own, and clamped down on Mohawk contact with the outside world, a move condemned by the European Parliament as a violation of basic human rights. The intent seemed clear: if the army was going to be forced to fire on Mohawk civilians, they didn't want any outside witnesses. The biggest blow came on September 14, when George Erasmus, the Grand Chief of the Assembly of First Nations, suddenly withdrew his support from the remaining warriors (although he continued to condemn Ottawa's handling of the crisis).

On September 25, the penultimate confrontation took place, and a strange one it was. It began when one of the warriors started walking around the perimeter, reaching across the razor wire with a long hooked stick and systematically setting off the trip-wire flares that the army had installed to detect attempted escapes. Angry, the soldiers turned a hose on the Mohawk man, but there was not enough pressure to knock over the tarpaulins the warriors had hung up to block the army's spotlights, let alone to disperse a crowd. The warriors taunted the soldiers, asking for more water so that they could shampoo and rinse. So the soldiers sprayed everyone. The Mohawk men and women responded by flinging water balloons back at soldiers. This response set off a full-scale water fight with much laughter and hilarity on both sides of the razor wire, until an enraged officer stomped over and yelled at his men to cease and desist. Sheepishly, the soldiers stopped their hijinks, even as the Mohawks taunted the officer and threw a few more water balloons.

The day after the Battle of the Water Balloons, the remaining Mohawks came to a decision. They were weary and they wanted to go home. They had blocked the golf course expansion and had focussed world attention on Canada's Native land claims. They could claim victory. In *This Land Is Our Land*, Michael Baxendale and Craig MacLaine write, "There would be no shame in laying down their weapons. It would not be a surrender. It would be a 'unilateral cessation of hostilities.' "

The Mohawks burned any incriminating evidence, dismantling their guns and dumping them into the septic tank, and then, after a final ceremonial burning of tobacco, they simply . . . walked away. Men, women and children. They used boards to cross the razor wire and then disappeared into the Pines. The soldiers scrambled to capture them, and as Mohawk protestors were wrestled to the ground, the Siege of Oka came to a flustered end.

Amid the confusion, a few Mohawk men managed to walk through the Pines and into the town of Oka. Stunned reporters saw a few notorious faces strolling down the main street. When asked "What are you doing?" one man replied, "We're walking home."

Among those captured by the army was a 14-year-old girl named Waneek Horn-Miller, who was stabbed in the chest by a bayonet during the scuffle. She carries the scar today in more ways than one. It was such a sad finale. What began with a money-making scheme to expand a local golf course ended with the Canadian army bayoneting a young girl. Not our most heroic moment.

The Oka Crisis lasted 78 days and caused the deaths of three people: SQ Corporal Marcel Lemay; Joe Armstrong, the 71-year-old Mohawk man who died after running the gauntlet of the Québécois mob; and an elderly Québécois man who was poisoned when the initial SQ gas attack of July 11 drifted downwind through Oka. (He lingered for a few months before dying.)

Almost 70 Mohawks were arrested, charged and put on trial in the months that followed. Most were acquitted, several were fined, and a few were sent to prison. The longest sentence handed out was four years. No one was ever charged with the murder of Corporal Lemay.

The situation at Oka represented the first time since 1970 that the Canadian army had been called in to quell a domestic crisis. More than 5,000 soldiers and SQ officers were involved, and the crisis cost the federal and Québec governments more than $150 million—plus the $1 Ottawa spent to buy the Mohawk cemetery.

In November 1991, Oka mayor Jean Ouellette was reelected in a landslide victory. When asked about the events of 1990, he replied that he had no regrets, none whatsoever: "If I had to do it all over again, I would."

Québec's own Human Rights Commission denounced the actions of the Sûreté du Québec. The International Federation of Human Rights, an organization based in Paris and accredited with the UN, publicly criticized the tactics of both the SQ and the Canadian army. Amnesty International raised allegations of torture and abuse following the final arrest of six Mohawk warriors, and added Canada to its list of human rights violators.

In *People of the Pines*, Waneek Horn-Miller, looking back on the Oka Crisis, put it as succinctly as anyone: "I think Canada isn't as great a place as people say it is."

Verdict

The Warrior Society: **Proud Bastards**

The Sûreté du Québec: **Not-So-Proud Boneheads**

Mayor Jean Ouellette: **Oblivious Bastard**

Robert "Boo Boo" Bourassa: What can I say? Once a **Bonehead**, always a **Bonehead**.

17

Ten Lost Years: The Decade of Discord

DEFYING GRAVITY AND common sense, and against all odds and expectations, Canada has managed to make it to the twenty-first century. Limping across the finish line, into the Glorious Second Millennium, we send up a weary sigh of relief, because, if nothing else, the nineties are finally over. Good-bye, and good riddance.

The nineties was the Decade of Disunity, the Decade of Discord, and it seemed to go on forever, like some kind of nightmare Möbius strip.

In the 1990s, Canada foundered and almost collapsed. Why? No reason. No reason at all. There were no wars, no economic disasters, no catastrophes, no conscription crises. There was just us, bumbling along. Led first by Brian Mulroney and later Big Jean, we managed to talk ourselves to the very edge of the abyss, shuffling papers and memos on our way to oblivion.

The nineties passed like a kidney stone: painful, drawn out and best forgotten. It was a decade of great kerfuffles and wrenching national debates that resolved nothing—absolutely nothing. For those of you who wisely chose to remain drunk or sedated through most of it, here are a few highlights of the last 10 years.

LOOK BACK IN EXHAUSTION: THE DECADE THAT WAS

1990
, The Meech Lake Accord collapses.
, Lucien Bouchard denounces the collapse of the accord as "a humiliation."
, Separatism in Québec soars to new heights.

1992
- The Charlottetown Accord is quickly patched together, and just as quickly rejected.
- Québec separatist leader Jacques Parizeau describes the death of the accord as evidence that Canada is unworkable.
- Separatism in Québec soars to new heights.

1993
- Brian Mulroney resigns, the Conservatives are defeated, and Lucien Bouchard's Bloc Québécois (a party dedicated to breaking up Canada) is named Her Majesty's Loyal Opposition.
- Separatism in Québec soars to new heights.

1995
- The Parti Québécois holds a referendum on Québec sovereignty and comes within a percentage point of winning.
- Québec Premier Jacques Parizeau blames the loss on "money and the ethnic vote."
- Separatism in Québec soars to new heights.

1998
- The Parti Québécois is reelected.
- Having made the leap from leader of the federal Tories to leader of the Québec Liberals, Jean Charest contemplates getting a new haircut.
- Separatism in Québec soars to new heights.

1999
- Montréal experiences unseasonably cold temperatures in early November.
- The Parti Québécois describes the bad weather as "a humiliation."
- Separatism in Québec soars to new heights.

2000
- A royal commission reveals that the sky is blue.
- The Parti Québécois denounces the study as "humiliating."
- Separatism in Québec soars to new heights.

That great, ethnically obsessed nationalist Lucien Bouchard once said, "Canada is divisible because Canada is not a real country." And he was right. To judge by the way we coddle separatists and allow them to set the national agenda, Canada is *not* a real country. It is a Theatre of the Absurd. And the performances have been getting a little stale and a little repetitive lately.

I mean, how much more humiliation can our poor, downtrodden separatist brethren endure?

The humiliation—the utter, abject humiliation—of the passing of the 1982 Constitution Act is what fuelled most of the rhetoric and boneheaded gestures that plagued us throughout the nineties. In theory, the act was fairly straightforward. It removed the last remnants of British parliamentary authority, as well as readjusting powers between the federal and provincial governments and adding an amending formula for future changes. But most importantly, it included a shiny new Charter of Rights and Freedoms, which established the human rights of the individual as both the final court of appeal and the philosophical foundation of Canadian society. At least, in theory. In practice, well, it wasn't quite that simple. There was a serious, almost fatal, flaw in the act. As a concession to the premiers, Section 33 of the charter contains a "notwithstanding clause," which allows any provincial legislature to override almost any part of the charter. A few years later, when the Supreme Court of Canada declared Québec's anti-English sign laws to be unconstitutional, provincial premier Robert Bourassa simply invoked the "notwithstanding clause" and ran roughshod over both the charter of human rights and the Supreme Court of Canada. (In Canada, you see, real power lies not with charters and the courts but with the peckerheads we elect to our provincial assemblies.)

Still, if nothing else, human rights had, in a typically muddled Canadian way, been enshrined in our constitution. Yay! Time to celebrate, right? Well, anywhere else on earth, perhaps, but not here in the Great White North, where the motto is "Logic? We don't need no steenkin' logic." In Canada, the 1982 patriation of the constitution, with the charter of rights and the full political independence it implies, is soulfully remembered not as a triumph but as a defeat. Instead of uniting us, it has become yet another Moment Divisive in our national history.

Why? Because the province of Québec refused to acknowledge the legitimacy of the 1982 Constitution Act, insisting that it was forced on them against their will. This is one of the Big Lies of modern Canadian history. René Lévesque, Québec's separatist premier at the time of patriation, would never have approved any constitutional agreement. Trudeau knew this, and Lévesque knew that Trudeau knew. Hence, the conscious decision on Lévesque's part to portray the 1982 act as "a betrayal." This assertion is simply not true. If anything, Québec "forced" the constitution on the rest of Canada. Consider: in 1982, the prime minister of Canada was from Québec, the Minister of Justice was from Québec, a third of the Cabinet was from Québec, 74 of 75 MPs from the province of Québec were members of the ruling party, and all but three of Québec's federal MPs approved the deal. And even with the separatists in power provincially, a full 60 per cent of Québec's elected representatives—federal and provincial combined—supported the Constitution Act.

One can certainly question Pierre Trudeau's wisdom in trying to bring the constitution home when a separatist government was entrenched in *la belle province*, but the 1982 act cannot be portrayed as invalid or illegitimate. Not by any stretch of the imagination.

Unfortunately, in 1987, Canada's stalwart helmsman, Brian Mulroney, decided to reopen the constitutional can of worms. Unlike Trudeau, he thought he could sweet-talk Québec nationalists into giving their approval. After meeting with the provincial premiers, Brian Mulroney—the "head-waiter of Confederation," in Trudeau's famous phrase—dutifully jotted down the premiers' various petty little demands and then typed them up nice and neat. The Meech Lake Accord, as the jottings were known, outlined these demands in the following manner:

1. Gimme
2. Gimme
3. Gimme

Central to the accord was the fact that it gave a veto to every single province, including tiny P.E.I., which, with a population of 130,000 (less than most midsize Canadian cities), would now be able to overrule legislation affecting the lives of some 27 million other Canadians. This was the new, inclusive approach to federalism: Canada would become a collection of self-cancelling fiefdoms. More ominous yet, Meech Lake also recognized the province of Québec (not French Canadians, mind you, but the actual provincial territory) as a "distinct society" within Confederation.

Constitutional authority Eugene Forsey called the Meech Lake Accord "a quagmire of ambiguities," and former prime minister Pierre Trudeau, reappearing from the mist like the Ghost of Hamlet's Father, savaged the Mulroney deal. The Trudeau-Mulroney feud quickly came down to a contest of manhood and implied sexual prowess—or lack thereof. Trudeau denounced Mulroney as "a weakling" and predicted that the accord would "render the Canadian state totally impotent," destined to be "governed by eunuchs." If Canada was going to end, it should be "with a bang, not a whimper." This was muscular, testosterone-driven language, and the target of Trudeau's attack wilted under the assault like a piece of limp celery. Trudeau hadn't just knifed Mulroney, he had twisted the blade.

It got worse.

Weeping crocodile tears over the impeding death of Meech Lake, Lucien

Bouchard, the Snidely Whiplash of Canadian nationalism, resigned from the Conservative cabinet to spearhead the separatist coalition of the Bloc Québécois. (Mulroney, of course, was the Dudley Do-Right of Canadian nationalism, a man brimming with bromides and bumbling boneheaded sincerity. Heck, he even had the cartoon chin.)

The Meech Lake Accord sputtered and died. It had gone up like a rocket, and it came down like a stick.

Now, if Brian Mulroney had had the sense God gave gravel, he would have quit while he was ahead. Thrown a couple of royal commissions at the mess. Made vague, meaningless speeches and appeased Québec in the usual way, with aerospace contracts and government grants. But no, not our Brian. Instead, like a punch-drunk boxer too stupid to know when to quit, he came back with the Charlottetown Accord. This agreement expanded on the themes of Meech Lake in the following way:

1. Gimme
2. Gimme
3. Gimme
4. More

Everybody was at the federal trough. Every two-bit provincial premier and special interest group bellied up for their share. Politicians were dishing out rights to every ethnic, linguistic and gender-based group in existence. Forget individual rights; Canada was about to become a nation based entirely on the rights of collectives, an entire nation of oppressed minorities, and a damn whiny one at that. Mulroney was practically stopping people on the street and offering to include them in his new, bloated and utterly unworkable constitution. The approach was beyond vague, it was garbled. (The French and English translations of the accord didn't match either, so you can imagine the type of fun that would have followed had it actually passed.)

Pierre Trudeau once again staged a strategic, one-man attack, striding out onto centre stage and denouncing the Charlottetown Accord as "a mess that deserves a big no." Speaking without notes, Trudeau tore apart both the accord and Brian Mulroney's credibility in a 40-minute after-dinner speech in downtown Montréal. If there is any doubt about the effect of personality on the events of history, one need look no further than the way a single, forceful individual, Pierre Elliott Trudeau, almost singlehandedly brought down a mighty alliance of political elites. Remember: Every province, every premier, every major political party backed Mulroney's new sweetheart deal. The entire machinery of the political establish-

❋ THE NONS HAVE IT! FIVE TO ONE

If the separatists in Québec really want to win, they should word the next referendum in the negative. Instead of asking Quebeckers to say *oui* to separation, they should ask them to say *non* to Canada. (That is, "Do you want Québec to stay in Confederation? Yes or No?") It is always easier to get the Québécois to reject a proposal than to accept it. This fundamental contrariness of character is something I find wholly admirable. It is a stubborn survival technique, and it has served them well over the years.

Quebeckers have voted in six separate provincial and national referendums/plebiscites since Confederation. In virtually every case, the "No" side won.

  1995   Referendum on sovereignty: Non! (51%)
  1992   Referendum on the Charlottetown Accord: Non! (55%)
  1980   Referendum on sovereignty association: Non! (60%)
  1942   Referendum on conscription: Non! (73%)
  1898   Referendum on introducing Prohibition: Non! (81%)
         (Québec was the only province who voted against it.)

There was, however, one glaring exception. As *Globe and Mail* columnist André Picard points out, Quebeckers did give their overwhelming support to the "Yes" side in one referendum. It happened on April 10, 1919, when nearly 80 per cent voted *oui*. The question? Whether to *end* Prohibition.

ment, from the government to the official Opposition, threw its full weight behind the Charlottetown Accord. These folks had money, resources and almost unlimited access to the media. And they *still* lost.

The Charlottetown Accord was rejected by 54 per cent of Canadians. In Québec, the number was 55 per cent. So you would think that, at least in this, the aspirations of Québec and the Rest of Canada were in line. But no; that is not how the separatists saw it. For them, it was another slap in the face for Québec, another "humiliation."

Mulroney, meanwhile, had denounced the opponents of the Charlottetown

Accord as "enemies of Canada" and had predicted that the entire country would fall apart if the agreement didn't pass. He was wrong on both counts. The only real casualty was Mulroney himself: his ham-handed attempts at amending the constitution had cost him his career, his political reputation and his place in history.

Let this be a lesson to any young politicians out there: constitutional reform is the Russian steppes of Canadian politics. Enter at your peril. Having marched boldly into the fray, Brian Mulroney was swept back by waves of Bolsheviks. Pandora's box had burst open. Separatism once again reared its ugly, tribal head. Lucien Bouchard was poised to become the leader of the Opposition, and the nation was on the brink of collapse.

"Well," said Brian. "My work here is done." And he rode off into the sunset.

By this point, the momentum was clearly on the separatists' side. The newly elected PQ government called for a referendum on Québec sovereignty and quickly commissioned four different studies on the economic effects of independence. (The PQ never released the studies because they didn't like the results.) As part of his separatist blueprint, Jacques Parizeau released a bizarre 84-page document entitled "Our Hearts in Our Work," which, among other things, listed the traits that made Quebeckers different from the rest of Canada. Among the irreconcilable differences that make separation inevitable: "Quebeckers like to ride bicycles more than the rest of Canada. They watch their calories more. They are more tolerant. [!] They spend more money on clothes than do other Canadians." All good, valid reasons for breaking up a country. One item, however, did stick out, if only because it so perfectly captured the tilt-a-whirl logic of the Québec separatists. According to the Parti Québécois, "Quebeckers spend more on lottery tickets *and* have more personal life insurance than other Canadians." In other words, they try to have it both ways. Kind of like separating from Canada, but still keeping a common currency and passport.

You would think that up against buffoons like Parizeau and opportunists like Bouchard, the federalist forces would have been able to win a referendum hands down. After all, separatism is such an irrational, emotional movement. Ah, but never underestimate the power of the irrational in human history. That, and the inept complacency with which the federalist forces were mustered. Jean Chrétien said, "Don't worry, be happy," and he damn near lost us the country.

Only a last-minute mass rally and love-in at Montréal's Place du Canada appears to have averted certain disaster. Coming just three days before the vote, the rally fought fire with fire, emotion with emotion. It was a direct appeal to the heart, and apparently it worked, pushing the *non* vote just a nudge ahead. On October 30, 1995, Québec voted *non* to sovereignty by a mere 50.6 per cent.

Jean Chrétien managed to get himself reelected in 1997, mainly by default:

"Anybody here know *why* we are having an election?" The following year, Québec Premier Lucien Bouchard was also reelected, and the separatist merry-go-round started back up again. Around and around and around we go.

There is, however, a lingering postscript. In 1998, the same year that Bouchard and the separatists were reelected in Québec, Martin Goldfarb released an intriguing poll. The results of this poll were largely lost amid the din and continuing hoopla about our imminent doom, but in its way, this seemingly innocuous survey may very well have far more long-term significance than any PQ bluster.

In January and February of that year, Goldfarb asked people whether they agreed or disagreed with the following statement: "I am proud to be a Canadian." The results were surprising. In a nation that is supposedly unpatriotic, 80 per cent of all Canadians said they felt "strongly" that they were proud to be Canadian. Only 5 per cent said they were not. In Québec, more than 80 per cent also stated that they were proud to be Canadian (50 per cent "strongly" and 33 per cent "somewhat"). Only 16 per cent of Québécois stated that they were *not* proud to be Canadian. This is hardly an insurmountable difference.

Separatist rhetoric, meanwhile, grows shriller and shriller, much like a small child whose antics grow more and more frantic as he begins to lose our attention. The separatists are wrong. Canada is not a seething cauldron of irreconcilable differences, nor is separation inevitable. If Canada does break apart, it will be because of a lack of national will on our part, and nothing more. In the 1990s, we put a shotgun to our heads and pulled the trigger. Twice. And we missed both times. Canadians: we can't even commit suicide properly.

And that, more or less, is the tale of that Dismal Decade, the nineties. Though I imagine, by this point, most of my readers have abandoned me and I am now talking to myself. That's understandable. The nineties, after all, was a decade best forgotten. Just writing about it is exhausting. I need a drink.

We all need a drink.

Verdict

Brian "Roll of the Dice" Mulroney: **A Bonehead in Bastard's Clothing**

Pierre "With a Bang, Not a Whimper" Trudeau: **A Bastard in Bastard's Clothing**

Jacques "Money and the Ethnic Vote" Parizeau: **Bonehead**. (Or, if he prefers, *La Tête d'Os.*)

Lucien "Canada Is Not a Real Country" Bouchard: **Bastard**. (Or, if he prefers, *A Real Bouchard.*)

"The Holy Terror."
Women's rights activist
Nellie McClung

"We've won! We've won!"
Judge Emily Murphy

*"An unexpected guest at
a dinner party."* Agnes
Macphail, Canada's
first female MP

*"Stalwarts in scarlet
coats."* Sam Steele,
Boer War veteran and
NWMP officer

*"Men, the world regards
you as a marvel!"*
Minister of Militia
Sam Hughes

*"The greatest general the
war produced."*
Canada's own
Arthur Currie

*"Senseless drumming
and dancing."* Poet and
bureaucrat Duncan
Campbell Scott

*"The perfect instrument
of government policy."*
Frederick Charles Blair

*"Loved, hated and
feared."* New-
foundland Premier
Joey Smallwood

"P'Tit Louis and the other Quiet Revolution."
New Brunswick Premier Louis Robichaud, at far left,
with (*left to right*) Lester Pearson, Jean Lesage
and Joey Smallwood

"Le roi nègre?"
The all-powerful
Maurice Duplessis

"My fast-living restless life." The seductive Gerda Munsinger

"The dangerous precedent of retroactive crime." Quebec Premier Robert Bourassa

"No, Mr. Speaker."
Native MLA
Elijah Harper

"Bastard, Bonehead, Bastard, Bastard."
Prime Minister Lester Pearson, at right, with three young cabinet ministers, each of
whom would one day become prime minister.
Left to right: Pierre Elliott Trudeau, John Turner, Jean Chrétien

Boneheads on Parade:

A Survey of Canadian Prime Ministers, Past and Present

18

More Sorry, Misguided Attempts at Evaluation (And Why Mine Is Still the Best Ever)

HAVING CONCLUDED OUR examination of some of the key players in Canadian history, we now turn our highly scientific and completely objective gaze upon the prime ministers of Canada. Many of them have already flitted across our pages and have even been classified as Bastards or Boneheads in relation to particular events, but in the chapters that follow we will look at them one by one, in chronological order, and attempt to evaluate them in light of their entire careers.

This final evaluation, then, will be the true test: if the Bastard and Bonehead System of Classification proves itself capable of handling the vast spectrum of Canada's prime ministers, then surely we can say—with something approaching mathematical certainty—that this system works. Or, at the very least, that it deserves further investigation by leading authorities in the field. Either way, it should qualify me for a couple more Canada Council grants.

Now then, as you may recall, at the beginning of this book we examined several competing systems of classification (Founders & Guardians, Winners & Losers, Dinks & Not Dinks). These, however, were based in *general* theories of leadership. Let us now look at some systems designed specifically for Canadian prime ministers. Although these, too, have proven woefully inadequate, there is still a certain value in examining their various shortcomings, if only to further illuminate the brilliant insights of my own B&B dichotomy.[†]

[†]Or "paradigm."

THE PIERRE TRUDEAU "NASTY/NICE" HYPOTHESIS

Pierre Elliott Trudeau once remarked that there were "nice guys" and "nasty guys," and that sometimes it took a nasty guy to get things done. There is some truth in this observation. It is the Bastards of the world who usually effect change, and Bastards are often (but not always) nasty.

In fact, at first glance it might appear that the two systems, Nasty/Nice and Bastards/Boneheads, are synonymous. But first impressions are deceiving. For although most Bastards are indeed nasty (Pierre Trudeau himself being a prime example) and most Boneheads are indeed nice (for example, Joe Clark), there have also been Nice Bastards (for example, Lester Pearson) and Nasty Boneheads (for example, Arthur Meighen). "Nasty" and "Nice" are simply qualifiers; they do not offer a final evaluation in and of themselves. The Trudeau System, therefore, fails to live up to our exacting standards, and as such must be discarded.

THE DOMINANT LEADER THEORY

In his study *The Origins of Canadian Politics*, Gordon Stewart defines Canada as a nation shaped primarily by a handful of what he calls "dominant leaders." Namely: Macdonald, Laurier, King, St. Laurent and Trudeau. Other than the somewhat surprising inclusion of St. Laurent on the list, this classification system ultimately fails because it doesn't make room for the likes of Diefenbaker, Mulroney and Bennett, who did as much damage as anyone. They too were dominant in that they had an immense *negative* impact on the nation. What we need is a theory that accounts for both the good and the bad, the winners and the losers, the bastards and the boneheads.

THE EET SYSTEM

In 1993, following Jean Chrétien's election to the PMO, the British newspaper *The Independent* offered its own classification system. It did this by dividing Canada's prime ministers into two broad categories: "The first comprises those whom the rest of the world has largely forgotten, if it ever knew about them; the second comprises Pierre Trudeau."

The *Independent* analyst goes on to note that although the world may remember Trudeau for the wrong reasons, the trivial reasons—his irreverence, his flamboyance, his feisty young wife—it at least remembers him. "[Trudeau] was a fashionable man from an unfashionable country, a bright spark struck from a dull flint." (The English, of course, being renowned for their sharp fashion sense and stylish joie de vivre.)

Other than the fact that the EET System (Everybody Except Trudeau) was devised by an insufferably smug Englishman—a redundancy, I know—it also fails because it doesn't take into account the rich assortment of eccentrics, nutballs, weirdos and visionaries Canadians have elected over the years. So the EET System too must be rejected.

FRIENDS AND ENEMIES

In *Stand Up for Canada*, Doreen and Robert Jackson divide our leaders into (a) Friends of Canada (Jean Chrétien and former NDP leader Audrey McLaughlin), and (b) Enemies of Canada (Preston Manning, Brian Mulroney, Jacques Parizeau). Former prime minister John Abbott is classified as "a scoundrel" for having once urged Canada's annexation to the United States. But "scoundrel" is just about as malicious as Jackson and Jackson ever get. They even go so far as to insist—vast archival evidence to the contrary—that "all Prime Ministers have been honest, upright Canadians." That's right, "honest and upright." Clearly, this is a tenuous theory at best, and as such, it too must be rejected.

ESTABLISHED BUREAUCRATS AND SOPHISTICATED LAWYERS

In his memoir *Straight from the Heart*, Jean Chrétien gives his own evaluation of past Liberal PMs:

King: "a sober bureaucrat"
St. Laurent: "an established lawyer"
Pearson: "a distinguished diplomat"
Trudeau: "a sophisticated intellectual"

I imagine you could combine the different elements of the Chrétien Classification System to give faint, innocuous praise to just about any public figure: "Mr. Jones is a sober intellectual," "a sophisticated lawyer," "an established bureaucrat." And so on.

Note also that, under the Chrétien System, it takes eight separate nouns and adjectives to classify just four prime ministers, whereas with my simpler, more concise method, only one term is required:

King: **Bastard**
St. Laurent: **Bastard**
Pearson: **Bastard**
Trudeau: **Bastard**

So, once again, we see just how efficient, intelligent and scientific the B&B System truly is. And good-looking, too.

TWO KINDS OF GOVERNMENT

Prior to the development of the "B&B Breakthrough" (as I like to call it), the best classification system devised was that of John W. Dafoe, the legendary editor of the Winnipeg *Free Press*, who once noted: "There are only two kinds of government: the scarcely tolerable and the absolutely unbearable."

I think this a splendid observation, and for a while I seriously considered dividing the prime ministers of Canada accordingly (for example, Pierre Trudeau: "scarcely tolerable"; Brian Mulroney: "absolutely unbearable"). But Dafoe was referring more to entire administrations, whereas I wanted to focus on specific personalities.

And with that, I rest my case. As the case studies in the following chapter will prove indisputably, no other scientific/academic system is better equipped to classify the full range of Canadian prime ministers than "Bastards and Boneheads."

19

John A. to Jean C.: An Overview

NOW, BEFORE WE review the careers of our various prime ministers, there is something you should keep in mind: every one of them (with a few notable exceptions) was put into office by *us*. By Canadians. That's the problem with democracy: the people have no alibi. We really do get the government we deserve. Brian Mulroney didn't stage a *coup d'état* and take Parliament by force; he was elected by his fellow citizens. Twice. So whatever the character of the rooster that makes it to the top of the dung pile, the ultimate responsibility lies with the average Canadians below. People like you and me. And I voted Rhinoceros, so it looks like this is all your fault.

Here then is the parade. Pay attention—there will be a test at the end.

1.
Sir John Alexander Macdonald
Nicknames: "Old Tomorrow"; "The Wizard of the North"
Party: Conservative
Terms: 1867–73, 1878–91
Words to live by:
"The public prefers John A. drunk to George Brown sober."
　　　　—self-assessment made by Macdonald in
reference to his upstanding and *very* sober arch-rival

Highlights

John A. was the alcoholic Father of the Nation, and with a father like that, is it any wonder we have been in therapy for so long? "I know my dad loved me, but . . ."

Born in Scotland, raised in Kingston, John Alexander was a tall, awkward man with a huge nose and a shock of unruly hair. He was handsome in an ugly sort of way, or ugly in a handsome sort of way, depending on your bias. (His own sister described him as "one of the ugliest men in Canada.") He charmed the ladies and sparred with opponents, and even his enemies admired him. Committed to the Empire but stubbornly supportive of French-Canadians, he was anti–free trade, anti-American and pro-British.

Once while in Washington to negotiate a treaty, John A. fell into conversation with the wife of a U.S. senator. She asked where he was from, and when he said Canada, she remarked that Canada's leader was a man named Macdonald who was known to be a "regular rascal."

"Oh, yes," said John A. "A perfect rascal."

"But why do they keep such a man in power?" she asked.

"Well, you see," said John A., "they cannot get along without him."

"But they say he is a real scalawag," the woman said, at which point her husband showed up and made a formal introduction. She was mortified and began apologizing profusely, but John A. stopped her.

"Don't apologize," he said. "All you've said is perfectly true, and is well known at home."

It was true. John A. Macdonald *was* a rascal, he *was* a scoundrel, and he *was* indispensable. He was, in many ways, the author of Canada, the key architect and greatest champion of Confederation. Although a late convert to the cause, it was John A. who drafted the terms of the BNA Act, which set both the tone and the structure Canada has retained ever since. That feat alone would make him one of the most important figures in our nation's history, but for John A. Macdonald, Confederation was not the peak of his career; it was just the beginning. It was under Macdonald that Canada became a country in name and in fact, starting as a cluster of colonies and ending as a dominion stretching from the Atlantic to the Pacific. In *The Prime Ministers of Canada*, Gordon Donaldson notes, "Every succeeding prime minister has to be matched against John A. and only a few stand the comparison . . . Several of them have been *better* humans than Macdonald, none has been greater."

Throughout his career, Macdonald's opponents were rarely ever able to pin him down. Some historians credit a commissioner with the North West Mounted Police for giving Macdonald the nickname "Old Tomorrow." Wherever it came from, the moniker seemed very appropriate.

Macdonald didn't win all his fights. In 1873, an incriminating telegram surfaced in which John A. shamefully begged for more campaign money from CPR backers. The public was outraged, and the ensuing Pacific Scandal, as it was known, forced Macdonald to resign in disgrace, making him the only prime minister ever to leave office due to unethical behaviour. In 1873, it appeared that his career was over, and so was the dream of a transcontinental railway.

Liberal leader Alexander Mackenzie took Macdonald's place, and he was as straight as John A. was crooked. But the public soon bored of Mackenzie's overly cautious approach to nation building, and, just four years later, a revitalized John A. Macdonald led the Tories back into power with a stunning victory over Mackenzie. Macdonald rode in on a wave of unabashed economic nationalism. He instigated a system of tariffs and internal trade known as the National Policy, which set the economic and political course for years to come.

Unfortunately, the National Policy had an unforeseen side effect. If Americans could not trade freely across the border, fine. They would build factories *inside* Canada, slipping behind the tariff wall. Thus, in many ways, the National Policy marked the unintentional start of Canada's branch-plant economy. Some historians have argued that the only thing the National Policy did was raise the Canadian cost of living, thereby subsidizing a few well-connected manufacturers. Some have argued that the National Policy hurt farmers, others that it pampered them too much. With such radically different criticisms from both ends of the political spectrum, John A. must have been doing something right.

The National Policy was soon expanded to cover the completion of the transcontinental railway, the settlement of the West, and the extension of sea transportation from Canadian ports, linking Canada to Asia at one end of the country and to Europe on the other. The policy was, in a sense, the economic equivalent of Confederation.

John A. Macdonald, a legend in his own time, was a gregarious man both beloved and reviled. His drinking binges were epic. He once puked on stage during a debate and then blamed his upset stomach on the speeches given by his opponent. Once, while in Opposition, he charged drunkenly across the floor of the House of Commons towards an opponent, bellowing, "I could lick him quicker than Hell could scorch a feather!" Although at times he seems like a character in a novel, Macdonald was in many ways a classic Canadian, impervious to oxymoron: a radical moderate, a pragmatic zealot, a self-described "progressive conservative" long before the title became official. (Macdonald originally ran under the banner of the "Liberal-Conservative Party," surely as Canadian a term as one could hope for.)

As historian P. B. Waite writes, John A. Macdonald "never forgot that popularity was power." When a party member assured him, "I will always support you when I think you are right," John A. retorted, "Anyone can support me when they think I'm right. What I want is someone that will support me when I am wrong."

However, as historian Cynthia Smith warns in her anecdotal history of Macdonald, in focussing on John A.'s foibles rather than his accomplishments "there is always a danger of leaving the distorted impression of a loveable drunk or a sozzled clown with a penchant for puns. No such person could have achieved what John A. did." Smith is right. Macdonald oversaw some of the most exciting and volatile events in our history: Confederation, the building of the CPR, the purchase of the Northwest, the creation of Manitoba, the bringing of British Columbia into Confederation, the great migration to the Plains, the founding of the North West Mounted Police, and, in 1885, the Northwest Rebellion and the subsequent execution of Métis leader Louis Riel.

John A.'s personal life, however, was marked by sadness and heartache. His first wife, Isabella, suffered from a long, debilitating disease that left her in constant pain. She became addicted to opium, and their first child, a baby boy, died at 13 months. Many years after Isabella's death, John married a second time, and his daughter from this marriage, Mary, was severely disabled. Encephalitic (suffering from an inflammation of the brain), she also appears to have had spina bifida and thus was confined to a wheelchair. John A. doted on Mary, but his personal tragedies took their toll, and he eventually became what is now known as "a functioning alcoholic." (Some historians deny that John A. was an alcoholic, but his blackouts and drinking binges speak for themselves.)

In 1891, at the age of 76, John A. Macdonald fought his last political battle under the banner of "The Old Flag, the Old Policy, the Old Leader." Throughout the campaign, he denounced the Liberals' proposal for free trade with the U.S. as little more than "veiled treason." "It might be that the lion and the lamb would lie down together," John A. warned, "but the lamb would be inside the lion." The 1891 election was his swan-song, a final triumph for Canada's grand old man. But the campaign exhausted him, and he never recovered. Just a few months later, John A. Macdonald was dead. Politics had been his life, and in the end, it had cost him his life.

Like most great men, John A. had great flaws. Most notably, he enshrined pork-barrelling as a Canadian tradition. But he had his idealistic side as well. A champion of quixotic enterprises, Macdonald argued in favour of giving Native Canadians the vote and granting women "complete equality," and though never a complete democrat (he thought the unlimited franchise of the United States was little more than "mob rule"), he did want to expand the electoral base and make it more inclusive.

He took bribes. He drank too much. He wrapped himself in the British flag. And when all is said and done, he built this nation of ours. "You'll never die, John A.!" the crowds yelled. *You'll never die!* And they were right.

Verdict

A Bastard, through and through.

2.

Alexander Mackenzie

Nickname: "Honest Sandy"
Party: Liberal
Term: 1873–78
Words to live by:
"I am ambitious to succeed in governing the country well and without any reproach, but beyond that my ambition is of a very humble kind."

Highlights

John A. Macdonald was a man of wild schemes and big, impractical dreams. Alexander Mackenzie was not.

Mackenzie interrupted John A.'s career, but he didn't end it. While at the helm, Mackenzie shelved his predecessor's grandiose nation-spanning railway and opted instead for a more cautious, piecemeal approach. His political style failed to capture the enthusiasm of Canadians, which isn't surprising. A stonemason turned newspaperman, Mackenzie was a dour, thin-lipped, humourless person. Historian J. M. Bumsted described him as "a hard-working man of exceptional integrity but little imagination." (Indeed, the two most common adjectives that come up when historians write about Mackenzie are "honest" and "unimaginative.") In every way, he was the opposite of Macdonald, a fellow Scotsman.

When John A. Macdonald resigned in disgrace following the Pacific Scandal, Mackenzie was unexpectedly swept into office. He had barely been named leader of the Liberal Party, and now he was prime minister. Unfortunately, he faced an economic downturn, and his constant dithering over the railway so infuriated B.C.

that the province threatened to secede from Confederation. Thus, within a matter of years, Canada faced two angry separatist movements: one in Nova Scotia and the other in British Columbia.

Alexander Mackenzie never really rose to the challenge of the PMO, but he did manage, during his short time in office, to give Canada two important institutions: the Supreme Court of Canada and secret ballots. The Supreme Court provided a much-needed, nonpartisan arm of justice and, like the secret ballot, was meant to make Canadian politics a less sordid affair. Up until this time, voters had declared their allegiance on a raised platform, something described as "the manly art of voting" because it took a certain amount of pluck to brave the brick- and club-wielding gangs of one's opponents. Election days in early Canada were riotous affairs in every sense of the word. Secret ballots were considered cowardly; it was felt one should have the courage to stand up in public and boldly declare one's loyalties. The open system also made it easier to buy votes. But Alexander Mackenzie put a stop to all of this.

Mackenzie instituted the Office of the Auditor General (an independent body to investigate government spending). He also sought, unsuccessfully, a free trade deal with the United States; plagued by a sluggish economy and growing regional discontent, he was overshadowed and outplayed at every step by his formidable opponent, John A. Macdonald.

Alexander Mackenzie was the only one of the early prime ministers to refuse the automatic knighthood that came with the office. Thus, one of the few politicians ever to deserve the title "Sir" didn't receive it. As Mackenzie himself later noted, he was a failure as a politician because he lacked the attributes of "a horse-thief or a railway chiseller." His dying whispered words: "Oh, take me home."

Verdict

A Well-Intentioned, Upright Bonehead. (Everyone knows that high moral standards and politics don't mix.)

3.
Sir John Abbott
Party: Conservative
Term: 1891–92
Words to live by:
"I hate politics."

Highlights

Not a lot. When John A. Macdonald died in office, there was a scramble to find a successor. The obvious heir apparent was Halifax lawyer John Thompson, but Thompson was a Catholic—a convert to Catholicism, at that—and many within the party adamantly opposed him. After much acrimonious in-fighting, a reluctant John Abbott was finally pressured into accepting the leadership because, as he put it, "I am not particularly obnoxious to anybody."

A corporate lawyer and one-time dean of law at McGill University, Abbott had served as mayor of Montréal before making the lucrative leap to Ottawa. Abbott had opposed Confederation and earlier had urged annexation to the United States—indeed, he even signed the Annexation Manifesto of 1849. But he soon recanted and even helped organize militia defences against a pending American invasion during the Civil War.

In spite of his somewhat fluid loyalties, John Abbott managed to become our first Canadian-born prime minister. He was no longer a member of the House when he was chosen to succeed Sir John, so he ruled from the Senate instead, as if by remote control. Citing ill health, Abbott eventually handed the reins over to Thompson, who had, in fact, been acting as unofficial head of the government ever since John A. had passed away. Abbott himself died the following year.

Verdict

A Reluctant Bonehead.

4.
Sir John Sparrow Thompson
Nickname: "Sir John the Lesser"
Party: Conservative
Term: 1892–94
Words to live by:
"These Yankee politicians are the lowest race of thieves in existence."

> —statement made during sensitive diplomatic talks with the United States over a trade dispute

Highlights

The John F. Kennedy of his day, though a bit tubbier, Thompson was young, dashing and Catholic: qualities unheard of in prime ministers of that time. A lawyer, judge and (briefly) the premier of Nova Scotia, Thompson had a piquant Maritime wit and a mind as sharp as any in the House. John A. Macdonald, always one with an eye for talent, had made Thompson his Minister of Justice, although John A. himself had had certain reservations: "Thompson has two faults. He is a little too fond of satire and a little too much of a Nova Scotian."

When Thompson became prime minister, he was dubbed "Sir John the Lesser," and everyone expected great things of him. He had been de facto leader since John A.'s death, and now that it was official, he proved himself both able and energetic. He drafted and introduced Canada's Criminal Code, and he was in the middle of strengthening and revitalizing his party when, two years after assuming office, he travelled to London to be sworn in by Queen Victoria as a member of the Imperial Privy Council. Shortly after the ceremony, amid the pageantry of Windsor Castle, he suddenly clutched his chest and keeled over, dead. He was only 49 years old. "Thompson's death," writes historian P. B. Waite, "left the Conservative Party bereft of moral courage and force."

Verdict

Unfortunate Bonehead. Had he lived, he might have become one of our greatest prime ministers, or at least one of our most interesting.

5.
Sir Mackenzie Bowell
Party: Conservative
Term: 1894–96
Words to live by:
"A nest of traitors!"
—Bowell's description of the mass revolt by Cabinet ministers
that eventually forced him out of office

Highlights

Tory leaders were dropping like flies. In the past three years, three party leaders and two reigning PMs had died. One might well wonder if there was a curse on John A.'s successors. And considering the Conservatives' next choice, curse might very well be the best word. As Gordon Donaldson notes, with the death of Thompson, "The Conservatives had lost their best man. To replace him, they produced one of their worst."

Senator Mackenzie Bowell was a virulently anti-Catholic Orangeman. Pompous. Blustering. A paranoid little Englishman with much to be paranoid about. When Thompson died, Bowell had been the acting prime minister and so, by default as much as anything, the office fell to him. He sort of stumbled into power. The Montréal *Herald* called Bowell "an irascible old gentleman who, despite his long political experience, works himself into a white heat on very slight provocation." A fellow member of Parliament, W. F. MacLean, described him as "an honest man, but a weak man." And that was just about the nicest thing anyone ever said about Mackenzie Bowell.

Still, he was not the cartoon character many have portrayed. For all his Orange Lodge bluster, the issue that ultimately brought him down was his support for French-Catholic minority rights in Manitoba. He was undone as much through his principles, shaky though they were, as through his abrasive personality.

Bowell was remarkably similar to John Diefenbaker in both his leadership style and his fate: like Diefenbaker, Mackenzie Bowell was eventually ousted by a group of disgruntled insiders, men he condemned as "a nest of traitors." Having been unceremoniously dumped, Bowell lived to the ripe old age of 94, outliving every one of those who had betrayed him.

Verdict

Bonehead. Had he remained in power, he might have become one of our worst prime ministers ever, or at least one of our most interesting.

6.
Sir Charles Tupper
Nickname: "War Horse of the Cumberland"
Party: Conservative
Term: 1896 (May to July)
Words to live by:
"It requires a great country and great circumstances to develop great men."

Highlights

The desperate procession of leaders trying to fill John A. Macdonald's enormous shoes continued. Charles Tupper had been premier of Nova Scotia and a key Father of Confederation; in fact, he had proposed a transcontinental union and railway years before the Charlottetown Conference. Tupper had been a close ally of John A.'s and a mentor to John Thompson. (Thompson's wife, Annie, called Tupper "that old tramp.") He was now offered up as a sacrificial lamb, leading the Tories to certain defeat against the much younger and far more charismatic Wilfrid Laurier. Like someone caught in a game of musical chairs on board a sinking ship, Charles Tupper was the last man in place when the ship went down. Seventy-four when he took office, he was one of our oldest PMs. He was also the shortest-reigning. He was in power less than 10 weeks, 69 days in all.

Tupper was an example of the Peter Principle in action: in any hierarchy, people tend to rise to their level of incompetence. The man had a brilliant pre–prime ministerial career, but once he reached the office of PM, he blundered his way into oblivion. Forty years of distinguished public service vs. two months as PM. He should have quit while he was ahead.

Verdict

Bonehead

7.
Sir Wilfrid Laurier
Nickname: "Knight of the White Plume"
Party: Liberal
Term: 1896–1911
Words to live by:
"The twentieth century belongs to Canada!"
(Described by John Robert Colombo as "the most celebrated of all Canadian aphorisms," this quotation is actually a paraphrase of what Laurier said in a 1904 address. The original was less pithy and less cocksure: "The nineteenth century was the century of the United States. I think we can claim that it is Canada that shall fill the twentieth century.")

Highlights

The 1896 election was one of the weirdest ever. During his brief reign as prime minister, Charles Tupper had tried valiantly to pass a bill guaranteeing French-Catholic school rights in Manitoba. Wilfrid Laurier, as leader of the Liberals, had opposed Tupper and fought for "provincial rights" (which in this case meant allowing Manitoba Anglos to run roughshod over a minority).

Thus, in 1896, Charles Tupper, an English Protestant, supported the rights of French-Canadian Catholics, and Wilfrid Laurier, a French Catholic, supported anti-French, anti-Catholic provincial legislation. Confused? Welcome to Canada. It was all very topsy-turvy.

Wilfrid Laurier was Canada's first French-Canadian prime minister. He was tall, handsome, dignified—and slippery as only a Liberal can be. A master of compromise, Laurier defended Québec but sold out Franco-Manitobans. In his youth, he had been an outspoken opponent of Confederation; in his dotage, he was the grand old man of Canada. Laurier waxed patriotic about being Canadian, yet pursued a policy of free trade with the U.S. that was greeted with annexationist cheers south of the border. In his first outing as leader of the Liberals he went head to head with John A. over this issue—and was trounced. With free trade rejected, Laurier soon renounced it himself and embraced the principles of Macdonald's National Policy.

Laurier was an intelligent, educated and literate man. He was also a great orator, perhaps the greatest Canada has ever produced. In politics, he successfully moved the Liberals from their original radical reform stance towards a more "sunny" middle ground. The Liberals had once been the NDP of their day (that is, an idealistic fringe party in constant danger of becoming terminally irrelevant). Now, they were just Tories in drag. This "Great Betrayal," as it was called, was part of the Laurier legacy as well.

For better or worse (and often for worse), many of Laurier's beliefs have become part of the Canadian Way. Unlike John A., Laurier championed a decentralized, regionalized nation. He described Canada as "a cluster of states." Not one country, but rather a union of separate provincial entities, foreshadowing Joe Clark's vague vision of "a community of communities." Above all, Laurier was a politician. He may have been progressive in certain ways, but overall he was relentlessly pragmatic in his allegiances.

In *Right Honourable Men*, historian Michael Bliss writes, "[Laurier] comes down to us as the great compromiser, the great Canadian conciliator, trying to bring a disunited people together." Laurier had an innate understanding of the moods and manners of Canadians. "The province of Québec," he once noted, "does not have opinions, it has only sentiments," a statement that rings as true today as it ever did.

Laurier was at the helm during the Klondike Gold Rush, and he oversaw the creation of two new provinces, Alberta and Saskatchewan. He was also instrumental in strengthening Canadian autonomy in the face of growing Imperial pressures to "consolidate the Empire." The twilight of the Victorian era had seen a move to draw British colonies and dominions into an international pact. Laurier resisted all such overtures, even as he flattered the royal family with eloquent speeches. He said "No" to an 1897 proposal to create a Great Council of the Empire. "No" to an Imperial Navy subsidy. "No" to a special Dominion military force to be at the beck and call of the Empire. "No" to proposals from Australia and New Zealand to tighten Imperial ties and colonial consultations. No. No. No. It was Laurier's stubborn "everlasting no" that marks him, ironically, as a nation builder.

Laurier has also been described as "the First Canadian." That is, he was neither fully French nor fully English, but something in between. "I am branded in Québec as a traitor to the French," he said. "And in Ontario as a traitor to the English. In Québec I am branded as a jingoist and in Ontario as a separatist. In Québec I am attacked as an imperialist and in Ontario as an anti-imperialist. I am neither. I am a Canadian."

By straddling the picket fence—never a comfortable position—Laurier managed to stay in power for 15 consecutive years and four straight election victories, the longest unbroken tenure of any Canadian prime minister. He was, in the words of biographer J. W. Dafoe, "a mix of Machiavelli and Sir Galahad."

Laurier also had the good fortune of presiding over an unprecedented economic boom. (This too was a legacy of John A. Macdonald's nation building. The National Policy and the CPR had paid off handsomely, and Wilfrid Laurier reaped the benefits.) He pursued railways with an unbridled, almost reckless optimism, launching three new lines that would eventually be consolidated into one massive transcontinental system: the Canadian Northern Railway. If the CPR was Macdonald's legacy, the CNR was Laurier's.

In the end, free trade and his all-too-clever navy scheme ended Laurier's reign as prime minister. Faced with demands that Canada help pay for Britain's Imperial Navy, Laurier came up with an inspired compromise that pleased absolutely no one. He proposed giving Canada its own navy, which would, in times of war, be put at Britain's disposal. Laurier launched his flotilla by borrowing two aged British cruisers. Tory humorist Stephen Leacock derided it as "a tin-pot navy," and that phrase would haunt, and eventually sink, Laurier's Liberals. The Conservatives said Laurier's navy was not enough. Québec anti-imperialists said it was too much. Add that to Laurier's ill-advised 1911 resurrection of limited reciprocity with the United States, and you have the seeds of his self-destruction. He went down graciously.

Laurier was, in the words of biographer Richard Clippingdale, "a giant among the pygmies." He is, of course, vastly overrated. But even that is part of his charm: Laurier is the sentimental favourite, a man of style over substance. Although he succeeded brilliantly as a politician, on the issues he cared most about he failed. He was never able to reconcile French and English Canada, and he was never able to convince Canadians of the value of free trade. But Laurier's vision of Canada as an ongoing compromise, patched up and self-contradictory though it was, has had an immeasurable impact on our history. Perhaps Laurier, the great decentralizer, the man who let the provinces call the tune, was in fact the first leader who saw Canada as it really was: chaotic, messy, discordant.

In some ways, he was ahead of his time. He believed in tolerance, openness and multicultural rights. "Mighty nations," said Laurier prophetically, "might well come to us to seek a lesson in justice and humanity." Unfortunately, a man ahead of his time is also a man out of his time, and one wonders whether Laurier was the right person to oversee the vast influx of settlers and the massive western expansion that occurred under his reign. Compromise and capitulation are not always the best approaches. Sometimes hard decisions and unwavering leadership are called for. I wonder: if Pierre Trudeau had been at the helm back then, what kind of nation would we have today?

When official bilingualism was proposed to Laurier in 1907, he brushed it aside as impractical. By which he meant: not politically expedient. No one could ever accuse him of putting his ideals ahead of politics. Wilfrid Laurier might have stood up to the British Empire, but when it came to provincial premiers, he caved in again and again. In some ways, this response was understandable: Canada was suffering acute growing pains and Laurier was under pressure from all sides. There were constant attacks by extremists, both French and English, east and west, and it is a testament to Laurier's political acumen that he survived for as long as he did. However, it should be duly noted that by appeasing English Protestants and abandoning French-Catholic rights in Manitoba, Alberta and Saskatchewan, Laurier allowed the dream (or was it just a delusion?) of a truly bilingual, bicultural transcontinental nation to wither and die. After Laurier, French Canada would be contained in the East. Under Canada's first French-Canadian prime minister, the West would become solely and irrevocably English-speaking.

As one of Laurier's friends noted, "Sir Wilfrid was unmoral, not deliberately immoral . . . He had no sentiment nor any strong conviction on any subject."

"Reforms," noted Laurier dryly, "are for Oppositions. It is the business of Governments to stay in power."

Spoken like a true Liberal.

Verdict

A real, Red Bastard.

8.
Sir Robert Laird Borden
Party: Conservative/Unionist
Term: 1911–20
Words to live by:
"Continuous consultation leading to concerted action."
　　—Borden's 1914 statement of policy regarding the controversial issue of drafting soldiers during World War I

Highlights

Robert Borden achieved, if not the impossible, the improbable. He defeated the White Knight.

When Laurier championed reciprocity with the U.S. during the 1911 election, Robert Borden and the Conservatives pounced on the issue. Under the anti–free trade slogan "No truck nor trade with the Yankees," Borden was swept into power, and Laurier spent the rest of his political life in Opposition.

Robert Borden had the unfortunate honour of being prime minster during World War I, when the contradictions and absurdities of imperialism were played out in graphic, gory detail. He was a steadfast, serious man, a Nova Scotian described by one journalist at the time as "the man who never laughs in public."

Above all, Robert Borden was a reformer. He overhauled an often corrupt political system and helped stem the worst of the patronage that had flourished under Macdonald and Laurier. Civil servants started to be appointed mainly due to merit, and the ethical standards Borden initiated were instrumental in cleaning up government graft. Robert Borden hated partisan party politics, and under his leadership the Conservatives were in fact far more progressive than the Liberals.

But Borden also oversaw the creation of the powerful War Measures Act, which allowed the government to strip citizens of basic civil rights in the name of national security. And it was Borden who, after a heart-rending wartime tour of hospitals in Britain, decided to begin drafting Canadians for overseas duty. The war came crashing to an end before conscripted servicemen could make much of a difference one way or the other, but the damage had been done on the home front. Canada was sharply divided along cultural/linguistic lines.

Borden was a man who took decisive action. He was never one to shirk responsibility or to avoid making the hard calls. He nationalized the bankrupt CNR. He introduced the "temporary" measure of income tax, and in 1918 he granted women the right to vote. At the same time, he also stripped the vote from antiwar pacifists and gerrymandered a wartime election win under his Unionist alliance, a coalition of Tories and dissatisfied Liberals. As always, Robert Borden played to win.

In the aftermath of the Great War, Borden used Canada's sacrifices to strengthen Canadian independence, especially in the area of foreign policy. In doing so, he made a crucial break with British authority. "Canada," he insisted, "must assume full sovereignty." It was a sovereignty that had been paid for with the lives of 60,000 young men, lost in a vainglorious and useless conflict.

Borden spearheaded the move that transformed the worn-out remnants of the British Empire into "a commonwealth of autonomous nations." World War I, it has been argued, was Canada's War of Independence. And Robert Borden, a strong leader in an age of upheaval, a good man in a bad time, has been greatly undervalued over the years. As columnist Dalton Camp writes, "After Macdonald, no prime minister did more to develop and define Canada, as an independent nation, than did Borden."

If John A. Macdonald was the Father of Canada, then Robert Borden was certainly the Father of Canadian Political Independence.

In 1918, Robert Laird Borden, having been reluctantly knighted himself, abolished all future hereditary titles in Canada. Such a class system was, in his words, "entirely incompatible with the ideas of democracy as they have developed in this country." On his deathbed, he specifically requested that the title "Sir" *not* be inscribed on his headstone. "None of this Sir 'stuff' at the cemetery," he said. "Just plain old Robert Laird Borden."

He began as a colonial. He ended as a Canadian.

Verdict

A true, Blue Bastard.

9.
Arthur Meighen
Party: Conservative
Term: 1920–21, with a brief interval in 1926
Words to live by:
"Ready! Aye, ready!"
                —the phrase Meighen insisted Canadians should use
                                to respond to any Imperial crisis overseas

Highlights

Arthur Meighen first rose to prominence as Robert Borden's hatchetman. Meighen drafted the Military Service Act, which allowed the government to conscript young men; it was he who first dreamed up the cunning gerrymandering of the Military Elections Act, and it was he who crushed the Winnipeg General Strike of 1919. Arthur Meighen was never afraid to play hard ball.

Meighen was a sharp man, a ruthlessly intelligent man, a man of focussed ideas, but in no way was he a great man. Or even a capable politician. Over the course of his long, unsuccessful career, he managed to alienate just about everybody: big business, labour, Québec, the West and, inevitably, his own party. He had all the arrogance of Pierre Trudeau and all the political savvy of John Turner. Not a good combination.

An arch-imperialist who had absorbed none of the hard-won lessons learned by his predecessor, Meighen began his career as a toadying colonial, and he ended it the same way. An observer described him thusly: "Meighen is clever, destructive in debate, crushing in criticism, but there it ends. No one possessed of such qualities can command heart loyalty."

"I never told a funny story in my life," Meighen once noted, and it wasn't clear whether he was bragging or complaining.

Meighen had originally been a schoolteacher, but he quit when the trustees would not give him a free hand in punishing his students: which more or less sums up his entire approach to wielding authority. You remember the worst teacher you ever had? The meanest, nastiest, most tight-assed terror of the classroom? That was Arthur Meighen.

In the House of Commons, he squared off against Mackenzie King, an old nemesis from his college days. The two men despised each other. Meighen described King as "the most contemptible charlatan ever to darken the annals of Canadian politics." King, in turn, considered Meighen to be "sarcastic, vitriolic, and the meanest type of politician." They were both right. But Mackenzie King was a Bastard, and in the game of life, Bastard always trumps Bonehead.

Meighen was outmanoeuvred and outplayed at every turn, and his career ended in a shambles. When he formed a government for a second time it lasted all of three days before collapsing, lost on a single vote, and in the election that followed he was booted out of office. He even lost his own seat, proving once again that only Meighen was enamoured with Meighen.

Years later, resurrected as leader of the Conservative Party, Arthur Meighen attempted to regain a seat in the House of Commons in a 1942 by-election. He lost.

Verdict

Bonehead. (Which is kind of a shame, since he wanted so much to be a Bastard.)

10.
William Lyon Mackenzie King
Nickname: "Rex"
Party: Liberal
Terms: 1921–30 (with a brief interruption in 1926), 1935–48
Words to live by:
"Not necessarily conscription, but conscription if necessary."
—King's wartime statement of policy

Highlights

Here are some questions that have divided historians and commentators for more than 50 years: Was Prime Minister Mackenzie King a bland, shapeless man steeped in the colour grey and remarkable only in his political longevity? Or was he a fascinating, mystical, spirit-intoxicated eccentric? Was he simply a capable but boring bureaucrat? Or was he our greatest leader ever? Answer: He was a bit of all these things.

Mackenzie King is the Great Enigma of Canadian politics, a man who managed to be both fascinating and incredibly dull. History has not always been kind to his memory, partly because he was so hard to grasp. Where Meighen was a union buster, King was a professional conciliator, a trouble-shooter who helped diffuse numerous strikes—and therein lay the secret of his success. King blunted extremes and always sought the middle ground. That was both his greatest talent and his greatest character flaw. In historian Frank Underhill's celebrated description, "Mr. King was the leader who divided us least." A backhanded compliment, at best. *He divided us least.* Not exactly words to inspire a nation, but then King was not a visionary, he was an administrator. A very adept administrator, a great administrator even, but an administrator nonetheless.

In *Right Honourable Men*, Michael Bliss argues that Mackenzie King was in fact "the greatest and most interesting of Canada's prime ministers." Indeed, among historians the tide has recently turned, and King has suddenly gone from being the most underrated politician in Canadian history to being the most overrated. But in my opinion we have confused longevity with greatness, management with leadership. I agree that King is one of our most fascinating figures; I am less convinced of King's "greatness."

Historian J. L. Granatstein, picking up on Bliss's theme, argued in a *Maclean's* survey that if Canadians do not consider Mackenzie King to be "a great man" the problem is not with King but with us. That is, we are somehow at fault for not being properly inspired by His Royal Blandness. But surely, if King fails to inspire Canadians, the blame lies with King and not with the average Canadian. Heroes are meant to be role models; they are meant to enlighten us and challenge us to become something more, something better. King may perhaps be an inspiration to history professors, or to university administrators and career bureaucrats—there are certainly lessons to be learned from his managerial style—but I defy anyone else to say, honestly, that they are personally inspired by the memory of Mackenzie King. (Indeed, I urge you to read Bliss's *Right Honourable Men* and decide for yourself.)

King's most scathing critic, the poet F. R. Scott, wrote of him, "He will be remembered wherever men honour ingenuity, ambiguity, inactivity, and political longevity." Even more cuttingly: "The height of [King's] ambition was to pile a Parliamentary Committee on a Royal Commission." In *The Lives and Times of the Prime Ministers*, historian Norman Hillmer describes the King phenomenon as follows: "Always to be elusive, always to be anonymous, always to be ambiguous—that was the King political style and strategy." Hardly the stuff of heroes.

King helped launch Canada's move towards a welfare state. He introduced old-age pensions, he led us into World War II more or less united, he brought in unemployment insurance and family allowances, and he laid the foundations for the economic boom years that followed the war. For all this, he is duly commended, but King's record is not without some very distasteful, very disturbing aspects.

In *Right Honourable Men*, Michael Bliss spends pages and pages on King's masturbatory obsessions and Victorian sexual hang-ups but relegates King's harsh indifference to Jewish refugees, thousands of whom died at the hands of the Nazis because of King's closed-door policies, to a footnote. And King's racism towards Asians—he was glad that the nuclear bomb at Hiroshima had been used on the Japanese and not on decent white people—is, incredibly, relegated by Bliss to a parenthetical aside *within* a footnote. Nor does Bliss mention either the role King played in the mass confiscation, sale and plunder of Japanese-Canadian property during his tenure *or* the blatantly racist immigration quotas King instigated, which stayed in effect right up until the 1960s.

Mackenzie King was a sad, reclusive man who sought solace among the spirits of the dead. He collected and reconstructed fake Roman-style ruins on his property. He had an unhealthy fixation on his mother. (He literally built a shrine to her.) He communicated with his dogs and the ghosts of his dogs. (At one point he even asked the long-dead Dr. Louis Pasteur for a medical prescription for his dog.) He liked to "redeem" prostitutes, and he often consulted the spirit of his late mentor, Wilfrid Laurier. During one seance, King asked a spirit, "Are you real or just a figment of my imagination?" When the spirit replied, "I am real," Mackenzie King was reassured. Yes, Canada's "greatest" prime minister was a complete muttonhead when it came to things private and mystical.

In public, however, he was a master politician. Cunning, quiet and relentlessly bland. In many ways, he was the ultimate Canadian: bizarre yet dull, passionate yet celibate, crafty yet thick, calm yet more than a bit mad. By striking that perfect Canadian balance, Mackenzie King became not only our longest-ruling PM, but also the longest-reigning elected leader in the history of the English-speaking world.

Mom would have been proud.

Verdict

In his public life: **a Monumental Bastard**.

In his private life: **Bonehead Supreme**.

11.
Richard Bedford Bennett
Nickname: "Bonfire Bennett" in younger, rabble-
rousing days; "Iron-Heel Bennett" in later years
Party: Conservative
Term: 1930–35
Words to live by:
*"One of the greatest assets any man or woman can have on
entering life's struggle is poverty."*
　　　　　—statement made at the height of the Great Depression

Highlights

R. B. Bennett was the wrong man in the wrong place at the wrong time. A self-made millionaire trying to lead a nation through the grips of the Great Depression, Bennett was always more aristocrat than democrat. Not the type of man you want at the helm during the greatest economic disaster in your country's history.

As farmlands blew away in dust clouds and hundreds of thousands of Canadians faced starvation and ruin, radical reforms were needed. No social security net was then in place and Bennett rode madly off in all directions, unable to fix anything or even to make much sense. He promised higher tariffs—and then promptly vowed to negotiate lower tariffs if reelected. He defended free-hand capitalism, and then tried to retreat into economic isolationism, building tariff walls to unscalable heights and then raising the drawbridge. It was all very confusing.

Like Mackenzie King, R. B. Bennett was a mother-fixated bachelor boy. But unlike King, Bennett was no career politician. A true capitalist who saw the market-place as the final, highest good, Bennett was a teetotaller who supported the temperance movement and made a fortune off a brewing company. At the height of economic desperation, he decided to cheer the country up by reinstating honorific titles (that is, knighthoods) for Canadians.

Bennett's vow to crush the forces of leftist propaganda earned him the nickname

"Iron-Heel" at the very time when "leftist" solutions were needed. (In his younger days, his rhetorical style had been compared to "a bonfire.") Ironically, his few achievements in office included launching the forerunner of the CBC (a veritable den of lefty propaganda) and creating the Bank of Canada, designed to control monetary policy and help regulate those very marketplace forces that Bennett held so dear.

Poor R. B. Bennett. Blustering, egotistical and self-righteous, he was an utter disaster as prime minister. When he was first elected, he had declared, "I will end unemployment or perish in the attempt," and these turned out to be prophetic words indeed. Bennett became a whipping boy and scapegoat for the country's frustrations. When farmers could no longer afford to run automobiles, they reverted to pulling them by horse team, and these symbols of capitalism's collapse became known as "Bennett buggies." Hot water and barley became "Bennett coffee," and so on. It didn't help that when thousands of relief-camp workers began a cross-country trek to confront Bennett in person, he had the march put down with force in Regina by RCMP thugs.

When Bennett finally did come up with a plan of attack, it was too little, too late. The Opposition called it a "death bed conversion," this flurry of New Deal–style reforms hastily thrown together in the face of an impeding election. During a radio address broadcast live across Canada, Bennett announced "the end of laissez faire." But it was too late. In the 1935 election, R. B. Bennett and the Conservatives were crushed, and the Liberals, under the banner of "King or Chaos," were swept back into power.

In many ways, Bennett was caught in circumstances beyond his control. The Great Depression might have destroyed Mackenzie King as well had the Germans not invaded Poland and plunged Canada into war—and prosperity. But Bennett's fate was to go down in history as a bombastic failure. He is second only to Brian Mulroney as the most unpopular prime minister ever elected.

Bennett is an important figure mainly for the angry *response* he provoked. The socialist Co-operative Commonwealth Federation (forerunner of today's NDP) was founded in 1932, and the following year the federation drafted the radical Regina Manifesto, which attacked the type of "old school capitalism" that was personified by men like R. B. Bennett. The CCF laid the groundwork for the Canadian social revolution. Medicare, welfare, unemployment insurance and minimum wage all trace their roots back to the prairie protests of the 1930s. (However, it was the Liberals under King who translated these ideas into practical policy. The old-age pension, for example, was instigated by Mackenzie King *before* the Depression began and *before* the CCF was formed.)

R. B. Bennett was just one of the many casualties of the Dirty Thirties. Bitterly disappointed, he would eventually abandon Canada entirely, and he ended his days in that bastion of aristocratic values, the British House of Lords. In the words of historian John English, "Bennett never forgave Canada for failing him." His body lies in Mickleham, England, making him the only PM buried in foreign soil. There have been ghoulish attempts lately to have his bones brought back and reburied in his native New Brunswick; if that were ever to happen, it would certainly be a last, ironic betrayal of the long-dead viscount.

Verdict

Bonehead. Once again, we see the Peter Principle at work. As a self-made man, Bennett was worth millions. As PM, considerably less.

12.
Louis St. Laurent
Party: Liberal
Term: 1948–57
Nickname: "Uncle Louis"
Words to live by:
"Canada is a Middle Power."
—that odd but typically Canadian boast, first popularized by St. Laurent

Highlights

Like John Abbott, Louis St. Laurent was a reluctant leader; he had to be talked into replacing the aged, retiring Mackenzie King as prime minister. When King first recruited St. Laurent in 1941, the latter protested, "I know nothing about politics." In spite of this deficiency—or perhaps because of it—St. Laurent proved himself to be a capable, if uninspired, leader.

Louis St. Laurent oversaw the economic boom years of the 1950s. Earlier, as King's Secretary of State, he had been one of the key architects and strongest advocates of the North Atlantic Treaty Organization (NATO), a military pact created to check Communist expansion. As the Cold War heated up, Prime Minister St.

Laurent sought to establish Canada as a strategic "middle power," one that could influence both superpowers while avoiding either extreme. This phrase was amended even further to suggest Canada become "a moderate mediatory middle power." Stirs the blood, don't it? If nothing else, it was an apt description of Canada under Louis St. Laurent. After all, he was a moderate, mediatory, middle-of-the-road type of prime minister. Middle years. Middle class. Fair-to-middling. They all apply to the droopy-eyed, sleepy satisfaction of the St. Laurent era. Political columnist Dalton Camp, writing in *Maclean's*, said of St. Laurent, "He was our Eisenhower, a safe man in a post-war age of euphoria and prosperity." In many ways, St. Laurent embodied the highest principles of Canadian leadership, those enshrined in the constitution as our noblest goals: "Peace, order, and good government." It is to yawn.

During St. Laurent's tenure, Newfoundland joined Confederation and (not coincidentally) equalization payments began between the have provinces and the have-nots. These payments, despite their bad reputation, have been instrumental in helping Canada avoid the brutal regional disparities one sees south of the border. If we are indeed a "kinder, gentler America," this difference can be traced back partially to the domestic policies of St. Laurent.

In spite of his legendary hair-trigger temper, St. Laurent was a cautious and methodical prime minister. He presented himself as a kindly statesman, but although his image was avuncular and his policies reserved, his back-room style was anything but. "St. Laurent ruled," writes author Gordon Donaldson, "with the quiet confidence of the chairman of the board." In *Renegade in Power*, Peter Newman, less enamoured, calls St. Laurent "a starchy corporation lawyer" who hid his true personality behind the patently false image of "Uncle Louis." Either way, the strategy was effective. Under his leadership, the Liberals won two back-to-back majorities, something they would not achieve again until Jean Chrétien led them to victory 44 years later. (The parallel is telling; St. Laurent is the leader Jean Chrétien most resembles.)

When the Liberals were finally ousted in 1957, St. Laurent shrugged off the loss. The Liberals had been in power for 22 years straight. "They just got tired of seeing us around," he said. In fact, the Liberals had become complacent to the point of unabashed arrogance. They rammed through legislation for a controversial Trans-Canada Pipeline and generally acted as though they were ruling by divine right rather than on the approval of the Canadian electorate. Their election slogan of 1957 demonstrated just how out of touch they had become: "You Never Had It So Good." The Conservatives under John Diefenbaker were more accurate in *their* choice of slogans: "It's Time for a Change." And boy, they weren't kidding.

Verdict

A Sweet, Ruthless Old Bastard.

13.
John George Diefenbaker
Nickname: "The Chief"
Party: Progressive Conservative
Term: 1957–63
Words to live by:
"I'll have my place in history."
(And he was right, though not perhaps in the way he meant.)

Highlights

John Diefenbaker had a Vision. It led him by night like a pillar of fire and by day as a tower of smoke. It was a vision of . . . *himself.* A vision of him leading the nation out of the wilderness and into the promised land.

It wasn't an easy journey. In 1925, Diefenbaker ran for the federal seat in Prince Albert, Saskatchewan, and was soundly defeated. In 1926 he ran again. Again he was trounced. (In fairness, he was running under Arthur Meighen's leadership, which made it virtually impossible to win.) Having failed at federal politics, Diefenbaker switched to provincial. He ran in 1929 and lost. He then tried municipal politics, running for mayor of Prince Albert in 1933. And he was again defeated. So he went back to provincial politics where—in a surprising turn of events—he was defeated.

As head of the Saskatchewan Conservatives, Diefenbaker led his party to a perfect record; they lost every single riding. In 1940, after 15 years of trying, Diefenbaker was finally elected to a seat in an obscure riding in rural Saskatchewan. This victory convinced him that he was destined to become prime minister.

Diefenbaker next sought the leadership of the federal Tories. He ran, alternately for the positions of party leader and house leader, in 1942, 1943, 1948 and 1953. His record? Defeated. Defeated. Defeated. Defeated. Now, any sane man would have reconsidered his career path at this point. But not Dief. As Peter Newman notes in his seminal work *Renegade in Power*, Diefenbaker "seemed to thrive on rejection."

He eventually won the party leadership in 1956, after almost 14 years of trying. Then, in the face of Liberal complacency, he won a surprise victory over St. Laurent, and suddenly, John George Diefenbaker was the PRIME MINISTER of CANADA!

The following year, Diefenbaker led the Tories to the greatest victory ever recorded in Canadian parliamentary history, taking an incredible 208 seats to the Liberals' 49 and the CCF's 8, a record that some thought would never be surpassed. (Indeed, Dief's record would stand, unchallenged, right up until 1984, when a Tory by the name of Brian Mulroney won by an even bigger landslide. John Diefenbaker and Brian Mulroney, our two worst prime ministers, between them won the two biggest victories in our nation's history.)

Diefenbaker even succeeded in Québec, in spite of his, how shall we say, *idiosyncratic* approach to French. (He once assured Quebeckers that he sincerely hoped "my baby cows will soon know how to shit." He was trying to say, "I hope my wishes will be well-received," but it came out wrong.)

After 37 years in the wilderness, Dief was convinced his time had come. The imagery and the personality were biblical. Old Testament biblical. Diefenbaker was a fire-and-brimstone prophet. A thundering, self-obsessed caricature of a man who preferred denouncing traitors, real and imaginary, to discussing issues. His life had been devoted solely to attaining power and personal glory, but once he achieved these things, he had no idea what to do with them. As Peter Newman writes, "It was not power, but the lack of power" that had corrupted Diefenbaker.

Diefenbaker was always more reactive than active. "He came to power with a few general objectives," notes Denis Smith in *Rogue Tory*, "[but] no timetable and no strategy."

Diefenbaker was paranoid, vindictive and obsessive. But he was, in his own quivering, jowly way, charismatic. He gave wonderfully stirring speeches even if they didn't, you know, make any sense. "Canadians have an appointment with Destiny!" said John, and Canadians cheered. What did it mean? No one knew, but it didn't matter. It was Destiny! And we had an appointment! Longtime MP Eugene Forsey compared Diefenbaker's bombastic style, long on theatrics, short on substance, to "loud detonations in a dense fog."

In their book *Derailed!* historians David J. Bercuson and Barry Cooper lay the blame for virtually all of Canada's current woes, everything from the deficit to bad breath, on the doorstep of Thundering John. But this view gives Dief way too much credit. The Chief was a great one for making dramatic gestures, but he had very little in the way of practical ideas. Having him as PM was like having one of the coffee-counter gang at the helm. You know the type, the guys in the John Deere hats who are always trying to tell you just what the hell is wrong with this country.

Diefenbaker's idea of constructive patriotism was leading the House in a warbled version of "O Canada" and "God Save the Queen." Very little of his fervent nationalism was ever turned into legislation, which is just as well, because whenever he did make an attempt to institute policy, the results were disastrous. The classic example was his infamous "15 per cent promise" to Great Britain.

Caught up in the glow of the Commonwealth spirit and egged on by reporters, Diefenbaker announced, without consulting his Cabinet or administrators, that Canada would henceforth divert 15 per cent of its total trade to the U.K. The promise sounded good at the time, but the ramifications were enormous. Diefenbaker's 15 per cent—a number apparently chosen on a whim—represented a mass diversion of trade to the tune of $625 million a year, something a socialist dictatorship might be able to achieve by decree, but which was all but impossible under the terms of the original 1947 GATT (General Agreement on Tariffs and Trade), which forbade one nation giving preferential treatment to another. The only way to achieve Diefenbaker's 15 per cent diversion was through the side door, by creating a special "free trade zone" between Canada and the U.K. and then setting up punitive tariffs aimed specifically at the U.S. The British were overjoyed and immediately began plans for implementing Diefenbaker's scheme. But even Dief's supporters were aghast. Amid a barrage of criticism from both within and outside his party, Dief quickly reneged, and in the end all he managed to do was piss off both the United States *and* the United Kingdom. Fortunately, the only real long-term damage was to Dief's reputation. As Bercuson and Cooper write, "Efforts to block or divert Canada-U.S. trade were as doomed to failure as efforts to amend the laws of gravity."

Diefenbaker's 1960 Canadian Bill of Rights, for all its high-flying rhetoric, was also fundamentally unworkable and unenforceable. A federal bill without jurisdiction in provincial courts, it was an empty-headed, empty-handed gesture. All it did was confuse the issue of individual rights and cause headaches and conflicts. Dief, however, saw the bill as his crowning achievement, somewhat on par with the Magna Carta. As author Denis Smith notes, with Diefenbaker, "there was always a larger destiny at work." He had a mythical, almost mystical view of his own self-importance. So, in the years to come, would Pierre Elliott Trudeau. But Trudeau could at least back up his own healthy self-regard with substance. Diefenbaker, alas, could not.

Oddly enough, the Chief's one concrete achievement is rarely commented on: he gave Native Canadians the vote, and he finally did away with the unabashedly discriminatory immigration barriers that had been put in place by King and maintained by St. Laurent. In striking down this distasteful colour criteria, Dief did a great service to Canadians. Mind you, by 1963 the notion of race quotas was already on its way out, and had these still been in place when Lester Pearson was elected, they would most certainly have been quickly dismantled. Still, give the old man his due. Unlike Mackenzie King, Diefenbaker was no racist.

Where John A. Macdonald recognized that popularity was power, Diefenbaker was equally as certain that power was personality. Sadly, it didn't work quite that way. In office Dief became, or was revealed to be, a blithering, dithering, indecisive crank, egocentric to the point of clinical megalomania. Although the two leaders couldn't have been more different, Diefenbaker nonetheless saw himself as the political reincarnation of Canada's first and greatest prime minister. "Sir John A. saw a Canada from East to West," said Dief. "I see a new Canada—a Canada of the North!"

As more than one insider has noted, Diefenbaker didn't really have any friends, he had only fans. Or foes. And as time went on, the number of his fans diminished rapidly, while the number of foes grew exponentially. Among them was party president Dalton Camp, who would eventually lead the forces that toppled the Chief.

"Everyone is against me except the people," Diefenbaker lamented, and by 1963, 17 Conservative ministers had either angrily resigned or been forced out. Never had a single personality so dominated a political party.

Like Macdonald, Dief had a rabid dislike of the Yanks, and he rekindled long-dormant anti-American feelings, gleefully fanning the flames. Yet, at the same time, he weakened Canadian military autonomy by cancelling the magnificent and exceedingly expensive Avro Arrow, a supersonic Canadian-made fighter plane, thus earning him the wrath of phallocentric nationalists everywhere.

Unyielding in debate, unethical in approach, Diefenbaker thought nothing of compromising national security and breaching codes of confidentiality simply to score minor political points. He blackmailed—or attempted to blackmail—opponents and allies alike.

It is frightening to think that, at the height of the Cold War, Canadians elected someone as mentally unstable as Diefenbaker to the helm. It was bad enough with Kennedy in the White House staring down the Soviets in a game of nuclear truth-or-dare; Diefenbaker only exacerbated the problem. This is a man who accepted nuclear weapons onto Canadian soil *by accident*. Having cancelled the Avro Arrow, Diefenbaker purchased American Bomarc surface-to-air missiles in its stead, without realizing that (a) the Bomarcs were designed to carry nuclear warheads, and (b) he had vowed to keep Canada a nuclear-free zone. Once these simple facts were pointed out, Diefenbaker frantically tried to come up with a solution. He ended up stuffing the Bomarcs with sandbags of ballast, making them the world's most expensive blanks: $685 million worth of duds. His Minister of Defence quit in disgust, and in the ensuing election, Diefenbaker was defeated.

He clung to the leadership of the party for several more years in a sad and unseemly way, until finally being overthrown by his own "nest of traitors" in a party revolt that stopped just short of actual beheading. It is just as well that Dief cancelled the Arrow (a plane that was designed to carry nuclear-tipped missiles). God help us if he had ever had access to nuclear weapons. For one thing, he probably would have ordered a tactical strike against Dalton Camp.

Verdict

Bonehead Definitive. Sound and fury, signifying very little.

14.
Lester Bowles Pearson
Nickname: "Mike" (given to Pearson while he was training with the Royal Flying Corps during World War I by a squadron commander who thought Lester wasn't a "tough enough" name)
Party: Liberal
Term: 1963–68
Words to live by:
"Not to seek success, but to deserve it."

—Pearson's personal motto

Highlights

At first glance, Pearson appears to have embodied the Peter Principle in much the same way as did Tupper and Bennett. As a diplomat, Pearson was inspired. In the PMO, he was shaky at the best of times.

A history professor with ambitions, Pearson joined the Department of External Affairs and quickly rose through the ranks to become Canada's top diplomat. In 1952 he was appointed president of the United Nations General Assembly. Four years later, Britain and France, in tandem with Israel, led an attack against Egypt at the Suez Canal. It was an act of imperial hubris that would bring the world to the brink of nuclear war, and Pearson, suddenly in the spotlight, performed brilliantly. His inspired solution to the Suez Crisis called for the creation of a neutral "peace-keeping force," a key element in world diplomacy today. For this, Pearson was awarded the Nobel Peace Prize in 1957, the first and only Canadian ever to be so honoured. In the words of the Nobel Committee, Lester B. Pearson had "saved the world." To which Pearson reportedly replied, "Gee, thanks."

Pearson's troubles began when he inherited the mantle of the Liberal Party just a few months after winning the Peace Prize. In a sort of "reverse evolution," Pearson had started as a statesman and worked his way down to politician. After two successive election defeats, he finally beat Diefenbaker in a nasty campaign that Pearson remembered as "the most degrading experience of my life." Pearson had rashly promised his government would start with "Sixty Days of Decision," a slogan that would come back to haunt him when he tried to rush through hastily drafted reforms and a completely botched budget. The Sixty Days became days of confusion, indecision and constant internal bickering. (Pearson seems to have been cursed with more churlish Cabinet ministers than any PM deserves. So not only did he have to face the tirades of Diefenbaker across the floor, he had to put up with the grandstanding emotional outbursts of people like Judy LaMarsh from within his own Cabinet. Hard to say which was more trying.)

As prime minister, Pearson made some disturbing decisions. Most notably, he allowed American forces to sneak across the border and install nuclear missiles at North Bay without public approval or even notification. An unavoidable decision, perhaps, but still an insult to Canadian sovereignty no matter what the rationale.

Pearson's greatest strength was also his greatest weakness: he was a diplomat, a very deft diplomat, but he lacked base political instincts. With his slight lisp, his polka-dot bow tie and his self-deprecating humour, Pearson was just too darn *nice* for the rough-and-tumble world of politics. Where Diefenbaker appealed directly to the emotions, Pearson tried to explain things rationally. He was largely non-partisan; he admired good ideas whatever the source, and he sought workable solutions rather than rabble-rousing visions. In a *Maclean's* profile, Robert Fulford described Pearson's outlook thusly: "He almost completely lacks ideology . . . His beliefs are eclectic, a compound of the best thoughts available." It was not enough to seek leadership, said Pearson. One had to *deserve* it.

On the surface, the Pearson Era, if it can be called that, was a time of great optimism marked by a booming economy, a new flag, Canada's hundredth birthday party and Expo 67. But underneath, there were dark currents and ominous portents of what was to come. Terrorists calling themselves the FLQ had been blowing up bombs in Montréal, the Quiet Revolution was underway, and Québec nationalism was growing. To outflank the separatist threat, Pearson came up with something he called "co-operative federalism." He created the Bilingualism and Biculturalism Commission, and he recruited a trio of talented Québécois: labour leader Jean Marchand, editor and activist Gérard Pelletier, and a somewhat flippant intellectual by the name of Pierre Elliott Trudeau. Dubbed "the Three Wise Men," Marchand, Pelletier and Trudeau would have an immeasurable impact on how Canada dealt with the French Fact.

Under Lester Pearson, Canada introduced a pension plan and universal medicare, continuing the move towards a welfare state that had begun with King. And although Trudeau usually gets the credit for carrying the policy forward, it was Pearson who first opened the door to official bilingualism. As Chrétien noted in his memoir *Straight from the Heart*, "Trudeau built on Pearson's groundwork."

But perhaps the most potent symbol of the Pearson years is our national flag. Canada had been using the Red Ensign, which included a prominently displayed Union Jack, and Pearson decided to replace this flag with a new, "all-Canadian" one. He proposed three red maple leaves bordered with blue, a design mocked by Diefenbaker as "the Pearson Pennant." This design was later simplified to one single stark maple leaf. It represented an intentional break with the colonial past: a symbol that was neither British nor French, but purely Canadian.

Although Diefenbaker and Pearson were born just two years apart, they might have been born in different centuries. Theirs was a clash not just of personalities but of world views, and the Pearson-Diefenbaker feud has gone down as one of the most wasteful, unproductive clashes in modern Canadian history. Diefenbaker was still fighting John A.'s "A British subject I remain" crusade. He was a populist, a reactionary and a monarchist. Pearson was a man who saw Canada in an international light; he was outward-looking, eclectic in his approach, and all too aware of how complex the world was. The Great Flag Debate brought out the best in Pearson and the worst in Diefenbaker. Dief wanted royal regalia. Pearson wanted a clean new emblem, one that stood for both unity and the future. In the end, Pearson won. After six weeks of raucous, divisive debate, Canada finally got a national flag. Its first official raising was on February 15, 1965.

Pearson managed to achieve much in just five years, without ever attaining a majority government and while facing one of the most vindictive, destructive Opposition leaders in Canadian history. That, in itself, is impressive.

Verdict

More than a Bonehead, yet somehow less than a Bastard. Judging his career as a whole, he can be classified as a Bastard—but just barely. (I would love to have seen what Pearson could have done with a parliamentary majority. He might have achieved greatness. Or complacency, that other great Liberal trait.)

15.
Pierre Elliott Trudeau
Nicknames: "PET"; "The Philosopher King";
"That %#@*&*#!" (western Canada only)
Party: Liberal
Terms: 1968–79, 1980–84
Words to live by:
"La raison avant passion" ("Reason before passion.")

—Trudeau's personal motto

Highlights

If Laurier was a mix of Machiavelli and Sir Galahad, Trudeau was a mix of Plato and Peter Pan.

Haughty, wealthy and a dead ringer for Napoleon (in attitude as well as appearance), Pierre Trudeau had travelled the world as a young man and come back with a healthy disdain for ethnic nationalism. Like St. Laurent, he grew up speaking French to his father and English to his mother, and this duality is what defined him. He came to Ottawa to fight Québec separatists and Anglo indifference. And for the most part, he won.

Pierre Trudeau was a playboy. An author. A critic. An intellectual. With Trudeau, one always got the feeling that he was lowering himself to become prime minister. The man redefined the meaning of the word arrogance. Love him or hate him, you could never feel neutral about Pierre Trudeau.

Although a civil libertarian, Trudeau didn't hesitate to suspend basic human rights in 1970 to crush the FLQ terrorist movement. Nor did he ever apologize or retract. He bullied the separatists into submission, he pissed off western Canadians, and he brought the Constitution home in 1982—without the approval of Québec's PQ government. He pirouetted behind the Queen's back and did backflips into swimming pools.

Trudeau has been dubbed "the philosopher king," but this is a slur on both philosophy and kings. A man of cutting and often crude vulgarities, Pierre Trudeau was less a leader than he was an Ego That Walked Like a Man. And yet, in spite of this—or perhaps because of it—he managed to transcend opposites without descending into self-contradiction: he was an aristocratic liberal, an ascetic hedonist, a Catholic humanist and—most compelling of all—a virile intellectual. (A virile intellectual? Was such a thing possible?)

In style and intellect Trudeau has been compared to a shaman, a Jesuit priest, a Zen master, an emperor, a Commie and a hippie. He was both a voyageur and an urbanite. He drove fast cars, dated beautiful women and paddled his own canoe. We had never seen the likes of him before, and we may never again. In *Mondo Canuck*, Geoff Pevere and Greig Dymond summed up Trudeau's appeal perfectly: "It was like having Jack Nicholson for prime minister."

As Pearson's Minister of Justice, Trudeau had been a progressive force. He reformed Canada's archaic divorce laws, he liberalized restrictions on abortion and homosexuality, and later, as PM, he lowered the voting age to 18. Adapting a line from a *Globe and Mail* editorial, Trudeau declared: "There is no place for the state in the bedrooms of the nation." Which was just as well, because at the height of his Trudeaumania bachelor days, it might just as easily have been Pierre in the bedroom as anyone else.

When Pearson retired in 1968, Pierre Trudeau ran for the Liberal leadership and won. Only a few years earlier, he had dismissed the Liberal Party as "a spineless herd." Now he was both their leader and the prime minister. Few people have risen so high so fast. Trudeau called a snap election and began barnstorming across Canada.

That 1968 campaign was one swinging, groovy scene. It saw the advent of "Trudeaumania" as crowds swarmed the new leader, young women asked for kisses, and dignified matrons fainted dead away. It was wild and hip, and for the first time ever, a Canadian prime minister had sex appeal. "I can't give you too many kisses," he told one pretty volunteer. "The press is watching. Perhaps later."

After meeting Trudeau in 1969, John Lennon and Yoko Ono declared, "He is Beautiful People."

"If all politicians were like Mr. Trudeau," said Lennon, "there would be world peace. You people in Canada don't realize how lucky you are to have a man like Mr. Trudeau."

A year later, Trudeau was sending troops into Montréal.

Pierre Elliott Trudeau would never again inspire the same degree of pop-star hysteria, but he would always be an icon, more myth than real man. Pollster Martin Goldfarb, as quoted in Ron Graham's book *One-Eyed Kings*, noticed that once the initial euphoria of Trudeaumania subsided, Canadians were never really comfortable with Trudeau. They respected him, but they never loved him. "This is a country that loves loggers and hockey players who can fight," said Goldfarb, "not philosophers and artists. Trudeau was truly an intellectual, and Canadians didn't know how to handle him because he wasn't a part of their psyche." Trudeau was, in the words of one colleague, "an easy man to hate."

If it is true, as Flaubert observed, that "you can judge the worth of a man by the number of his enemies," then Pierre Trudeau was a very, very worthy man. Almost priceless, in fact. In a letter to the PM, media guru Marshall McLuhan gushed, "You are immeasurably the greatest Prime Minister Canada has ever had." But poet Irving Layton was not quite as awe-stricken. "In Pierre Elliott Trudeau," wrote Layton, "Canada has at last produced a political leader worthy of assassination."

Nixon referred to him as "that asshole Trudeau," which didn't bother the Canadian prime minister in the least. "I've been called worse things by worse men," said Pierre.

Of Voltaire, it was said that "while he loved humanity, he couldn't stand people." The same might be said of Trudeau. For all his Enlightenment ideals about the sanctity of the individual, he could be completely insensitive. When farmers complained of government indifference, Trudeau said, with a shrug, "When there is too much sun, they complain. When there is too much rain, they complain. A farmer is a complainer."

Comments like these did not endear him to people in western Canada. Mind you, the West did not treat Trudeau with much respect either. Trudeau was the Father of Official Bilingualism, and his Languages Act of 1969 was denounced—wrongly and hysterically—as an attempt to "shove French down our throats." Later in his career, while on vacation with his children, Trudeau was travelling in a train car that was pelted with garbage by angry protestors in Salmon Arm, B.C. When he pulled back the curtains and gave them the finger they had the gall to act aghast. "How dare he be so rude!" said the garbage throwers. (If it makes western Canadians feel better, Trudeau was just as blunt with francophones. In 1970, he told striking postal drivers to "*Mangez d'la merde.*" "Eat shit!")

During a heated exchange in the House on February 16, 1971, Trudeau leaned over and, mouthing the words, told a member of the Opposition to "Fuck off." When confronted later, Trudeau denied that he had used unparliamentary language: "What I said was, ah, 'fuddle-duddle.' " A new word, and a new Trudeauism, was born. "Fuddle-duddle" became a catch-phrase of the 1970s, adorning T-shirts and bumper stickers and appearing regularly in newspaper columns.

Trudeau was often bored with the mundane (but important) minutiae of economic issues, and it showed. Instead, he was concerned with long-term, life-and-death matters, matters affecting the very structure of the state: constitutional reform, entrenching individual rights, ensuring a place for French Canada, containing separatism, keeping the country from falling apart. For Trudeau, economic policy was a distraction at best. Much like R. B. Bennett, our other millionaire prime minister, who had vowed to defeat unemployment "or perish in the attempt," Trudeau vowed to "wrestle inflation to the ground." And like Bennett, he failed. Trudeau also ran up huge deficits and allowed unemployment to reach levels that seemed scandalous at the time but would pale considerably when compared with the excesses of the Mulroney years.

The gap between Trudeau's rhetoric and his actions was often vast. An outspoken opponent of economic protectionism, Trudeau would nonetheless introduce an energy policy that outdid the policies of any of his predecessors in its nationalism. Pierre Trudeau, the great world citizen, was in fact the biggest economic nationalist since John A. himself. In 1973, Trudeau implemented FIRA (Foreign Investment Review Agency) in an attempt to gain some control over Canada's branch-plant economy. In 1974, he campaigned against proposed wage and price controls and won a solid majority. He then imposed wage and price controls. And in 1980, he brought in the disastrous NEP (National Energy Program), which set Canadian oil prices and was based on the erroneous assumption that prices would continue to rise. Unfortunately, prices soon plummeted, and Trudeau's massive government intervention only managed to heighten the growing rift between Ottawa and western Canada.

And yet, in spite of his autocratic image, Trudeau oversaw one of the biggest devolutions of power in Canadian history. Taxation, law, communication, resource management: massive powers were handed over to the provinces. Instead of a united federation, the country became more and more balkanized and threatened to turn into a collection of feuding provincial fiefdoms. As political author Ron Graham notes, Trudeau was always "bolder in image than in fact."

In 1979, Pierre Trudeau was defeated by the Conservatives under Joe Clark, and Trudeau duly handed in his resignation to the Liberals. The role of leader of the Opposition held no appeal for him. Trudeau wanted it all, or nothing. But then Joe Clark lost a vote of confidence and a snap election was called. The Liberals, now leaderless, talked Trudeau into coming out of retirement. In February 1980, just three months after announcing his retirement, Pierre Trudeau was re-elected and back in office with his biggest majority since 1968. "Welcome to the eighties," said Trudeau with a smile.

He returned just in time to save Canada. With bumbling "Super Anglo" Joe Clark in power, the separatist government of René Lévesque had made its move, calling for a referendum on Québec sovereignty, and they might very well have won had Joe Clark still been leading the federal forces. But under Trudeau, the separatists were defeated. Even with a watered-down, vague "sovereignty-association" question, the PQ lost the 1980 referendum, 60 per cent *Non* to 40 per cent *Oui*.

Trudeau followed up on this victory by kicking the PQ while they were down. He called a series of conferences with the provincial premiers, where he isolated Premier Lévesque (cutting him from the herd, as it were), and in 1982 Trudeau brought home a new constitution with an entrenched Charter of Rights and Freedoms. It was one of the most important legal, moral and jurisdictional watersheds in modern Canadian history.

When he finally retired for good in 1984, Pierre Trudeau went out a champion. He had accomplished virtually everything he had set out to achieve: official bilingualism was now a fact, the separatists had been defeated, and the constitution had been patriated. On the last day of a leap-year February, Pierre Trudeau went for a walk in the middle of the snowy Ottawa night, alone. He was looking for signs of destiny in the sky. "But there were none," Trudeau reported wryly at a news conference the following day. "There were just snowflakes." He then announced his resignation.

Veteran journalist Val Sears, writing in the *Toronto Star*, probably put it best. "Pierre Trudeau was, for many of us, the Canadian we would like to be—a bilingual, intellectual, clever, handsome fellow and a devil with women. A Canadian who never before existed except in the eye of God."

In his passionate dislike of ethnic nationalism and his elevation of the individual as the final court of appeal, Pierre Trudeau was, of course, right. The problem was, he *knew* he was right, and from this he incorrectly deduced that everyone else was wrong. Logic such as this tends to feed one's sense of superiority. Most politicians attempt to compromise and soothe, but Trudeau came out guns blazing. He was never intimidated by anyone. He could have stared down Medusa herself. Shrill provincial premiers, rock-throwing hooligans, angry-voiced Albertans, rabble-rousing separatists: no one was ever able to shake him. Almost singlehandedly, he moulded the image of Canada into the type of nation he wanted it to become: a bilingual, rational, just society based on the ideals of freedom and individual autonomy. In other words, a country just like him.

Pierre Trudeau, you see, had a Vision. It led him by night like a pillar of fire and by day as a tower of smoke. It was a vision of . . . *himself.* A vision of himself, projected outwards onto the nation.

And we are all Trudeau's children, whether we like it or not.

Verdict

Bastard Maximus Supremos.

16.

Joe Clark

Nickname: "Joe Who?"

Party: Progressive Conservative

Term: From the late seventies to the early eighties. (That is, from June 4, 1979, to March 2, 1980. Nine months. Pregnancies have lasted longer than Joe Clark's reign of power.)

Words to live by:

"If I'm beaten, it will be because of image."

—statement made during the 1980 election campaign.
(Joe was beaten. It was because of image.)

Highlights

Joe Clark, the kid from High River, Alberta, was just 36 years old when he came from behind and captured the Tory leadership in 1976. "Joe Who?" asked the headlines the day after. It was a moniker that would dog him all the way to the House, where, three years later, he became known proudly as "Prime Minister Who?" In a somewhat lame attempt to turn things around, Clark started referring to Trudeau as "Pierre Pourquoi?" but that nickname never stuck.

Joe Clark and Pierre Trudeau were just about as different as any two human beings could be. As Ron Graham explains in *One-Eyed Kings*, "Trudeau was what Canadians wished to be—suave, intellectual, worldly, independent, and spontaneous. Clark was what Canadians feared they were—earnest, nice, honest, predictable, and rather dull."

Or, as journalist Charlotte Gray wrote about Poor Joe in *Saturday Night*, "Certainly he's living proof that power is not always an aphrodisiac."

Joe Clark, the chinless wonder, was a cartoonist's dream come true: a dopey, clumsy, decent man thrust into the limelight—and then smashed with a pie in the face. One of history's many casualties, Joe Clark was elected with a parliamentary minority but decided to rule as though he had a majority. Big mistake. His went down as the shortest elected government in Canadian history, a great hiccup in time.

Joe's downfall came when he tried to push through a hard-line budget. Without bothering to count the seats, or even make sure that all of his MPs were in the country, Joe faced a vote of non-confidence—and lost by three votes. In the subsequent election, he was trounced by Pierre Trudeau, fresh back from the wilderness.

The defeat devastated him. "What did I do wrong? What did I do wrong?" he asked. And then he started to cry. He had been in power just 259 days. (And even this term was rounded down to 200 by political biographer Warner Troyer.)

As columnist Allan Fotheringham says in *Look Ma . . . No Hands!*, "The problem is that Joe Clark really is a nice guy. He is kind, he is considerate. He would never do anything intentionally rude. He is, in a way, a sort of sociological freak."

And yet, I have always wondered if a small matter of birthdays didn't hasten Joe's downfall. One of his enduring problems, the one that lost him his second election, was that no one—absolutely no one—took Joe seriously. After all, he was just a kid, right? Prime minister at the age of 39? Give me a break. In fact, Joe Clark turned 40 just two weeks after the 1979 election and well before taking office, but the impression stayed. I remember more than one commentator asking, "Can someone still in his thirties really hope to run this country?" Had the 1979 election been held just two weeks later, if Joe had been "in his forties" when he won, I wonder whether the media, and in turn the public, might have been less dismissive. (Trudeau, after all, was also "in his forties" when he first became prime minister.)

Mind you, Clark did tend to fall down open manholes without too much help from anyone else. Joe Clark's worst enemy was always Joe Clark. Case in point: Having been tossed back out of office, Joe, a glutton for punishment, next sought approval from his party to continue as leader. He got a solid majority of support, almost 67 per cent, but Joe decided it wasn't a *big enough* majority, so he launched a leadership race anyway, even though he had nothing to gain and everything to lose. It was a typical, self-destructive Joe Clark strategy, and at the 1983 Conservative convention Joe Clark was defeated by a man with an enormous chin.

His loss of the leadership should have ended Clark's aspirations to the PMO, but there is a bizarre, yet oddly Canadian, footnote to the Saga of Joe Who. In 1998, long after Brian Mulroney had ridden the venerable Conservative Party into the ground and after Jean Charest had abandoned it to fight separatist dragons in Québec, Joe Clark—carefully assessing the situation—decided that the time was ripe for a comeback.

Poor Joe. He doesn't know when to quit.

Verdict

Boooooonehead!

17.
John Turner
Party: Liberal
Term: The mid-eighties. (Namely, from June 30 to September 17, 1984. A grand total of 80 days. Summer holidays have lasted longer than Turner's reign of power.)
Words to live by:
"I had no option."

Highlights

A stammering, blue-eyed mannequin, John Turner exuded warmth the way a ventriloquist's puppet exudes humanity. He was a tightly wound man who looked physically incapable of ever relaxing. (The poor guy looked as though he were cramming for midterms every day of his life.) Still, he was certainly the *prettiest* prime minister we've ever had, with his ga-ga eyes, his tousled silver hair and his athletic physique. In a sense, John Turner embodied the highest level of WASP sex appeal.

He first lost a leadership bid to a young upstart named Pierre Trudeau back in 1968. Trudeau eventually made him Finance Minister, but John Turner left in a huff and decided to wait Trudeau out. He waited. And he waited. And he waited. In a very real sense, John Turner was "yesterday's man," a matinee idol who had been out of the picture for more than a decade when he finally got the chance to launch his great comeback.

In February 1984, when Pierre Trudeau took his famous "walk in a snowstorm," John Turner was basking in the warm Caribbean sun. Almost immediately a cry went up for Turner to return and save the Liberal Party. As always, Turner was at his most attractive when he was absent. Brian Mulroney called him "the Liberal dream in motion." If only he hadn't shown up and ruined it all. John Turner was worse than a media darling; he was a media creation. And when the media was tired of him, they spit him back out. As his career crumbled around him, he became more and more strained; he had the look of a rabbit caught in the glare of a semitrailer's headlights.

There were portents of disaster right from the start. After his hard-fought victory over Jean Chrétien at the Liberal leadership convention, Turner stood waving to the crowds. Behind him, also on stage, sat Pierre Trudeau. Amid the hoopla, Turner, grinning ear to ear, gestured for Trudeau to join him at the podium. Trudeau smiled enigmatically—and stayed seated.

Trudeau screwed Turner one last time by leaving a trail of patronage appointments, like carefully placed depth charges. Turner reluctantly approved them all. When, during a live televised debate, Brian Mulroney demanded to know why Turner had bowed to such blatant cronyism, Turner stammered, "I had no option."

"You did have an option," retorted Mulroney. "You could have said no."

That moment, more than any other, lost Turner both the momentum and the campaign. Mulroney, of course, went on to get elected *twice*, and he elevated cronyism and patronage to new, near-pornographic levels. Not that any of that was a comfort to John Turner.

Verdict

Booooooonehead II: The Sequel. (In fairness to Joe Clark, we should note that John Turner was never democratically elected prime minister by his fellow Canadians. Joe was.)

18.
Brian Mulroney
Nicknames: "Lyin' Brian"; "The Boy from Baie-Comeau"
Party: Progressive Conservative
Term: Forever. Or at least, that's how it felt. Technically, from 1984 to 1993.
Words to live by:
"Let's face it, there's no whore like an old whore."
—Mulroney on the fine art of patronage

Highlights

Brian Mulroney rode into town promising national unity and fiscal responsibility, and he left nine years later with Canada in the worst debt it has ever seen and on the brink of a national breakup. Brian Mulroney was, absolutely and without doubt, the worst prime minister in Canadian history.

I make my assessment based on four criteria: (1) economic management (promising restraint, Mulroney managed to run up the largest peacetime debt in our nation's history), (2) national unity (he pandered to the separatists, and he launched two dismal, botched attempts at "bringing Québec into the Constitution," all of which nearly tore Canada apart), (3) public confidence (he was by far the least-liked, least-trusted PM in Canadian history, achieving record-setting rates of disapproval), and (4) political legacy (Mulroney all but destroyed the venerable Conservative Party, taking it from an unprecedented parliamentary majority to utter defeat and disgrace—just two seats in the post-Mulroney fallout of 1993). Economically, politically and in terms of posterity, Brian Mulroney, Canada's very own bush-league Margaret Thatcher, was an abject failure.

He didn't start out that way. When Brian Mulroney steamrollered over John Turner in 1984, he was unstoppable, a titan, a giant among men. As promised, he had delivered Québec to the Tories. He had also set a new record, with the largest parliamentary majority in Canadian history: 211 seats to the Liberals' 40 and the NDP's 30.

"Give us 20 years and you will not recognize this country," said Brian. What Canadians didn't realize was that this was a threat, not a promise. We only gave him nine years, and look what he did. Imagine another 11?

Brian got cozy with the separatists right from the start. He honestly believed he could "convert" Québec separatists to the federalist cause (in much the same way, I suppose, that Mackenzie King had really believed he could "redeem" prostitutes to Christianity). Egged on by his good buddy and close advisor Lucien Bouchard, Mulroney gave passionate speeches—written by Lucien Himself—harping about the historic "humiliations" of Québec and the betrayal of the 1982 Constitution. Brian Mulroney had, quite cheerfully, become a tool of Québec nationalists. He fanned the flames of separatism to score political points; he played with fire, and he damn near burned down the house.

During the campaign for party leadership, Mulroney had been notoriously vague when it came to dealing with Québec's position within Confederation. Too vague. Reporters kept demanding specifics, and the voters were starting to catch on. So, while on an airplane, in one of life's oh-so-symbolic moments, Mulroney scribbled down a "Nine-Point Statement of Principles" on the back of a barf-bag. His First Statement of Principle read: "Canada is a great country and Québec is an integral and important part of it." When his aides urged him to round his list out to an even 10, he scratched his head for a while and had to decline. He couldn't come up with any more "principles." Nine had pretty much exhausted his supply.

Fortunately for lovers of political wisdom, Brian later decided to expand his Barf-Bag Principles into something more substantive: a notably thin book entitled *Where I Stand*, published in 1983, just as he was poised to take over. Deep pensées culled from *Where I Stand* include the following: "Québec is different, very different. It is not strange or weird, it is just different." Gee, Brian. Thanks for clearing that up.

Even more ironically, Mulroney goes on in the book to scold Trudeau over the size of the federal deficit. Indeed, there is an entire chapter on the importance of controlling government spending. So how did Brian measure up in comparison? Well, under his astute helmsmanship, Canada incurred more than half the total debt accumulated since Confederation. And if you exclude wartime deficits, Mulroney actually managed to run up a larger accumulated debt than all previous peacetime debts *combined.* Incredible. Unbelievable. But true. If the Trudeau years had been financially erratic, the Mulroney years were almost criminally irresponsible.

Economically, Mulroney's "limited austerity" program was an even greater disaster, much like an indecisive dentist who can't make up his mind and pulls a tooth halfway out and then says, "Well, if it hurts I could always pound it back in." Mulroney didn't go far enough to please the staunch fiscal conservatives, but he did go just far enough to trigger a recession and widespread voter dissatisfaction.

Here are some sound bites and assorted snippets from Brian Mulroney before being elected prime minister: "Don't talk to me about free trade . . . Free trade is a danger to Canadian sovereignty. You'll hear no more of it from me . . . This country could not survive with a policy of unfettered free trade . . . This is a separate country, we'd be swamped. It's bad enough as it is." And so on.

Free trade was seen as a threat: it would undermine Canadian economic autonomy—shaky at the best of times—and it would endanger medicare, arts subsidies and fledgling industries that relied on protective tariffs to stop them from being, in the words of Mulroney, "swamped." So Brian dutifully denounced the very notion of free trade.

He then got himself elected, and next thing you know, suddenly he is Mr. Free Trade. Talk about pulling a 180-degree reversal. It's surprising he didn't get whiplash. Of Mulroney's Road to Damascus–like conversion, Norman Hillmer and J. L. Granatstein, in *Empire to Umpire*, write, "The years after 1984 marked a decisive shift in Canadian history. For the first time Canada apparently cast its lot wholly with the United States." Brian even managed to win a second-term majority *based* on free trade, the first time any Canadian PM has ever successfully waged an election on the platform of closer ties to the United States. Free trade was, historically, a Liberal issue. After all, it was a Liberal-appointed commission that had recommended Canada take "the leap of faith" required. But Brian Mulroney quickly made free trade something of a Conservative crusade, and in doing so he became (electorally) the most successful Tory leader since John A. Macdonald. Brian Mulroney won back-to-back majorities, something Trudeau himself never achieved. (Free trade was later expanded to include Mexico, a country with a population of more than 90 million, and Canada found itself an increasingly small cog in a very large economic machine.) The Americans were very upfront about the whole thing. U.S. trade representative Clayton Yeutter chortled, "The Canadians don't understand what they have signed. In 20 years, they will be sucked into the U.S. economy."

But Brian was only warming up. In 1991, his crowning glory came into effect: the GST (Goods and Services Tax, also known as the "Gouge, Snatch and Take"). The GST replaced an older manufacturers' tax and shifted fiscal responsibility from companies onto the individual consumer. True, Mulroney had to abuse parliamentary process and stack the Senate with extra Tories just to get the GST to pass, but pass it did.

The GST, of course, was brought in largely to compensate for the import duties and excise taxes on American goods that were now being lost under—you guessed it—free trade. Remember that the next time you cough up your share of the GST. Free trade is not free; we are subsidizing the American takeover of our economy every time we buy a pack of cigarettes or a magazine. Another proud Mulroney legacy.

Brian Mulroney was also the undisputed King of Patronage. John A. Macdonald had once noted that "given a government with a big surplus, and a big majority and a weak opposition, you could debauch a committee of archangels." Brian Mulroney was living proof of this (except for the part about the surplus). In his first year alone, he set an all-time record: making an incredible 1,280 patronage appointments, filling the ranks with school chums, old business associates and friends of friends.

Mulroney was elected on the promise of "fiscal restraint and national reconciliation," which in retrospect was like having a nymphomaniac run on a chastity ticket. Or, as Brian himself so crassly put it, "There's no whore like an old whore."

In one final, farewell six-month feeding-trough frenzy (from December 1992 to June 1993), Mulroney made more than 500 patronage appointments. Former aides, senior party members, regional fundraisers, failed candidates, party workers, volunteers, donors, backroom organizers: it was all the press could do just to keep up. At times, it seemed as if anyone with a Tory membership card was being offered a government appointment of some sort, from Supreme Court judgeships to VIA Rail management positions. It was the last hurrah on the Tory *Titanic*. "Damn the icebergs! Full steam ahead."

In fairness, Brian Mulroney didn't invent patronage appointments, he merely perfected their use. As Gordon Stewart notes in *The Origins of Canadian Politics*, unbridled patronage has long been one of the defining characteristics of Canadian politics. John A., for one, was notorious in this regard. Compared to the American and British systems, patronage is endemic in Canada. Brian Mulroney was, in a way, simply the *reductio ad absurdum* of this fact. He didn't employ patronage to win political points, however; he did it for the sheer joy of it. He wallowed in patronage the way hogs wallow in mud.

Journalist Claire Hoy outlined Mulroney's lusty approach to patronage as far back as 1987 in *Friends in High Places*, but Canadians reelected Brian anyway, so we have only ourselves to blame. Stevie Cameron's exposé, *On the Take*, is subtitled "Crime, Corruption and Greed in the Mulroney Years," though one might argue that having "crime, corruption and greed" in the same sentence as "the Mulroney years" is a redundancy.

In her book, Cameron reveals a complex web of bribes, kickbacks, graft, tax shelters, extortion, influence-peddling, conflict-of-interest scandals, shady land deals, criminal investigations, bagmen, bank accounts in the Cayman Islands, suitcases filled with unmarked bills, secret money-laundering trips to Bermuda, Cabinet ministers rubbing shoulders with Mafia hit men. It reads like a chronicle of some second-rate banana republic. Anywhere but here. Anywhere but in Canada.

Not surprisingly, lately there has been a backlash *against* the backlash. Among Brian's most ardent defenders is newspaper tycoon Conrad Black. In a recent editorial, the *National Post* tried to stroke up some reverence for Brian by insisting that "the issues of patronage and influence-dealing are now irrelevant. Brian Mulroney is a Canadian natural resource that should not be ignored." That's right: according to His Royal Lordship Conrad Black, "issues of patronage" are now "irrelevant," and Brian Mulroney is a natural resource. (In much the same way that swamp gas can be considered a natural resource, I suppose.) Mind you, Stevie Cameron has also been accused of overstating her case, and certainly some of her accusations do seem, well, unbelievable. But it should also be noted that Brian, who has been quick to sue over perceived libel in the past, has never legally challenged Cameron's allegations. His silence on the matter speaks volumes.

Canadians, Brian Mulroney once said, "simply will not buy leadership that so blatantly has one code of conduct for itself and quite a different one for the rest of us." And you know something, Brian? You're right. Eventually Canadians will catch on.

Blarney and bullshit only go so far, and when Canadians finally turned on Brian, they turned with a vengeance. His popularity sank to unheard-of depths, plummeting to single digits and hovering at around 8 per cent. Like both his patronage trail and the size of the national debt, it was an all-time record: the lowest level ever recorded for any Western democratic leader, making Brian Mulroney—according to the *Globe and Mail*—the least-liked, most-hated prime minister in Canadian history.

Still, a master of patronage like Mulroney naturally has his share of loyal friends and faithful cronies, and there is no shortage of Mulroney apologists out there. (Huge Seagull being the largest one—in every sense of the word.) Who knows?

Maybe Conrad Black is right. Maybe 92 per cent of Canadians were wrong. Maybe 92 per cent of Canadians were dumb, uninformed and misguided in their evaluation of Brian Mulroney. Maybe 92 per cent of Canadians were completely out to lunch. Maybe the man who gave us Lucien Bouchard, the GST, a crippling national debt, obscene federal deficits, rampant patronage, two divisive failed constitutional accords and unbridled free trade with the U.S. was actually a swell guy and a great leader. But somehow I doubt it.

Brian Mulroney, with his raspy baritone and fake concern, always reminded me of an undertaker, a man frowning thoughtfully and offering his deepest condolences to the widow while mentally calculating the profit on the funeral. "Let's see, I'll hire my old college chum Marcel to drive the limo. I'll rent the tuxedos from Lucien . . ."

Though perhaps undertaker isn't the right image. Snake-oil salesman is probably more accurate. As Claire Hoy noted, "Watching Mulroney, one got the feeling, as always, that beneath the plastic exterior of the studied politician there was an impenetrable layer of more plastic."

"He oozes unctuousness" is how political economist Mel Watkins put it in *If I Were Prime Minister*. And that was the heart of the problem. Mulroney was all gloss and no depth. He wore what biographer John Sawatsky called "the veneer of substance." As Ron Graham writes, "It wasn't that Mulroney lied. He said everything with heartfelt oozing sincerity." The only problem was that, a moment later, he would say the exactly opposite thing with the same oozing sincerity.

Ultimately, Brian Mulroney was his own biggest benefactor. Cameron closes her exposé with the following observation:

> Ever since Brian Mulroney left elected office in November 1993, he has prospered in the private sector, even though most Canadians, including Tories, do not like him, admire him, or respect him. Indeed, the feeling across the country for the man who led Canada for nine years is one of contempt.

If nothing else, Canadians could take pride in the fact that they had, somehow, made it through alive. After all, if we can survive nine years of Brian Mulroney, we can survive just about anything.

Verdict

As noted, Brian Mulroney managed the remarkable feat of being both a Bastard *and* a Bonehead. However, in the interests of scientific accuracy, and considering the way his career self-destructed and how he unleashed forces he had no way of controlling, Brian Mulroney was, ultimately, a **Bonehead**.

19.
Kim Campbell
Party: Progressive Conservative
Term: That swingin' summer of '93
Words to live by:
"Gee, I'm glad I didn't sell my car!"
—comment made after conceding defeat in the 1993 election,
when she failed to win even her own seat

Highlights

Kim Campbell said that "style without substance is a dangerous thing," and then went out and proved it.

Like Lucien Bouchard, Kim Campbell was one of Brian Mulroney's pro-tégées—and boy, didn't that man have an eye for talent! Kim Campbell may have become Canada's first female prime minister, but this happened through party machinations. It doesn't really count. She was not elected; she simply won a party convention.

Campbell was flippant, glib and absolutely vacuumesque. She was all style and no substance, a media-created and media-rejected icon. "John Turner with breasts" is how one of my colleagues described her. And on October 25, 1993, after a mere 123 days in office, she went down in flames. Kim Campbell led the party of John A. Macdonald to the worst parliamentary defeat in Western democratic history. The old man must be spinning in his grave like a gyroscope. It was incredible. The Conservatives were left with only two seats. Two seats, mind you. And one of those belonged to New Brunswick MP Elsie Wayne, a woman so beloved in her Saint John riding that she could have run under the Nazi Fascist Puppy-Kickers banner and still have won. The other seat was, of course, that of Jean Charest, giving the Tories, if nothing else, complete gender equality.

Hard to believe that just nine years earlier, the Conservatives had won the largest majority in Canadian history, taking 211 seats. From those heady heights they plummeted to just two in 1993. The Decline and Fall of the Conservative Party was unprecedented.

True, taking over the party leadership from Brian was a lot like taking over the controls of a 747 just before it plunges into the Rockies, but at least some of the blame for the massive voter revolt of 1993 must rest squarely on Kim Campbell's curvaceous shoulders—the same shoulders she so teasingly bared from behind her attorney general's robes in that now notorious portrait. This coyness contained a hard edge, however, and her mean-spirited campaign ads mocking Jean Chrétien's physical disabilities rank as the lowest point ever reached in a Canadian election campaign. (Apparently, Kim's message was, "Vote for me cuz I'm so cute. Not like that old creepy guy.")

Still, Canadians didn't hate Kim Campbell, they were simply using her to get at her political godfather. You could have run Jesus Christ Himself and the Tories still would have been crushed. It wasn't an election, it was a public lynching: in 1993, Brian Mulroney was tried, judged and executed in absentia. The Tories lost everything, even official party status, meaning that technically the Conservative Party no longer existed. There would be no time specifically alloted for them during question period, no party research funds, no full-scale offices or any other party perks. Brian Mulroney had once boasted that he would give appointments to Liberals only when "there isn't a living, breathing Tory left" who could fill the job. In the wake of the 1993 massacre, that possibility now loomed.

Brian Mulroney destroyed the Conservative Party of Canada. Kim Campbell was simply the fall guy. Brian had left her holding the bag—not that the bag was empty. No sir. It was filled with rancid horseshit and wads of IOUs: an annual deficit of more than $35 billion, an unemployment rate of over 11 per cent and a staggering $500-billion national debt, the largest debt per capita in the industrialized world. Mulroney had "managed" Canada to the point of bankruptcy and had "led" Canada to the point of disintegration.

"Here you go, kid," he said to Campbell as he handed over the reins of power. "It's all yours."

Kim Campbell took a bullet for Brian Mulroney.

Verdict

Bonehead.

20.

Jean Chrétien
Nickname: "The Little Guy from Shawinigan"
Party: Liberal
Term: 1993–present
Words to live by:
"If I say I'll do something, I make sure I do it . . . There will not be a promise that I will make in the campaign that I will not keep!"

—Jean Chrétien on the election trail.
(Apparently, he was just kidding.)

Highlights

On February 15, 1996, Jean Chrétien celebrated Flag Day by wading into a crowd of flag-waving children and festively choking a labour protestor. Big Jean was wearing shades at the time as well, which gave him the appearance of a Goodfella in a Martin Scorsese flick. When asked about the incident, Chrétien said with a shrug, "If you're in my way . . ."

The public response? Canadians loved it. They thrilled at it. That was their leader throttling a citizen on national televison. It was exciting and delicious, and that reaction tells you everything you need to know about the twisted, ongoing love affair between Jean Chrétien and the Canadian public.

Jean Chrétien was once dismissed as "yesterday's man," but not any more. After losing a party leadership bid to John Turner in 1984, he quit politics entirely. But then, in 1990, Big Jean came back from the grave. (Canadian politicians are like mythical beasts. You have to kill them three times before they finally stay down. Turner, Trudeau, Clark, Chrétien: each one of them retired from politics only to resurface later. Who knows but we may yet have to drive a stake into the chest of Brian Mulroney.)

Where Mulroney was all gloss and polish, Jean Chrétien is folksy and down-home. He is a man of broad strokes and simplified summaries. He sees the larger pattern and hates to get bogged down in details. Early in his career, he sat in on a high-level meeting on Liberal economic policies, including tariffs and balance of payments. After the meeting, one of the ministers approached him and said, "Remember, Jean, what you have heard today is very secret. You must not say a word to anybody about it." To which Jean replied, "Don't be worried, I didn't understand a bloody thing."

Jean Chrétien lied to us about the GST. He defended his home from a knife-wielding separatist loony while armed only with an Inuit sculpture, and he brags about being a "street fighter from Shawinigan." When university students protesting Chrétien's cozy snuggle-fest with the Society of Third-World Murderous Dictators (also known as APEC) were assaulted by police officers armed with pepper spray, Jean just laughed. He laughed and laughed, our Jean. "For me, the pepper it's what I put on the plate." Hee hee, har har. What a funny, funny guy. Never mind that those protests were peaceful, legal and wholly within the constitutional rights of Canadians. Bring on the pepper spray and tell us another bedtime story, Uncle Jean.

Jean Chrétien almost lost the 1995 referendum on Quebec sovereignty simply through complacent inaction. He promised to bring more women MPs into the House, but then said it was too complicated. And he *still* has not revoked free trade or gotten rid of the GST as he promised. Jean Chrétien flip-flops like a live fish on a hot grill. In short, he is a true Liberal. As the Saint John *Telegraph Journal* so acerbically put it, "Most people can hold their breath longer than Liberals can hold their principles."

My favourite quote on Jean? Montréal *Gazette* columnist Paul Wells: "Mr. Chrétien said last week that he doesn't govern by polls. Perhaps his pollster told him to say that."

Where some politicians have ideas, Jean Chrétien has anecdotes. Indeed, Jean Chrétien is living proof that if you hang around in politics long enough you will eventually become prime minister. He has held practically every Cabinet portfolio available, from Indian Affairs to Industry, from Trade to Finance, from Justice to Energy, and finally, through sheer political longevity, the prime ministership itself.

Pop Quiz: Jean Chrétien and Brian Mulroney: what's the difference?

If you go by policy, not much. Aside from avoiding a repeat of Brian's monumental blunder in reopening the constitutional can of worms, Jean has pretty much kept Brian's platform intact. Brian wanted to cut social programs. Jean did. Brian wanted to establish free trade with the United States. Jean has pursued it with an even greater passion. Brian gave us the hated GST, and Jean vowed to get rid of it. Then he realized what a Lord Almighty cash cow it is for the federal government, and suddenly Jean Chrétien was Mr. GST! (Or HST or BST or whatever the hell they are calling it now.)

Indeed, Brian Mulroney even has a certain begrudging admiration for Chrétien's track record. "[Chrétien's Liberals] endorsed our agenda pretty well," said Brian, "and I'm very pleased with that. The free-trade agreement with the United States, the North American free-trade agreement, the GST, privatizations and our low-inflation policy. I was very pleased to see that those main policies have been maintained intact by the new government and—," he noted ominously, "—they're taking them a little further."

Mulroney may have given CP passenger trains the axe, but it was Chrétien's Liberals who sold off the CNR. When Mulroney awarded a multimillion-dollar defence contract to a Québec aerospace company even though a Winnipeg-based firm had made a lower and better bid, the public outcry was intense. Mulroney's obvious pandering to Québec was loudly—and rightly—condemned. However, when Chrétien's Liberals simply *gave* a $3-billion contact to the Québec firm Bombardier, without even tendering offers or contacting other companies, there was only muted protest.

The question remains: Jean Chrétien and Brian Mulroney, what's the difference? Why is Jean beloved and Brian reviled? The answer is one not of policy but of *personality*. Jean Chrétien has managed to blend Brian Mulroney's economic policies with John A.'s down-home charm. And charm is the essential ingredient. Thus, where Brian failed miserably, Jean has succeeded brilliantly. If I ever have to have my throat slit, I hope Jean Chrétien is the one who does it. He would cajole and chuckle and coax you into believing that having your throat slit was the best possible thing for you to do.

The Liberal Party used to stand for a social safety net; for the notion that, no matter how bad things got, by the very virtue of being Canadian you would never be allowed to fall too far. If this philosophy blunted our economic growth and prevented us from being a land of free-wheeling millionaires, so be it. There has always been a price to be paid for the privilege of being Canadian. At least, that was the old soft-left position. But the Canadian public, jaded by Mulroney's excesses and horrified at the degree of deficit spending, demanded a right turn in fiscal policy, and Chrétien cheerfully complied.

In their book *Straight through the Heart*, Maude Barlow and Bruce Campbell seem genuinely shocked at the fluidity of Liberal values: "The party that built our social safety net is now shredding it; the party that gave us the just society is now turning its back on its history and its people." But the history of the Liberal Party suggests that Chrétien is no anomaly.

Under Laurier, the Liberals stood for low tariffs and increased trade with the U.S. Under King, they stood for the welfare state; under Trudeau, for economic nationalism and the Just Society (the notion that individual rights must be balanced with social responsibilities); under Chrétien, for fiscal belt-tightening and massive cuts to social programs. Other than a party name, the only common denominator among Laurier, King, Trudeau and Chrétien is this: they all enjoyed impressive tenure as leaders. The Liberal Party is in the business of staying in power. In this, Jean Chrétien *is* a true Liberal.

So far, Chrétien has pulled off two impressive feats. He has led back-to-back majority governments, something that no Liberal has achieved since Louis St. Laurent. Even more impressive, Jean Chrétien—or rather, Finance Minister Paul Martin—has managed to bring in a balanced budget, the first in nearly 30 years. True, they had to slash medicare funding and allow an already shaky infrastructure to crumble even further, but our books certainly were put in order. So let's give the Liberals credit on that score. After all, they had a tough assignment; following the excesses of Brian Mulroney's Conservatives was like being asked to sweep up after an orgy.

And it was Jean Chrétien, that protestor-throttlin', pepper-sprayin', promise-breakin' guy from Shawinigan who would lead Canada into the twenty-first century. Yup. We started the twentieth century with Wilfrid Laurier and we ended it with Jean Chrétien. A lateral move at best.

Verdict

Bastard.

So there you have it. Of Canada's 20 prime ministers, past and present, the score now stands at 8 Bastards, 12 Boneheads.

This number is deceptive, however, because the Canadian electorate clearly prefers Bastards to Boneheads. Of the 13 prime ministers who were legitimately elected, the score is 8 Bastards, 5 Boneheads. The lesson being, if you want to succeed in Canadian politics, you should be a bit of a Bastard.

20

Ranking Our Prime Ministers, from Best to Mulroney

ON ONE THING, our prime ministers have all agreed:

"Canada is a hard country to govern."

—John A. Macdonald

"This is a difficult country to govern."

—Wilfrid Laurier

"It has been said that Canada is the most difficult country in the world to govern. I am perhaps more aware of that than I used to be."

—Lester Pearson

"This is a difficult country to govern."

—Brian Mulroney

"It's a very difficult country to run."

—Jean Chrétien

To which author and columnist Richard Gwyn, in *The 49th Paradox*, replies, "While Canada is not in any way the 'difficult country to govern' it is often claimed to be, since it is inherently orderly, democratic, and affluent, it is an almost impossible country to lead."

How, then, do we *rank* our prime ministers? How do we compare one to another? Bastards naturally outrank Boneheads, but the B&B System is primarily one of classification. Within that larger scheme, how does one rank specific Bastards and Boneheads from top to bottom, best to worst?

THE JACKSON AND JACKSON SYSTEM OF EVALUATION

In *Stand Up for Canada*, Jackson and Jackson, as noted, classified our leaders as "friends of Canada" and "enemies." When it came to ranking specific PMs, they used three categories: Great, Mediocre and Failure. The great prime ministers were those who "exhibited outstanding capacities of intelligence, will and character." The "Great" list comprises the following six men:

Macdonald
Laurier
King
St. Laurent
Pearson
Trudeau

The failures?

Abbott
Borden
Bennett
Diefenbaker

But Borden was hardly a failure, by any standard. And if one is to judge prime ministers on "intelligence and will," Arthur Meighen would surely rank among the greats. So clearly this is a flawed system of ranking our PMs.

THE MONETARY EQUIVALENCY SYSTEM

The Canadian Mint has rated and ranked several of Canada's prime ministers in terms of their buying power:

Borden $100
King $50
Macdonald $10
Laurier $5

But you can see the flaw in this system. If we continue in descending degrees of monetary worth, we will soon end up with the Joe Clark Penny, the John Turner Ha'Penny and the Kim Campbell One-Eighth of One Half-Penny Divided by Four.

In February 1997, *Maclean's* put together a committee of 25 academic historians. All but two were professors, assistant professors or former professors. They represented 18 university campuses, and together they submitted "a collective judgement" on Canada's prime ministers.

The *Maclean's* panel included many of Canada's most respected historians. Several had written prime ministerial biographies. Individually, the members of the committee were giants. Together? Well, together they were a committee. (A camel, as they say, is a racehorse designed by a committee.)

Here, then, is what our academic blue panel came up with. [Editorial exclamation marks are my own.]

Great:
1. King
2. Macdonald
3. Laurier

Near-Great:
4. St. Laurent

High-Average:
5. Trudeau
6. Pearson
7. Borden

Average:
8. Mulroney (!)
9. Chrétien
10. Thompson
11. Mackenzie
12. Bennett (!)
13. Diefenbaker (!!!)

Low-Average:
14. Meighen
15. Clark

Failures:
16. Tupper
17. Abbott
18. Turner
19. Bowell
20. Campbell

That's right, the committee ranked St. Laurent ahead of Trudeau, and they put Brian Mulroney in the Top Ten. They considered Diefenbaker "average" and they rated Mackenzie King as the "Greatest Prime Minister Ever."

(Indeed, members of the Mackenzie King Redemption Committee have been working overtime lately. A similar panel a year later anointed Mackenzie King the "Most Important Nation Builder in Canadian History." That's right, *nation builder*. Not John A. Macdonald. Not Samuel de Champlain. Not John Graves Simcoe. But William Lyon Mackenzie King. This has gone beyond strange. It's downright silly.)

THE OFFICIAL BASTARDS AND BONEHEADS RANKING OF CANADIAN PRIME MINISTERS

In spite of recent, relentless attempts at convincing Canadians otherwise, Mackenzie King remains an uninspiring and ambiguous figure. King is a professor's hero, not a people's hero. He is admired by academics precisely because he possessed the traits so valued in their line of work: he was a highly competent and methodical administrator. King was not especially creative or innovative, but he was very adept both at playing office politics and at maintaining his tenure. (The fact that King managed to squirm his way through the conscription crisis with a minimum of political and social fallout, for example, has typically been heralded as an example of his "genius.") No: for true greatness, we must look beyond the halls of academe.

So who *was* Canada's greatest prime minister? The answer is painfully obvious. It may not be a risqué or a titillating choice, but the fact remains that the man most responsible for launching this country of ours, the man who continues to inspire, charm, challenge and enrage us, is John A. Macdonald. He was our first prime minister and our greatest. Macdonald was a rogue and a rascal and a *true* nation builder. He made hard choices, he achieved near-impossible goals, and more than any other single individual he is responsible for the shape Canada first took: "As the branch is bent, so grows the tree."

John A. Macdonald is at the top of the list. As for the others, in ranking the prime ministers of Canada, we must ask ourselves the following questions about our candidates: Did they have a strong vision? Did they make a lasting, positive impact on the evolution of Canada? Did they succeed, were they inspiring, did they dominate their era? Did they challenge us to become something greater, better, grander? Or did they unleash forces they could not control? Did they get steamrollered by history? Did they damage Canada? Or strengthen it? In short, did they leave the country better than they found it—or worse?

Based on these criteria, here is the Official Bastards and Boneheads Ranking of Canadian Prime Ministers, which I gladly admit has not been reached by a committee vote or by consensus, and has never been vetted by a panel of academic historians. Note that because he is still prime minister, Jean Chrétien's rank has been deferred. He is classified as a Bastard, but his final position on the list can only be determined after he leaves office.

First, the Failures.

These are the prime ministers who held office for a short time, often only a few months, and never had a chance to make much of a difference one way or the other. All of the prime ministers judged as Failures were, of course, Boneheads. They are listed below in simple chronological order:

Abbott
Bowell
Tupper
Meighen
Clark
Turner
Campbell

Of the remaining 12 prime ministers, the ranking from best to worst is as follows:

The Greats:	1. Macdonald
	2. Trudeau
The High-Averages:	3. King
	4. Laurier
	5. Borden
	6. St. Laurent
	7. Pearson
The Adequates:	8. Mackenzie
	9. Thompson
The Disasters:	10. Bennett
	11. Diefenbaker
	12. Mulroney

There you have it. The prime ministers of Canada from best (John A. Macdonald) to worst (Brian Mulroney).

You may be surprised at the position of Laurier on the list. He is usually automatically assigned a designation of "great," but the evidence just doesn't hold up. Laurier remains one of the most overrated prime ministers in Canadian history, just as Borden remains the most *under*rated.

As for the order of the top three (John A. Macdonald, Pierre Trudeau and Mackenzie King), in comparing these three leaders, the real key is this: Canada without Mackenzie King would no doubt have muddled through somehow. Canada without Trudeau might very well have split apart. But Canada without John A. Macdonald is impossible to imagine, if only because, without John A. Macdonald, Canada as we know it might never have existed at all.

Other than a bizarre encounter with a Japanese sumo wrestler, I don't have a lot of celebrity anecdotes to share. However, I should point out that no fewer than *three* of Canada's prime ministers have sought me out. Namely, Pierre Trudeau, Brian Mulroney and John Turner.

I hobnobbed with Trudeau back in '86, after his retirement. I was in Ottawa during Senator Jacques Hébert's hunger strike (Hébert was protesting Mulroney's cuts to the youth budget) when, lo! Pierre Trudeau sauntered by, and he and I had the following, now immortal conversation, given here in its entirety:

Me: "Mr. Trudeau! How are you?"

Pierre Trudeau: (smiling) "Yes, it certainly is."

There you have it, a true meeting of minds. Granted, Pierre's response was a bit enigmatic, but, hey, the man was an intellectual. You have to expect a certain amount of ambiguity.

Two years later, in 1988, Brian Mulroney came to my hometown of Fort Vermilion, Alberta, and hung out for a while, but we never really clicked, you know?

With John Turner, it was even worse. I met him at West Edmonton Mall. That was in 1988 as well. (Can you say "election year"?) I was on shore leave from York University and was hanging out with my sister. It was fairly early in the day, and we were waiting for the mall's Fantasyland Amusement Park to open. There was almost no one around—and then, in a burst of flashbulbs and hoopla, the reigning prime minister of Canada, John Turner, came sweeping through with his entourage, kissing hands and shaking babies (or something to that effect).

Unfortunately, there were very few "average Canadians" about, so the prime minister came at me and my sister instead, his hand extended from 40 paces, grinning away like the dumbest kid in daycare.

"Hello there," he said in that braying voice of his. "What are you young people up to today?"

"Well," I said. "We're going to go on the roller coaster. Why don't you join us? You can come along for the ride."

I was trying to trip him up, but son of a gun if he didn't come right back with some quick repartee. Without missing a beat, he replied, "Listen, my entire life is one big roller coaster."

It was an exchange caught on the TV cameras, and it made the PM look good. His aides chuckled, the reporters nodded, and I thought: Great, I'm playing straight man to John Turner. That's like playing straight man to a slab of Formica.

"Boy," said my sister dryly after he left. "You really showed him."

In Conclusion:
The Point to All of This
(There's a Point?)

OCTOBER IN TORONTO. It was a cold, grey, dismal day, and I couldn't get the chill of impending winter out of my bones. I was huddled over a cup of coffee in a diner on Yonge Street, shivering and trying my best to be pithy and quotable. I was being interviewed, you see. This was the tail end of a Book Tour from Hell, and across from me was an earnest young man from my alma mater, writing a profile for a campus paper. He was as sincere and polite as I was hungover and incoherent. Still, we persevered, with the young man asking insightful questions about my latest work, *I Was a Teenage Katima-Victim!* ("This is supposed to be a humorous book, right?") and then dutifully recording my wry, witty bon mots ("Um, yeah, it's supposed to be.").

At the end of the interview, the young man thanked me, and as he was packing up his tape recorder and notepad, he asked what I was working on next. I said, "A book on Canadian history."

He pulled the type of face you usually make after discovering a dead gerbil in your Cream of Wheat. "*Eeew,*" he said, "Canadian history. Why? It's so boring."

When I pressed him on this, he said, "Well, we've never had a civil war or anything. I mean, nothing interesting ever happened here."

We were sitting in a café at Yonge and Eglinton, not far from where the Rebels of 1837 had gathered at Montgomery's Tavern, and when I pointed this out to him he just looked at me blankly.

"Montgomery's?"

"You know," I said. "Mackenzie. Papineau. The armed uprisings. The executions. The deportations. The battle for responsible government."

"Papineau?" he said.

"In 1837."

"Eighteen thirty-seven?" he said.

He and I didn't speak the same language. The boy was illiterate. No doubt he was up-to-date on pop music and fashion and the latest, shifting trends, but when it came to his own country, when it came to Canadian history and culture, he was illiterate. I do not mean he was unintelligent. Far from it. He was simply a product of the Canadian educational system. In Canada it is quite possible, and perhaps even quite common, to go through twelve years of education, graduate from high school and then spend four years or more in university and still come out completely, utterly, culturally illiterate.

There are degrees of literacy, of course. But surely any Canadian should know what happened in 1837, and who Lord Durham was, and what LaFontaine and Baldwin achieved. Surely every Canadian should have a basic working knowledge of the country's prime ministers, should know who Borden and Bennett and John A. Macdonald were and why they are important. Surely one needs to be aware of Joseph Howe and James Douglas, of Nellie McClung and Joey Smallwood.

Bastards and Boneheads is partially intended as a crash course in cultural literacy. I have emphasized key personalities and pivotal events, but one could just as easily emphasize government policies, demographics, gender, race, or class conditions. You may, if you are so inclined, denounce the Fathers of Confederation as an amoral gang of capitalist, phallocentric, bourgeois oppressors. You may denounce them for being white, you may denounce them for being male. Indeed: denounce them as much as you want. But you cannot deny their importance. The constitutional deal that they cobbled together has had an immeasurable effect on how we live our lives as Canadians. The basic structure and underlying patterns in our society, the strengths and weaknesses, the quirks and defining traits, can largely be traced back to those first early meetings of 1864 and the swirl of champagne that surrounded them. Whether you despise the Fathers or admire them, you must at least be aware of who they were and what they did.

A feminist interpretation of Canadian history will no doubt contrast starkly with my own, as will a separatist interpretation or that of a rah-rah monarchist. But if we are going to choose from among the various interpretations presented to us, we must first be culturally literate.

History, after all, is a series of verdicts, and the final sentence is inevitably carried out in the court of public opinion. The more literate the public, the more incisive the judgements made and the more decisive the actions that will follow. The lessons we *choose* to learn, the events we *choose* to forget and the issues we *choose* to ignore have a lasting impact both on present policies and on future goals. A nation with no sense of its past has very little understanding of its present—and very little chance of controlling its future.

History is a verdict, and we are all on the jury.

Sources

WHILE WRITING *Bastards and Boneheads*, I used the *Origins* and *Destinies* text-books as my standard references, along with the two-volume *Readings in Canadian History: Pre-Confederation* and *Post-Confederation*. I recommend *Origins* and *Destinies* highly; the feature "Where Historians Disagree" is especially valuable.

The best single-volume overview of Canadian history remains *The Illustrated History of Canada*, which really should be read alongside Daniel Francis's provocative meta-histories, *National Dreams* and *The Imaginary Indian*, which examine the codes and hidden biases through which we view our past.

I have focussed on key personalities, and as such I relied heavily on biographies, autobiographies and political memoirs. Many of these, such as William Kilbourn's wonderful look at William Lyon Mackenzie, *The Firebrand*, and Donald Creighton's classic two-volume study of John A. Macdonald, *The Young Politician* and *The Old Chieftain*, rank with the best of literature: engrossing, informative, entertaining. Having slogged through John Diefenbaker's ponderous three-volume autobiography, however, and having waded through Lester B. Pearson's equally plodding three-volume set, I can vouch for the fact that official political memoirs are often only for those readers who have a great deal of patience and an unwavering interest in historical minutiae.

Fortunately, for the casual reader there are several excellent biographical surveys of Canada's prime ministers. The two I found most rewarding are Gordon Donaldson's *The Prime Ministers of Canada* and Michael Bliss's *Right Honourable Men*. Although I find Donaldson's repeated use of the word "squaw" somewhat disturbing, *The Prime Ministers of Canada* remains one of the best overviews available. Bliss goes into more depth in *Right Honourable Men*, with a sizable chunk devoted to defending the reputation of Mackenzie King. The two books actually work well together, with Donaldson providing the broad outline and Bliss filling in the gaps.

Martin Lawrence's *The Presidents and the Prime Ministers* offers a fascinating look into how the personality clashes—and congruencies—of various presidents and prime ministers have played a crucial role in the directions the two nations have taken. And though Susan Merritt's two-volume survey, *Her Story I* and *Her Story II*, is ostensibly written for a younger audience, I read and enjoyed it. As well as introducing some lesser-known women from Canada's past, her books also underline the importance of personality in the flow of history.

Throughout *Bastards and Boneheads*, I have tried to draw on as wide a range of sources as possible, from separatist polemics to Pierre Berton's classics, but I should also make special note of the following works, which I relied on heavily in the areas they covered: Christopher Moore's *1867: How the Fathers Made a Deal*, Irving Abella and Harold Troper's *None Is Too Many*, and Geoffrey York and Loreen Pindera's *People of the Pines*. Although it was published in 1983, I still find Susan Mann Trofimenkoff's social history of Québec, *A Dream of Nation*, to be the best single overview available. I also highly recommend Gerda Lerner's persuasive and articulate book *Why History Matters*.

A list of sources follows. Where I discovered discrepancies in dates, ages, spellings, and so on among various sources, I used as my final arbiter the CD-ROM version of the *1999 Canadian Encyclopedia, World Edition*. Any errors or oversights are my own.

Abella, Irving, and Harold Troper. *None Is Too Many: Canada and the Jews of Europe 1933-1948*. Toronto: Lester, 1983; revised 1991.

Adachi, Ken. *The Enemy That Never Was: A History of the Japanese Canadians*. Toronto: McClelland & Stewart, 1976.

Armstrong, Joe C. W. *Champlain*. Toronto: Macmillan, 1987.

Arnopoulos, Sheila McLeod, and Dominique Clift. *The English Fact in Québec*. Montréal: McGill-Queen's University Press, 1980.

Atwood, Margaret. *Survival: A Thematic Guide to Canadian Literature*. Toronto: Anansi, 1972.

Axworthy, Thomas S., and Pierre Elliott Trudeau, editors. *Towards a Just Society: The Trudeau Years*. Toronto: Penguin, 1992.

Barlow, Maude, and Bruce Campbell. *Straight through the Heart: How the Liberals Abandoned the Just Society*. Toronto: HarperCollins, 1995.

Baxendale, Michael, and Craig MacLaine. *This Land Is Our Land: The Mohawk Revolt at Oka*. Montréal: Optimum, 1991.

Bercuson, David J., and Barry Cooper. *Derailed: The Betrayal of the National Dream*. Toronto: Key Porter, 1994.

Bercuson, David J. *Confrontation at Winnipeg*. Revised edition. Montréal: McGill-Queens University Press, 1990.

Berger, Thomas R. *A Long and Terrible Shadow: White Values, Native Rights in the Americas, 1492–1992.* Vancouver: Douglas & McIntyre, 1991.

Berton, Pierre. *The Last Spike: The Great Railway, 1881–1885.* Toronto: McClelland & Stewart, 1971.

Berton, Pierre. *The National Dream: The Great Railway, 1871–1881.* Toronto: McClelland & Stewart, 1970.

Betcherman, Lita-Rose. *The Swastika and the Maple Leaf: Fascist Movements in Canada in the Thirties.* Toronto: Fitzhenry & Whiteside, 1975.

Black, Derek. *Winners and Losers: The Book of Canadian Political Lists.* Toronto: Methuen, 1984.

Bliss, Michael. *Right Honourable Men: The Descent of Canadian Politics from Macdonald to Mulroney.* Toronto: HarperCollins, 1994.

Bothwell, Robert. *Pearson: His Life and World.* Toronto: McGraw-Hill Ryerson, 1978.

Bourgault, Pierre. *Now or Never! Manifesto for an Independent Québec.* Toronto: Key Porter, 1991.

Bourne, Paula, et al. *Canadian Women: A History.* Toronto: Harcourt Brace Jovanovich, 1988.

Bowsfield, Hartwell, editor. *Louis Riel: Rebel of the Western Frontier or Victim of Politics and Prejudice?* Toronto: Copp Clark, 1969.

Brooke, Jeffrey. *Breaking Faith: The Mulroney Legacy of Deceit, Destruction and Disunity.* Toronto: Key Porter, 1992.

Brown, Craig, editor. *The Illustrated History of Canada.* Toronto: Key Porter, 1997.

Cahill, Jack. *John Turner: The Long Run.* Toronto: McClelland & Stewart, 1984.

Cameron, Stevie. *On the Take: Crime, Corruption and Greed in the Mulroney Years.* Toronto: Seal, 1995.

Campbell, Kim. *Time and Chance: The Political Memoirs of Canada's First Woman Prime Minister.* Toronto: Doubleday, 1996.

Carr, E. H. *What Is History?* New York: Penguin, 1964.

Chadderton, H. Clifford, editor. *Hanging a Legend: The National Film Board's Shameful Attempt to Discredit Billy Bishop, VC.* Ottawa: War Amputations Publications, 1986.

Champagne, Lyse. *Double Vision: Reflections of a Bicultural Canadian.* Toronto: Key Porter, 1990.

Chatwin, Bruce. *Anatomy of Restlessness.* London: Picador, 1997.

Chrétien, Jean. *Straight from the Heart.* Toronto: Key Porter, 1985; revised 1994.

Clark, Gerald. *Montréal: The New Cité.* Toronto: McClelland & Stewart, 1982.

Clarkson, Stephen, and Christina McCall. *Trudeau and Our Times: The Magnificent Obsession.* Toronto: McClelland & Stewart, 1990.

Clippingdale, Richard. *Laurier: His Life and World.* Toronto: McGraw-Hill Ryerson, 1979.

Cohen, Andrew. *A Deal Undone: The Making and Breaking of the Meech Lake Accord.* Vancouver: Douglas & McIntyre, 1990.

Colombo, John Robert. *The Dictionary of Canadian Quotations.* Toronto: Stoddart, 1991.

Colombo, John Robert. *1001 Questions about Canada.* Toronto: Doubleday, 1986.

Comeau, Pauline, and Aldo Santin. *The First Canadians: A Profile of Canada's Native People Today.* Toronto: James Lorimer, 1990.

Cook, Ramsay, editor. *French Canadian Nationalism.* Toronto: Macmillan, 1969.

Coucill, Irma. *Founders & Guardians.* Second edition. Toronto: John Wiley & Sons, 1982.

Creighton, Donald. *Canada: The Heroic Beginnings.* Toronto: Macmillan, 1974.

Creighton, Donald. *John A. Macdonald: The Old Chieftain.* Toronto: Macmillan, 1955.

Creighton, Donald. *John A. Macdonald: The Young Politician.* Toronto: Macmillan, 1952.

Creighton, Donald. *The Story of Canada.* Toronto: Macmillan, 1959; revised 1971.

Dafoe, J. W. *Laurier: A Study in Canadian Politics.* Reissue of 1922 edition. Toronto: McClelland & Stewart, 1963.

Daigle, Jean. *The Acadians of the Maritimes.* Moncton: Centre d'études acadiennes, 1982.

Dancocks, Daniel G. *In Enemy Hands: Canadian Prisoners of War 1939-45.* Edmonton: Hurtig, 1983.

Dancocks, Daniel G. *Sir Arthur Currie: A Biography.* Toronto: Methuen, 1985.

Dancocks, Daniel G. *Spearhead to Victory: Canada and the Great War.* Edmonton: Hurtig, 1987.

Dancocks, Daniel G. *Welcome to Flanders Fields: The First Canadian Battle of the Great War: Ypres, 1915.* Toronto: McClelland & Stewart, 1988.

Daniels, Robert V. *Studying History: How and Why.* New York: Prentice-Hall, 1966.

Davies, Alan, editor. *Antisemitism in Canada.* Waterloo: Wilfrid Laurier University Press, 1992.

Deveau, Alphonse, and Sally Ross. *The Acadians of Nova Scotia: Past and Present.* Halifax: Nimbus, 1992.

Dickason, Olive Patricia. *Canada's First Nations: A History of Founding Peoples from Earliest Times.* Second edition. Toronto: Oxford University Press, 1997.

Diefenbaker, John G. *One Canada: The Crusading Years (1895–1956).* Toronto: Macmillan, 1975.

Diefenbaker, John G. *One Canada: The Tumultuous Years (1962–1967)*. Toronto: Macmillan, 1977.

Diefenbaker, John G. *One Canada: The Years of Achievement (1956–1962)*. Toronto: Macmillan, 1976.

Dodge, William, editor. *Boundaries of Identity: A Québec Reader*. Toronto: Lester, 1992.

Donaldson, Gordon. *The Prime Ministers of Canada*. Toronto: Doubleday, 1994.

Dufour, Christian. *A Canadian Challenge: Le défi québécois*. Lantzville, B.C.: Oolichan, 1990.

Dulong, Gaston. *Dictionnaire des Canadianismes*. Québec: Larousse, 1989.

Dumont, Gabriel. *Gabriel Dumont Speaks*. Vancouver: Talonbooks, 1993.

Durham, John George Lambton, Earl of. *Report on the Affairs of British North America*. First published, 1840. Abridged as *Lord Durham's Report* by G. M. Craig. Ottawa: Carleton University Press, 1992.

Dymond, Greig, and Geoff Pevere. *Mondo Canuck*. Scarborough: Prentice-Hall, 1996.

Eccles, W. J. *France in America*. Toronto: Fitzhenry & Whiteside, 1972; revised 1990.

English, John. *Borden: His Life and World*. Toronto: McGraw-Hill Ryerson, 1977.

Ewen, Jean. *Canadian Nurse in China*. Halifax: Formac, 1983.

Ferguson, Ted. *Desperate Siege: The Battle of Hong Kong*. Toronto: Doubleday, 1980.

Fetherling, Douglas, editor. *The Broadview Book of Canadian Anecdotes*. Peterborough: Broadview, 1988.

Flanagan, Thomas. *Louis "David" Riel: Prophet of the New World*. Toronto: University of Toronto Press, 1979.

Forsey, Eugene A. *A Life on the Fringe: The Memoirs of Eugene Forsey*. Toronto: Oxford University Press, 1990.

Fotheringham, Allan. *Look Ma . . . No Hands! An Affectionate Look at Our Wonderful Tories*. Toronto: Key Porter, 1983.

Francis, Daniel. *The Imaginary Indian: The Image of the Indian in Canadian Culture*. Vancouver: Arsenal Pulp Press, 1992.

Francis, Daniel. *National Dreams: Myth, Memory and Canadian History*. Vancouver: Arsenal Pulp Press, 1997.

Francis, Douglas R., and Donald B. Smith, editors. *Readings in Canadian History: Post-Confederation*. Third edition. Toronto: Holt, Rinehart and Winston, 1990.

Francis, Douglas R., and Donald B. Smith, editors. *Readings in Canadian History: Pre-Confederation*. Second edition. Toronto: Holt, Rinehart and Winston, 1986.

Francis, Douglas R., Richard Jones, and Donald B. Smith. *Destinies: Canadian History since Confederation.* Second edition. Toronto: Holt, Rinehart & Winston, 1992.

Francis, Douglas R., Richard Jones, and Donald B. Smith. *Origins: Canadian History to Confederation.* Second edition. Toronto: Holt, Rinehart & Winston, 1992.

Franklin, Stephen. *The Heroes: A Saga of Canadian Inspiration.* Toronto: McClelland & Stewart, 1967.

Fraser, Graham. *PQ: René Lévesque and the Parti Québécois in Power.* Toronto: Macmillan, 1984.

French, Doris, and Margaret Stewart. *Ask No Quarter: A Biography of Agnes Macphail.* Toronto: Longmans, Green & Co., 1959.

Friesen, John W. *When Cultures Clash.* Second edition. Calgary: Detselig, 1993.

Frink, Tim. *New Brunswick: A Short History.* Saint John: Stonington, 1997.

Frye, Northrop. *The Bush Garden: Essays on the Canadian Imagination.* Toronto: Anansi, 1971.

Fryer, Mary Beacock. *Battlefields of Canada.* Toronto: Dundurn, 1986.

Fryer, Mary Beacock. *More Battlefields of Canada.* Toronto: Dundurn, 1993.

Ganong, William Francis. *Champlain's Island.* Saint John: New Brunswick Museum Publications, 1945; reprinted 1979.

Garrett, Richard. *General Wolfe.* London: Arthur Barker, 1975.

Graham, Ron. *One-Eyed Kings: Promise and Illusion in Canadian Politics.* Toronto: Collins, 1986.

Granatstein, J. L. *Mackenzie King: His Life and World.* Toronto: McGraw-Hill Ryerson, 1977.

Granatstein, J. L. *Who Killed Canadian History?* Toronto: Harper Collins, 1998.

Granatstein, J. L., and Desmond Morton. *Marching to Armageddon: Canadians and the Great War 1914–1919.* Toronto: Lester & Orpen Dennys, 1989.

Granatstein, J. L., and J. M. Hitsman. *Broken Promises: A History of Conscription in Canada.* Toronto: Oxford University Press, 1977.

Granatstein, J. L., and H. Graham Rawlinson. *The Canadian 100: The 100 Most Influential Canadians of the Twentieth Century.* Toronto: Little, Brown, 1997.

Granatstein, J. L., Patricia Roy, Masako Iino, and Hiroko Takamura. *Mutual Hostages: Canadians and Japanese during the Second World War.* Toronto: University of Toronto Press, 1990.

Gratton, Michel. *French Canadians: An Outsider's Inside Look at Québec.* Toronto: Key Porter, 1992.

Graubard, Stephen R., editor. *Daedalus: Journal of the American Academy of Arts and Sciences.* "In Search of Canada." Fall 1988, Vol. 117, No. 4. Cambridge, MA: Daedalus, 1988.

Griffiths, Naomi. *The Acadians: Creation of a People*. Toronto: McGraw-Hill Ryerson, 1973.

Gwyn, Richard. *The 49th Paradox: Canada in North America*. Toronto: McClelland & Stewart, 1985.

Gwyn, Richard. *Nationalism without Walls*. Toronto: McClelland & Stewart, 1995.

Hamilton, Robert M., and Dorothy Shields. *The Dictionary of Canadian Quotations and Phrases*. Toronto: McClelland & Stewart, 1979.

Hannon, Leslie F., editor. *Maclean's Canada: Portrait of a Country*. Toronto: McClelland & Stewart, 1960.

Haycock, Ronald G. *Sam Hughes: The Public Career of a Controversial Canadian, 1885–1916*. Waterloo: Wilfrid Laurier University Press, 1986.

Henderson, John. *Great Men of Canada*. Toronto: Southam Press, 1928.

Hill, Daniel G. *The Freedom-Seekers: Blacks in Early Canada*. Toronto: Stoddart, 1992.

Hillmer, Norman, and J. L. Granatstein. *Empire to Umpire: Canada and the World to the 1990s*. Toronto: Copp Clark Longman, 1994.

Hitsman, J. Mackay. *The Incredible War of 1812: A Military History*. Toronto: University of Toronto Press, 1965; revised 1978.

Horwood, Harold. *Joey: The Life and Political Times of Joey Smallwood*. Toronto: Stoddart, 1989.

Hoy, Claire. *Friends in High Places: Politics and Patronage in the Mulroney Government*. Toronto: Key Porter, 1987.

Hume, Stephen. *Ghost Camps: Memory and Myth on Canada's Frontiers*. Edmonton: NeWest, 1989.

Hurtig, Mel, editor. *If I Were Prime Minister*. Edmonton: Hurtig, 1987.

Hutchison, Bruce. *The Incredible Canadian: A Candid Portrait of Mackenzie King*. Toronto: Longmans, 1952.

Hutchison, Bruce. *Macdonald to Pearson: The Prime Ministers of Canada*. Toronto: Longmans, 1967.

Hutchison, Bruce. *The Struggle for the Border*. Toronto: Longmans, Green, 1955.

Jackson, Doreen, and Robert J. Jackson. *Stand Up for Canada: Leadership and the Canadian Political Crisis*. Scarborough: Prentice Hall, 1992.

Johnston, Gordon. *Duncan Campbell Scott and His Works*. Downsview: ECW, 1983.

Jones, Donald. *Fifty Tales of Toronto*. Toronto: University of Toronto Press, 1992.

Jones, Richard. *Duplessis and the Union Nationale Administration*. Ottawa: Canadian Historical Association, 1983.

Kilbourn, William. *The Firebrand: William Lyon Mackenzie and the Rebellion in Upper Canada*. Toronto: Clarke Irwin, 1956; revised 1977.

Knowles, Valerie. *Strangers at Our Gates: Canadian Immigration and Immigration Policy, 1540–1997*. Revised edition. Toronto: Dundurn, 1997.

Kobayashi, Cassandra, and Roy Miki. *Justice in Our Time: The Japanese Canadian Redress Settlement*. Vancouver: Talonbooks, 1991.

Lalande, Gilles. *In Defence of Federalism: The View from Québec*. Toronto: McClelland & Stewart, 1978.

LaPierre, Laurier. *Canada, My Canada: What Happened?* Toronto: McClelland & Stewart, 1992.

LaPierre, Laurier, editor. *If You Love This Country: Facts and Feelings on Free Trade*. Toronto: McClelland & Stewart, 1987.

LaPierre, Laurier. *1759: The Battle for Canada*. Toronto: McClelland & Stewart, 1990.

Layton, Irving. *The Whole Bloody Bird*. Toronto: McClelland & Stewart, 1969.

Lee, Dennis. *Civil Elegies and Other Poems*. Toronto: Anansi, 1972.

Lefolii, Ken. *The Canadian Look: A Century of Sights and Styles*. Toronto: McClelland & Stewart, 1965.

Lerner, Gerda. *Why History Matters*. New York: Oxford University Press, 1997.

Lewis, Jane, et al. *Newfoundland and Confederation: Jackdaw Portfolio C38*. Toronto: Clarke Irwin, 1974.

Longfellow, Henry Wadsworth. *The Poetical Works of Longfellow*. Originally published in 1893. Boston: Houghton Mifflin, 1975.

McCaffery, Dan. *Billy Bishop: Canadian Hero*. Toronto: James Lorimer, 1988.

MacDonald, M. A. *Fortune and La Tour: The Civil War in Acadia*. Toronto: Methuen, 1983.

McDonald, Marci. *Yankee Doodle Dandy: Brian Mulroney and the American Agenda*. Toronto: Stoddart, 1995.

Macdougall, Angus J. *Martyrs of New France*. Midland: Martyrs' Shrine Publications, 1972.

McKague, Ormond, editor. *Racism in Canada*. Saskatoon: Fifth House, 1991.

McKenzie, Ruth. *Laura Secord: The Legend and the Lady*. Toronto: McClelland & Stewart, 1971.

McMillan, Alan D. *Native Peoples and Cultures of Canada*. Second edition. Vancouver: Douglas & McIntyre, 1995.

Marsh, James H., editor. *The 1999 Canadian Encyclopedia, World Edition: CD-ROM*. Toronto: McClelland & Stewart, 1998.

Martin, Lawrence. *Pledge of Allegiance: The Americanization of Canada in the Mulroney Years*. Toronto: McClelland & Stewart, 1993.

Martin, Lawrence. *The Presidents and the Prime Ministers*. Toronto: Doubleday, 1982.

Mathews, Georges. *Quiet Resolution: Québec's Challenge to Canada.* Toronto: Summerhill, 1990.

Merritt, Susan E. *Her Story: Women from Canada's Past.* St. Catharines: Vanwell, 1993.

Merritt, Susan E. *Her Story II: Women from Canada's Past.* St. Catharines: Vanwell, 1995.

Milne, David A. *The Canadian Constitution.* Toronto: James Lorimer, 1991.

Molyneux, Geoffrey. *British Columbia: An Illustrated History.* Vancouver: Polestar, 1992.

Monkman, Leslie. *A Native Heritage: Images of the Indian in English-Canadian Literature.* Toronto: University of Toronto Press, 1981.

Moore, Christopher. *1867: How the Fathers Made a Deal.* Toronto: McClelland & Stewart, 1997.

Moore, Christopher. *The Loyalists: Revolution, Exile, Settlement.* Toronto: McClelland & Stewart, 1984.

Morrison, R. Bruce, and C. Roderick Wilson, editors. *Native Peoples: The Canadian Experience.* Toronto: McClelland & Stewart, 1995.

Morton, Desmond. *A Military History of Canada: From Champlain to the Gulf War.* Toronto: McClelland & Stewart, 1992.

Morton, Desmond. *A Short History of Canada.* Edmonton: Hurtig, 1983.

Morton, W. L., editor. *Alexander Begg's Red River Journal and Other Papers Relative to the Red River Resistance of 1869-1870.* Toronto: Champlain Society, 1956.

Mowat, Grace Helen. *The Diverting History of a Loyalist Town.* Fredericton: Brunswick Press, 1932; 1990.

Mulroney, Brian. *Where I Stand.* Toronto: McClelland & Stewart, 1983.

New, Chester. *Lord Durham's Mission to Canada.* Abridgement of *Lord Durham: A Biography*, 1929. Toronto: McClelland & Stewart, 1963.

Newman, Peter C. *The Distemper of Our Times: Canadian Politics in Transition, 1963–1968.* Toronto: McClelland & Stewart, 1968; revised 1990.

Newman, Peter C. *Empire of the Bay: An Illustrated History of the Hudson's Bay Company.* Toronto: Viking, 1989.

Newman, Peter C. *Renegade in Power: The Diefenbaker Years.* Toronto: McClelland & Stewart, 1963; revised 1989.

Nicol, Eric. *Say Uncle: A Completely Uncalled-for History of the U.S.* New York: Harper, 1951.

Nicholson, Norman L. *The Boundaries of the Canadian Confederation.* Toronto: Macmillan, 1979.

Nuffield, Edward W. *The Discovery of Canada.* Vancouver: Haro Books, 1996.

Ondaatje, Christopher. *The Prime Ministers of Canada: Macdonald to Mulroney, 1867–1985*. Toronto: Pagurian, 1985.

Orchard, David. *The Fight for Canada: Four Centuries of Resistance to American Expansionism*. Toronto: Stoddart, 1993.

Ouellet, Fernand. *Louis Joseph Papineau: A Divided Soul*. Ottawa: Canadian Historical Association, 1972.

Pearson, Lester B. *Mike: The Memoirs of the Right Honourable Lester B. Pearson: Volume One*. Toronto: University of Toronto Press, 1972.

Pearson, Lester B. *Mike: The Memoirs of the Right Honourable Lester B. Pearson: Volume Two*. Toronto: University of Toronto Press, 1973.

Pearson, Lester B. *Mike: The Memoirs of the Right Honourable Lester B. Pearson: Volume Three*. Toronto: University of Toronto Press, 1975.

Pelletier, Gérard. *The October Crisis*. Toronto: McClelland & Stewart, 1971.

Pennington, Doris. *Agnes Macphail: Reformer*. Toronto: Simon & Pierre, 1989.

Pindell, Terry. *Last Train to Toronto*. Vancouver: Douglas & McIntyre, 1992.

Read, Colin. *The Rebellion of 1837 in Upper Canada*. Ottawa: The Canadian Historical Association, 1988.

Richler, Mordecai. *Oh Canada! Oh Québec! Requiem for a Divided Country*. Toronto: Viking, 1992.

Sanders, Byrne Hope. *Emily Murphy: Crusader*. Toronto: Macmillan, 1945.

Savage, Candace. *Our Nell: A Scrapbook Biography of Nellie L. McClung*. Saskatoon: Western Producer Prairie Books, 1979.

Sawatsky, John. *Mulroney: The Politics of Ambition*. Toronto: Macfarlane, Walter & Ross, 1991.

Schull, Joseph. *Laurier: The First Canadian*. Toronto: Macmillan, 1965.

Schull, Joseph. *Rebellion: The Rising in French Canada, 1837*. Toronto: Macmillan, 1971.

Scott, Duncan Campbell. *Powassan's Drum: Poems of Duncan Campbell Scott*. Selected and edited by Raymond Souster and Douglas Lochhead. Ottawa: Tecumseh, 1985.

Senior, Hereward. *The Last Invasion of Canada: The Fenian Raids, 1866–1870*. Toronto: Dundurn, 1991.

Simard, Francis. *Talking It Out: The October Crisis from Inside*. Montréal: Guernica, 1982.

Sinclair, Gerri, executive producer. *Lives & Times of the Prime Ministers: CD-ROM*. Toronto: McClelland & Stewart, 1998.

Sloan, Thomas. *Québec: The Not-So-Quiet Revolution*. Toronto: Ryerson, 1965.

Smith, Anthony D. *National Identity*. London: Penguin, 1991.

Smith, Cynthia M., and Jack McLeod, editors. *Sir John A.: An Anecdotal Life of John A. Macdonald.* Toronto: Oxford University Press, 1989.

Smith, Denis. *Rogue Tory: The Life and Legend of John G. Diefenbaker.* Toronto: Macfarlane, Walter & Ross, 1995.

Smith, Melvin H. *Our Home or Native Land?* Toronto: Stoddart, 1995.

Stacey, C. P. *A Very Double Life: The Private World of Mackenzie King.* Toronto: Macmillan, 1976.

Stanley, Della M. M. *Louis Robichaud: A Decade of Power.* Halifax: Nimbus, 1984.

Stanley, George F. G. *Louis Riel.* Toronto: McGraw-Hill Ryerson, 1963.

Stanley, George F. G. *The War of 1812: Land Operations.* Ottawa: Canadian War Museum Historical Publications, 1983.

Stewart, Gordon T. *The Origins of Canadian Politics.* Vancouver: University of British Columbia Press, 1986.

Stewart, Roderick. *Bethune.* Toronto: New Press, 1973.

Stewart, Walter. *But Not in Canada!* Toronto: Macmillan, 1976.

Stich, K. P., editor. *The Duncan Campbell Scott Symposium.* Ottawa: University of Ottawa Press, 1979.

Sunahara, Ann Gomer. *The Politics of Racism: The Uprooting of Japanese Canadians during the Second World War.* Toronto: James Lorimer, 1981.

Swainson, Donald. *Sir John A. Macdonald: The Man and the Politician.* Kingston: Quarry Press, 1989.

Sweeny, Alastair. *George-Étienne Cartier.* Toronto: McClelland & Stewart, 1976.

Thomson, Dale C. *Alexander Mackenzie: Clear Grit.* Toronto: Macmillan, 1960.

Thomson, Dale C. *Jean Lesage and the Quiet Revolution.* Toronto: Macmillan, 1984.

Thomson, Dale C. *Louis St. Laurent: Canadian.* Toronto: Macmillan, 1967.

Titley, E. Brian. *A Narrow Vision: Duncan Campbell Scott and the Administration of Indian Affairs in Canada.* Vancouver: University of British Columbia Press, 1986.

Trofimenkoff, Susan Mann. *The Dream of Nation: A Social and Intellectual History of Québec.* Toronto: Gage, 1983.

Troyer, Warner. *200 Days: Joe Clark in Power.* Toronto: Personal Library, 1980.

Trudeau, Pierre Elliott. *With a Bang, Not a Whimper: Pierre Trudeau Speaks Out.* Toronto: Stoddart, 1988.

Trudeau, Pierre Elliott. *Federalism and the French-Canadians.* Toronto: Macmillan, 1968.

Trudeau, Pierre Elliott. *Memoirs.* Toronto: McClelland & Stewart, 1993.

Trudeau, Pierre Elliott. *A Mess That Deserves a Big No.* Toronto: Robert Davies, 1992.

Turner, Wesley B. *The War of 1812: The War That Both Sides Won*. Toronto: Dundurn, 1990.

Vallières, Pierre. *The Assassination of Pierre Laporte*. Toronto: James Lorimer, 1977.

Vallières, Pierre. *White Niggers of America*. Toronto: McClelland & Stewart, 1971.

Waddington, Miriam. *Driving Home*. Toronto: Oxford University Press, 1972.

Waite, P. W. *The Life and Times of Confederation, 1864–1867*. Second edition. Toronto: University of Toronto Press, 1962.

Waite, P. W. *Sir John A. Macdonald: His Life and World*. Toronto: McGraw-Hill Ryerson, 1977.

Watkins, Ernest. *R. B. Bennett*. Toronto: Kingswood House, 1963.

Wilbur, Richard. *The Rise of French New Brunswick*. Halifax: Formac, 1989.

Woodcock, George. *British Columbia: A History of the Province*. Vancouver: Douglas & McIntyre, 1990.

Woodcock, George. *100 Great Canadians*. Edmonton: Hurtig, 1980.

Wright, Ronald. *Home and Away*. Toronto: Alfred A. Knopf, 1993.

Wright, Ronald. *Stolen Continents*. Toronto: Penguin, 1991.

York, Geoffrey, and Loreen Pindera. *People of the Pines: The Warriors and the Legacy of Oka*. Toronto: Little, Brown & Company, 1992.

Acknowledgements

Permission to use the following excerpts is gratefully acknowledged: From Miriam Waddington, "Canadians," *Collected Poems*. © Miriam Waddington, 1986. Reprinted by permission of Oxford University Press Canada. From R. Douglas Francis, Richard Jones and Donald B. Smith, eds., *Destinies: Canadian History since Confederation*, third edition. Toronto: Harcourt Brace & Company, 1996. From *On the Take: Crime, Corruption and Greed in the Mulroney Years* by Stevie Cameron. A Seal Book published 1995 by arrangement with Macfarlane, Walter & Ross. From *The Prime Ministers of Canada* by Gordon Donaldson. © 1994 Gordon Donaldson. Reprinted with the permission of Doubleday Canada Limited. From *Straight from the Heart* by Jean Chrétien, Key Porter Books, 1994. Used with permission. From *French Canadians: An Outsider's Look at Quebec* by Michel Gratton, Key Porter Books, 1992. Used with permission. From *None Is Too Many: Canada and the Jews of Europe 1933-1948*, third edition, by Irving Abella and Harold Troper, Lester and Orpen Dennys, 1991. Used with permission. From *The Firebrand: William Lyon Mackenzie and the Rebellion of Upper Canada*. © 1956 by Clarke, Irwin and Co. Reprinted by permission of Stoddart Publishing Co. Ltd., 34 Lesmill Road, Toronto, Ontario, Canada M3B 2T6. From *A Military History of Canada* by Desmond Morton. Used by permission of McClelland & Stewart, Inc. *The Canadian Publishers*. From *1867: How the Fathers Made a Deal* by Christopher Moore. Used by permission of McClelland & Stewart, Inc. *The Canadian Publishers*. From *China Nurse 1932-1939* by Jean Ewen. Used by permission of McClelland & Stewart. *The Canadian Publishers*. From *The Dream of Nation: A Social and Intellectual History of Quebec* by Susan Mann Trofimenkoff, Gage, 1983. Used with the permission of the author. From *But Not in Canada!* by Walter Stewart, Macmillan, 1976. Used with the permission of the author. From *National Dreams: Myth, Memory and Canadian History* by Daniel Francis, Arsenal Pulp Press, 1997. Used with permission. From *The First Canadians: A Profile of Canada's Native People Today* by Pauline Comeau and Aldo Santin. Used by permission of James Lorimer and Co. From *National Identity* by Anthony D. Smith, University of Nevada Press, 1991. Used with permission. From *The Swastika and the Maple Leaf: Fascist Movements in Canada in the Thirties* by Lita-Rose Betcherman. Used by permission of Fitzhenry & Whiteside.

Every reasonable care has been taken to trace ownership of copyrighted material. Information that will enable the publishers to rectify any reference or credit is welcome.

PHOTOGRAPHY CREDITS

Page 100: *Top row, left to right:* National Archives of Canada (NAC)/PA 20123; NAC/C2113; NAC/C70293. *Middle row, left to right:* NAC/C27665; NAC/C6296; NAC/C82656. *Bottom row, left to right:* NAC/C100404; NAC/C11075; NAC/C1991.

Page 101: *Top row, left to right:* NAC/C121846; NAC/C988; NAC/C69900. *Middle row, left to right:* NAC/C26415; NAC/C8007; NAC/C22002. *Bottom row, left to right:* NAC/PA 139073; NAC/PA 178147; NAC/PA 25397.

Page 230: *Top row, left to right:* NAC/PA 30212; NAC/PA 138847; NAC/PA 165870. *Middle row, left to right:* NAC/PA 28146; NAC/C20240; NAC/PA1606. *Bottom row, left to right:* NAC/PA 135698; NAC/PA 114064; NAC/PA 117105.

Page 231: *Top row, left to right:* NAC/C52329; NAC/C9338. *Middle row, left to right:* NAC/PA 152498; NAC/PA 129677; CP Picture Archive (Wayne Glowacki). *Bottom row:* NAC/PA 117107

Page 239: NAC/C8447; page 243: NAC/C4953; page 245: NAC/PA 33933; page 246: NAC/C68645; page 247: NAC/PA 27222; page 248: NAC/C10109; page 249: NAC/RD 2073; page 252: NAC/RD 2076; page 254: NAC/C5799; page 255: NAC/C13225; page 258: NAC/C7731; page 260: NAC/C10461; page 262: NAC/C80883; page 266: NAC/PA 165516; page 269: NAC/PA 184701; page 274: NAC/PA 116450; page 276: NAC/PA 197391; page 277: CP Photo Archive (Chuck Mitchell); page 283: NAC/PA 197391; page 285: NAC/PA 197391.

Index

Hudson's Bay Company, 86, 88, 102–3, 109

Hughes, Sam, 134–35, 138, 144, *230*

Hull, William, 51–53, 60

Humphrey, John, 185

Hutchison, Bruce, 58

I

Ice storm, 16–17

Imperialism, 5, 14, 19, 23, 26, 66, 74, 122, 129, 133, 141, 197, 250, 253

Indian Act, 148; and assimilation, 148, 154–55; and enfranchisement, 148, 154; and reserves, 148, 152

Indian and Northern Affairs Canada, 156

Indians. *See* First Nations; Native peoples

Institute Canadien, 78

Inuit, 154, 156

Irving, K.C., 33

Isomura, Hirokichi, 184–85

J

Jackson, Andrew, 58

Jackson, Doreen, 237, 290

Jackson, Robert, 237

Jacquelin, Françoise-Marie. *See* La Tour, Madame

James Bay, 19

Jamieson, Alice, 126–27

Japan, 9, 17; immigrants, 168; military strategy, 173, 175; in WWII, 142, 178

Japanese Canadians: evacuation of, 177, 182–84; forced labour, 177; internment of, 5, 173, 176, 200; Redress Agreement, 184; stolen property, 179, 183–84

Jefferson, Thomas, 62

Jewish WWII refugees, 163–64, 166–70, 256

Johnson, Albert, 136

Johnson, Daniel, 194

K

Kilbourn, William, 65, 69, 70

King, Martin Luther, 67

King, William Lyon Mackenzie, 2, 71, 131, 141–44, 168–71, 236–37, *255*, 255–58, 259, 260, 265, 278, 290–94; and 1942 conscription plebiscite, 142; treatment of Japanese Canadians, 177, 179, 181–83, 185

Kingston, 77

Kitchener, 135

Knowles, Valerie, 168

L

LaFontaine, Louis-Hippolyte, 78, 80–81, *101*, 298

Lake Champlain, 58

Lalande, Gilles, 44

LaMarsh, Judy, 267

Lambton, John George. *See* Lord Durham

Lanctôt, Jacques, 201

Lanctôt, Louise, 201

LaPierre, Laurier, 80

Laporte, Pierre, 91, 199, 199–204, 207

La Tour, Madame, 24–25, *100*

Laurier, Wilfrid, 90, 111, 134, 139, 142, 236, *249*, 249–51, 253, 287–91, 293–94

Lawrence, Col. Charles, 27–30, 34, 75, *100*

Lawrence, James, 55

Lawson, John, 174

Moore, Christopher, 82, 85

Morton, Desmond, 42, 51, 64, 92, 103, 193

Mowat, Grace Helen, 32

Mulroney, Brian, 2, 96–97, 184, 222–29, 236–38, 239, 259, 263, 272, *277*, 277–83, 284, 285, 286, 287, 288, 289, 291–95; and Meech Lake Accord, 158–59; in Oka Crisis, 217

Munsinger, Gerda, 190, *231*

Murphy, Emily Ferguson, 124–25, 127–28, 132, 230

N

Napoleon, 45, 48, 55, 57, 78, 269

National Defence Act, 217

National Energy Program, 272

National Policy, 89, 241, 249–50

Native peoples, 12–13, 56, 58, 66, 96, 115, 178; land claims, 10, 147–48, 153–54, 156–58, 210–20; land reserves, 148, 152, 154, 155–56; reaction to 1969 White Paper, 154; in residential schools, 152; resurgence of, 5; self-government, 158; treaty rights, 145, 147; vote, 153, 242, 264; in wars, 36–37, 45, 49–59

NATO (North Atlantic Treaty Organization), 260

Nazis: death camps, 162; neo-Nazis, 164; war criminals, 169

NDP (New Democratic Party), 204, 249

Nelson, Dr. Robert, 64

Nelson, Dr. Wolfred, 63

New, Chester, 75

New Brunswick, 9–10, 15, 22, 26, 30,

32–34, 89, 94; Official Languages Act, 33–34

New England, 15, 26–27

Newfoundland, 11, 13–14, 73, 94, 112, 137, 261

New France, 15, 18, 23, 37–38, 43, 45, 47, 66, 86, 146, 194, 208, 213

Newman, Peter, 261–62

New Zealand, 121, 250

Niagara Falls, 74

Niagara River, 54, 70

Nichol, Eric, 48

Ninety-Two Resolutions, 62, 63

Northcote (ship), 109

Northwest, 94, 98, 103, 107, 109, 242; Rebellion, 108–11, 242

North West Mounted Police, 96, 98, 107–109, 240, 242

Northwest Passage, 19

Nova Scotia, 13, 15, 26–27, 30, 44, 67, 79, 90, 92–94, 101, 122, 244, 248

Nunavut, 112, 156

O

October Crisis, 80, 111, 196–209; myths surrounding, 207–8

Oka Crisis, 209–21; Châteauguay, 216–17; Kahnawake, 214–18; Pines, 210–16, 220

Olsen, Kirsten, 126–27

Onasakenrat, Joseph, 209–10

Onderdonk, Andrew, 96

O'Neil, Wilfrid, 196

Ontario, 47, 94, 102, 133, 134

Orangemen, 80, 104, 133, 138, 247

Osborn, John, 174

Ouellet, Fernand, 62, 191

WILL FERGUSON's debut book, *Why I Hate Canadians*, sold more than 25,000 copies and made both the *Globe and Mail* and the *Toronto Star* best-seller lists, climbing as high as number three nationally. His follow-up book, *I Was a Teenage Katima-Victim!*, is a hilarious memoir of his days as a cross-Canada volunteer. Ferguson is also the author of the critically acclaimed travel narrative *Hokkaido Highway Blues*, as well as the nuts-and-bolts budget traveller's bible, *The Hitchhiker's Guide to Japan*. Although long considered an honorary Maritimer, he now lives in Calgary with his wife, Terumi, and young son, Alex.